PEN

A Day in the

'You will love Harry Sidebo
study of the life of a gladiator,
of the crowds . . . Was I not entertained? I absolutely was.'
Dominic Sandbrook

'A grippingly original way of making the alien world of the Roman amphitheatre both accessible and comprehensible.'
Tom Holland

'Wonderfully panoramic . . . as an account of the games and the lives of the gladiators alone it is endlessly informative, rich with unexpected detail but never heavy to read.'
Literary Review

'Blends extensive research with a talent for vivid storytelling to distil 700 years of gladiator history into the 24 hours around match day, from eve-of-fight rituals to stripping the corpses.'
The Times

'Vivid [and] gripping . . . a detailed chronicle of what a gladiator's life was actually like.'
Economist

'Sidebottom brings the ancient world dazzlingly to life. A thrilling book . . . every page sizzles.'
Alice Loxton

'A masterful journey which takes the reader into the heart of Roman culture by exploring the lives of its gladiators. Sidebottom combines meticulous scholarship with electrifying storytelling, revealing how the arenas shaped Roman ideals of courage and freedom. A vivid window into the ancient mind.'
Donald J. Robertson

Previously published in 2025 in hardback under the title *Those Who Are About to Die*

Also by Harry Sidebottom

Warrior of Rome Series

Fire in the East

King of Kings

Lion of the Sun

The Caspian Gates

The Wolves of the North

The Amber Road

The Last Hour

The Burning Road

Falling Sky

Throne of the Caesars Series

Iron & Rust

Silence & Lies

Blood & Steel

Shadow & Dust

Fire & Sword

Smoke & Mirrors

Other novels

The Lost Ten

The Return

The Shadow King

Non-fiction titles

Ancient Warfare

The Mad Emperor

HARRY SIDEBOTTOM

A DAY IN THE LIFE OF A GLADIATOR

AN ALTERNATIVE HISTORY OF ANCIENT ROME

PENGUIN BOOKS

PENGUIN BOOKS

UK | USA | Canada | Ireland | Australia
India | New Zealand | South Africa

Penguin Books is part of the Penguin Random House group of companies
whose addresses can be found at global.penguinrandomhouse.com

Penguin Random House UK,
One Embassy Gardens, 8 Viaduct Gardens, London SW11 7BW

penguin.co.uk

Penguin Random House UK

First published in the UK by Hutchinson Heinemann 2025
Published in Penguin Books 2026
001

Set in 11.31/13.7pt Bembo Book MT Pro
Typeset by Six Red Marbles UK, Thetford, Norfolk

Printed and bound in Great Britain by Clays Ltd, Elcograf S.p.A.

The authorised representative in the EEA is Penguin Random House Ireland,
Morrison Chambers, 32 Nassau Street, Dublin D02 YH68

A CIP catalogue record for this book is available from the British Library

ISBN: 978–1–804–94852–1

Penguin Random House is committed to a sustainable future
for our business, our readers and our planet. This book is made
from Forest Stewardship Council® certified paper.

FSC
www.fsc.org
MIX
Paper | Supporting
responsible forestry
FSC® C018179

To my mother, Frances Sidebottom

Contents

Introduction

Twenty-Four Hours in the Colosseum

The gladiator takes counsel in the sand. The air is scented with saffron, wine and flowers, almost masking the reek of close-packed humanity, recently spilled blood and the smell of his own sweat, his own fear. Just watch the blade! Shut out everything else: the blare of the trumpets, the swirl of the water organ. Ignore the two white-clad referees, let alone the emperor in his box, the crowd beyond the nets and the sheer wall topped with rollers. Just watch the blade. The gladiator is on his own. He takes his own counsel in the sand.

Diodorus drops into the first stance: left foot forward, body half-turned, chin tucked down behind the rim of his shield, sword held underarm, low at his side. Balanced and ready, his world has narrowed to the restricted view through the grill of his helmet. Nothing matters but the man he will fight, and the few feet of sand between them.

A coward dies a thousand times, a brave man once. Diodorus moves forward fast. Just within sword reach, he steps off to the right and thrusts at the thighs. The blow is turned by the shield of his opponent, who stabs down overhand at his head. Diodorus fails to get his shield up in time. The blade glances off the side of his helmet. No real impact, but the noise of the blow reverberates inside the heavy, closed helmet. Both fighters, off-balance, step back.

Diodorus knows his opponent well. They are from the same school. Cellmates, they drink and eat together, use the same bars and brothels. Identically armed – helmet, crescent-shaped breastplate covering the top of the chest, banded protection on the right arm, wide belt, tall greave on the left leg, rectangular shield and short sword – both are the type of gladiator called a provocator. *They train together. No wonder Demetrius was not unsettled by the sudden attack.*

Demetrius takes the initiative. He comes in cautiously, feints left, jabs to the right. Diodorus counters with his shield. They slip into the rhythm of the training ground: strike, repost and recover. Demetrius does not want to kill Diodorus, any more than Diodorus wishes to kill Demetrius. Gladiatorial combat is about skill, courage and endurance, not about slaughter. Yet accidents happen, a man can lose control, and at the end there is always the will of the crowd and the giver of the Games.

Diodorus is panting, his breath hot and damp in the confines of the helmet. There is a tremor in his left arm from the weight of the shield. The hilt of the sword is slick in his hand. Time has lost all meaning. It seems like an age, but no fight lasts long. As if by arrangement, both men pull back, just out of reach. They circle the sands, watching for an opening: a false move, a stumble, or a misstep.

In a fight 'to the finger', to submission, the giver of the Games usually defers to the decision of the crowd: life or death. It is time to court the 'Lords of the Day', the tiered ranks of the populace. Demetrius shouts some boasts and insults, well-worn from repetition in the arena. They are muffled by his visor. Diodorus contents himself with a couple of fancy passes with his blade. They are veterans; they have done this before.

It is time to end the fight. Demetrius comes in fast, using his shield as a battering ram. Diodorus had been waiting for his friend's favourite move. He sidesteps, swings the edge of his own shield up into the grill of the other man's helmet. Demetrius clatters to the floor; shield and sword slip from his grip. The wind knocked out of him, Demetrius pulls off his helmet and raises his right hand in submission.

It is over. Diodorus casts away his own shield and helmet, picks up Demetrius' sword. Now he feels drained. With a blade in each hand, he turns to claim the palm branch set up for the victor. A confused roar from the crowds. They sound surprised, angry. Diodorus turns back. The Summa Rudis, *the chief umpire, is handing Demetrius his helmet. The treacherous bastard is not accepting the submission. He orders Diodorus to give Demetrius his sword back. The fight will go on.*

The gladiator is at the centre of our modern image of ancient Rome: a troubling figure, both fascinating and repulsive to us now. Likewise, he was in his own time a deeply ambiguous figure, by turns reviled and idealised, at the heart of Roman culture. If we return to the ancient sources, guided by the latest modern scholarship, we can begin to understand the gladiator in his own context.

Gladiators first appeared in Rome in the third century BC. The earliest recorded contest was in 264BC. These fights, unlike chariot races, were not part of official festivals. Instead, they were privately-funded events at the funerals of senatorial families. They were *munera*, from *munus*, a gift – perhaps to the shades of the dead, certainly to the spectators. Gladiators became a key element in politics. The goodwill senators obtained from lower-class voters by staging gladiatorial contests led to an increase in both the frequency of the bouts and the numbers of participants during the rest of the Republic (509–31BC).

Once Augustus (31BC–AD14) had reintroduced monarchy to Rome, after five centuries of republic, the emperors gave shows of ever-increasing elaboration and scale. The emperors replaced the traditional senatorial elite as the main patrons of the urban plebs, and the opportunities for the latter to give Games in the city of Rome were severely curtailed. Yet, in the first two centuries AD, gladiatorial shows and, in the West, the amphitheatres in which they were staged, spread across the whole empire. They were a very public, and hugely expensive, way for the provincial elites to advertise their adherence to Roman ways, to *Romanitas*.

Contrary to the view most of us will have encountered in Hollywood films, gladiatorial combat was not a slaughterhouse. A gladiator had a good chance of survival. The risk of death in a bout was perhaps only one in eight. Gladiators fought just once or twice a year, and a career in the arena might not extend beyond three years. Success brought financial rewards, which is why freemen volunteered to fight.

The justification for the Games remained ever the same. They were a preparation for war: if even gladiators showed spirit close to the steel, how much more would be exhibited in battle by the Roman citizens watching? Even when the professional army was stationed on distant frontiers, and with war an unlikely prospect for most civilians, gladiatorial combat enacted *virtus*, or courage, a crucial foundation of Roman self-identity. Gladiators lasted some 700 years. Until changes in patterns of munificence – the types of gifts the upper classes gave to the lower – caused by the Christianisation of the elite eventually brought the demise of the Games, at some point in the mid-fifth century AD.

Gladiators were at the heart of Roman culture. They haunted people's dreams. Elite philosophers took them as role models, even though socially they were the lowest of the low. Gladiators were sex symbols, despite being overweight, and often having bad teeth, bad breath and bodies marked and altered, sometimes to the point of deformity, by combat and their hard, repeated physical training.

This book was inspired by Colin Jones' brilliant *The Fall of Robespierre: 24 Hours in Revolutionary Paris*. But the materials and the methods are very different. Jones had hundreds, perhaps thousands, of precisely dated documents, often timed to the hour – diaries, letters, government reports – to construct a minutely detailed picture of one specific night and day in Paris: 27 July 1794, or, as it was then, 9 Thermidor Year II of the Revolutionary Calendar.

We must gather our evidence from across the Roman empire, and from across several centuries, to build a composite picture of a typical night and day at the gladiatorial Games. Despite the many depictions in art and literature through the ages, we have no ancient blow-by-blow account of twenty-four hours at the Colosseum, or any other amphitheatre. The Latin poet Martial wrote a small book, *On the Spectacles*, to celebrate the opening of the Colosseum. It used to be thought that the order of his poems reflected the running order of the events at the first show put on by the emperor Titus in June AD 80. But there was always a problem with this idea – Titus' Games stretched over 100 days – and now it is thought that some of the poems were composed to mark the completion of the building by

Titus' successor Domitian (AD 81–96). The content and order of the poems reflect Martial's interests.

A sculptural relief from the cemetery outside the Stabian Gate at Pompeii shows three phases of a gladiatorial show (**Plate One**). The top register depicts a procession (a *Pompa*). There was a flourishing genre of fiction, in both Latin and Greek, under the Roman empire, and in one of the Latin novels, a procession opens the day's events. Although some Roman narrative art was designed to be 'read' from the bottom to the top (Trajan's Column is an obvious example), that is not the case here. Reading the Pompeiian relief top down gives a running order of procession, gladiatorial combat, then beast-hunt. We are told, however, that the emperor Commodus, now best known from Ridley Scott's *Gladiator*, killed wild beasts in the morning and fought as a gladiator in the afternoon, and that seems to have been the normal order. Most likely, the man who commissioned this relief to immortalise the Games he had given elevated the gladiators to the centre, and made that register much bigger, because they had been the main attraction.

Something we might expect is missing from the relief. We know from a philosophical anecdote, and a line of dialogue in a novel, that it was customary at the Games to stage both non-lethal entertainments and executions at midday. Often the executions were theatrical; the condemned acted a role from pagan myth. Christians viewed the entire day through the lens of the midday executions. But it was always in their interest to vastly inflate the number of martyrs. Most victims were pagan criminals. The man who paid for the show at Pompeii either decided to edit the executions out of the monument, or the programme did not include any.

So, our typical day at a full show in the amphitheatre had a procession first thing, wild beast hunts in the morning, executions and other entertainments at midday, and gladiators in the afternoon. But we should be aware of two things. First, only one ancient source, a Greek novella, has all the events in the 'right' order. Second, the programme was always flexible. Novelty was appreciated in the arena. The man giving the Games could add or subtract elements, alter the order of their appearance. Not just within one day, but across shows over several. We are told that at Lyons (Lugdunum), instead of gladiators fighting with each other, a whole day was devoted to executing Christians in inventive ways.

Our day is a composite. The Roman ordering of time was in some ways similar to ours, but in other ways different. They divided the day into twenty-four hours, but the length of the hours varied with the seasons. With precision hard to achieve, most inhabitants of the empire resorted to vaguer measures of time, and it is these we will employ – from *Vesper* (evening), through the four 'Watches' (*Vigilia*) of the night, and then on through the hours of daylight, from *Conticinium* (just before dawn) back to the evening after the Games.

Following twenty-four hours of the Games in the amphitheatre offers many unique viewpoints, some surprising and all insightful, onto the world, and the worldview of the Romans. It offers the perfect vehicle to explore the lived realities and mentalities that shaped their ideas about freedom and servitude, diet and body shape, privacy and gambling, sex and desire, sleep and dreams, despair and suicide, music and perfume, man and the gods, status and honour, animals and the natural world, crime and punishment, pagans and Christians, Greeks and Romans, civilisation and barbarity, courage and cowardice, virtue and vice, philosophy and pain, the empire and the past, the emperor and his subjects, wounds and medicine, hope and astrology, and death and the afterlife. It illuminates everything that mattered in the Classical world, much of which still matters now. A night and a day seeing the world through the eyes of a gladiator changes how we think about both the ancient Romans and ourselves.

That is a long list of promises. It is time to start – time to go to the evening before the Games, to the 'Last Supper' of the gladiators.

1

VESPER
(Evening)

The men reclining at the tables are heavy-set, with great rolls of flesh; very different from the stick-thin spectators watching them eat. The bodies of those dining are scarred from the edge of the blade and the track of the whip; their necks ridged with muscles; their faces lined and callused from wearing helmets. Some are almost deformed, with one arm longer than the other. They are all the subject of intense scrutiny. Some laugh and joke, talking lightly; others are calmly ordering their financial affairs; many are silent, pale and sweating, unable to choke down their food. Some drink heavily. By this time tomorrow some, perhaps one in eight of them, will have died a violent death. But no one knows which one in eight. This is the cena libera*, when the public are admitted to the barracks to watch the last supper of the gladiators.*

The Cena Libera

The *cena libera*, a kind of public meal for gladiators, was a strange ritual: thin men observing fat men eat. Like so much ancient history – like the structure of a day at the Games itself – it must be stitched together and reconstructed from scattered fragments of evidence: a line in a Latin novel, a passing example in Greek philosophy, a couple of pieces of Christian propaganda, and a humorous mosaic. It raises many questions: of diet and body shape, of privacy and dining, of courage and disgrace, of the purpose of *this* odd custom and of what drew the spectators, of how the fat men became gladiators. In the *cena libera* the gladiators offer us our first window into the Roman mind.

Diet and Body Shape

The thin men watching habitually ate a vegetarian diet. This had nothing to do with modern concerns about health, or morality, or animal rights, let alone saving the planet. In antiquity vegetarianism was very much a minority choice. It was best left to eccentric philosophers, like the motley band of charlatans and wizards that liked to think of themselves as the school of Pythagoras. For the Pythagorean vegetarianism was all about the transmigration of souls. There was always the danger of eating your deceased parents. In his youth, Seneca the Younger flirted with Pythagoreanism and gave up meat, until set right by his father: vegetarianism was un-Roman and might bring accusations of adherence to one of the dubious, if not illegal, eastern cults, with their bizarre dietary restrictions.

The vegetarianism of those viewing the gladiators was caused by poverty. They existed in a time when the social pyramid was as steep as in any modern country in the developing world. The elite (maybe about 10 per cent of the population) was well-off, if not fabulously wealthy in contemporary terms, while the vast majority existed on or below the subsistence level. The *plebs*, or *hoi polloi* (respectively in Latin and Greek – both pejorative terms in elite mouths, usually coupled with adjectives like *dirty* or *superstitious*), lived on what is often called the 'Mediterranean triad' of grain, olives and the vine. They also ate other vegetables – mainly beans and legumes – though they have not made it into popular understanding of the 'triad'. Although nowadays endlessly lauded in colour newspaper supplements for the affluent middle classes, the Mediterranean triad makes for a limited and repetitious diet. When animals were sacrificed at religious festivals the plebs gleefully seized the opportunities for a dinner of roast meat. The moral philosopher Plutarch felt the need to remind people that festivals were more enjoyable for those who attended with genuine religious belief.

The gladiators were also usually vegetarian, but they had a different and distinctive diet. Pliny the Elder said they were nicknamed the 'Barley-men' (*hordearii*), from the stew or soup of beans and barley that was the main component of their rations. In the Roman army barley was a punishment food. Pliny goes on to say it was mainly used to feed animals. Gladiators were given large amounts of food. The emperor Vitellius, in a doomed attempt to increase the loyalty of his soldiers, increased the level of their wheat-based, better-quality rations to match the quantities given to gladiators. A member of the elite wrote that gladiators were crammed with food, which was worse than any hunger. The word used – *sagina*, 'stuffing' – was more appropriate to feeding animals. As we will see, the elite often equated gladiators, or at least *most* gladiators, to beasts. But there again the elite tended to see everyone except themselves – the plebs and barbarians alike – as 'bestial'.

Gladiators not only ate different food; to strengthen their bones they drank a unique concoction of ash (either from burned wood or bone) dissolved in watered wine. Just outside the ancient Greek city of Ephesus (in modern Turkey) archaeologists have excavated a graveyard of gladiators. It contained the remains of at least sixty-seven men and one woman (we will return to this important site frequently). Scientific analysis has shown that the bones of some of the men exhibited exceptionally high levels of calcium.

Gladiators were fattened up by their barley stew 'stuffing' (it is all too easy for us to slip into the attitudes of the ancient elite, as they wrote all our literary texts). Those depicted on the Borghese Mosaic (named after the owners of the estate outside Rome on which the seven panels were found) look very heavy indeed (**Plate Two**). Why was it thought desirable for them to be so bulky? As Cyprian, an ancient Christian bishop and opponent of the Games, put it: 'The gladiatorial Games are prepared, that blood may gladden the lust of cruel eyes. The body is fed up with stronger food, and the vigorous mass of limbs is enriched with brawn and muscle, that the wretch fattened for punishment may die a harder death.' In modern terms, gladiators needed a strong frame to support short bursts of intense and violent physical activity, and their carbohydrate-rich diet produced a thick layer of subcutaneous fat which shielded the vital organs. This enabled the combatants to take flesh wounds that would bleed profusely but would not prevent them from continuing to fight. Fat gladiators made a better visual spectacle.

Food and Participants

The *cena libera* literally translates as the 'free dinner', but the gladiators' rations probably were always provided for them free of charge. *Libera* could be translated as 'unlimited', but quantity was never an issue. It should best be understood as 'unconstrained', as in the type and quality of what they consumed. The Roman expression for 'mansplaining', spelling obvious things out in tedious detail, was to go 'from the eggs to the apples'. Formal Roman dinners, like modern Italian ones, tended to consist of three courses. Eggs, often hard boiled, usually featured in the first, apples, fresh or dried out of season, in the last. Greeks under the empire continued to divide a meal into the *sitos*, the staple (almost always bread), and the *opson*, sometimes translated as 'relish', but really covering everything else: the meat, the fish, the sauces, the pies, all the good stuff. Plutarch says that gladiators about to enter the arena had set before them many expensive foods. For once, instead of stodgy stews and cheap wine that tasted of grit, the gladiators could enjoy meat and other delicacies copiously washed down with fine wines. Perhaps among the emotions of the thin men watching them eat were hunger and envy.

Apart from the gladiators, who partook of the *cena libera*? In his *Apology*, a defence of the Christian way of life, Tertullian writes that at the pagan festival of the *Liberalia* he will not feast in public, as is the custom for the beast-fighters, when those unhappy men take their last meal. The word he uses is *bestiarii*. Technically these were the men who managed the animals used for performances and executions, not the *venatores* who hunted and fought beasts in the arena. But the two roles overlapped and were often conflated. By extension *bestiarii* came to be applied to those who were executed by exposure to fierce animals. Unsurprisingly, given their sole role as victims in the arena, Christians tended to view the whole day of gladiatorial spectacle through the lens of the midday executions. In another work, *On the Spectacles*, Tertullian has the lion stand for the entirety of gladiatorial Games (*munera*), as the horse does for chariot racing in the Circus Maximus, bodily strength for athletics, and sweetness of voice for the theatre. Needless to say, as a Christian moralist, Tertullian is vehemently opposed to all of them.

Alongside the gladiators, the *venatores* and the *bestiarii*, some modern scholars include among the diners those condemned to execution the next day. They point to *The Passion of Perpetua and Felicitas*. This is an important text that can yield many insights, but it is a complicated document. It recounts the last days of six Christian martyrs (four male, and the two young women of the title) in Carthage in North Africa in the spring of AD203. This text tells its story in three voices: an unnamed narrator, supposedly a contemporary, frames what it claims are the actual words of two of those killed: Saturus, the male leader of the group, and Perpetua, the female main character. Modern readers are keen to take the narrative at its word about Perpetua. It would give us a very rare female voice from antiquity. No one seems all that bothered about the authenticity of the words of Saturus. Whether by three hands or one, the *Passion* is an explicit piece of Christian religious propaganda: miracles now are as good as those in the past, if not better. Now even delicate young women endure martyrdom, and this converts many pagans. Actually, it can only convert *some* pagans. Martyr literature needs a baying mob. If they were all converted the divine plot would shudder to a halt as there would be no martyrdom.

The anonymous narrator claims that the martyrs transform their *cena libera* into an *agape*, the Christian 'love-feast' based on the last supper of Jesus and his disciples. At an *agape*, Christians sat, rather than reclined. It shows that the condemned could be allowed a *cena libera* at least in fiction if not necessarily in reality. But it is unwise to generalise from this sole piece of evidence. In the previous section, the narrator has given Perpetua strong arguments to win this privilege from the Roman officer in charge: *Why do you not permit us to refresh ourselves – we, the most noble of the condemned belonging to Caesar, who are to fight on his birthday? Would it not be to your credit, if we were brought forth well fed?* The implicit threat worked – *the tribune was horrified and flushed* – the condemned were granted a one-off privilege. It is most unlikely that those sentenced to the beasts or the flames – Christian or otherwise – were normally allowed such a treat.

Backgrounds

Those drinking the sweet wine and eating choice meats must have wondered how they came to be at the *cena libera*. How did a man end up as a gladiator? What were their backgrounds?

After victorious Roman campaigns many were barbarian prisoners of war. In AD70, having crushed the Jewish revolt and destroyed Jerusalem, Titus, son of the new emperor Vespasian, marched to the town of Caesarea Philippi, 'where he stayed a long time exhibiting shows of every kind. Many of the prisoners perished here, some thrown to wild beasts, others forced to meet each other in full-scale battles.' From there, Titus went to another Caesarea – Caesarea on the Sea – and celebrated his brother's birthday, 'reserving much of his vengeance on the Jews for this notable occasion. The number of those who perished in combats with wild beasts or in fighting each other or by being burned alive exceeded 2,500. Yet all this seemed to the Romans, though their victims were dying a thousand different deaths, to be too light a penalty.' At the next city, Berytus, he celebrated his father's birthday, 'with a still more lavish display . . . vast numbers of prisoners perished in the same way as before'. Later, 'he passed through a number of Syrian towns, exhibiting in them all lavish spectacles in which Jewish prisoners were forced to make a show of their own destruction'. Despite having also presented great numbers of prisoners to appear in the arenas in the provinces, and sent others to hard labour in Egypt, there were thousands left – 'the tallest and most handsome' – to adorn a triumphal procession in Rome, then fight in the newly opened Colosseum.

The greater the number, and the more diffuse the origins, of the prisoners the better. At times the elaborations of ancient fiction give a clear picture of the values of Roman culture. A lengthy Latin historical novel, set out as a series of biographies of emperors, written about AD400 and now known to historians as the *Augustan History*, says that the emperor Probus (AD276–82) exhibited 'three hundred pairs of gladiators, among whom fought many of the Blemmyae [from Sudan], who had been led in his triumph, besides many Germans and Sarmatians [a nomadic tribe from the Great Hungarian Plain], and even some Isaurian brigands [from Asia Minor]'. In the world created by this text Probus' events were vastly overshadowed by the triumph and subsequent Games of the emperor Aurelian (AD270–5), which featured 800 pairs of gladiators, as well as captives from the Blemmyae, Axomitae (from Abyssinia), Arabs, Indians, Bactrians (from Afghanistan), Iberians (from Georgia), Saracens, Persians, Goths, Alans (nomads from the Steppes), Roxolani (nomads from north of the Danube),

Sarmatians, Franks, Suebians (from the headwaters of the Rhine and Danube), Vandals, Germans, Palmyrenes (from Syria), and Egyptians. To gild the lily, among the Goths were ten women armed for war, 'these, a placard declared, were from the race of Amazons'.

Spartacus, who had been a Roman auxiliary soldier, deserter and bandit, before being condemned to the arena, was the leader of the great slave revolt which convulsed Italy from 73 to 71BC. At funeral Games for his fallen comrades, he ordered 300 Roman captives to fight as gladiators. In about AD 117 Jewish rebels in Cyrene in North Africa, among many other outrages, including cannibalism and making belts of human entrails, were accused of giving prisoners to wild beasts and forcing others to fight as gladiators. For the Romans such a role reversal was a terrible humiliation, which, somewhat paradoxically to our eyes, marked the utter inhumanity of their enemy.

After the battle of Cannae (216BC), Hannibal was said to have made senators and other distinguished Roman prisoners fight each other. With a refinement of cruelty, typical of Carthaginians in Roman thinking, he compelled fathers to fight sons, and brother against brother. In another version, Hannibal promised freedom to a Roman matched against an elephant. When the Roman unexpectedly won, with characteristic Carthaginian untrustworthiness (*Fides Punica* – Carthaginian good faith – meant the opposite in Latin), Hannibal sent horsemen to kill the victor as he left. The two sources for these tales were written long after the supposed events. As nothing of the sort appears in the earlier and more reliable *Histories* of Polybius, most likely they reflect Roman mentalities rather than reality. Spartacus and the Jews, of course, knew Roman customs all too well from the inside, but it is surprising that, apart from the imagined cruelties of Hannibal, we do not hear of any external enemies, the demonised barbarians beyond the frontiers, turning this powerful symbol back against Rome.

Only once, in the aftermath of the civil war between Julius

Caesar and Pompey the Great in the 40 BC, do we hear of a Roman forcing a defeated Roman into the arena. Asinius Pollio, the governor of the province of Further Spain, wrote a letter to Cicero denouncing his own quaestor (deputy in charge of finances). Among other crimes, including absconding with the pay chest, and condemning Roman citizens to the beasts, Cornelius Balbus had compelled a veteran called Fadius, who had served Pompey, to fight as a gladiator. Fadius survived two bouts, presumably winning both, as the aftermath shows that he would not have won a pardon. Having fought without pay, Fadius refused to take the oath to become a professional gladiator and appealed to the crowd. Infuriated, Balbus ordered him to be confined ('half buried') in the gladiatorial school. Stones were thrown by the spectators as Fadius was dragged away, and Balbus unleashed a squadron of Gallic horses on the crowd. Finally, Balbus had the unfortunate veteran burned alive. Balbus' attitude compounded his actions: 'while this was being done he walked about after dinner without his boots, with tunic ungirdled, and his hands behind his back, and in answer to the unhappy man crying out "I am a born Roman citizen," he replied: "Off with you then, and appeal to the people."'

Criminals convicted of heinous crimes were another source of gladiators. A character in an imaginary courtroom speech, designed to teach Latin oratory, says that when in the gladiatorial barracks he was confined with men convicted of sacrilege, arson and murder. A Greek novel, *The Life of Apollonius of Tyana* by Philostratus (composed in the third century AD, but set in the first), talking about Athens under Roman rule, adds several categories: 'adulterers and male prostitutes and burglars and cut-purses and kidnappers and such-like people'. It is hard to be precise about which crimes might incur this penalty. The legal texts we have were compiled in late antiquity, in the reign of Justinian (AD 527–565), when gladiatorial combat no longer existed, and largely edit the institution out of the earlier sources they quote. In all probability, application of the sentence was flexible, and at the discretion of the judge. The passage of Philostratus perhaps suggests that there was a lack of uniformity across the empire, that different crimes might send a man to the arena in different cities.

As with prisoners of war, the number of criminals varied over time and across the empire. Sometimes supply exceeded demand. When Pliny the Younger was sent by the emperor Trajan to govern the province of Bithynia-Pontus in Asia Minor (c.AD 110–112), he was puzzled to find men who had been convicted to the arena instead working relatively comfortably as public slaves and receiving an annual salary. Investigating, he found no satisfactory reason to explain why they had been released from their original sentence. Pliny wrote to Trajan asking for advice. The emperor replied that those convicted in the previous ten years must be sent back to the arena, but if they were elderly, and tried more than ten years ago, they should be 'employed in work not far removed from penal labour, cleaning public baths and sewers, or repairing streets and highways'. More usually, one suspects, demand outstripped supply. The emperors Septimius Severus and Caracalla (AD 198–211) ruled that prisoners condemned to the arena should not be transferred from one province to another without imperial permission. Instead, those of strength and skill should be sent to be displayed in Rome.

Condemnation to fight as a gladiator was considered milder than straightforward execution. This was beheading for Roman citizens, crucifixion for slaves, while non-citizens might suffer either, until the later empire (after AD 212 everyone was a citizen) when the elite lost their heads, and the non-elite were nailed to the cross. Certainly, being sentenced to the arena was less severe than being condemned to the wild beasts, or to be burned alive, or to labour in the mines (a sort of living death sentence, where you worked in terrible conditions until you died). As we will see, the gladiator at least had a chance of surviving.

'It is a good thing when the guilty are punished,' noted

Tertullian. 'Who will deny this except the guilty?' However, the theologian, an inveterate critic of Roman customs, went on: 'Who will vouch that it is always the guilty that are condemned to the beasts, or some other fate, and that it is never inflicted on the innocent through the vindictiveness of the judge, or the weakness of the defence, or the intensity of the torture?' In his view 'it is certain that innocent men are sold as gladiators to serve as victims of public pleasure'. As a Christian, Tertullian had a highly jaundiced attitude, but his doubts were shared by pagans. The impeccably traditional Roman soldier and author Varro (116–27BC) lived through the trauma of the great slave revolt, yet a late source quotes him as saying that 'although he was an innocent man, Spartacus was condemned to the gladiatorial school'.

Slaves were the third main source of gladiators. Aulus Vitellius owned a slave called Asiaticus. 'As a youth Asiaticus had been his partner in libidinous disgrace but grew tired of this and ran away. Later, Vitellius found him again, working as a seller of *posca* in Puteoli, and threw him in chains, but quickly released him and restored him to his former position as a favourite. Then, once more angry with him because of his insolence and petty thefts, he sold him to a travelling trainer of gladiators, but, when he was held in reserve for the end of a gladiatorial show, suddenly bought him back, giving him his freedom.' When Vitellius improbably became emperor (AD69), he elevated Asiaticus to the equestrian order (the second rung down on the social ladder) and followed his advice on governing. This story, as presented in Suetonius' biography of the emperor, carried a whole freight of meanings for ancient readers. It paints Vitellius as a weak, vacillating sexual deviant (*mutua libidine constupratum* sounds a lot worse than my translation as partner in libidinous disgrace), who hung out with lowlifes. *Posca* was a cheap drink of sour wine or vinegar and water; Puteoli (modern Pozzuoli) a seaport near Naples. Both were disreputable. What was Vitellius doing there? Perhaps worst of all Vitellius disrespected the values of his class (making an ex-slave an equestrian, let alone taking advice from him), as well as being both cruel and a terrible judge of character.

For Suetonius' readers, Vitellius was not cruel for owning a slave, but for how he treated him. The Greek philosopher Aristotle had written that 'there are others who hold that controlling another is contrary to nature', and the late Latin legal text called the *Digest* stated that slavery was contrary to the natural order. But Aristotle's *others* were few and far between and the *Digest* upheld slavery by regulating the laws governing it. The institution was almost entirely unquestioned. In a notorious passage Aristotle described slaves as an animate piece of property, a tool that could speak. There was no ancient abolition movement, not even among the slaves who joined Spartacus' revolt.

Under the Republic an owner could sell a slave to a gladiatorial school on a whim. According to the *Digest*, in 19BC a law was passed that a slave had to have committed some wrongdoing, which had to be presented in court, before his owner could hand him over to fight with wild beasts. Most likely, the *Digest*, compiled in the sixth century AD, with gladiatorial combat long defunct, edited out that the edict included slaves also fighting as gladiators. As we saw with Vitellius, the law did not work. The emperor Hadrian legislated again, 'prohibiting the sale of a male or female slave to a pimp or gladiatorial trainer without the case being presented in court'. There is no reason to think that Hadrian's prohibitions were any more effective. How was a slave to get access to the courts? If they did, whose word would the judge take – theirs or that of their owner? Most alarmingly, the evidence of a slave could only be accepted after torture. It was probably better for the slave to just go quietly to the gladiatorial school.

Some slaves decided that running away and selling themselves to a gladiatorial school was preferable to remaining with their masters. For them, the evident dangers of the arena were less bad than the continuing brutality of their servitude. A ruling of the emperor Antoninus Pius (AD 138–161) ordered that those slaves who were discovered doing this should be restored to their owners. The grounds given were that they may have 'embezzled money, or committed some other greater breach of the law'.

The final source of gladiators is the most puzzling to us: the free men who volunteered (the *auctorati*). Why did men choose a career that was not only dangerous but degrading? To become a gladiator brought *infamia* (disgrace). This was a Roman legal concept which branded someone as intrinsically untrustworthy. They could not represent themselves or anyone else in court, witness a will, vote, serve in the army, act as a magistrate or juror, or go to the theatre. They had no recourse from arbitrary physical punishment by magistrates. *Infamia* came from specific acts: any conviction in court, bankruptcy, a soldier shirking his duty, or showing cowardice in battle, a judge taking a bribe. It also adhered in general to certain professions: prostitutes, pimps, actors, and trainers of gladiators (*lanistae*). Along with gladiators, all these brought disgrace on themselves by taking money to exhibit their bodies, or the bodies of those they controlled, for the pleasure of others.

We have an eyewitness account of a free volunteer. In the mid-second century AD Toxaris and Sisinnes, two Scythians from the steppes, on their way to study Greek culture (*paideia*) in Athens, stopped at the Greek city of Amastris on the southern shore of the Black Sea. They took lodgings at an inn and went shopping. While they were out, the door of their room was forced. All their possessions were stolen, and they were reduced to penury. As strangers in the town, they decided there was no point in taking legal action. (Once again Roman law appears not as accessible as it is imagined by some now.) Initially Sisinnes laboured as a stevedore at the docks, but then in the agora he saw a procession of high-spirited and beautiful young men who had enrolled in a troupe of gladiators. A herald announced a prize of 10,000 drachmas for anyone who would volunteer to fight one of them. Two days later, in the theatre, Sisinnes stepped forward. He was given the money, which he handed to his friend. Armour was provided for Sisinnes, but he declined to wear a helmet. Sisinnes took the first wound, a cut to the back of the thigh with a curved blade. His blood flowed copiously, and in the stands Toxaris was almost dead with fright. But then the gladiator rushed forward too confidently, and Sisinnes ran him through the chest. Sisinnes collapsed onto the corpse of his opponent. Toxaris took his friend, and the prize money, back to their lodgings, where he nursed him back to health. Sisinnes travelled back to Scythia, where he married Toxaris' sister, although he carried a limp for ever. Toxaris returned to somewhere in Greece, although not Athens or Amastris, but to an unnamed city where there were many Amastrians who remembered and could confirm his account of the fight.

Although written as straight reportage, this exciting tale turns out to be something else. It is the ninth of ten stories – five Greek, five Scythian – of friendship in the *Toxaris*, a skilfully crafted and playful work of literature by the Greek intellectual Lucian of Samosata. Another story in the collection in which Toxaris is a participant names two contemporary kings of the Bosporus (a Greek client kingdom of Rome based in the Crimea): Leucanor and Eubiotus. From coins and inscriptions, more than literature, we have a seemingly complete list of Bosporan kings in the second century AD; none have these names. But a fragment of a Greek novel preserved on papyrus has a Eubiotus, ruler of the Scythians. Just like the Bosporan kings, Toxaris is an invention of Lucian. The name is not Scythian, but created from *toxon*, the Greek word for a bow, the typical weapon of steppe nomads. Lucian had used the name before in an earlier work for another, otherwise unattested Scythian, who was equally keen on Greek culture. Sisinnes and his friend Toxaris are inventions of Lucian. But, as we have already seen, fiction often provides a window onto the Roman mind.

Poverty – sudden and unexpected, and importantly not his

fault – drove Sisinnes to volunteer as a gladiator. It is a frequent motive in our sources. A young man down on his luck, according to the poet Horace, had three choices: become a gardener, a carriage driver or a gladiator. A speaker in a practice courtroom speech fears that lack of means might force him back to a gladiatorial school. As Seneca put it, a gladiator paid for his food and drink with his blood.

Most ancient commentators – although emphatically not Lucian on Sisinnes – believed that the descent into poverty that led to the gladiatorial school was the new gladiators' own fault. It was caused by morally bad habits. These could be either general extravagance, or something more specific. Idleness and a whore had led the man in Horace to the point where he was forced to choose between demeaning occupations. For others, gluttony led to the frittering away of fortunes, which in turn led to the arena. The Christian Tatian, obviously no fan of the arena or its inhabitants, held that, 'some, giving themselves up to idleness for the sake of profligacy, sell themselves to be killed; and the indigent barters himself away, while the rich man buys others to kill him'. The pervasiveness of the underlying moral dimension is demonstrated when a pagan turns it on its head. In the same fictional legal speech mentioned above, the very 'goodness' of a character, stepping into the arena to replace his friend, turned him into a gladiator: 'Has anyone ever heard of such a thing?'

Idleness, extravagance, whoremongering and gluttony are unlikely to appear in any modern historian's analysis of the motives for volunteering to fight as a gladiator. Surely, we think, they are cultural fears of the Roman elite, rather than objective realities. But modern historians are sometimes closer to Classical writers than we like to think. Things look more plausible to us if we substitute modern concerns for Roman ones: the mindless pursuit of vacuous celebrity, an addiction to the adrenaline-rush of extreme risk-taking, and, above all, the glamorisation of violence in the media, and the effect it has on the behaviour of young men. Less morally suspect, but equally lacking in any ancient evidence: a love of adventure is sometimes advanced as a reason to step out onto the sand.

Sisinnes' fee of 10,000 drachmas was a great deal of money. A Greek drachma was roughly equivalent to a Roman *denarius*. At the time the annual pay of a Roman legionary was 300 *denarii*. A legionary served for twenty years, plus five in the reserves, and on discharge received a bonus of some twelve years' pay. For one fight Sisinnes collected almost the entire earnings of a lifetime in the army. Lucian's *Toxaris*, of course, is a collection of fictional tales. The sum of 10,000 drachmas appears in another of the stories, this time as a gift from a governor. It means no more than 'a very large amount of cash'.

Nevertheless, the hope of gain, rather than just escaping grinding poverty, encouraged some to become gladiators, and, away from the fiction of Lucian, we for once have relevant official documentary evidence. Sometime between late AD176 and 180, Marcus Aurelius attempted to limit the cost of gladiators. Ironically, he did so in his own name, and that of his gladiator-obsessed son and co-emperor Commodus (hence the date – between the elevation of Commodus and the death of Marcus). Two inscriptions survive recording the same debate in the Senate. Both are fragmentary. The one in better condition (the other is so damaged it adds little) preserves only part of a speech by an unnamed senator, who was replying to a now lost letter from the emperors, which had been read out. At times it is not altogether certain if the senator is quoting the emperors, and if so how accurately, or whether the senator is amending and adding to the emperors' proposal. The many difficulties of interpreting this text have generated much debate. Whether suggested by the emperors or by the senator, the law laid out a complicated scheme of how much a *lanista* (a commercial dealer in gladiators) could charge the man giving the Games for fighters (almost certainly to purchase, but just possibly to lease, see below) depending on the total cost of the Games. The highest prices were 12,000 *sesterces* for a freeman, and 15,000 for a slave. With four *sesterces* to the drachma or *denarius*, at 3,000 and 3,750 drachmas, this was much less than Sisinnes received in the fiction of Lucian. But it was still a lot of money: ten or twelve times the pay of a legionary (1,200 *sesterces*), and enough to keep a family of four for at least a dozen years, at the modern estimate of 1,000 *sesterces* per annum.

If the gladiator was a member of the elite, negotiating directly with the giver of the Games for a one-off performance, he would keep all the fee. The vast majority of gladiators, however, were part of a troupe, a *familia*. Things were not so good for them. The *lanista* who ran the *familia* took the money and passed on a proportion to the gladiator (perhaps 20 per cent to a slave, and 25 per cent to a freeman). So, for each fight, a star gladiator who was a slave got only 3,750 *sesterces* from the fee of 15,000, while one who was free would get 3,000 from the 12,000 paid for his participation. In reality, the sum might have been lower. Gladiators, especially in the western half of the empire, liked to see themselves as soldiers. The army kept back part of a soldier's pay to cover their food and subsistence. Although there is no ancient evidence, and next to no modern discussion, quite possibly a *lanista* did the same.

Yet three factors suggest that a top gladiator's earnings might have been considerably higher. First it must be remembered that Marcus was attempting to lower prices, evidently significantly. The inscription says that previously prices had been so flagrantly high (*flagrabant*, literally 'blazing') that priests of the imperial cult – very wealthy members of the provincial elite whose duties included providing Games – were being ruined. Marcus' predecessor, Antoninus Pius (AD 138–61), had also attempted to fix prices. Obviously, this had not worked. Given the complexity and imprecision of the legislation, the openness to abuse, and difficulty of overseeing it, it is highly unlikely that Marcus' attempt was any more successful.

Second, if a gladiator won a fight, there was prize money.

As far as we know, Marcus did not legislate to limit this. What survives of the inscription merely states that a slave gladiator should take 20 per cent and a free one 25 per cent of the prize (these percentages have been transferred above to also apply to the charge for a gladiator). Presumably, the amounts involved varied wildly but could be considerable at the top end.

Third, a gladiator was likely to fight more than once a year. If he survived, his fees and prizes would begin to mount up.

So far, we have been thinking about superstar gladiators. Most would have been at the other end of the scale. In Marcus' legislation the lowest gladiators were priced at 3,000 *sesterces* a fight. Yet the inscription features a group of fighters who were lower still: the *Gregarii*. Outside the complicated price grading, and hardly ever mentioned in other sources, the *Gregarii* are mysterious. Presumably they were very B-list gladiators. The 'better' among them, Marcus decreed, were worth only 2,000 *sesterces*, the rest just 1,000. Any free volunteers among the latter collected at 25 per cent a miserable 250 *sesterces* on each occasion they risked their lives. These were slim pickings indeed – only enough to feed a family for three months. But young men did not enter the arena resigned to mediocrity or worse. They had in mind the highest fees ever charged – the 100,000 *sesterces* with which the emperor Tiberius tempted famous gladiators back into the ring. Young free volunteers had their eyes on the country estate to which, according to the poet Horace, a gladiator might retire.

These figures, however, illustrate only one method by which a man giving Games acquired gladiators: outright *purchase*. Our only other source shows something completely different. The jurist Gaius, writing a handbook for aspiring lawyers in the second century AD, set out the law on *hiring* gladiators. If a gladiator hired for 20 *denarii* (80 *sesterces*) was killed or maimed, the giver of the Games (the *editor*) had to pay 1,000 *denarii* (4,000 *sesterces*): in effect turning the hiring into a (sometimes posthumous) purchase at fifty times the cost of the original renting.

We do not know if Gaius wrote before or after the decree of Marcus Aurelius. Yet as Gaius' treatise continued to be used to train lawyers into the fifth century and beyond, it suggests the continuing relevance of his scheme, and that the decree of Marcus did not stand the test of time. If we transport from Marcus' decree to Gaius' text the percentages given to the gladiators, the combatants got next to nothing per fight: twenty *sesterces* if free, only sixteen if a slave. But if purchase prizes of gladiators were 'blazing' in the second half of the second century, it is likely the cost of renting was equally inflated. Gaius is setting out a legal principle, not prescriptive prices. Quite likely his figures are merely theoretical, designed to illustrate the fifty-to-one ratio of purchase to hiring.

The acclaim of the crowd, the desire to win glory, was another motive for free volunteers. A modern contention holds that over time the number of free volunteers increased. It is based on the study of two types of inscriptions: lists of gladiators, and their tombstones. There are two major problems. First, there are only seven extant lists. Two of these are from Pompeii and together number nine free men and twenty-seven slaves. The five from the rest of the empire have twenty-one free men and thirty slaves. Statistically this is an insignificant sample from which to draw any conclusions spanning centuries across an empire which stretched from modern Scotland to Iraq. Each gladiatorial troupe and every gladiatorial show was different. Second, while there are many more tombstones – 259 feature in a recent survey – the evidence they provide is skewed in significant ways. Putting up inscriptions is not a universal activity. Some cultures erect lots of inscriptions, others do not. Of those that do, the numbers can vary over time. The Romans got what is now sometimes called the 'epigraphic habit' (from epigraphy, the study of inscriptions) in the last century BC. It flourished in the first two centuries AD, before dropping away in the third. Some groups in society are more likely to commission inscriptions than others. To put up an inscription was to declare a

Roman identity. Only the 'Romanised' bought into the habit. *Venationes*, who hunted the wild beasts in the arena, were often imported from outlying, barbaric areas of the empire. Unsurprisingly we have very few tombstones for these men, and none from the western half of the empire. Among the gladiators, those embedded in Roman society would be more likely to receive a tombstone. Put simply, a free volunteer was more likely to be commemorated in this way than a gladiator who had begun life as a foreign slave or a barbarian prisoner of war.

The evidence from the inscriptions is insubstantial and yet it could still be true that in the first two centuries AD increasing numbers of free men chose to pursue a career in the arena. Military glory (*gloria* or *laus* in Latin) was central to Roman culture. Under the Republic it was won on the battlefield by a display of *virtus*, which included our concept of virtue, moral goodness (obviously without any Christian humility or mildness), but also physical courage and manliness. Rome had a rich tradition of tales of solo combat, such as Horatius holding the bridge, and Titus Manlius Torquatus winning his third name by stripping the torque from the neck of a Gallic chieftain. In Greek this was *monomachia*, the same word used for gladiatorial combat. From the late second century BC all elite Romans were fluent, and could think, in Greek, having learned the language in early childhood. The problems posed by unrestrained pursuit of individual glory were illustrated by stories such as Torquatus himself executing his own son for fighting a duel against orders. When the first emperor Augustus (31BC–AD14) introduced autocracy and professionalised the army, he curtailed the opportunities for all levels of Roman society to win *Gloria*. As the legions were stationed on distant frontiers, their recruits came to be drawn from Roman citizens in the provinces. Only very rarely were new legions raised in Italy, so in normal times the only access to a military career for the inhabitants of Italy was in the garrison of Rome, principally in the Praetorian Guard, who protected the emperor. In AD193 the

Praetorians were on the losing side in a civil war. The victor, Septimius Severus, disbanded the Guard, and reformed it with men from the legions based along the Danube, from where its recruits henceforth would be drawn. A contemporary, the senatorial historian Cassius Dio, was outraged: 'it became only too apparent that he had incidentally ruined the youth of Italy, who, instead of their former service in the army, turned to brigandage and gladiatorial fighting (*monomachia*)'.

For some men, signing up as a gladiator was a substitute for war. 'Now they sell their persons to provide the spectacle of death and to perish in the arena, when, warfare in abeyance, they find themselves foes to attack.' It was down to the stars, being born under the sign of the Scorpion, according to the poet Manilius. The Christian Tertullian took a predictably more censorious view.

> Earthly glory has so great a power over the strength of body and mind, that men despise the sword, the fire, the cross, the beasts, the tortures, for the reward of the praise of men . . . How many men of leisure does a display of weapons hire to the sword! Truly they go down to the very beasts for the motive of display, and see themselves as more beautiful for their bites and their scars.

Such passages should not be dismissed as literary commonplaces. Literature and life do not operate in separate worlds. Literature not only reflects but also shapes life – never more so than in the extremely bookish culture of Classical antiquity. Elite Romans interpreted what happened to them through the lens of literature; the non-elite through the same stories told in the theatre and by street-corner storytellers. What they read or heard influenced what they did. The idea of entering the arena to prove your courage made it into legal tomes. Discussing who was ineligible to make a claim on behalf of another, the third century AD jurist Ulpian stated, in convoluted legalistic prose: 'it is not the man who has fought against beasts who will be liable, but only the man who has hired out his services for this purpose; accordingly, the old authorities say that those who do this without pay to demonstrate their manliness will not suffer *infamia*, unless they have accepted prizes in the arena'. Given that Ulpian's words were collected in the *Digest*, in the sixth century AD, by which time gladiatorial combat had long been defunct, we can assume that the references to gladiators in the original text have been edited out. Demonstrating their manliness, and the prospect of glory that this could win them, encouraged some free men to choose a path that led to the *cena libera*.

Disgrace and the Elite

Eating at the *cena libera* was a mark of disgrace, and disgrace (*infamia*) mattered to the elite. They were the ones who were appointed magistrates, served as jurors, made speeches in court, and liked to be seen attending the theatre. Disgrace corroded their *dignitas*: the public recognition of the self-worth and influence – manifested in a slow walk, cultured accent, refined manners, ability to produce apposite literary quotations in Greek and Latin, and iron self-control – which was at the heart of their identity. Julius Caesar, famously, had said that his *dignitas* was more important to him than life itself. *Infamia* was maybe not so important to the plebs.

It is sometimes suggested that the free men who volunteered to become gladiators were shady characters from socially marginalised groups: ex-slaves, ex-gladiators, ex-soldiers. There is no evidence for the latter, and it is implausible. Veterans got comparatively large retirement bonuses; enough to set them up as a member of the local elite in most provincial settings, say as a town counsellor in a small town. Besides, even if they had enlisted at sixteen, after a quarter of a century with the standards, they would have been rather middle-aged novices in the arena.

We have already seen the emperor Tiberius luring famous

gladiators out of retirement. At a less exalted level, gladiators of servile status who had won their freedom might have found it hard to reintegrate into society. If they did not find work as a trainer in a gladiatorial school, they may well have signed on again as a volunteer. In the dinner of Trimalchio, the most famous scene from Petronius' novel *The Satyricon*, one of the reasons that the rag-merchant Echion is keenly looking forward to a gladiatorial show is that the performers are freedmen for the most part. It has been suggested that the appeal is such volunteers would fight better. But interestingly Echion himself is an ex-slave. Maybe part of the anticipated thrill was 'there but for the grace of the gods'.

The disgrace (*infamia*) that came with performing in the arena was a major problem for the elite. Under the rule of the emperors the elite constructed a narrative that exculpated them. Members of the upper orders had been forced to fight by 'bad' emperors, those all too frequent 'tyrants' on the throne, who had been 'bad' precisely because they had been at odds with the elite. Caligula compelled a prominent equestrian to fight, on the grounds of him having insulted the emperor's mother. When the equestrian won, he was executed anyway. Another twenty-six equestrians were condemned to the arena by that emperor; some because they had practised gladiatorial combat. It was said that Nero 'put on a show as fighters four hundred senators and six hundred equestrians, some of whom were wealthy men of good reputation . . . even those who fought the wild beasts and served as assistants in the arena were drawn from the senatorial and equestrian orders'. This narrative was an ideological construct designed to condemn certain (safely dead) emperors, and generally to make the elite feel better about the conduct of some of its members. Although almost certainly exaggerated (400 senators, out of a total of 600), there may be some truth in these tales. But they are far from telling the whole story.

Marcus Aurelius once gave sharp advice to a 'man of abominable reputation' who was standing for office. The candidate replied that he saw many men who had fought with him as a gladiator serving as praetors in the senate. In a culture where children commonly played at being gladiators, and even a baby's bottle could carry the image of a gladiator, unsurprisingly the desire to enter the arena was not confined to the socially marginalised and to those at the lower levels of the social pyramid. Some of the elite – senators, equestrians, even emperors – were prepared to face *infamia* to tread the sand. Far from being forced by 'bad' emperors, they actively wanted to fight as gladiators. When Julius Caesar was preparing a lavish series of Games, in 46BC, some equestrians and one senator volunteered. Caesar refused the senator, but allowed the equestrians to contend. General restrictions soon followed. In 38BC a law was passed prohibiting any senators or their sons from appearing as a gladiator. The emperor Augustus, in 22BC, restated the ban, extending it to the grandsons of senators, and (if it was not already in place) to the whole equestrian order. Later, in AD11, Augustus permitted those equestrians who were flouting the law to fight, because, as Cassius Dio put it, 'these guilty men seemed to require a greater punishment . . . they incurred death instead of disenfranchisement'. Evasions of the law continued. The emperor Tiberius decreed exile for those senators and equestrians who were deliberately acquiring *infamia* in order to lose their status, so that they could appear in the arena, and extended the ban to the grandchildren of equestrians, and the great-grandchildren of senators. Henceforth, those who broke the law were to be denied due burial. A minimum age limit of twenty-five was set for volunteers (presumably imagined as from the lower orders) to the arena. In AD69 the emperor Vitellius passed unspecified further 'strict laws' on equestrians; ironically his own great-uncle had been notorious for fighting as a gladiator. The reiterations and evasions of the laws demonstrate the continuing desire of some of the elite to become gladiators. As the anecdote about Marcus Aurelius and the ex-gladiator shows, the fascination with the arena was pervasive in the highest echelons of society. Once securely in power, Septimius Severus castigated the senators for their hypocritical attitude towards the deceased emperor Commodus: 'you will say, he actually fought as a gladiator, and do none of you fight as a gladiator? If not, how and why is it that some of you bought his shields and famous golden helmets?'

The elite's desire to be in the arena was matched only by the desire of their social inferiors to see them there. According to Tacitus, various Italian towns vied with each other, offering financial inducements to get Roman equestrians to perform at their Games. One, quite benign, interpretation of this behaviour is that high-status volunteers were likely to fight with enthusiasm. Another, more jaundiced, view is that the non-elite enjoyed seeing their betters degraded. The Greek historian Herodian, who had a thoroughly elite outlook, believed that the masses revelled in the misfortunes of the rich.

Elite morality applied a sliding scale of degradation to things gladiatorial. No matter, as Septimius Severus pointed out, the hypocrisy. People could go to the gladiatorial schools (*Ludi*) and watch the gladiators train. It was the first step on a slippery slope. In court on a charge of being a magician, Apuleius, best remembered as the author of the Latin novel *The Golden Ass* (also known as *The Metamorphoses*), blackened the character of one of his accusers – he was the sort of man who allowed his nephew, Apuleius' stepson, to be a frequent visitor to a gladiatorial school, where the youth learned from the *lanista* the names of the combatants, the fights they had fought, and the wounds they had received.

Watching the training was bad, participating in it was worse. It was an easy step to make, as elite Romans often did military weapons-training. Even the philosopher-emperor Marcus Aurelius participated as a young man. The techniques were considered somewhat different, as we will see, but it was the context that was crucial. A law passed in AD 19, under Tiberius, fulminated against any senators, equestrians, or their descendants who took the practice sword or participated in any similar subordinate role in gladiatorial schools.

Actually fighting in private, with either blunt or real weapons, was another step down. According to Septimius Severus, that was why senators had bought Commodus' equipment, and that was how the candidate for office with the abominable reputation recognised others who had fought as gladiators serving as praetors, while Marcus Aurelius did not. Perhaps the most bizarre example, which was thrown in the faces of the senate by Septimius Severus, was the elderly ex-consul who had acted the part of a beast-fighter against a leopard played by a prostitute.

To enter the arena to fight in public was a further descent. We have seen the jurist Ulpian invoking 'old authorities' to argue that to do so without being paid, and without receiving any prizes, brought no *infamia*. Many contemporaries would not have agreed. The anecdotes of members of the elite forced into the arena by 'bad' emperors do not mention pay or prizes; the disgrace came from being out on the sand exposed to the public. Fadius, the Pompeian veteran, was shamed when compelled to fight in the arena. When Balbus tried to make Fadius swear the gladiatorial oath, and thus take pay, it was too much: the old soldier refused and was executed.

Fighting in public for pay was the nadir of moral delinquency. The satirist Juvenal gives us the lowest of the low. Gracchus, bearer of a noble name, chose to fight as a *retarius*, a gladiator armed with a net and trident. This was especially bad in two ways. Most gladiators wore helmets that covered their faces. A *retarius* did not, and Gracchus' face, and thus his shame, was exposed for all to see. Also, a *retarius* fought at a distance: 'watch him gather the folds of his net, and cast it, and miss, and run for his life round the arena'. Since Homer, the Classical cultures had considered there was something inherently cowardly, and thus effeminate, about not fighting face to face. Courage, true manliness, was found 'close to the steel'.

Emperors, until the rise of the 'barracks emperors' who

rose from the ranks of the army in the mid-third century AD, were themselves always from the elite. But wearing the purple provided no immunity from the dark glamour of gladiatorial combat. Not all were affected, and we should assume keenness on the Games varied among individuals at all levels of society. Three emperors – Tiberius, Vespasian and Marcus Aurelius – were uninterested in the *munera*. But the imperial princes Caracalla and Geta trained as gladiators. The *Augustan History* claimed that Hadrian, Lucius Verus and Didius Julianus continued the practice as grown men on the throne. It goes further with Macrinus, suggesting that as a young man he made his living as a professional gladiator and male prostitute. In reality, he was neither, working instead as a provincial lawyer. Suetonius, the biographer, says that Nero wanted to emulate Hercules slaying the Nemean lion, and had a beast 'prepared' for him to fight in public with a club while naked like the god. Suetonius also has Caligula fighting in private with wooden swords against the type of gladiator called a *murmillo*. When the gladiator deliberately threw himself to the ground, the emperor killed him with a real dagger, before rushing about with the palm of victory, 'as real gladiators do'. And then there was Commodus.

In the early autumn of AD 192, spectators flocked to Rome to see 'something they had never seen or heard of before': fourteen days of the emperor fighting in the Colosseum. There are two eyewitness accounts. Commodus entered the Colosseum carrying the wand of the god Mercury and preceded by attendants holding the lion-skin and club of Hercules. In the mornings the emperor killed animals. Dangerous beasts were despatched, either with a bow or javelins, from raised walkways that divided the arena into four. Then he descended to the sand to slaughter unfettered domestic animals and wild ones brought to him in nets. The numbers were prodigious – including a hundred lions or a hundred bears – and his accuracy amazing; always one shot one kill, ostriches decapitated and still running. More a demonstration of skill than courage, one observer tartly noted. As part of his identification with Hercules, when Commodus became weary he tossed down in one gulp chilled sweet white wine from a cup shaped like the club of the god. Immediately the whole crowd, including the senators, shouted out the familiar words from a drinking party: 'Long life to you!' In the afternoons Commodus appeared as a gladiator. He fought left-handed as a *secutor*. In private bouts he used sharp steel, sometimes slicing off the noses or ears of his opponents. Now in public he refrained from shedding human blood, wielding a wooden sword against his opponents' *narthex* (cane or stick). The emperor charged a million *sesterces* a day, which was the property qualification to be a senator, one of the 600 richest men in the empire (although as the money ultimately came from the imperial *fiscus*, he was actually paying himself). Commodus had the colossal statue of the sun god outside the amphitheatre (from which later the name Colosseum derived) kitted out with the lion-skin and club of Hercules, and its face remodelled to resemble his own features. To its base was added an inscription giving the emperor the title 'Champion [*Primus Palus*] of the *secutors*', the only left-handed fighter to have won a huge number of, variously recorded, fights (620, 735, 1,000, even 12,000). An even stranger story places Commodus in the Colosseum, seemingly participating in the midday executions, some time before the fourteen-day extravaganza. According to Cassius Dio, the emperor rounded up all the men in Rome who had lost their feet, because of disease or accident. Their legs were dressed to resemble the tails of serpents, like those of the giants of myth. They were armed with rocks made of sponge. Commodus then beat them to death with a very real club of Hercules.

The rehabilitation of 'bad' emperors like Commodus has become a standard scholarly response. It runs on these lines. The emperor did not get on with the elite. They wrote all the literary accounts once he was safely dead. So anything they say can be dismissed as posthumous propaganda. All the really strange anecdotes are just *topoi* (literary commonplaces; it sounds more authoritative in Greek), and *topoi* were where ancient writers 'played'. If similar stories are told of two or more 'bad' emperors, somehow they are both proved to be untrue. Sometimes the mundane functioning of the empire – roads being repaired, laws issued – is enlisted to show the efficiency of the emperor's regime. Sometimes art is adduced – coins, statues – to reveal the well-thought-out promotion of a new, and often original, image of the role of the emperor. The results are that the 'bad' emperor – far from capricious, perverse, or mad, or however our literary sources portray him – was a rational, if radical, politician. In essence he always turns out to be a 'good' emperor, who was approved by everyone, except, of course, the elite.

Such rehabilitation is in many ways fundamentally flawed. Art does not give us a window into the mind of the emperor. Changes in the style of the emperor's portrait busts can be remarkably similar across the empire. Clearly, they respond to a central model, but we have no information on who at the centre chose those models, or how they were disseminated. We are on slightly firmer ground with what appeared on imperial coins. However, we hardly ever hear of emperors choosing coin types. Instead, they were usually chosen by the *tres viri magistrales*, a board of junior magistrates, who were not yet senators. The pictures and words on coins were images offered up by subjects, not evidence of a coherent imperial policy. Similarly, roads got repaired, and laws were promulgated, with little or no input from the emperor. No matter who was on the throne, the day-to-day machinery of government continued. Then there was the literature. *Topoi* were indeed where ancient authors 'played', but it was not always a game without any rules. Some writers, like the unknown novelist of the *Augustan History*, felt free to invent. But those writing in a more realistic register, like the historian Cassius Dio, were constrained by appositeness and plausibility. They selected and shaped *topoi* to fit with the perceived truth. If *topoi* were no more than free fiction, they should have been applied indiscriminately. All 'bad' emperors would have been accused of the same things, and they were not – only Commodus is said to have fought as a gladiator in the Colosseum.

At a fundamental level, these standard rehabilitations rest on both allowing too much and too little imagination. On the one hand, it depends on imagining, despite a lack of evidence, the feelings of the non-elite, which are assumed to be in opposition to the elite. On the other, it refuses to imagine that autocrats often do irrational, even deranged things. In any event, no rehabilitation can deny that Commodus fought in the Colosseum.

On New Year's Eve AD 192 Commodus announced that the following morning he would start the procession to be inaugurated consul from the gladiatorial barracks, where he would spend the night, presumably in the *Ludus Magnus*, where he had a cell as the highest-ranked *secutor*. Instead of a toga, he would be equipped as a gladiator and escorted by the rest of the imperial gladiators. His mistress, Marcia, the chamberlain of his bedchamber (*a cubiculo*), Eclectus, and the Praetorian prefect, Laetus, desperately begged the emperor to change his plan. Their advice was rejected. When the emperor threatened them, they decided Commodus had to die. Interestingly, only the equestrian Laetus had any claim to be a member of the elite, the other two, as members of the *Familia Caesaris* (palace staff), were ex-slaves. Commodus took some killing. Poison was administered to his lunch, either in his wine or beef. As emperors built up their immunity by taking a daily dose of a tiny amount of every poison known to man, Commodus merely felt ill and vomited. While he was recovering in the bath, the conspirators sent in a burly Greek athlete to strangle the gladiator-emperor.

Commodus, murdered after lunch in the palace, never made it to his last *cena libera*. Had he done so, a gladiator hoping for the sort of elaborate delicacies that their subjects liked to imagine emperors ate – the *pentepharmacum* of Hadrian, a pie of pheasant, peacock, ham, sow's udder and wild boar; let alone the force-meat of lobster, crab and prawn, washed down with wine flavoured with mastic and pennyroyal, or the tongues of peacocks and nightingales of Heliogabalus – might have been disappointed. Emperors could take their roleplay very seriously. Acting the common soldier, the emperor Caracalla had the hair-cut and the clothes, marched on foot carrying a standard, and in camp sat on the ground eating the porridge and bacon and drinking the sour wine of legionary rations.

Privacy

The big, burly, scarred men dining at the *cena libera* had their every mouthful studied, their every expression analysed. To watch people eat is alien to our culture now; it feels intrusive, makes both sides uncomfortable. Not so for the Romans, who drew different parameters around privacy.

Take the public baths. Across the empire the baths were a self-conscious and distinctive marker of Roman identity. Everyone went to the public baths, at times even those rich enough to have a private bathhouse. When Hadrian saw a veteran rubbing the oil off himself against a wall, because he could not afford a slave to scrape him down, the emperor gave him both slaves and the cost of their maintenance. On a subsequent day Hadrian was confronted by several old men doing the same; the emperor told them to rub each other down. Like Scandinavians in saunas, Romans normally bathed naked. Unlike Scandinavians, men and women usually bathed separately; either there were separate suites, or different times. Mixed bathing aroused the indignation of Roman moralists. In the fiction of the *Augustan History*, emperors' attitudes to mixed bathing was employed as a kind of moral shorthand: the appalling Heliogabalus encouraged it; the virtuous Alexander Severus banned it. Single sex bathing did not remove the sexual charge. Public baths were like multiple-use leisure centres: not just bathhouses, but places for eating and drinking, exercising and having a massage, maybe consulting a doctor, looking at art, listening to music or lectures, the grandest even had libraries. Among the facilities, some shadier establishments offered prostitutes. Again, elite moralists were outraged; the non-elite, one suspects, less so, as they were accustomed to taverns, where the serving girls also provided sexual services for money. The baths remained steamy with sex, even without the prostitutes. The moral philosopher Plutarch recorded that it was not proper or decent for fathers and sons to bathe together. *The Confessions* of Saint Augustine provide a reason. Aged fifteen, when the 'brambles of lust grew high above my head', the future saint seems to have had an unwanted erection in the baths. His pagan father was delighted at the thought of grandchildren; on the other hand, his Christian mother, when informed later, was 'alarmed and apprehensive'. Any man visiting the baths could expect to have his penis closely scrutinised. Those lacking a foreskin, either naturally or through circumcision, sometimes resorted to cosmetic surgery. The procedure for the latter, the medical writer Celsus assures his reader, 'is not so very painful'. Size mattered and attracted attention. Martial describes a man of outwardly austere morality who at the baths 'keeps his gaze below waist level, devouring the boys with his eyes, his lips twitching at the sight of a luscious prick'. Martial again says that if you hear a round of applause in the baths, 'Maron's giant cock is the cause.' Seneca talks of an individual who scoured the baths for well-endowed men, then took them back to his house, where he liked to watch himself having sex with them in a room equipped with distorting mirrors, which both magnified and multiplied their cocks (or, as Seneca puts it, 'revealed scenes of revolting and abominable iniquity'). Heliogabalus was said to have added an element of compulsion, employing the *frumentarii* (Rome's nearest equivalent to a secret service) to take well-hung men from the baths to the palace for the emperor's pleasure.

Another area where the Romans drew the boundaries of

privacy very differently from us was the use of communal latrines, whose ruins are so loved by modern tourists. Even the elite used them at times. At Hadrian's villa at Tivoli the rooms where the emperor and his guests dined were served by single-seat lavatories, but multiple-use ones were attached to the baths. Perhaps access was controlled: 'Don't go in there, an important senator is having a shit.' At the other end of the social spectrum, female slaves must have used communal ones. Again, at Hadrian's villa quarters for perhaps 600 servants had one communal latrine with just fifteen seats. Perhaps here too access was controlled: 'Don't go in there, it is the women's turn.' There was a certain amount of privacy from the outside world. Staggered entrances prevented passers-by from seeing in, but there was not always an actual door. (Interestingly, some of the most luxurious single lavatories at Hadrian's villa had a big picture window with a fine view. It has been suggested that these were screened by a translucent cloth, although again control might be the answer: 'Don't go into the garden, the emperor is having a shit.') But there was no privacy *inside* a communal latrine. There were no cubicles or partitions. There has been a modern attempt to provide a little privacy in the form of suggestions that the keyhole cutaways at the front of the seats, and the voluminous folds of a toga, might allow unobserved arse-wiping with the supposedly ubiquitous sponge on a stick. The former idea has some merit, although such discretion would not always have been possible, as some latrines lack the keyhole, and the manoeuvre perhaps called for more dexterity from men. The suggestion about clothing is less convincing – Romans hardly ever wore the toga, which was reserved for certain formal contexts. An overly modest man, according to Tertullian, can hardly bring himself to lift his tunic in public to relieve himself. As a Christian savaging pagan behaviour, Tertullian goes on that in the Circus the very same man gets so carried away that he strips off his tunic completely, 'as if bent on exposing himself before everybody'. In a communal latrine the seats were very close together, usually allowing only about twenty inches for each user, and sometimes as few as twelve. Everyone was exposed to a close and personal range of sensory experiences: sights, smells and sounds. They drew comment. Suetonius tells that the poet Lucan once farted so loudly in a latrine that all the other users ran out. The poet called out after them an apposite line of the emperor Nero's dreadful verse: 'You'd think it had thundered underground.' As the anecdote indicates, humorous conversation was normal. A wall painting in the 'Tavern of the Seven Sages' at Ostia depicts the seven wise men holding objects that resemble sponges on sticks, and discoursing on bowel movements: 'Thales of Miletus advised those having a difficult shit to push hard', while 'Cunning Chilon taught how to fart silently'. Below the sages, ordinary men are talking to each other. One advises, 'Shake yourself about, and you will finish your crap faster'; his neighbour testily replies, 'I am hurrying' (one word in Latin, *propero*). Some moments were less suitable for conversation: 'No one says many words to you, Priscianus, while you are using the sponge on a stick.' Indeed, it would be hard to argue against the words of another: 'Shit well, and the doctors can suck your dick.'

Nothing in life is more hedged around with cultural norms than privacy and sex. The painted walls of two rooms that survive of the Villa Farnesina, excavated in Rome, and dated to about 20BC, depict a Greek-style art gallery (a *pinacotheca*). Set in a fake architectural background of painted columns and marble slabs are pictures represented as if hanging on the walls. Artfully arranged among them are erotic images. In each a man and a woman on a richly furnished bed are in the early stages of making love: they are about to kiss, or are already kissing; the breasts of one of the women are exposed. The setting is domestic, and the couples are married; one woman wears a bridal veil. What comes as a shock to us is that servants are in the room, on hand with refreshments. The House of Caecilius Iucundus at Pompeii has a more explicit image. A male servant approaches a well-upholstered bed on which a woman, whose breasts and bottom are exposed, is straddling a man in the 'reverse-cowgirl' position, and reaching behind her for his penis, either just before or after penetrative sex. The servant looks straight into her face. His head is closer to hers than that of her husband.

These erotic images were not tucked away in some 'private' part of the house. The rooms they decorate were *cubicula*. The usual translation of 'bedrooms' is somewhat misleading. With a few exceptions – kitchens, lavatories, baths – the function of rooms in Roman houses was not as 'fixed' as in ours. *Cubicula* – a house of any size would have more than one – were places for both sleeping and sex, but they were also where you received visitors. Outsiders viewed this erotic art. The painting in the house of Caecilius Iucundus is in a prominent spot, just off the open space at the centre of the building, which suggests visitors were positively encouraged to stop and look. How are we meant to understand these images where servants are present while their owners have sex?

One interpretation could be that slaves, those 'instruments with voices', were beneath consideration. As they were not completely human, it really did not matter what you did in front of them. It is true that none of the couples look at the servants, and the majority of the latter do not look at those making love. Another interpretation might run as follows. There are endless stories in Roman literature of either the master or the mistress of a house having sex with a slave. This was socially acceptable for the master. In a work of advice to married couples, Plutarch recommends a wife should ignore such a peccadillo on the part of her husband. But such a dalliance was totally unacceptable for the wife. It was grounds for divorce and disgrace. The consequences for the slave were worse. In Petronius' *Satyricon* one of the attractions in a gladiatorial show anticipated by the freedman Echion is a slave-steward who had been caught having sex with the mistress of the house being thrown to the lions. Echion predicts that the sympathies of the audience will divide between jealous husbands and ardent lovers. Such anecdotes, coupled with other works of art that depict servants surreptitiously peering round doors to watch elite couples making love, might suggest that the servants in the room offered a transgressive thrill.

The most credible modern interpretation, however, discounts such 'documentary' readings. The servants are an artistic convention. They, like the wine jugs they hold, and the rich cushions on the beds, symbolise luxury, and thus the wealth and status of the household. The style of the scenes recalls fourth-century BC Greek art, and thus points to the taste and sophistication of the owners of the villa. On this reading the erotic images play with chronology, conflating two moments in time: the servants had already left the room before the start of the lovemaking, or, in the Villa Farnesina, are about to leave before the action gets any hotter, or, perhaps in the House of Caecilius Iucundus, have come back in afterwards. Even in these cases, the servants in the room remain unsettling to us. It is very easy to imagine a modern affluent and aspirational Western couple commissioning or buying art that they intend to indicate their wealth, status and good taste. But much harder to think that they would hang on their walls pictures that invited the viewer to speculate on the intimacies of their sex life, let alone that might open implications of socially unacceptable deviancy. It reminds us that the ancient Romans placed the boundaries of privacy in different places from us, not only in their actions, but also in their innermost thoughts.

The boundaries of Roman privacy were moveable. Pliny the Younger, in a speech of praise to the emperor Trajan, claimed that 'one of the chief features of high estate is that it permits no privacy, no concealment, and in the case of a *princeps* [a *leading man*; a tactful way to refer to an emperor], it throws open the door not only to their homes, but to their bedrooms [*cubicula*], and their most intimate retreats'. In one sense this is completely untrue – an example of Pliny viewing the world solely through the eyes of his own class. Only the elite had the wealth to afford, or the authority to command, even a temporary seclusion. Ironically, Pliny himself, never exactly one of the boys, boasted in a letter that the part of his seaside villa he loved best was a suite of rooms where at night 'neither the voices of my young slaves, nor the noise of a storm can penetrate'. It was an ideal retreat, 'especially during the Saturnalia when the rest of the house resounds with festive cries in the holiday freedom'. Yet, in another sense, Pliny's words to Trajan had some truth. Any elite desire for isolation fuelled rumour and scurrilous gossip: *he must hide himself away for nefarious activities*. It was a sign of Domitian's bad character that he spent hours every day on his own. Popular imagination filled that time with brooding and killing flies with a sharp stylus. Any such solitude brought danger. A Greek athlete was able to strangle Commodus because the emperor was on his own in the baths. At least Commodus probably was drowsy from poison; the emperor Caracalla's death was more demeaning. On a journey in Mesopotamia Caracalla had an upset stomach and needed to relieve himself. His bodyguards and entourage drew back, out of respect for the emperor's dignity and honour. They looked away, although remaining within sight. This allowed an assassin to pretend the emperor had summoned him with a nod. Caracalla was stabbed to death with his trousers round his ankles.

The Romans were as aware as we are that privacy was culturally coded. Long before, in the fifth century BC, Herodotus had stated that 'everywhere custom was King'. The 'Father of History' was remarkably non-judgemental about other cultures, but the majority of his followers abandoned his moral relativism. The fourth-century AD historian Ammianus Marcellinus thoroughly disliked the Sassanid Persians. Which is not to say that he was uninformed, or made up what he wrote about them. Rather, he selected and nuanced his ethnographic comments to contrast them, usually to their detriment, to the Romans. The Persians had very different attitudes to privacy. They had no set times for meals, at which they were abstemious with food and drink. Though the Persians were voluble and boastful, those serving them at the table were forbidden to open their mouths. Far from bathing naked, Persians took care never to expose any part of the body from their neck to their feet. Similarly, they were notable for an insistence on absolute seclusion when urinating or defecating; you seldom saw them doing either.

No one in Roman society had any expectation of privacy when dining. The elite always had servants in attendance at every meal. The poor and slaves, crammed together in narrow tenements and servile quarters, or eating in busy taverns, of course, had no privacy at all. Everyone from highest to lowest was completely accustomed both to watch and to being watched at the table. Such scrutiny caused neither the gladiators nor the spectators the slightest discomfort at the *cena libera*.

Reasons

What reasons lay behind the strange cultural construct of the *cena libera*?

Various explanations are on offer. It was a way for the *editor* to compensate or thank the participants for the dangers and possible death they would face the next day; for their suffering, which would bring the *editor* popularity with the crowd. Another suggestion is that it was to raise the lowly status of slaves and the like, to make them worthy of taking part in the exalted ritual in the arena. A third has it forming a dramatic contrast with the forthcoming violence, thus acting as a form of mediation between the living and the dead.

All these operate at a deep structural level below the consciousness of those involved, and, to my mind, do little to explain the *cena libera*. The *editor* had no need to thank the gladiators and those who would fight the wild beasts. Apart from free volunteers, who had chosen their status, the rest – the prisoners of war, criminals and slaves – had already been compensated. They had not been executed, as they could have been. Instead, they had been given a chance of life, even acclaim, money, and eventual freedom. The argument that the meal was to raise the status of the participants depends on understanding the gladiatorial Games as a type of human sacrifice. It is true that later Roman antiquarians speculated, without any evidence, that in the distant past the Games had originated out of human sacrifice. Perhaps unsurprisingly, Christian polemicists not only leaped on this idea, but invented fiction which wrote such sacrifices back into the real world of the contemporary arena. But at no point in recorded history did anyone involved in the Games (except, of course, the Christians) see themselves as taking part in human sacrifice. The final suggestion that the contrast between the conviviality of the meal and the bloodshed on the sand in some way mediated between the living and the dead seems, to me at least, too vague to explain anything.

Another proposal feels more plausible: advertisement. The *cena libera* existed in the same category as the parade of gladiators through the marketplace of Amastris that caught the attention of Sisinnes, or the posters painted on the walls of Pompeii listing the attractions of coming Games. The *cena libera* was part of ratcheting up the anticipation that would bring a big crowd.

Another way of thinking about the reasons behind the *cena libera* is to move to the surface level and explore the conscious motives of the spectators. Why did the thin men come to watch the fat men eat? Some had specialist interests. First and foremost, of course, there were the serious aficionados of the Games; those, like Apuleius' stepson, who hung out in the schools with the gladiators.

The other group we can identify who had a special reason to attend is far odder to our mind. One of the key sources for trying to reconstruct the *cena libera* is a passage in Plutarch: 'Why even among the gladiators, I observe that those who are not utterly bestial, but are Greeks, when about to enter the arena, though many expensive foods are put before them, find greater pleasure in recommending their women to the care of their friends and setting free their slaves than in gratifying their stomachs.'

Now mainly remembered as a biographer, the author of parallel lives of Greek and Roman statesmen, which inspired several of Shakespeare's plays, Plutarch was first and foremost a Platonic philosopher. He was an important player in the Greek cultural renaissance of the first three centuries AD (now usually labelled the Second Sophistic), which placed a central importance on high Greek culture (*Paedeia*) and its intellectual and moral benefits. The brief passage on the *cena libera* is found in one of two linked, and lengthy, treatises refuting the views of the rival school of Epicurean philosophers. The argument at this point is that the pleasures of the flesh are nothing compared with those of the mind.

Plutarch is not giving us unbiased reportage on the ritual of the last dinner. We may well doubt that only Greek gladiators behaved well at the *cena libera*. But the point here is that Plutarch has gone to the meal to observe the gladiators to draw a philosophical moral. Not only that, but he expects his philosophically-minded readers to be able to verify his point from their own experience. The highly educated (the *pepaideumenoi*) attended the *cena libera* searching for insights into human nature.

A less cerebral, but no doubt more common, motive among the spectators was *Schadenfreude*, pleasure in the misfortune of others. By the same time the next day some of those dining were going to die, but the viewer was not. With an uncertain faith in an afterlife, Roman culture was fascinated by death. Innumerable artistic and literary *memento mori* reminded you to enjoy what little time you had in the light. At Trimalchio's dinner the host had an articulated model of a skeleton in silver. Having thrown it on the table once or twice, so its flexible joints fell in different postures, Trimalchio recited some of his execrable verse.

O woe, woe, man is only a dot:
Hell drags us off and that is the lot;
So let us live a little space,
At least while we can feed our face.

Or, as Horace famously put it, *carpe diem*; seize the day. You were never more alive than when faced with death.

There was another, much more prosaic, draw for the spectators: gambling. It must be admitted that we have no direct evidence for betting on gladiatorial Games. Scholars are divided on its existence. Yet all levels of Roman society were obsessed with gambling. It was not left at the entrance of the arena. Gaming boards have been found scratched into the stones of the amphitheatre at Aphrodisias (in modern Turkey), and the Colosseum itself in Rome. We know they bet on cock fighting and chariot racing. Gambling was seen as a social problem when others, especially the lower classes, indulged. (It obviously wasn't an issue when you or your friends did it.) Repeated laws sought to regulate it. Three laws from the late Republic, mentioned in the sixth-century AD *Digest*, suggest the people were betting on gladiatorial Games. It was legal to bet on athletic contests – javelin- and spear-throwing, running, jumping, wrestling and boxing are named – where the contest involved *virtus* (courage or strength). We have already seen another passage from the *Digest* where men fought wild beasts in the arena explicitly to prove their *virtus*. As mentioned before, given that the texts were compiled long after gladiatorial combat was extinct, it is most probable that gladiators have simply been edited out from lists like these.

If people did gamble on the arena, it would not have been like modern horse racing or other sporting events. There were no professional bookmakers, let alone a Tote or pari-mutuel. A closer comparison would be the individual wagers staked on racing or boxing in the eighteenth and nineteenth centuries. Which is not to say there were no odds. Only a fool, or someone with inside knowledge, bets even money on an outsider. It is important, as well as honest, that a historian is open about how their own background has shaped their views. Brought up in racing stables, I find it very difficult to imagine going to the Games and *not* wanting to have a bet. For me, the *cena libera* was like the pre-parade ring at the July Course at Newmarket, where those in the know go to study the condition and behaviour of the contestants.

A Mosaic and Conversations

We have one visual representation of a *cena libera*: a mosaic dating to the third century AD found in a house in the North African city of El Djem (**Plate Three**). Within a border of four stalks of millet, five men recline on the top level of an amphitheatre. All are elaborately dressed. Two of them wear crowns: one has three prongs, with a cross in the centre, the other five, with a blue fish in the centre. Each of the three bareheaded men holds an object: a leaf on a long stem, a stalk of millet, and a staff which ends in a crescent. Their conversation is inscribed above their heads: (from left to right) 'We will take off our clothes'; 'We have come to drink'; 'You are all talking too much'; 'Let's have fun'; and (more enigmatically) 'We are holding three'. Below them on the floor of the arena, in the bottom register, five bulls are lying down; each has a different brand: a leaf, a fish, a millet stalk, a gladiator, and a design like a *sistrum* (a kind of rattle). In the middle register, still on the arena floor, two servants flank a mixing bowl and two jugs on a table. One holds a drinking cup up to the reclining men, the other puts a finger to his lips, and says, 'Silence, don't wake the bulls.'

After some debate, scholars agreed the mosaic depicts a *cena libera*. The various symbols are those of organisations of beast-hunters (*venatores*), based in different cities across North Africa. Some have been identified from other works of art. The crescent-headed staff, apart from being an instrument to physically control animals, was a symbol of the *Telegenii*; the fish, one of the *Pentasii*. Most likely the symbols refer to the patron deity of each group of *venatores*: in art, Dionysius sometimes holds a crescent on a stick, Diana a stalk of millet.

The composition of this mosaic was unique, not chosen from a stock repertoire of a workshop. The man who commissioned it was making a series of interlinked statements about himself. Obviously that he was rich – high-quality polychrome mosaics like this cost a lot of money. Also that he was civic-minded – he had funded a beast-fight in the amphitheatre of El Djem for its citizens. Not just any beast fight, but a lavish one; he had brought various groups of *venatores*, and their animals, from across the province. Finally – *Silence, don't wake the bulls* – that he had a sense of humour. As well as these evocations, guests dining in his house, looking down at the *venatores* dining, might reflect that unlike the beast-fighters, they would not have to venture into the arena the next day.

The mosaic is not a form of 'photo-realism'. There are elements of fantasy. It is highly unlikely that servants would attempt to go about their duties next to dangerous wild animals. Certainly, they could not physically serve men in the upper reaches of the amphitheatre from the sands in the centre. But the image opens several avenues of interpretation.

Take the location of the *cena libera*. Walking through the gladiatorial barracks at Pompeii, or looking down at the exposed ruins of the *Ludus Maximus* in Rome, it is hard not to imagine that these were the settings for the last meal. In the *Passion of Perpetua and Felicitas* the Christians had their version of the *cena libera* in the prison in which they were confined. But in the El Djem mosaic the venue is the amphitheatre itself. For such costly edifices, amphitheatres were very underused. There were only a few days of Games each year. Holding the *cena libera* there added another day of use to the arena for each show.

The mosaic tells us something about the nature of the dinner.

This was no free-for-all boorish food fight. Reclining in fancy clothes, while servants handed you wine, indicates a symposium, the Greek style of elite drinking party, which had been enthusiastically adopted by the Roman upper classes. The giver of the Games had opened the purse strings. The conversation among the *venatores* might not have been at the intellectual level of literary symposia, like Athenaeus' *Sophists at Dinner* (*Deipnosophistae*), or Plutarch's *Table-talk* (*Symposiaka*), but that just adds to the humour.

The inscriptions make us think about conversation – who talked to who? At the *cena libera* of Plutarch the gladiators talk to each other. Here in the mosaic the servants talk to those dining. We have to turn to the Christian adaptation of the meal in *The Passion of Perpetua and Felicitas* for the missing piece. The Christians speak harshly to the spectators, warning them of the judgement of God, and ridiculing their curiosity: 'Today you are our friends, tomorrow our enemies, but take careful note of what we look like, so that you will recognise us on the day.' The Christians were doomed, the gladiators were not necessarily. It is unlikely any of the latter would have adopted the truculent tone of the Christians. If a gladiator appealed for mercy in the arena, his fate was decided by the giver of the Games, but the latter was expected to be swayed by the crowd. The spectators at the *cena libera*, especially the aficionados of the arena, would be influential in the stands. Any gladiator in his right mind would want to be remembered – hoping the friendship of the evening would last until the following afternoon.

Which one of the five figures in El Djem would you bet on? Certainly not the one on the left, 'We will take off our clothes', with his slouched posture and inebriated gesture. Probably not either 'We have come to drink', or 'Let's have fun'; although at least they can sit up straight, and you might think they are showing an admirable sangfroid. 'You are talking too much' is more promising, but maybe he is just an aggressive drunk. My money goes on the man on the right. 'We are holding three' probably means 'We have had three drinks, and that is enough'. Something else suggests both that he is in control and a figure of some authority. Where individuals look is often significant in ancient art. The other four drinkers all look at the man on the right, who returns their gaze calmly with a hand gesture that recalls those of triumphant generals. Definitely worth a few *sesterces*.

Revenge

No subjects of Rome had more reason to hate the empire in general, and the gladiatorial Games in particular, than the Jews. Many thousands of Jews died in the arena after the First Jewish Revolt of AD66–70. The same can be assumed after the crushing of the less well documented Diaspora Revolt of AD115–7, and the rebellion led by Bar Kokhba in AD132–5. Although there is some slight evidence of Jews attending the Games in the audience, nothing conclusive points to them ever volunteering to fight. But in fiction they could volunteer, and they could get their revenge.

The *Babylonian Talmud* was compiled in the sixth or seventh century AD, long after the end of the Games, and outside the empire, in Babylonia, where gladiatorial combat had never happened. Far from a reliable source, the *Babylonian Talmud* embroidered a colourful early life for the third-century AD Rabbi Reish Lakish (also known as Shim'on ben Lakish): either he was a bandit in the wilderness, or he sold himself into a gladiatorial school. Described as very strong and fat, the future rabbi appeared well suited to the latter life. This version adds a 'condemned man's last wish' to the *cena libera* – an evident fiction, given both the lack of other evidence, and what follows in the story. When asked what he wanted, Reish Lakish said he would like to tie up each of them, sit them down, and hit them all one-and-a-half times (the identity of Reish Lakish's interlocuters is ambiguous in the original text). Almost inexplicably – did they assume it was some sort of game? – they agreed. What Reish Lakish had not told them was that he had a rock in a bag, with which he duly beat them to death one by one, before making his escape.

Revenge is best served with a good one-liner. When one of the gladiators gnashed his teeth, Reish Lakish said, 'Are you laughing at me? You still have half a strike remaining, as I have only hit you once,' and finished him off – a sanguine end to the strangest *cena libera*.

2

Prima Vigilia
(The First Watch of the Night)

The cena libera *is over. At last the slaves can sweep up, and eat and drink the leftovers. For the gladiators, drunk or sober, it is time for bed. They see themselves as sex-symbols: Lords of the Girls. But no matter where, or with whom, he usually spends the night, before a fight a gladiator sleeps in the barracks of his* ludus *or school.*

The Schools

Spartacus was owned by a man called Batiatus. The cruelty of Batiatus, unjustly keeping his gladiators shackled all the time when they were not fighting, caused them to break out of their school in Capua, triggering the great Italian slave revolt of 73–71BC. Putting the blame on the individual bad behaviour of Batiatus, as Plutarch does, was useful to the slave-owning elite. It served both as a warning, and as a reassurance – few slave owners would have seen themselves as particularly cruel. Batiatus was easy to blame. He was not a member of the elite, but instead a morally reprehensible, and socially marginalised *lanista*. Batiatus is the first of the *lanistae* to be named in our sources. These were shady, lower-class figures who made their living by directly buying, training, leasing and selling gladiators. In elite eyes they were worse than ordinary slave traders. Contaminated by the shedding of human blood, they were the evil that had made themselves necessary.

A troupe of gladiators was a 'family' (*familia gladiatoria*). This term implies no affection. Slaves were part of an owner's extended *familia*, and any group of slaves was a *familia*. Where the gladiators were quartered was a *ludus*. Under the Republic, troupes of gladiators were owned by individuals. Apart from Batiatus, all those whose names are known were members of the traditional elite. Of course there were many *lanistae* like Batiatus, but they were of no interest to our literary sources, unless their appalling actions caused a disaster. The elite could own gladiators for pleasure or profit. Cicero had heard great things of the gladiators bought by his friend Atticus: they had fought magnificently; had he hired them out he would have recouped his outlay in two shows. Unlike a *lanista*, Atticus was not involved in the day-to-day running of his troupe, so avoided any social stigma. Such social distancing was perfectly familiar. A member of the elite could appoint a freedman or slave to manage their interests in trade, manufacture or usury so that they could rake in profits without being tainted by the sordid nature of these activities.

Atticus was a wealthy equestrian, who kept out of the dangerous business of politics. The other named owners of gladiators were senators. For them pleasure and profit took second place to politics. While Rome remained a republic, senators needed the votes of the plebs to pass laws proposed by themselves and their friends, and to reject those of their enemies. Even more importantly, they needed those votes to further their careers, to elect them to the higher magistracies – from quaestor to praetor to consul – to help them ascend the *cursus honorum*, the 'ladder of offices'. It is impossible to overestimate the importance of the *cursus honorum* in the self-fashioning of senators. If you were one of the two consuls appointed every twelve months, not only was your family ennobled for ever, but, as the year during which you served was known by your name, you achieved a sort of immortality. By the last century BC there was no better vote-winner than giving lavish gladiatorial Games. Julius Caesar owned a gladiatorial *familia* in Capua, said to contain 5,000 fighters. Desperate as always to excel, in 65BC he gave a show starring 320 pairs of fighters, a previously unparalleled number.

Such gladiatorial troupes were objects of suspicion. Although there never was another great slave revolt after Spartacus, the fear remained that gladiators might make a bid for freedom and lead a rebellion. As late as AD61, according to Tacitus, an attempted breakout by gladiators in the town of Praeneste was still capable of evoking the spectre of Spartacus. Under the Republic a more pressing apprehension was that the gladiators' senatorial owners would use them for political violence. Trained for combat, gladiators made good bodyguards. Faustus Sulla, the son of the Dictator, surrounded himself with 300 men from the arena. The fear was very real, as the line between bodyguards and an armed gang existed only in the eye of the beholder. In 62BC Metellus Nepos brought men with weapons, including gladiators, into the Forum, and stationed them on the steps of the temple of Castor and Pollux to intimidate voters. He intended to force through a law recalling Pompey in order to crush a conspiracy led by a disaffected senator called Catiline to overthrow the elected government. At first it appeared to be working. When the gladiators charged with terrifying shouts, the voters ran, and Cato the Younger, who was opposing the bill, was pelted with sticks and stones. Seeing the area empty, and thinking he had succeeded, Metellus ordered the armed men to leave. His opponents rallied, then chased Metellus and his remaining partisans away.

Extremist senators at both ends of the political spectrum turned to gladiators to help them further their ambitions and priorities: both the minority of *populares*, who argued that all citizens should be active in politics, and the majority of *optimates*, who held that the Roman people should follow the lead of the Senate. The arch *popularis* Clodius could put men on the street from many sources, including gladiatorial schools. His conservative enemy Milo had to rely more heavily on gladiators to fill out his gangs. In the 50BC fighting between their supporters threatened to make Rome ungovernable. The climax came with a chance encounter mid-afternoon on 17 January 52BC, some ten miles from Rome, on the Appian Way. Clodius, accompanied by three friends and thirty slaves armed with swords, was riding back to the city. Milo was leaving the city. He was in a carriage with his wife and a close friend, but was escorted by a large contingent of slaves, including gladiators. Two of the latter, the famous Eudamus and Birria, riding at the head of the column, charged Clodius' party. As more of Milo's men rushed up, Birria wounded Clodius with a sword thrust to his shoulder. Clodius' men carried him into a nearby inn, but Milo ordered him dragged out and hacked to death. His corpse was left by the side of the road. In an eloquent statement of political allegiance, when Clodius' body was returned to Rome, some three hours later, the plebs used the senate house as its funeral pyre.

At times of crisis the Senate moved to forestall gladiatorial violence. In 63BC, during the panic caused by the conspiracy of Catiline, all gladiatorial troupes were expelled from Rome, split up, and sent to Capua and other towns, where they could be guarded. At the same time, one Gaius Marcellus was expelled from Capua, where he had joined a gladiatorial troupe under the pretence of training in arms. In 49BC, at the start of the civil war, a supporter of Pompey had the men in Caesar's gladiatorial school in Capua distributed among the rural slave gangs in the area. Later Pompey himself, perhaps with Spartacus in mind, removed the gladiators from this dangerous source of potential servile rebels, and had them confined two to a household in Capua itself.

Augustus' reintroduction of monarchy to Rome, which saw him supplant the senatorial order as the chief patron of the plebs, sounded the death knell for private schools of gladiators in the city. Augustus did not ban them; that would have smacked of tyranny, which would have run counter to his carefully crafted image as first among equals (*primus inter pares*). Augustus contented himself with regulating and limiting the few gladiatorial shows given by magistrates. Some private troupes still existed under Augustus. The poet Horace tells of a *ludus* owned by one Aemilius, which was a landmark. In 29BC Statilius Taurus, one of Augustus' generals, dedicated the first stone amphitheatre in Rome, on the Campus Martius, the 'Field of Mars', down by the Tiber. Four years later a praetor, Publius Servilius, gave a wild beast hunt at which 300 bears and 300 'African animals' (lions, or perhaps big cats in general) were killed. But for the elite the rules of the game had changed. Senatorial advancement no longer came from the votes of the populace, but from the favour of the emperor. Not only had the key reason for senators to own a troupe of gladiators been removed, but their possession had become potentially dangerous. Given the legacy of gladiatorial political violence during the Republic, a senator under the principate who owned a school of gladiators was potentially opening themselves up to a charge of treason (*maiestas*). It is likely that by the mid-first century AD all private schools in Rome had disappeared.

It is sometimes argued that Roman senators continued to stage combats in private once giving public gladiatorial shows had become the prerogative of the emperor, or magistrates overseen by the authorities. Writing under Augustus, Nicolaus of Damascus claimed that the Romans had adopted gladiatorial combat from the Etruscans, and that some Romans put on two or three pairs of gladiators at dinner parties. The Greek Nicolaus thoroughly disapproved: 'sated with food and drink, they called in the gladiators . . . as soon as one had his throat cut, they applauded with delight'. Nicolaus linked this decadent behaviour to a Roman whose will specified that his most beautiful slave girls should fight each other, and another who did the same for his favourite slave boys. If the practice continued, it has left little trace.

It is true that the elite could legally own gladiators. Consuls, praetors and others were compelled by Caligula to buy imperial gladiators at auction for vastly inflated prices. It was said that when one senator fell asleep the emperor instructed the auctioneer to take his nodding head as bidding, and the man woke up to find he had bought thirteen gladiators for nine million *sesterces*. In one version of the story some bankrupted by their unwanted purchases opened their veins and took their own lives. In another, Caligula subsequently had the best and most famous of the gladiators poisoned. But by the time the passage of Nicolaus was quoted by Athenaeus in the *Sophists at Dinner*, in the early third century AD, the events he described were no more than an antiquarian curiosity, just like tales of naked serving girls at Etruscan dinners, or Parthians eating like dogs on the ground. Quite possibly, Nicolaus had been writing about the baleful influence of the Etruscans on Rome in the long distant past. The Greek geographer Strabo, a contemporary of Nicolaus, illustrated the extravagant luxury of the ancient inhabitants of Campania by claiming they exhibited gladiators at dinner parties; he gave no indication that contemporary Romans indulged in the same custom.

The imperial schools grew out of that established by Julius Caesar in Capua. Gladiators owned by the emperor were known as *Iuliani*. Nero founded another school, the *Neroniani*. The two schools coexisted, and their members could be hired by private givers of Games. A graffito from Pompeii reproduced the programme from a show given by a man called Marcus Mesonius. Over several days *Iuliani* and *Neroniani* fought both against each other and members of their own *ludus*. After the suicide of Nero, and the end of the Julio-Claudian dynasty in AD69, the names *Iuliani* and *Neroniani* were no longer used, and fighters from an imperial *ludus* were known interchangeably as gladiators of Caesar, Augustus, or the princeps. The emperor Domitian reorganised the imperial gladiators, building four schools in Rome: the *Ludus Magnus*, *Ludus Matutinus*, *Ludus Dacicus* and *Ludus Gallicus*. Almost half the *Ludus Magnus* can be seen about a hundred yards to the east of the Colosseum. A late-antique list of buildings in the regions of Rome places all four close to the Colosseum. An excavation in 1938 found traces of a smaller building with a similar plan just south of the *Ludus Magnus*, which has tentatively been identified as the *Ludus Matutinus*. The name, 'School of the Morning' (*Ludus Matutinus*), suggests this was for training animal fighters, who performed before noon. We know from a letter of Seneca that a *ludus* for beast fighters (*ludus bestiarius*) already existed. It is often said that the other two schools were built to house Dacian and Gallic prisoners of war, who had been condemned to fight in the arena. The former might be true. The Dacian wars of Domitian were disastrous, but even unsuccessful campaigns produced some captives, and imperial propaganda was quite capable of turning defeat into victory. That the *Ludus Gallicus* was designed for defeated Gallic warriors is much less convincing. The last brief and localised revolt in Gaul had been over for more than a decade before Domitian came to power in AD81. It is more likely that it was named after a kind of professional gladiator long known as a 'Gaul'; although it is commonly held that the type had dropped out of use by this time.

Imperial schools of gladiators soon sprang up all over the empire, including in the cities of Capua, Praeneste and Ravenna in Italy, Barcelona in Spain, and Alexandria in Egypt. Strabo tells us the one in Ravenna – planned by Julius Caesar, completed by his posthumously adopted son Augustus – was sited there because the tides of the Adriatic cleansed the air, making it a healthy place to feed and train gladiators. The others also get sea breezes – trained gladiators were an expensive investment; they needed looking after.

Just as the emperor became the single biggest landowner in every province, so – more quickly, and far more comprehensively – he became the greatest owner of gladiators everywhere. The imperial schools were overseen by procurators (financial officials). These were members of the elite: equestrians making a career in imperial service. They were not specialists. Cominius Clemens, procurator of a gladiatorial school in northern Italy, had previously commanded the fleets at Misenum and Ravenna, and served as procurator in the province of Dacia (modern Romania). Another procurator went on to administer the important empire-wide 5 per cent tax on inheritances. In Rome, at least one man was procurator of the *Ludus Magnus* and the imperial mint, which produced coinage, while Bassilius Crescens ran the *Ludus Matutinus* at the same time as overseeing the vital grain supply of the city.

Outside Rome, procurators could be responsible for imperial gladiators over wide swathes of territory. One supervised those in northern Italy, and at the same time the two provinces of Pannonia, as well as Dalmatia. Lucius Didius Marinus was responsible for the provinces of Asia, Bithynia, Galatia, Cappadocia, Lycia, Pamphylia, Cilicia, Pontus, Paphlagonia, as well as Cyprus (roughly modern Turkey and the island of Cyprus). Remarkably, at another point in his career, he oversaw the emperor's gladiators in Gaul, Britain, Spain, the German provinces, and Raetia (the latter equating roughly to modern Switzerland and Bavaria). These imperial procurators had a deputy and staff. Like Cicero's friend Atticus in the Republic, they remained aloof from the mundane running of the schools. No one was going to mistake these highly paid imperial functionaries for lowly, moneygrubbing *lanistae*.

Away from Rome, out in Italy and the provinces, troupes of gladiators could still be owned and exhibited by members of the local elite, both magistrates and private citizens. The high priest of the imperial cult in the province of Asia (the *Asiarch*) owned a *ludus* in Pergamum. As the priesthood was annual, each year the incumbent sold it on to his successor. An inscription from the island of Cos mentions the wife of an *Asiarch* using the *familia* of gladiators as a guard, which kept them occupied as they only fought once a year at a festival in the summer. Permanent troupes were not maintained by the high priests of all provinces. In Gaul, newly appointed high priests had to obtain gladiators from *lanistae*. We lack unambiguous evidence for members of the elite, who were not high priests, keeping a long-term *familia*. Presumably, though it could be ruinously expensive, it was still cheaper to go to private dealers or imperial procurators for combatants on those rare occasions civic office or family pride necessitated you give a show.

Below the level of the elite there were men in pursuit, not of honour and status, but straightforward profits. The cataclysm that overwhelmed Pompeii preserved on painted advertisements and graffiti the names of three men who owned troupes of gladiators and gave commercial shows, the so-called *munera assiforana*, or 'penny shows'. (Not that we should assume the price of admittance was always a single low-denomination Roman coin called an *as*. The contemporary term 'penny dreadful' is a judgement of literary quality, not a statement of the actual price of a novel.)

Away from Pompeii, the *lanistae* lurk in the shadows. The inscription of the senatorial debate on Marcus Aurelius' attempt to fix the price of gladiators shows there were lots of them; enough to provide the manpower for the immoderately expensive Games presented by the imperial high priests in Gaul. It also indicates that senators regarded them as intrinsically greedy and unscrupulous. Seneca described them as the 'most contemptible and shameful' of men. Usually, they were beneath the contempt of elite writers. No matter how much money they made, they were still legally ranked with prostitutes, pimps and their own gladiators. Few *lanistae* would have put their profession on their tombstone. On an inscription from Arles in Gaul a man describes himself as a *negotiator familiae gladiatoriae*: a euphemism for his disreputable trade.

The Oath

The midwinter *Saturnalia* was a time of drinking, feasting and gambling; an occasion for presents and suckling pig; a chance to 'sing stark naked, clap and shake, sometimes even get pushed headfirst into cold water, with a face smeared with soot'. The festival looked back to the Golden Age ruled by Saturn, when all men were equal, before slavery was invented. For a few days in December the world was turned upside down. A roll of the dice chose the 'king' of the revels. Slaves ate with their masters or even dined before them; they could speak their minds and not be punished.

Davus, a slave in a satire by Horace, takes advantage of the *Saturnalia* to upbraid his master (let's not call him Horace – the poem is a *Satire*, not an *Autobiography* or a *Confession*). His master is more unfree than Davus – enslaved by his inconsistency, his jumping to obey his social superiors, his belly, and, above all, by his lust. To commit adultery the master is prepared to be burned, beaten and killed by steel, just as a gladiator swears to submit to a *lanista*. Even the *Saturnalia* had its limits. Davus' criticisms are cut short when his master first threatens violence, then to send him to a slave gang on a farm.

We do not have an ancient discussion of the gladiatorial oath. Instead, it was so well known that it was used to illustrate oaths taken in other circumstances – both good and bad, but always profound. For Seneca the 'most honourable' oath a philosopher takes to virtue is the same as the 'most disgraceful' one taken by a gladiator: 'to be burned, bound, and killed by steel'. The fullest version is offered during the course of an attempted scam by the anti-heroes of Petronius' novel the *Satyricon*. 'We swore an oath dictated by Eumolpus, that we would be burned, bound, beaten, and killed with steel, or whatever else Eumolpus ordered; like real gladiators we most solemnly [*religiosissime*] handed ourselves over, body and soul, to our master; after swearing the oath, we saluted our master, in our role as slaves.'

The slight variations in these oaths can be explained by their literary contexts. Horace does not include being bound because Davus goes on to imagine his master confined in a box with his head stuffed between his knees, where he has been bundled by a maid when his mistress's husband returns unexpectedly. Petronius has a lengthy exposition because Eumolpus is a verbose poet. Yet, as the sly 'or whatever else Eumolpus ordered' suggests, not only is Eumolpus not to be trusted, but the gladiatorial oath itself was malleable, and might vary from *ludus* to *ludus*.

One piece of evidence puts a time limit on the oath. A late legal source preserves the third century AD jurist Ulpian commenting on an edict of the emperor Hadrian (AD 117–38). Cattle rustlers in Spain who were condemned to the arena could be released from fighting after three years and freed from the *ludus* altogether after five. It is unwise to see this as a universal timescale. Hadrian was ruling on cattle-rustling, not other crimes, and specifically in Spain, not in all provinces. But it establishes a general principle of minimum sentencing. If a gladiator survived, he might begin to hope for release from combat after a set number of years, and then for freedom some years later.

Who took the terrible oath? Condemned criminals, slaves and prisoners of war had no choice. But even taken under compulsion it was important for the discipline, morale and performance of the *familia*. There was a light at the end of the tunnel. The oath added a carrot to the burning torches, whips, shackles and sharp steel. A law of AD 4, the *lex Aelia Sentia*, stated that such freed gladiators would not become full citizens. They would be ranked at the bottom of free society, as if they were foreigners who had surrendered to Roman armies (*peregrini dediticii*). But that was better than the alternatives of summary execution or perpetual slavery.

Even after taking the oath, a free volunteer was in a slightly different legal position to the rest of a *familia*. He had sworn to submit to the punishments of a slave, but in a sense retained an element of freedom. The second-century AD jurist Gaius included an abducted gladiatorial volunteer, along with children, a wife, and a legally 'judged' (*iudicatus*) debtor, as the potential victims of the paradoxical crime of the 'theft of free people'. One way in which a volunteer differed from the other inhabitants of the school was that he, or his family, could buy him out of his contract at any point. Quintilian imagines a case where a sister has frequently bought her brother out of a *ludus* but he keeps re-enlisting. Finally, exasperated, she cuts off his thumb while he is asleep. When he brings a legal action for compensation, she snaps that he deserved to keep his hand entire, so that he could have fought, and presumably died. For most free volunteers the oath offered the hope that they could wipe out their *infamia*, not through family money, but through their own manly courage, and thus win back their honour and their place as a full citizen.

The only gladiators who did not take the oath were those members of the elite who contracted directly with the *editor*, the giver of the Games, to appear in one show. To do so would have reduced the upper-class *editor* – sometimes the emperor himself – to the status of a reviled professional *lanista*.

It is tempting to think that the hope of freedom was what mattered, and that the oath was no more than empty ceremony. This would be a mistake. A brilliant study of modern combat has shown that, even in secular Western armies, the military oath is surprisingly psychologically important to those in the firing line. For the Romans there was a special place in Hades for the gruesome punishments of oath-breakers. The gladiatorial oath meant something. Remember Fadius, the veteran of Pompey, persecuted by the Quaestor Cornelius Balbus. Fadius reluctantly was prepared to fight twice in the arena, but rather than take the gladiatorial oath, he suffered himself to be burned alive. For Fadius, the oath meant more than the excruciating pain of death itself.

Training

The sources for the training of gladiators could hardly be more oblique: a misogynist satire and an unrealistic antiquarian proposal to reform the late Roman army. But Juvenal's sixth *Satire*, and the *Epitome of Military Science* by Vegetius, are the best we have.

Juvenal was a man full of loathing. He, or the persona he adopted in his poems, detested, among others, decadent aristocrats, social climbers, passive homosexuals and foreigners, especially Jews and other easterners – in his view, the shit from the Orontes was flowing into the Tiber. Written in the second century AD, the *Satires* are savage, ironic, and very funny; unless you are upset by other cultures not sharing your attitudes. In the sixth *Satire*, to dissuade a friend from marriage, Juvenal turns his jaundiced eye on women. They are quarrelsome, nagging, grasping, spendthrift and cruel; they drive away all your old friends, drink too much, talk too much and wear too much makeup. When they grow old, they look awful. Addicted to religious charlatans, they are quite likely to poison you. They criticise your performance in bed, while taking endless lovers.

A lot of the sex in Juvenal's work is linked to gladiators. Even a *lanista* would not tolerate the perverts your wife will invite to dinner. You will be presented with a son and heir whose features, if not black, will resemble those of a gladiator who fights as a *murmillo*. Eppia, a senator's wife, runs off to Egypt with a battered old gladiator called Sergius, fondly calling him her 'darling Sergius' (Sergiolus). Then your wife might turn out to be one of those elite women who confound respectable gender roles by training for the arena. She will wear a heavy helmet and full kit: either the two greaves of a small shield gladiator (probably a *Thraex* or a *Hoplomachus*), or just the one greave of a type using a big shield (possibly a *murmillo*). She grunts as she strikes the wooden training stake (the *palus*) with both sword and shield in the rhythm (*numerus*) recommended by her instructor. The only thing that reveals she is a woman is her use of a chamber pot. According to Juvenal, late at night drunken upper-class women like to take turns pissing on a statue of the goddess Chastity.

Vegetius, a bureaucrat and expert on the ailments of horses and cattle, was not a military man. In spite of this, at some point between AD 383 and 450, he took it on himself to write a pamphlet proposing a reform of the Roman army and sent it to the emperor. Offering advice to an autocrat is a tricky business. In an ingratiating preface Vegetius says he is just reminding the emperor of things he already knows. According to Vegetius the emperor asked for more, and books two to four were added to the *Epitome of Military Science*. Disavowing expertise and originality, in their place Vegetius claimed to offer painstaking scholarship: the fruits of long hours studying many books by ancient authorities. The claim was threadbare. He mainly drew upon later summaries of the authors he cited. From these, largely ignoring contemporary realities, he assembled items from wildly different periods to create an ahistorical picture of the pristine 'antique legion'. Tactfully, the central message of the *Epitome* was mostly implicit: 'stop employing barbarian mercenaries'. Instead, the emperor was to recruit the right sort of Roman youths from the countryside, equip and organise them properly, and subject them to rigorous training. Which is where gladiators come in, because Vegetius believed that in the past basic training for the arena and the army had been the same.

Recruits set up a six-foot-high wooden post. With a wooden sword and a shield woven from withies, both twice the weight of their real equivalents, they practised against the stake, 'as though it were an actual opponent', both in the morning and the afternoon. Veterans might exercise just once a day. They aimed, as it were, at the head and face, the flanks, the hamstrings and legs, backed off, came on, and sprang forward: 'Let them grow used to executing jumps and blows at the same time, rushing at the shield with a leap and crouching down again, now eagerly darting forward with a bound, now giving ground, jumping back.' They were taught to strike with the point, not the edge of their sword – not only was it more likely to inflict a fatal wound, it exposed less of their right arm and side. When a recruit took up real, lighter arms, 'he fought with more confidence and agility, being liberated from the heavier weight'. Vegetius declared, 'neither in the arena or on the battlefield has a man proved invincible, unless he has been thoroughly trained at the post'.

From Juvenal and Vegetius, a few other passing literary allusions, and scraps of archaeological material, we can construct a tentative programme of gladiatorial training. Novices (*novicii*) began with the *palus*. To build up strength and stamina, as Seneca the Elder said, 'gladiators train with heavier weapons than those used in combat, and their trainer keeps them longer in arms than will their opponents'. They were taught attacking and defensive moves, using both shield and sword as offensive weapons. These moves formed a sequence, or, as Juvenal put it, a 'rhythm'. The next step was to fight each other with the heavy wooden equipment. Several of the skeletons from the gladiatorial cemetery in Ephesus show healed wounds caused by blunt force trauma. From this they graduated to sparring with blunted real weapons. Commodus made a mockery of this by using a sharp sword, while his opponents had a foiled blade: 'he managed to kill a man now and then, and in making close passes with others, trying to sheer a bit of their hair, he sliced off the noses of some, and the ears of others'. Finally, like a trainee orator moving from imaginary speeches to those of the courtroom, gladiators trained with real weapons. The *novicius* was now a *tiro*, a trained, but as yet untried, gladiator. If he survived his first fight in the arena, he would become a veteran (*veteranus*) and hope to begin his ascent of the ranks within his school.

An instructor in a *ludus* was called either a *doctor* or a *magister*. They were senior or ex-gladiators. Martial praised the famous fighter Hermes: skilled in all the styles of fighting, he was both gladiator and trainer. After Hadrian's edict, Spanish cattle-rustlers, who had survived at least three years in the arena, might expect to serve out the rest of their time in the *familia* passing on the skills they had acquired. In a small, private *ludus* there might be only one trainer (*doctor gladiatorum*), perhaps the *lanista* himself. In the larger schools, including all the ones of the emperor, there were specialist trainers for the different types of gladiators: *doctores myrmillonum*, *hoplomachorum*, *retiariorum* and so on.

A nearly naked *retiarius*, equipped with a trident, net and dagger, needed very different training from, say, a *murmillo* wearing a heavy helmet and greaves and wielding a large shield and short sword. We find an echo of this in a law passed under Tiberius which banned the elite, and their descendants, not only from appearing in the arena, but forbade them in the gladiatorial school 'either to snatch the feathers (*pinnas*) of gladiators, or take up the *rudis* (practice sword), or take part in any way in a similar subordinate role'. Most types of gladiators fought with a sword and wore a helmet, which was often decorated with feathers. A slang term for gladiator was 'feather-wearer' (*pinnirapus*). Juvenal complains that in the seating at the Games a decent poor man would have to give way to the sons of pimps, auctioneers, *pinnirapi* and *lanistae*. A few types of gladiators, notably the *retiarius*, had neither sword nor helmet. They relied on speed, agility and guile. Snatching the feathers from the helmets of heavier armed gladiators was an excellent form of training. It reminds me of an afternoon watching Provençal bullfighters training in pairs in the Roman amphitheatre in Arles. One took the part of the bull, wielding a wooden board with flowers pinned between the attached horns. The other worked the 'bull' with a cape, plucking the flowers as it passed.

Who decided what sort of gladiator a *novicius* would become? In the late Republic Cicero claimed that a political enemy, Vatinius, assigned types of gladiators (Samnites, or *Provocatores*) in his *familia* of 200 by lot. However, this was a troupe intended for just one show and raised on the cheap. Its men were not carefully selected from slave markets but bought wholesale from rural chain gangs. Vatinius later claimed that only one of them was a gladiator, all the rest were beast-fighters. In the permanent schools of the principate, criminals, slaves and prisoners of war were most likely assigned their roles by the trainers or the *lanista* himself on the basis of their physique, strength, agility and perceived natural aptitude. Free volunteers to a *ludus* presumably chose the type of gladiatorial combat in which they would be trained. Certainly, elite volunteers, who negotiated with the giver of the Games for an appearance in a single show, selected the style in which they would fight. The disgrace of the noble Gracchus who fought in the arena was exacerbated by his choosing to appear as a *retiarius*.

Sex

After dinner was a good time for sex. For the Romans it was not the only good time. The emperor Vespasian liked to have sex with a concubine in the afternoon, before going to the baths. His biographer Suetonius approved. It was infinitely better than Caligula dragging senators' wives away from the dinner table and then returning to discuss their performance with their husbands.

'Cresces the net-fighter (*retiarius*) sorts out the girls in the night, in the morning and all the other times.' Far from being written by a gladiator groupie, let alone by an 'innocent girl', as is often assumed, this famous piece of graffiti from one of the two gladiatorial barracks in Pompeii was almost certainly scratched by Cresces himself. It was a bit of competitive boasting with his friend, and fellow gladiator, Celadus the Thracian (*Thraex*). One of them had inscribed their names together as 'lords of the girls', while Celadus hailed himself the 'heartthrob' and the 'pride' of the girls.

The remains of a woman wearing an emerald necklace, two

armbands, rings and other ornaments, and carrying a cameo in a small casket, was found in the other gladiatorial barracks at Pompeii. Excitable tour guides, and some sober scholars, will assure you this was an upper-class woman caught out visiting her gladiator lover. If so, she had a taste for Messalina-style orgies. In the same room were found the remains of eighteen people and two dogs.

Nevertheless, there is ample evidence that gladiators had a strong sexual charge. Martial praised the famous fighter Hermes as the 'darling and passion of the gladiators' women [*ludiarum*]'. A *ludia* was a slang term for a woman with a sexual interest in gladiators. Tertullian bemoaned that men give their souls and women their bodies as well as their souls to charioteers, actors, athletes and gladiators. It has been suggested that because we have no erotic literature expressing male desire for gladiators, they had no sexual appeal for Roman men. That is a lot of weight to be carried by a silence that could be explained by literary fashions. We have already seen that *retiarii* could be considered effeminate. Sometimes these net-fighters took stage names – *Softy* or *Depilated* – that implied effeminacy. Other types of gladiators also adopted names suggesting softness or delicacy – Columbus (*Dove*) or Palumbus (*Ringdove*) – or called themselves after famous 'pretty boys' of myth: Narcissus, who spurned the nymph Echo, Hippolytus, who rejected all women, and Hyacinthus or Hylas, the boy-lovers respectively of Apollo and Heracles. Look again at the Borghese Mosaic (**Plate Two**) – doesn't all that muscly flesh on display almost resemble soft-core gay porn?

Roman sexuality was different from ours. There were no words in Latin or Greek that equate to heterosexual, bisexual or homosexual. Roman male elite sexuality – that is the group we know best, as they wrote the books – focused much more on being the 'active' as opposed to the 'passive' partner in sex, than it did on the sex of the person you were penetrating. There would have been nothing 'unmanly' in being the active partner in sex with a gladiator. Conversely there was a small minority of elite males, like the emperor Heliogabalus, who openly flaunted their pleasure in taking the passive role with other men. A funerary relief, now in Maastricht, shows two gladiators (**Plate Four**). The victor, on the left, advances, sword in hand, ready to strike, virile and masculine. The loser, weapon discarded, turns his back, and raises a hand to appeal for mercy. He stands knees together, one leg straight, the other angled out from the knee – a stance that in art had signified femininity since the fifth century BC, when Praxiteles had used it for his famous nude sculpture, the Aphrodite of Knidos. Sex was often thought of in terms of fighting: of striking, cutting, splitting, wounding and killing. Just like winning a bout in the arena, sex with a gladiator would have enhanced the masculinity of the penetrator and feminised the penetrated.

What gave gladiators their erotic appeal? They were far from the classical ideal of male beauty – the ripped young athlete of Polyclitus' famous statue the Spear-carrier. Stuffed with *sagina*, gladiators were fat. They had bad teeth, worse than the rest of the population. This was caused by their pulpy, carbohydrate-rich diet, and their lifestyle: the physical and psychological stresses they were under reduced their production of saliva. It would have given them even worse breath than most of the poor. Their trade was inscribed on their bodies: scars from blades and whips, bites from wild animals. By the early fourth century AD men condemned to a gladiatorial school or the mines were tattooed on their faces. An edict of the first Christian emperor, Constantine, in AD 316 banned this – the face was in the likeness of the divine – instead they could be tattooed on their hands and legs.

Some chose to use their appearance to advertise their profession. Commodus had his hair cut short, like a gladiator. On a mosaic from Zliten in North Africa, a *bestiarius*, one of those that handled the animals, can be seen sporting a topknot as he encourages a boar to dance (**Plate Five**). Other physical peculiarities that marked gladiators were involuntary, the result of long hours of repeated training. Sergius, the gladiator that Juvenal said ran away with the wife of a senator, had a furrow on his forehead and a hump on his nose, caused by the rubbing of his helmet. Some were almost deformed. According to Pliny, it was well known that a gladiator called Studiosus, a *Thraex* belonging to Caligula, had a right arm longer than his left. Archaeology seems to confirm that repeated, heavy gladiatorial training could cause such asymmetry. A Roman cemetery excavated in York (from 2004 onwards) contained eighty-two skeletons, seventy-four of which were young, adult males deposited between the second and fourth centuries AD. Interestingly, forty-six had been beheaded. Blunt and sharp force traumas, some of which had healed, comparable to those in the cemetery in Ephesus suggests they were gladiators. An individual, with bites from a large carnivore (a bear, lion or tiger) to collar and hip, probably was a beast-fighter. The stress lesions to the collarbone of another, caused by constant circular movements of his arms, would fit with training as a *retiarius*. Of the others, one in seven had one arm longer than the other, presumably from long sessions with a sword at the *palus*.

Despite their gnarled, battered and hefty bodies, gladiators were often described as 'beautiful'. Sometimes this was irony. Cicero described the troupe of Vatinius as 'so beautiful, noble, and magnificent'. But they were the sweepings from rural slave-prisons, and Cicero was making a snide dig at the ill-favoured Vatinius, who 'himself was the finest specimen'. But there was no irony when gladiators were described as 'beautiful' on their tombstones. The majority of these come from the Greek eastern half of the empire, where gladiators tried to equate themselves with high-status athletes. For the latter, being 'beautiful' (*kalos*) had been almost as important as prowess for centuries. But not all 'beautiful gladiators' were found in the east. According to the elder Seneca, 'all the best looking' of the condemned were thrown into gladiatorial schools. Perhaps we should invoke the

French concept of *jolie laide*, the attractively ugly, as exemplified by the magnetic sex appeal of bruised and lived-in actors such as Thierry Godard? Tertullian claimed that free volunteer gladiators 'see themselves as more beautiful for their bites and scars'.

The dark glamour of violence was a major component of the sexual appeal of gladiators. Juvenal was clear about what attracted Eppia the senator's wife to Sergius: 'He was a gladiator, that makes each one an Adonis . . . it's the steel they love.' The steel (*ferrum*) was his sword (*gladius*), and both were slang for penis. In Ovid's *Art of Love* the poet asks Briseis, the concubine of Achilles, 'was that what you found so exciting – the hands of a killer on your limbs?' The other major part of the sexual appeal of gladiators was transgression. A maid in Petronius' *Satyricon* says her mistress is one of those women whom the arena sets on heat; what gives her pleasure is kissing the tracks of the whip. For some women, and most probably for some men, gladiators were the ultimate Roman rough trade.

Thinking about sex with a gladiator was exciting, transgressive and dangerous, but it could also be very funny. A terracotta lamp from Arles in Gaul shows a woman and man making love on a well-upholstered bed (**Plate Six**). She has been interpreted as wearing five bracelets on her right arm, and, presumably with some difficulty, combining vigorous sex and working out with weights. More likely, she has the equipment of a Thracian gladiator: a guard on her right arm (*manica*), curved sword in her right hand (*sica*), and small rectangular shield (*parmula*) in her left. Has she taken them from her gladiator lover, or is she one of those women satirised by Juvenal who train for the arena? Although being penetrated, she has reversed the normal gender roles. She is riding him – *mulier equitans*, the Romans called it – in total control. She brandishes her shield and sword. At any moment she could wound, even kill her partner. No wonder the man spreads the fingers of his left hand in alarm (or is it perverse pleasure?), and raises his right hand, like a gladiator submitting.

This startling image was not pornography to be hidden away and brought out in solitude for furtive arousal. This was a lamp to light a room. In a catalogue of well over a thousand Roman lamps now in Switzerland, but mainly found in Gaul, the third largest category of scenes is erotic. The second largest is gladiators and their equipment. This lamp would have been seen by everyone in the house: women, children, visitors, perhaps slaves (although its relatively cheap materials and mass production might mean its owners could not afford any slaves). The image is a talking point. It is meant to make viewers laugh.

3

Secunda Vigilia
(The Second Watch of the Night)

In the barracks the gladiators are snoring. They sleep on camp beds or straw pallets. Unless they are high in the ranking in their Ludus, *there are three or four in a room. The time they have to rest varies with the seasons. Most Romans go to bed at sunset and get up at dawn. There is a nightlight burning. For these rough, violent men are afraid of the dark.*

The Measure of Time

The Romans had more time than us, or at least so they thought. Even after they adopted the seven-day week from the Jews and Christians, they continued to reckon dates from fixed points in the future. Each day was counted as so many days before whichever of the following came next: the *Kalends*, the first day of the subsequent month, or, if that was passed, the *Nones* of the current month (the fifth in the short ones the seventh in long), then the *Ides* (the thirteenth, or the fifteenth). Unlike us, they counted inclusively. Writing this on 29 April, for me, 1 May is two days away. For a Roman, who would include 29 April, it would be three days off. Conceptually they bought themselves another day.

Like us, the Romans divided the day into twenty-four hours. Unlike us, the length of their hours varied with the seasons. For them there were always twelve hours of daylight and twelve hours of darkness. So, at midsummer in Rome, by our reckoning, each hour of their night was about forty-five minutes long, giving a little under nine hours in which to sleep, while at midwinter each hour stretched out to almost seventy-five minutes, allowing the best part of fifteen hours' rest. Roman civilians also adopted from the army another, complementary way of conceptualising the hours of darkness, dividing the night into four watches, each notionally of three hours.

Some later European cultures practised what is known as segmented sleep. You went to bed for your first sleep, then got up and did something – maybe had a snack, went for a walk – before returning to bed for your second sleep. The concept is best known now from Robert Harris' novel *The Second Sleep*. It has been suggested that the Romans practised something similar. Certainly, they had time for it, especially in winter. There are plenty of references to the 'first sleep' (*prima quies*, or *prima nocte*). But what is lacking is any mention of getting up habitually to do things in the middle of the night, or any expression in Latin or Greek for such activity, or a phrase for a 'second sleep'. It seems that *prima quies* meant no more than the first part of the night. If Romans wanted to burn the midnight oil, as we will see, they either stayed up late, or got up very early.

It was difficult to tell the time with much accuracy. In the day there were sundials. Pliny the Elder claimed that if you were in the countryside you could tell the time by watching lupins turn to follow the sun. Elaborate water clocks could be used at night, the most sophisticated calibrated to take account of the changing seasons. But these were the toys of extremely rich men. Oil lamps were preferred to candles, which could be marked to show the hours as they burned down. The latter were for barbarians and odd eastern sects like Christians. In a military camp, trumpets sounded the changing watches. There was nothing like that in the city. At night the streets of Rome were patrolled by the Watch (the *Vigiles*), and in some cities in the Greek East by the men under local officials with various titles:

the 'Night Guard' (*Nyktophylakes*), 'Prefect guarding the Night' (*Praefectus nocturnae custodiae*), or 'Peace Officer' (the *Eirenarch*). But they were looking for criminals and fires. It was not part of their duty to call out 'Midnight, and all is well!' Unlike the bells of an English cathedral, or the Muezzin that fragments sleep in modern Istanbul, in the night the pagan temples were silent. If a gladiator in the *Ludus Magnus* wanted to know the time, he had to either walk out into the courtyard and look at the moon and the stars, or resign himself to waiting for the cocks to crow.

'Truly, I say to you, this very night, before the cock crows, you will deny me three times.' No wonder that most inhabitants of the Roman empire, like Jesus, fell back on very vague conceptualisations to order the night: *crepusculum* (twilight), *vesper* (evening), *prima nocte* ('first part of the night') or *prima quies* ('first sleep', or 'first quiet time'), *nox intempesta* ('unseasonable night', i.e. the dead of night, from the appearance of the evening star to sunrise), *concubium* ('sleep time'), *silentium noctis* ('silent night'), *gallicinium* ('cockcrow'), *conticinium* (when the cocks have stopped crowing, but men are still asleep), and *Prima lux* ('first light').

But in the city of Rome the night was seldom quiet, let alone silent.

The Difficulties of Sleeping

'Now the rest of the gods, and the chariot-fighting warriors slept through the night, but sweet sleep did not embrace Zeus.' The educated remembered the lines of Homer from their schooldays. It was something everyone in Rome knew from experience. Sleep was hard to entice into your bed in Rome. Something less sweet was certain to join you. Bedbugs were ubiquitous. Smearing the legs of your bed with vinegar and ox gall might help. If, of course, gladiators slept in beds, not on pallets stuffed with straw. Quite likely beds were not allowed.

According to Seneca, comfortable beds made soldiers afraid to die.

The main barrier to sleep was the noise. All big cities were noisy, and, as by far the largest, Rome was much the worst. In the darkness dogs barked, while drunken revellers laughed, shouted, and sang to discordant musical accompaniment. Even a member of the elite, such as Cicero, might be disturbed by a snoring neighbour. Oddly there is no mention of the scream of gulls, which was my soundscape for a sleepless night in Rome.

After Julius Caesar had banned most wheeled traffic in Rome from sunrise until the tenth hour of daylight, the evening and night were filled with the rumbling and grinding of wagons, the lowing of animals, the cries of carters, and the crack of their whips, as food and building materials were brought into the city, and night soil and the unclaimed or impecunious dead taken out. Sometimes the dark streets echoed with the sound of mourning; children were buried at night. To some extent, the level of nocturnal noise was dependent on location. Proximity to some trades did not aid slumber. Millers worked all night, and bakers began before sunrise. Down at the docks by the Tiber stevedores might unload vessels through the night. An inscription tells us that at Vipasca, a settlement in what is now Portugal, the baths stayed open until the end of the second hour of darkness. In two passages where almost everything looks like fiction, the *Augustan History* claims that while the emperor Alexander Severus (AD222–35) donated oil to light the public baths in Rome through the night, the emperor Tacitus (AD275–6) ordered them to be closed at the hour the lamps were lit, to prevent disturbances in the dark. These uncertain few decades aside, in Rome at least the baths closed in the evening and reopened at first light. The same was not true of bars (*popinae*) some of which stayed open late, or all night. Brothels, however, seem to have shut before morning. An anecdote has the empress Messalina returning to her bed in the palace sexually frustrated – 'still burning with desire in her rigid clitoris', according to Juvenal – when the brothel in which she had serviced many men finally shut.

For some the answer was to take a sleeping draught. Anise, cinnamon, saffron and mandrake were among the recommended ingredients. The soporific benefits of eating cabbage – another popular solution – must have been psychosomatic. More effective were drinking wine, and the use of opium poppies.

The remedy for others was to leave the city for the countryside, or a peaceful rural town. Some of the elite, like modern well-off Romans, did it every summer to escape the heat. Some made the move permanent. Juvenal's *Third Satire* comprises Umbricius telling the poet why he is quitting Rome. Apart from the awful nouveau riche social climbers, and all the ghastly foreign immigrants, Umbricius wants to get a decent night's sleep.

The main thoroughfares were the noisiest places to live. The Via Labicana, which ran right past the *Ludus Magnus* to the gate leading to the town of Praeneste (the *Porta Praenestina*, now the *Porta Maggiore*), was very busy, as is its modern successor. The *Ludus Gallicus* was probably on the other side of the street; the *Ludus Dacicus* not far away. The night before the Games would be filled with the roaring and bellowing of the caged wild beasts transported by wagon from the imperial *vivarium*, a holding place for animals, outside the *Porta Praenestina*, to the secure enclosures underneath the Colosseum, adjacent to the gladiatorial schools. It would not have aided the sleep of the inhabitants of the *Ludus Matutinus* just a few yards away, who would have to fight these dangerous animals in the morning.

The Cult of Sleeplessness

Cicero was disturbed by the snoring of his neighbour. In Roman towns the rich and poor lived very close together. Although some districts were more salubrious than others, and traders gathered in certain locales, there was nothing like the zoning of modern cities. The affluent and the impecunious did not just live in the same areas, but in the same buildings. Affluent home-owners commonly rented out the rooms of their dwelling that faced the street as small shops, in which the tenants lived and worked.

Despite the proximity of others, if anyone could obtain nocturnal silence it was the elite. They had the money to afford the necessary architecture and space. Pliny the Younger designed his secluded suite of rooms in his villa at Laurentum so that he would not be disturbed even by the sounds of merrymaking at the *Saturnalia*. In town there were no openings in the solid wall separating the rented shops from the other rooms in an elite house. We should not underestimate the level of social control. Few tenants would want to keep their landlords awake. At the very top, the emperor could enforce silence. There were servants named *silentarii* in the imperial household. When Caligula was disturbed in the middle of the night by a crowd waiting to get free tickets to the Circus Maximus, he had them driven away with cudgels. According to Suetonius, more than twenty Roman equestrians, and the same number of ladies of that rank, 'along with a vast number of others', were trampled to death in the confusion.

Ironically, the elite – the one group who could hope to obtain sufficient peace for a good night's sleep – cultivated a cult of sleeplessness. Intellectuals stayed up late, struggling against fatigue, to work at their books, reading and writing serious literature. Or they got up before daybreak to continue their studies. Quintilian had a point that there were fewer distractions at these times; there was nothing to see out of the window, and no one around (except maybe a slave or two, tending the lamp, taking dictation, or actually doing the reading out loud). This high-status voluntary sleep deprivation was given a name: *Lucubratio* ('Night-Work'). It was Roman virtue signalling. Those who indulged made sure others knew. It signalled valuing the mind over the body. It also underlined commitment to public duty – undertaken at night, *Lucubratio* did not consume the hours of daylight that should be devoted to serving the *Res publica*. To emphasise the virtue of frugality, *Lucubratio* was best done by the light of a solitary light. This caused many intellectuals problems with their eyesight. The deleterious effects on health were noted, even boasted about; not just impaired vision, but thickened speech, bad complexion and poor digestion – all physical manifestations of inner virtue.

For almost all Romans there was no service to the *Res publica* as praiseworthy as military service. The night was a perilous time on campaign or in camp. Generals should not be caught slumbering. Ulpius Marcellus, the general sent by Commodus to crush the tribes of Britain, was efficient and conspicuously incorruptible, but lacked a pleasant or kindly nature. 'He showed himself more wakeful than any other general . . . for nature had made him able to resist sleep, and he had developed this faculty by the discipline of fasting.' Every day he wrote orders on twelve wooden tablets, and had aides deliver them throughout the night, so his officers, 'believing the general to be always awake, might not themselves take their fill of sleep'.

The role of the emperor was created by Augustus out of successful warfare (almost entirely civil wars, under armies commanded by his subordinates, but all that was quietly forgotten). Every subsequent emperor, even if they never led troops in person, was the commander in chief of all the Roman army. They monopolised military glory. Every battle was fought under their auspices. Only they, or favoured members of their families, could have the ultimate accolade of the military parade called a triumph. The imperial image projected – in every media available: coins, sculpture, laws, speeches, literature – had to be that of a capable and successful general. This included cutting down on sleep. Vespasian always rose while it was still dark to work on reports. Likewise, Septimius Severus was busy before dawn. As so often, fiction about emperors tells us a lot about the expectations of their subjects. The *Augustan History* depicted the ineffectual Alexander Severus as the perfect emperor. Another early riser, he either worshipped the gods, or, if ritually unclean because he had had sex with his wife, did some healthy physical activity. However, 'if necessary he would give his attention to public business even before dawn, and continue to a late hour, never growing weary, or giving up in irritation or anger'. In his bedroom he had records of his troops, 'and when he was alone constantly went over their budgets, numbers, ranks, and their pay, so that he knew every detail'.

The image of the unsleeping emperor filtered down to civic officials, as bureaucrats came to see themselves as military men. Aphrodisias in Caria (in modern Turkey) is an unusually well-preserved site. Enough statues of members of the local elite from the late empire have been found to draw generalisations about their self-fashioning. Many of these rich and leisured men liked to be depicted in marble as unshaven, haggard and drawn, with unnaturally large and staring eyes. Their brows are furrowed with cares, their mouths unsmiling and turned down. These are men who want to be seen as serious and hardworking, who don't have time for fripperies like shaving, because they are up half the night for the good of the community. Like a member of the elite from Ephesus, they want to be thanked for their 'sleepless labours'.

Out in the country, the best slaves were those who did not need much sleep. Such was the opinion of the agricultural writers Cato and Columella. The same was unlikely to have been the case in a gladiatorial school. A commercial *lanista* would want his expensive investments well rested, and in peak condition, so that, if they did not win, they might fight creditably enough to be spared their lives. There was no financial risk for an officer in charge of an imperial school – he did not own the gladiators – but there were other hazards. In Carthage, Perpetua secured better conditions for the Christians condemned to the beasts from the military tribune running the prison: 'We belong to the emperor; we are to fight on his birthday; would it not be to your credit if we were brought forth on the day in a healthier condition?'

Sleeping as Weakness and Wickedness

Sleep was 'sweet' in Greek poetry. For Homer it 'loosened the limbs and released the cares of the heart'. It was a necessity that relaxed and restored tired minds and bodies. Latin poets could desire its embrace like that of a lover.

But sleep had a dark side. Too much of it, along with idleness, gambling and drinking, weakened your spirit. Go down those lines, Ovid warned, and you might end up falling in love. However, when Cicero wrote of Mark Antony sending away important embassies because he was sleeping during the day, it was not because of his concern about its potential bad effects on the future triumvir. Instead, Cicero was criticising Antony's pre-existing vices of indolence, drunkenness and arrogance. Sleeping at the wrong time was bad. Those men, like Antony, or the emperor Heliogabalus, who turned night into day, and day into night, were the worst of all. According to Seneca, those who 'lived by the lamp' were unnatural; like growing roses in mid-winter, or mature men who wanted to be sexually penetrated.

An acceptable summertime siesta aside, good men who took a chunk out of the night for good reasons, like reading and writing morally and intellectually improving literature, did not catch up on their sleep during the day. Therefore, those who did slumber in daylight had been up all night indulging in the usual litany of vices: drinking, feasting, gambling, idle tittle tattle and illicit sex. There were those who were yet more wicked.

Criminals – burglars and muggers – were active at night. The law treated them more harshly than those who operated in the day. If you discovered a thief in your house in the dark, you could legally kill him, even if he was unarmed. In daylight he had to be carrying a weapon.

The Roman authorities, with the weight of defending the *Res Publica*, and upholding traditional morality on their shoulders, were profoundly suspicious of nocturnal gatherings. Such things reeked of alien cults and conspiracy. The authorities rarely intervened, but when they did it was with a heavy hand. In 186BC the Senate ordered the suppression of the nocturnal rites of Bacchus. Followers were to be hunted down across the whole of Italy, funds confiscated, altars demolished, and initiates executed. Only ancient shrines were exempt, and henceforth only officially sanctioned rituals were to be allowed, with no more than five priests and worshippers in attendance. The followers of Bacchus were condemned for introducing an alien cult, sexual immorality between men and women, as well as men and men, especially the homosexual rape of young men, fiscal crimes (including forgery and perjury), poisoning, and the ritual murder of those youths reluctant to submit to penetrative sex. All of which, in ways unspecified, ultimately amounted to an intention to take over the state.

Catiline was the archetype of the Roman conspirator, thanks to the literary fame of Cicero's speeches denouncing him, and Sallust's monograph. Perverting the Roman virtue of endurance, Catiline eschewed sleep, to stay up all night plotting the overthrow of the *Res Publica*. On the night of 6 November 63BC, Catiline and his followers met in the house of Laeca in the Street of the Sickle-Makers in Rome. There they finalised their plans to bring down the state in a cataclysm of murder and arson. To bind themselves together, they swore a terrible oath, and, according to Sallust, drank human blood mixed with wine. Later sources made the human sacrifice explicit. Plutarch said they sacrificed a man, Cassius Dio a boy; both added that they ate the flesh of the victim.

Christians, who met before dawn, and after sunset, could not but remind educated pagans both of the followers of Bacchus and of Catiline. If one considers the centrality of the consuming of the body and blood of Christ at a love-feast (*agape*), at which the worshippers called each other 'brother' and 'sister', it is no surprise that the early Church Fathers (as the most influential ancient Christian writers are known) felt the need to devote a lot of time and effort to denying that Christians indulged in incest and cannibalism. More obviously than had the followers of Bacchus, Christians posed a threat to the empire. It was problematic, given the history of Jewish revolts, that the Christians worshipped a man who had styled himself king of the Jews and promised to return. On the other hand, although their pacifism ('thou shalt not kill') ruled out armed insurrection, it also implied disloyalty, as they could not, or should not, join the army, and fulfil the key obligation of citizens: fighting to defend Rome.

At a deeper level, the Christians posed an existential threat to Rome. In pagan eyes Christians were atheists who denied that the traditional gods existed, or demoted them to evil daemons (early Christianity never reconciled these logically incompatible views). Any traditional-thinking pagan knew that the safety and health (in Latin, *salus* covered both) of the empire, and of the whole order of the universe, depended on the *pax deorum* (the 'peace', or better the 'pact with the gods'). In essence, if the Romans did right by the gods, the gods would do right by them. Allowing the existence of atheist Christians, who denied or demeaned the gods, was not doing right by the traditional gods. This was not too great a source of anxiety while the empire was strong. Persecutions of Christians, although later Christian apologists inflated them, were small scale and localised until the second half of the third century AD. Then, when the great crisis struck (endless civil wars, very short-lived emperors, and unprecedented barbarian victories), empire-wide persecutions of increasing severity were ordered. The emperors Decius, Valerian and Diocletian acted to restore the *pax deorum*. Of course, they failed. Some have thought it was too little, too late. Or it could all have been a series of chance events. Decius was the first emperor to die in battle against the barbarians. Valerian was the only emperor ever captured alive by the barbarians. Christians exulted – that was how God punished those who persecuted the true faith! It must have given traditional pagans pause for thought – maybe there was something in this crucified god?

Far from being Christians, gladiators boasted of their adherence to the traditional gods. After the death of Spartacus, no gladiator conspired against the *Res publica*. Clandestine nocturnal meetings were not their thing. In normal circumstances, they might drink late in taverns, or expend their energy in lamp-lit bedrooms, but the night before they fought they needed all the sleep their anxious minds would allow.

Sleep and Darkness as Fear and Death

Alexander the Great said that only sleep and sex reminded him that he was mortal. Which was odd, as in epic poetry – and Alexander kept a copy of the *Iliad* under his pillow – Sleep (*Hypnos*) was the 'Lord of mortal men and all the gods', for the gods also slept.

Hypnos was the fatherless son of Night (*Nyx*), the eternal darkness that preceded even the gods. His twin brother was Death (*Thanatos*). They lived in Hades, the realm of the dead. Together they carried the souls of men down to the darkness of the Underworld.

Romans were afraid of the dark. For good reasons. At night the streets were gloomy. A few cities, all in the Greek East (including Alexandria, Ephesus, Antioch and Caesarea), had oil lamps as street lighting, but the vast majority did not, including Rome itself. If you ventured out at night, there were many dangers. In the darkness accidents were waiting to happen. A chamber pot, discarded because it was cracked, or clumsily dropped from a high window, might knock your brains out. If you were lucky, it would splinter on the pavement and you would just get covered in piss. St Andrew the Fool lay down on a dung heap and was run over by a drunken waggoneer.

Not all the dangers lurking in the streets were accidental. Andrew the Fool had escaped from some drunken youths before taking his ill-advised nap. Venturing out alone into the streets at night was asking for trouble. According to Umbricius in Juvenal's third *Satire*, you were a fool if you did not make a will before accepting an invitation to dinner. A drunken thug will pick a fight. With characteristic xenophobia, he may accuse you of being a Jew. It makes no difference if you try to talk your way out of the situation, or steal away without speaking. You will be kicked and punched, reduced to begging to be allowed to go home with a few teeth remaining. You might be robbed or murdered. The arrival of the Watch might not save you. They could take you for a malefactor and arrest you. At least in cities the streets seem to have been largely free of supernatural dangers. Once you stepped out of the town, even only as far as the necropolis beyond the gates, the night was full of ghosts, werewolves and assorted *daemons*.

A bedroom, behind locked doors, perhaps held more terrors than the dark streets outside. The poor lived crowded in badly constructed tenements. Fears of a sudden collapse, or of being burned to death, were ever present. All the locks and chains in the world could not keep out determined burglars armed with sharp steel. When Dionysius, bishop of Alexandria, was arrested, a gang of very militant Christians came to the rescue. They chased away the soldiers guarding the house and burst into the bishop's bedroom. Dionysius automatically assumed they were robbers. Sleeping in nothing but a linen shirt, Dionysius offered them the rest of his clothes. The anecdote tells us not only that a good Christian did not sleep naked, but that poverty was no defence against violent home invasion.

Bedrooms, unlike a city street, were places of supernatural anxiety. Ghosts came in the night. Classical ghosts, unlike modern ones, were not pale, white and insubstantial, although they might have clanking chains. Usually, they were dark brown or black skinned – no matter their ethnicity when alive – and they were quite capable of tearing a man apart. *Daemons* were also a problem. Plotinus, the Platonist philosopher, cut down on sleep by taking little food, and continuous exercise of his intellect. This was fortunate. When a rival philosopher sent a *daemon* one night, which attempted to smother him, 'like a money-bag pulled tight', he was awake, and his powerful soul thwarted the attack. There was no strict division between *daemons* and ghosts. Neither presaged anything good. Brutus, the assassin of Caesar, never slept during the day, and only a few hours at night. Taking a short sleep after dinner, he spent the rest of the night in public business or reading. One night on campaign, before the third watch, a strange and horrible figure entered his dimly-lit tent. Brutus was admirably calm. 'What man or god are you, and what do you want with me?' The ghost answered, 'I am your evil *daemon*, Brutus; you will see me at Philippi.' Brutus replied, 'I will see you then.'

Darkness and night intensify emotion and make the natural weird and frightening. The barking of dogs or the shrieking of owls could be the sounds of witches. As they were shape-shifters, night-hags could enter a bedroom as a mouse, weasel, or even a fly. Witches stole babies and body-parts of adults. If you were lucky, they merely urinated all over you. Christians, with their new and uptight sexual morality, worried about supernatural beings that came in the night to have sex with people.

Precautions were advisable. Pagans made offerings to their household gods (the *lares*) before going to bed and placed statuettes of guardian deities in their bedrooms. If the danger was imminent, it was advisable to touch the doorposts and threshold of your home three times with arbutus, to sprinkle water on the entrance, put a rod of whitehorn in the window and to sacrifice a pig.

Sleep was too close to death and darkness was too close to Hades. Many adults, not just lovers, kept a lamp burning at night. Having failed to have his mother drowned in the dark in a fake accident with a collapsible boat, Nero sent marines to finish the job. Bursting into her bedroom, they found Agrippina with a single maid. They surrounded the couch on which the empress was reclining. A naval officer struck her on the head with a club. When a centurion drew his sword, she pointed to her womb, saying 'Strike here!' Crowding round, they stabbed her repeatedly until she was dead. The whole hellish scene was illuminated by one dim nightlight. On an altogether lighter note, Lucian joked about a fool who thought he could stop a bedbug biting him by extinguishing the lamp: 'You can't see me now!'

Gladiators were the second most popular images, after erotic scenes, for decorating Roman lamps. The night before the gladiator appeared in the arena, as he fell asleep, he could gaze at an image of one of his kind, or even of himself, shedding a light that held at bay both the darkness and Hades.

4

Tertia Vigilia (The Third Watch of the Night)

The gladiator turns in his sleep and mutters. What dreams haunt his slumber? It is after midnight. The food and drink of the cena libera *have died out of him. It is the time the gods send true dreams through the Gates of Horn. If ever a man needed a glimpse into the future, or divine advice, it was a gladiator the night before a fight.*

The gladiator, many years before, had dreamed that some people lifted him up and carried him about in a sarcophagus full of human blood; he ate the blood where it had congealed; his mother appeared and said that he had brought dishonour on her; the people put him down, and he went home. Like him, we will have to wait to see what it all means.

The Importance of Dreams

Everyone dreams. Gladiators were no exception. Roman culture invested much thought in the significance of dreams.

Septimius Severus dreamed that the emperor Pertinax was riding through the Forum, when he was thrown by his horse, which then took Severus on its back. After he became emperor, Severus commissioned an equestrian statue of himself at the spot indicated in the dream. Having written a little book about the dreams and portents that gave Severus reason to hope for the imperial power, Cassius Dio was instructed by a *daemon* in a dream to write a history of the wars of the emperor, which he expanded into a monumental history that covered from the foundation of Rome to his own lifetime. Whenever he tired of the task, the goddess Tyche (Fortune), who had become his constant companion, sent dreams to encourage him. Later, a dream told him when and how to end the book.

Some thought all dreams were meaningless. Chief among them were the epicureans – who believed that either the gods did not exist, or they had no interest in humanity. But they were in the minority. From emperors and senators, like Septimius Severus and Cassius Dio, down to illiterate slaves, most considered that dreams could be significant. The late-second-century AD philosopher and medical doctor Sextus Empiricus listed dreams as things 'believed by all men', along with divination, divine inspiration and astrology. The popular view was that they were sent by the gods. This belief fuelled an industry in the temples of the healing god Asclepius and other oracular divinities. After ritual purification, and various other ceremonies, the worshipper slept in a special area of the sanctuary to facilitate the nocturnal appearance of the god. In the morning they paid a fee. The process is known as incubation. Dozens of ancient inscriptions attest a successful outcome. The man of letters Aelius Aristides – either a chronic invalid or a terrible hypochondriac, depending on how charitable you are – spent two years in the temple of Asclepius at Pergamum and left six books of *Sacred Tales*, detailing decades of divine dreams.

Some specialists – dream diviners and philosophers – disagreed: dreams did not come from the gods, but from the soul itself. Of course they disagreed. To maintain their status, like any group of self-styled specialists, they had to claim greater insight than the rest of humanity. Dream diviners had an additional motive – they were competing with the oracular shrines for the same customers.

Not all dreams were significant. It was unwise to pay too much attention to the ones that came in the first half of the night. The mind then was clouded by wine and either too much food, or too little. Such dreams were no more than jumbled fragments of the thoughts from the previous day. The educated remembered from Homer or Virgil that these false dreams came through the Gates of Ivory. True dreams came through the Gates of Horn, later in the night, when the fumes of the evening's wine had dispersed (which is strange, given the number of recipes that existed for preventing or ameliorating hangovers). True dreams foretold the future or offered advice that could help to influence the future.

Some true dreams seemed straightforward. A man dreamed a javelin fell from the sky and wounded his foot. It was a premonition of an injury to that foot. Some were complicated. A man dreamed his absent son said that he had brought him 3,800 coins. Returning from abroad, the son brought him nothing. You needed a dream diviner to explain that. To indicate 3,000, a Greek, counting on his fingers, closed the third, fourth, and fifth fingers of his right hand; the sign for 800 was to close the index finger, placing the thumb on the middle joint; the resulting closed fist gave the meaning of the dream – 'nothing'. Actually, according to a dream diviner, you still needed his services to fully understand the simple one – the man was bitten by a snake, called a 'javelin-snake', he caught gangrene and died. Either way – simple or complex – if you wanted to be sure what a dream meant, you needed a dream diviner.

How to be a Dream Diviner

Dream diviners covered the whole spectrum of society. At the bottom there were illiterate diviners peddling their wares in the marketplace, at the top there was a flourishing genre of literature on interpreting dreams. One book survives. *The Interpretation of Dreams* (*Oneirocritica*) by Artemidorus offers unique and fascinating insights into the thought-world of the Greek half of the Roman empire, and intimate access to the minds of gladiators and their audience. It is worth spending some time with this text.

Artemidorus was born and lived in Ephesus, the great city on the eastern shore of the Aegean, which was the capital of the Roman province of Asia. In his previous works (unspecified, and all now lost) he had written as 'Artemidorus of Ephesus'. In the surviving *The Interpretation of Dreams* he explains why he has now styled himself 'Artemidorus of Daldis': many distinguished men had made Ephesus renowned, but Daldis, the birthplace of his mother, was 'a small and not very notable town in Lydia, which had remained in obscurity up to our time'. But presumably not any longer, which shows a certain confidence.

Artemidorus was writing in the later second and early third centuries AD. He might be the same Artemidorus who was a civic magistrate in Daldis responsible for minting coins between AD 198 and 211. However, all we know for certain about Artemidorus the dream diviner is what he tells us in his book. The latest individual he mentions who can be dated is Paulus the lawyer, who misinterpreted a dream when he was pleading a case before the emperor. Most likely this was the famous Roman jurist Iulius Paulus, who served on the councils of Septimius Severus (AD 193–211) and Alexander Severus (AD 222–235).

The Interpretation of Dreams has a complex structure. Artemidorus wrote books one and two together, and dedicated them to a man called Cassius Maximus, an equestrian from Phoenicia, who he described as 'the most accomplished Greek orator ever to take a public platform'. This is usually thought to have been the philosopher and public speaker Maximus of Tyre, forty-one of whose orations survive, who was active in the reign of Commodus (AD 180–192). Artemidorus later added book three, covering omissions from the first two, also dedicated to Cassius Maximus. Later still, he wrote books four and five as advice for his son, an aspiring dream diviner. Fascinatingly, Artemidorus urged his son not to share these books with anyone. We have no idea how they came to be published with the other three.

Perhaps Artemidorus changed his mind. The first three books contain just one cross-reference to the last two. Perhaps his son ignored his father's wishes and edited all five into one volume.

Artemidorus' methods of dream divining rest on empiricism – collecting case studies of past dreams and their outcomes – and analogy. The latter is underpinned by some basic oppositions: white is good, black is bad; right is male, left is female; the east is young, the west is old; and so on. Often, he turns to wordplay and etymologies or numerology (ancient Greek numerals were written using a modified version of the alphabet; alpha for 1, beta for 2, and so on). But empiricism always trumps analogy. The case studies tell you the outcome, the analogies the causes. Artemidorus encouraged his son, who, as we have seen, was not meant to share the text with anyone, to be creative when providing causes. Clients would not be happy with just an outcome, they wanted reasons.

Sigmund Freud read Artemidorus and claimed him as a forerunner of his own work on dreams. In fact, their thinking about dreams could hardly be more different. Freudian psychoanalysis, and its trite popular derivatives, is about the present and the past – teasing out the subject's unconscious, which has been shaped by their previous life, all too often how they got on with their mother. Ancient writers – especially historians, epic poets and novelists – used dreams to illustrate character. But this holds almost no interest for Artemidorus. For him, dreams are not shaped by the past of the individual but sent by their soul to predict their future.

Artemidorus implicitly aligns himself with the educated and intelligent, claiming to be widely read and travelled. He proudly boasts of his links to the renowned intellectual Maximus of Tyre. Artemidorus was almost definitely a citizen both of Ephesus and Daldis. He certainly had money, enough to travel in the province of Asia, and to the Aegean islands, mainland Greece and Italy. His destinations were famous athletic festivals; attending these was a typically elite activity.

On the other hand, Artemidorus did not move in the highest circles of the empire, those of provincial governors, let alone in the court of Roman emperors. There is no evidence that he had Roman citizenship or knew Latin. The range of classical literature that Artemidorus quotes is limited, smacks of the schoolroom, and is sometimes misunderstood. His prose is workmanlike, far from the elevated and self-consciously antique Atticism of the high-status intellectuals of the time; although this is because *The Interpretation of Dreams* is a technical manual.

Artemidorus divided the world into the *rich* and the *poor* (and very occasionally the *middling*), identifying himself with the former. We should place him among the elite of two provincial cities – with the backwater Daldis being much less impressive than the wealthy port of Ephesus. He seems comfortable in the world of civic magistrates, priests, landowners, merchants and ship owners. But, by his own account, his research took him outside his own class. Not only did he collect material from books, but over many years 'also spent time with the much-maligned diviners of the marketplace, paying no attention to the disparagement of those po-faced eyebrow-knitters who call them beggars, frauds, and parasites'. For once in the ancient Mediterranean, we might hear the voices of the non-elite, get a view of the world from the bottom of society. Perhaps we might hope for even more.

In *The Cheese and the Worms*, Carlo Ginzburg used the records of the Inquisition to recreate the thought-world of a peasant miller in sixteenth-century Friuli in Italy. The punctilious bureaucracy of the inquisitors, Ginzburg claims, preserves very rare evidence of an illiterate and non-elite subordinate counter-culture locked into a continuous and unequal conflict with the dominant, literate elite culture. Such a counter-culture, Ginzburg suggested, was widespread in pre-industrial European societies. Do the stories the beggar-diviners of the marketplace told Artemidorus support the idea that something similar existed in the Roman empire?

Just a handful of dreams in Artemidorus are autobiographical. Quite a large number are said to be drawn from previous writers. The vast majority, however, have no provenance. Artemidorus does not tell us if he read them in a book or was told them by a diviner in the marketplace. That we cannot tell their origin is significant. The types of dreams people had, whatever their background, were remarkably similar. Social status only came into play with the interpretation. The same dream could mean different things for elite and non-elite. If a rich man dreamed of being crucified it was bad, because the condemned are stripped naked, and once on the cross lose their flesh. If a poor man had the same dream it was good, because 'someone who has been crucified is elevated, and has the substance to keep many birds well fed'.

The evidence of Artemidorus argues against the existence of a non-elite counter-culture as imagined by Ginzburg. It fits much better with the model proposed for Rome by Jerry Toner in *Leisure and Ancient Rome*: elite and non-elite inhabit the same culture, but their different resources mean they express themselves differently. In Toner a member of the elite threatened with loss of face initiates a legal action, while in the same circumstances one of the non-elite starts a barroom fight. In Artemidorus social status remains important *within* dreams. If you dream that a poor friend shits on your head, it is very bad, signifying that you will be covered in shame. If, however, the friend is rich, this is very good. It foretells that you will inherit his wealth.

The world of *The Interpretation of Dreams* is viewed from the city. Farmers and farming frequently appear, but in a rather vague and unengaged way. The stance is that of an urban-dwelling absentee landowner. The rural estate of a gentleman farmer is inhabited by males, because the owner does not live there. Two sons, sent by their father to work an outlying farm, were killed by a band of robbers; a not altogether exceptional outcome, as the countryside was full of bandits. While the farmed countryside was auspicious, all natural landscapes – mountains, valleys, glens, ravines and forests – were forbidding. The best thing about the countryside were the roads that got you out of it.

The thought-world of *The Interpretation of Dreams* was a dangerous place, full of rumours and plots, of fears of ridicule and disgrace, of being cuckolded or kidnapped, of losing loved ones or your property or livelihood. It was a world of sickness and death, where a capricious judge may strip you of your civic rights, send you into exile, condemn you to hard labour in the mines or treadmills, or have you beheaded or crucified. The appearance of the Roman state is almost always ominous. As might be expected, there are men lying low, or on the run. It is an uncertain territory where, all too often, things that appear good turn out to be bad. For the free sometimes things that at first glance seem bad are actually good – success in your career, an agreeable spouse, or coming into an inheritance – although often only after a nasty illness or shock. Although many bad things happen to slaves, there is hope: over half their dreams promise freedom.

You need to be alert, observant, and have a good memory, even in your sleep if you want to interpret your dreams correctly. Absolutely anything could be of crucial importance. It is not just the physically impossible events – flying among the rooftops of Rome, or feeding your penis bread and cheese – or the supernatural – playing a ball game with Zeus, or having sex with the Moon – or the socially taboo – urinating in a crowded theatre, or having sex with your mother – that hold meaning. So do the completely mundane: washing your face, brushing your hair, or leaving your house.

Artemidorus creates a strongly fatalistic world. Only four dreams out of hundreds offer advice. The balance is very different in Aelius Aristides and the temples where the gods come in dreams. Here, Artemidorus tells you what is going to happen, and that is that. There is nothing you can do. Resign yourself, there is no point in looking for a way out. You dreamed your hands turned into the paws of a bear – you are going to be condemned to the arena.

The Interpretation of Dreams opens a unique, and very strange, window onto the hopes and fears, and the attitudes and values, of the Greek-speaking inhabitants of the Roman empire. It offers many new paths, still largely unexplored, to approach important themes: Greek and Roman identities, marriage and families, the roles of philosophers and sophists, popular ideas about violence and warfare, and a surprising amount about gladiators.

Dreams about Gladiators

A poor man dreams he is struck by lightning, a slave that he is serving in the army, a passenger about to board a ship that he is crucified, a bachelor that he is fighting as a gladiator. Artemidorus tells us that all these dreams are internally bad (no one wants to be crucified), but externally good (they foretell a change for the better). The first three respectively signify wealth (those struck by lightning are honoured, as are the wealthy), freedom (only freemen can serve in the army), and a prosperous voyage (a cross resembles the mast of a ship). When Artemidorus returns to gladiators and marriage in an extended passage things take a less promising turn.

The type of gladiator indicates the character of the wife the dreamer will marry. Artemidorus says a clear demonstration requires clarity and implicitly apologises for using Latin words transliterated into Greek. If you fight a *Thraex*, your wife will be rich, but devious and eager to put herself first; rich because that type of gladiator has full armour, devious because he has a curved sword, and domineering because he advances to attack. If you dream that you are fighting in 'silver armour' (the type of gladiator is obscured by a corrupt line in the manuscript) your wife will be beautiful, moderately rich, faithful, a good housekeeper and obedient; because this type gives ground and is well protected by armour that is more handsome than that of the *Thraex*. Fight a *Secutor* and your wife will be beautiful and rich, but with a high opinion of herself because of her wealth, and, because the *Secutor* always goes after his opponent, will cause you endless trouble. If you are matched against a *Retiarius*, she will be poor and lecherous and have sex with anyone who wants it. An *Eques* (mounted gladiator) means she will be rich and well born, but devoid of any sense; an *Essedarius* (chariot-mounted gladiator) points to a lazy and stupid wife; a *Provocator* to a beautiful and charming, but flirtatious and randy one. Worst of all are the *Dimachaerus* (a gladiator armed with two daggers) and the *Arbelas* (armed with one normal dagger and a semi-circular blade like a leather-worker's knife) – dream of one of those and your wife will be a witch, or malicious, or just plain ugly.

Artemidorus tops and tails his 'gladiators and wives' exposition with assurances that none of this is based on conjecture or probability, but instead all derives from direct observation and actual outcomes. If true, an awful lot of people had very detailed dreams about fighting as gladiators. If not, Artemidorus at least thought his readers would find it plausible that in their dreams many people entered the arena. Artemidorus also assumes that his Greek readers had a good knowledge of the technicalities of gladiatorial combat. He does not feel the need to explain the meanings of six of the nine types. A contemporary reader knew these things. We must infer them. In the logic of the text a *Retiarius* represents poverty because he has no armour, and likewise the defensive equipment of a *Provocator* makes him beautiful and charming. Presumably the sexual promiscuity of the former comes from his running here and there in the arena; why the latter shares this characteristic is less obvious. For the *Eques* there was a long-standing association of horsemanship with wealthy aristocrats, who could be thought of as lacking common sense. Maybe the *Essedarius* was lazy because he rode in a chariot, but his stupidity is elusive. Where the magic, malice and ugliness of the *Dimachaerus* and *Arbelas* come from is anyone's guess.

Why were gladiators associated with marriage? Three explanations can be offered. They are not mutually exclusive. First, there was the strong sexual charge of the figure of the gladiator. Then there was the gladiatorial oath that bound him to his *ludus*, as a wife and husband should be bound to each other. Finally, there was an ancient Roman ritual, so old its meaning was unknown to the Romans and much debated. A bride's hair should be parted with a bent iron spearhead. One with which a gladiator had been killed was best.

It is unfortunate that the identity of the only type of gladiator that predicts an agreeable wife is hidden in a corruption in the manuscript. But it seems significant that the only good outcome occurs when the sleeper dreams about the equipment *he* is using, rather than that of his opponent. Perhaps in gladiatorial dreams, as in attitudes to sex, it is better to be the active partner.

An overwhelming majority – eight out of nine – of the types of gladiators predicts a bad wife. In the world of Roman dreams the prospect of marriage is seldom enticing. If a bachelor dreams of being crucified, it foretells marriage, because the victim is tied to the cross, as a husband to his wife.

Before launching into his extended analysis of what gladiator dreams meant for bachelors, Artemidorus offered a brief explanation of what they foretold more generally. Unsurprisingly it is nothing good. You will be caught up in a lawsuit or some other dispute or fight. Yet in another passage dreaming of being beheaded in gladiatorial combat – or through judicial condemnation, or by bandits; he assures us it makes no difference – can be good. It all depends on who is dreaming. A defendant on a capital charge will get off; you can't lose your head twice. A debtor will escape what he owes. A man living in a foreign country will return home, and anyone in court over the ownership of land will win his case; because a severed head falls to the ground. For most slaves a dream about beheading signifies freedom, because the head is master of the body, or maybe it just foretells being sold. But here too the bad connotations vastly outweigh the good. Anyone with parents, children, a wife, a friend, a good steward, or a house, will lose the one they most cherish. Anyone who accumulates money – bankers, moneylenders, presidents of an *eranos* (a credit lending society), shipowners and merchants – will lose their capital. A slave in a trusted position will lose that trust. Those in lawsuits about civic rights or money will lose their case. For a passenger at sea it indicates grave danger – the ship will lose its yardarm. For a member of the crew, somewhat reassuringly, it foretells the death of their immediate superior. Finally a Greek, who Artemidorus knew, had this dream and obtained Roman citizenship, and 'so lost his former name and status'.

The outcome of dreaming of fighting wild beasts as a *Bestiarius* was largely dependent on your social status. It was a good dream for a poor man, indicating that he would be able to feed a large household, because the *Bestiarius* feeds the beasts with his own flesh. But, if you were rich, it foretold injuries inflicted by people with beastly characters. It signified freedom for a slave, if he dreamed he was killed by the animals. For many, social status unspecified, animal fighting presaged sickness, as beasts consume flesh like a wasting disease.

Artemidorus thought it was vital that the interpreter got to hear the whole of the dream, and all its details, as well as finding out as much as he could about the background of the dreamer. The latter included his geographical origins and ethnic customs. As a rule 'local customs are indicators of good outcomes, foreign of bad'. Bullfighting is almost universally an ordeal imposed on the condemned. Unless you are from Athens or Ephesus, where young men do it as part of a religious ritual, or from Larissa in Thessaly in northern Greece, where the 'best of the gentry' enjoy the sport. A day at the gladiatorial Games followed the same broad outlines across the empire, but Artemidorus reminds us that there were local variations.

The Dreams of Gladiators

Athletes receive many dreams in the Artemidorus' book, gladiators very few. Of course this reflects their social status: athletes were young men of the elite, gladiators were slaves, or freemen reduced to a sort of servitude. But we should not rule out the possibility that Artemidorus had gladiators as clients. Galen, who became physician to the emperors Marcus Aurelius and Commodus, started his career treating the gladiators of Pergamum.

Some dreams foretold that a man was destined for the arena. A man dreamed that he had sex with a lump of iron, as if it were a woman. Artemidorus mentions another diviner, Antipater, who on the basis of a previous outcome of the same dream, predicted that the dreamer would be condemned to fight as a gladiator. Quite wrong, declares Artemidorus. The same outcomes will follow the same dreams unless some new significance arises. Evidently something did change in this case, although Artemidorus does not tell us what, for the dreamer was castrated.

Possibly Artemidorus has not been totally fair to his predecessor here. A man could not be condemned to be castrated, which was illegal in the Roman empire. As we will see later, there was an exception – very rare condemnation to self-castration in the gladiatorial arena.

A man dreamed that his hands turned into the paws of a bear. There was a widespread belief that a hibernating bear sucked its own paws for nourishment. The interpretation was obvious. The dreamer was condemned to death in the arena; tied to a stake, he was eaten by a bear.

Gladiators already enrolled in a *ludus* twice feature as the hypothetical recipients of dreams in the *Oneirocritica*. Dreams of the personifications of Terror and Fear (Deimos and Phobos), and their father Ares, the god of war, signify conflict and damage for everyone, as they are the cause of it. The exceptions to this role are those for whom conflict and damage are their stock in trade. The fearsome divine triumvirate are auspicious for generals, soldiers, gladiators, bandits and gamblers. At first sight the inclusion of gamblers is odd, but gambling, along with drunkenness, was thought to lead to fights. In a series of paintings on the wall of the 'Inn of Salvius' at Pompeii, betting on a game of dice escalates into violence; the landlord issues the timeless command: 'If you want to fight, take it outside.'

The other dream of gladiators was inauspicious. For an athlete, a gladiator, or anyone in physical training, dreaming that they had milk in their breasts foretold sickness; 'as it is the bodies of the weaker sex that have milk'.

Finally, we can return to the dream which introduced this chapter – the man who signed up as a gladiator in the sarcophagus full of blood. Teasing out its meanings, Artemidorus illuminates contemporary views of life as a gladiator. The words of the mother show the choice of career was dishonourable; eating the congealed blood that it was savage and godforsaken; and the sarcophagus, whose 'contents are inevitably consumed to nothing', illustrate its constant danger. The full meaning was not revealed until, after many years fighting to the finish, 'late in the day some people urged him to abandon his gladiatorial career, and he did so' – just as the dream had prophesied when the people had put down the sarcophagus, and the man had returned home. Artemidorus expects his readers to find it entirely believable, even normal, that someone might volunteer as a gladiator, have a long career fighting in the arena, before a comfortable retirement.

One key interpretive question remains, at least to me, unanswerable. How did Artemidorus' clients respond when they were told they were going to lose a loved one, all their property, or their own life, quite possibly in the arena?

5

QUARTA VIGILIA
(The Fourth Watch of the Night)

Just before dawn a man is at his lowest. Especially the night before he enters the arena. The gladiator says he needs to relieve himself. At this hour the communal latrine is empty. It is the only place where he is not watched by a guard. In the dark, damp room the gladiator picks up a sponge on a stick, for wiping arses. He brings the repulsive thing close to his face. He opens his mouth, and rams the sponge down his throat, blocking his windpipe. The gladiator chokes himself to death.

Security

The gladiator here, who we come across in Seneca's writing, would rather kill himself in a degrading way than fight in the arena. And on the night before the show he can only find solitude for his suicide in the deserted latrine. It raises questions about the motives and methods of suicide, of whether gladiators were particularly prone to killing themselves, and about the levels of security in the barracks. But first, where were gladiators normally quartered?

Seneca, as a stern moral philosopher, roundly condemned the effeminacy of contemporary men. Among many examples, 'one man cuts off his genitals, another flees into the obscene part of the gladiatorial school [*obscenum ludi partem*], and, hired for death, he chooses a disgraceful [*infame*] type of armament in which to practise his sickness'. Seneca is castigating free men who have not just volunteered to fight as gladiators, but have chosen to appear in the arena as the most effeminate type, as the net and trident fighter, the *Retiarius*. According to Seneca such men are quartered in the 'obscene' part of the barracks.

The satirist Juvenal provides more on this line.

> The lightly armed [literally, *naked*] are required to keep away from the heavily armed. Even the nets are separated from the tunics that signal disgrace. The one who fights naked hangs up his shoulder-guard, along with his trident, in a separate locker. The school's remotest cells are given to the most despised; they even have a different chain in prison.

This is not a straightforward passage. But it seems to suggest that not only are the lightly armed quartered away from the heavies, but that among the *Retiarii*, those of slave origins, who fight 'naked' (actually in a loincloth), are separated from the free volunteers, who wear the 'tunic of disgrace'.

Seneca and Juvenal are giving us highly charged moral judgements, but they imply that the different types of gladiators bunked with their own sort. It makes sense. Each type trained together. In a *Ludus*, bonds were formed between the men who fought within each style (*armatura*). Gladiators often erected tombstones for men who fought in the same style: *murmillo* for *murmillo*, and so on. But it did not preclude other relationships. Sometimes the deceased were commemorated by gladiators who fought as other types, and sometimes by other members of the staff of the school. Relationships could also be forged with people outside the gladiatorial *familia*: remember Sergiolus, the battered old gladiator who ran off to Egypt with the wife of a senator?

Can any of this be mapped onto the archaeological evidence? Five gladiatorial barracks have been located. Two are in Rome. The *Ludus Magnus* is adjacent to the Colosseum. Almost half the site can be viewed from the outdoor tables of the restaurants along Via San Giovanni in Laterano, the rest is unexcavated under your feet. To the south of the *Ludus Magnus* a similar, although smaller complex was briefly investigated in 1938, and tentatively identified as the *Ludus Matutinus*; the School of the Morning, where beast-fighters were trained. It is now buried under modern buildings.

Two of the other gladiatorial barracks are in Pompeii and have been visited by innumerable tourists over the years. The smaller is in the north-east of the city, on the way to the Nola Gate. Technically it is V 5.3 (all buildings in Pompeii are identified by three numbers; the first [Roman] numeral is the region of the city, the second the block, and the third the main entrance of the individual building). It was here that Cresces the *Retiarius* and Celadus the Thracian boasted of their sexual appeal to girls. The style of writing of over a hundred gladiatorial graffiti found on the site point to them being written in the early first century AD, perhaps as early as the reign of Augustus (31BC–AD14). The building was damaged in an earthquake in AD62, and it is thought that the gladiators were moved out then. The building collapsed after heavy rains in November 2010. Sometime after the earthquake of AD62, it is thought that the gladiators moved to the second, larger barracks in Pompeii (VIII 7.16). This lies in the south-west of the city, next to the Temple of Minerva and Hercules, and the two theatres, close by the Stabian Gate. It was in use in AD79, when Vesuvius erupted, as fifteen gladiatorial helmets, and many other items of equipment for the arena, were found on the site.

The fifth and final barracks was identified next to the civilian amphitheatre outside the city of Carnuntum on the Danube in the province of Pannonia. It has not been excavated, but brilliant and methodical use of sophisticated modern archaeological techniques, including airborne imaging spectroscopy, electromagnetic induction, and ground-penetrating radar, have allowed firm interpretation of the site.

The two barracks in Rome, and almost certainly the one at Carnuntum, were specifically designed to house gladiatorial troupes. The two in Pompeii were not. The smaller (V 5.3) was previously a private house, and the larger (VIII 7.16) was designed as a spacious portico in which spectators from the two theatres could meet and stroll during intermissions. Despite their different original uses, all the barracks share a broadly similar layout. A rectangle of cells, on more than one level, surrounds a central open area, which was used for training. The *Ludus Magnus* has a brick-built amphitheatre, only 25 per cent smaller than the Colosseum itself, and thus of equivalent size to most provincial arenas. At Carnuntum two circular training enclosures, one with stands for spectators, have been identified. All the sites have other, larger rooms. And here the interpretive problems start. Apart from a few rooms whose purpose is clear – a kitchen, a prison, and a stable in the larger barracks at Pompeii, and a bathhouse at Carnuntum – we must guess their function. Was a room a mess hall or an indoor training area, an armoury or a mundane storeroom, a medical area or a place for laying out corpses, a punishment cell or accommodation for the staff of the school or the higher-ranked gladiators (the emperor Commodus slept in the quarters of the *Primus Palus* of the *Secutors* in the *Ludus Magnus*)? Similarly, we have no idea which types of gladiators occupied which cells. Which cells in a rectangle are the 'remotest' (Juvenal), especially if we are not certain where was the main entrance? How do we recognise which are 'obscene' (Seneca)? Ancient moralists, like Seneca and Juvenal, ordered domestic space in different terms from modern archaeologists.

The gladiator choked himself to death with a sponge in the deserted communal latrine because on the night before a fight he was watched by a guard everywhere else in the *Ludus*. As the anecdote in Seneca is one of only a handful of bits of evidence, utterly divergent views can be held on the normal levels of security in a gladiatorial barracks.

It is possible to argue that security was tight. Spartacus and the other gladiators in the *familia* of Batiatus were kept shackled when they were not fighting. When they broke out, they had to equip themselves with kitchen implements – indicating that weapons were either in an armoury they could not access, or were stored offsite. In a room in the later barracks at Pompeii shackles were attached to the wall in such a way that a prisoner could only sit or crouch. In the same complex, a small room by the main entrance has been identified as a guard post. Two inscriptions refer to a man in the *Ludus Maximus* as a *Cryptarius*; which can be translated as a warder. A character in a Latin fictional courtroom speech talks of his time in a gladiatorial barracks, 'locked up in a foul gaol, in the fetid neglect of the cells'. By comparison the gaol of a slave work gang was a palace. All of which fits the modern popular image: dank, dark cells, strict confinement and brutality.

On the other hand, security in a gladiatorial barracks can be seen as surprisingly light. Spartacus lived in the barracks with his wife. Numerous inscriptions from the principate record married gladiators, several with children. Various daggers, and a lance, were discovered scattered throughout the later barracks at Pompeii. In the same complex, although four men were discovered in the prison when it was excavated in the eighteenth century, it seems none of them was shackled, and we have no idea if the door was locked. The 'guard room' was not exceptional – all private houses of a certain size tended to have a porter's lodge by the main entrance. No increased security is visible in the archaeological record when the smaller barracks at Pompeii was converted from an ordinary house. A *Cryptarius* can be translated less ominously: either the functionary in charge of the training ground, or just a cellar man. We have seen gladiators outside their barracks acting as bodyguards to important men, and even to the dignitaries' wives. In one of his interminable and depressing homilies, Saint John Chrysostom admonished his audience not to think that the gladiators they saw feasting in taverns were happy – their fleeting pleasures could not be compared to their fate: presumably both likely death in the arena, and the eternal punishment that monotonously awaited everyone that did not share the beliefs of a Christian moralist. The pagan satirist Juvenal did not speculate on the happiness of the veteran gladiator Sergiolus, but nothing stopped him from eloping to Egypt with the wife of a senator. Finally, returning to Spartacus, we are told that the regime of Batiatus was exceptionally cruel.

To search for a 'normal' level of security might be futile. Quite likely it varied from one *Ludus* to another. It definitely would have varied over time. Security would have to be stepped up on two obvious occasions: when there was an influx of new men condemned to the school, and in the run-up to the Games, especially the night before a fight.

Which begs the question – who were the guards? Here our evidence fails us completely. Soldiers, almost certainly, guarded the schools owned by the emperor. As we will see, they provided security at the Games, and we know of soldiers detached from their units guarding imperial mines worked by slaves and condemned criminals. But soldiers were not available to private *Ludi*. The best guess is that these were to some extent self-policing, with a system something like 'trusties' in modern American gaols.

There was a hierarchy in a gladiatorial school. You arrived as a *novicius*, became a *tyro* after training, and a *veteranus* after surviving your first fight. Veterans then progressed through a ranking system, named after the *palus* (the wooden stake at which gladiators practised). At the top were those ranked *Primus Palus* (First Stake) of each type of gladiator. Commodus liked to be honoured as *Primus Palus* of the *Secutors*. Usually there were five ranks in a school, although occasionally we hear of up to eight. Advancement, presumably, depended on a combination of the number of fights survived, victories won, the ranking of opponents, and the gladiator's favour with the owner of the school.

A man at the top might train those further down. Aelius Marcion, trainer and *Primus Palus*, set up a gravestone for one of his charges. A trusted *Primus Palus* could have guarded lower-ranked gladiators; although not the nights before he fought – it was in no one's interest to have an acclaimed combatant enter the arena sleep-deprived. The emperor Hadrian's ruling on Spanish cattle rustlers condemned to gladiatorial schools might provide an answer to the identity of the guards. The condemned had to serve a minimum of three years as fighters and a minimum of five in the school. It is usually assumed that they served as trainers in the time between retirement from the arena and discharge from the school. Such experienced men could have also made excellent guards.

Roman Suicides

'I am a Christian, and I want to die!' The voice came from outside the courtroom. The governor replied, 'Whoever shouted, bring him in.'

Voluntary martyrs were a problem for the Roman authorities. Arrius Antoninus, governor of Asia, was once confronted by the entire Christian community in the town where he was holding court. At least that was the story told by a Christian almost twenty years later in distant Africa. Arrius Antoninus ordered a few executed and sent the rest away with the words, 'Cowards, if you want to kill yourselves, there are cliffs and ropes round here.'

It is easy for a modern reader to feel sympathy for overworked Roman governors harassed by these insistent and often abusive zealots. Equally it is hard not to smile at the governors' deadpan, black humour.

Aemilianus the governor said to Fructosus: 'You are a Bishop?'

'Yes, I am.'

'You were,' said Aemilianus, and sentenced him to be burned alive.

Sympathy and amusement are emphatically not the responses intended by the authors of early Christian Martyr Acts. The words of Arrius Antoninus are meant to demonstrate both his ignorance – he mistakes Christian desire for paradise with common suicide – and his boorish offensiveness.

Arrius Antoninus suggested the Christians made use of cliffs and ropes out of scorn; neither jumping from a height nor hanging yourself was a respectable way for a Roman man to die. They were methods of suicide associated with women, slaves and barbarians. A later story (told by men) had Sappho, the original lesbian, leap off a cliff out of unrequited love for a man. For an author of the third century AD, it was remarkable that when the mythical Evadne took her own life, she did not 'hang herself as women usually do'. According to a Latin legal text, jumping and hanging were two of three ways a 'bad slave' might do away with themselves, thus in effect robbing their master of his property. In the fiction of the *Augustan History*, the emperor Heliogabalus – from Syria, and seen as the archetypal eastern despot – 'prepared cords entwined with purple and scarlet silk', and built a gilded and jewelled tower, so that 'even his death would be costly and marked by luxury'. A Roman man, who jumped out of a high window, went to a 'hasty and unseemly death'. When the aged emperor Gordian I hanged himself, after his son had been killed in battle, it was seen as a sign of weakness. An inscription records the gift of a public cemetery to a town in Umbria – those who had hanged themselves were excluded from burial, along with volunteer gladiators and others who had followed immoral professions for profit.

There were other disreputable ways to kill yourself. Poison was one. Again, it was employed by 'bad slaves' and barbarians. Heliogabalus laid in a supply, contained with characteristic extravagance in precious stones. Women had special expertise in poison but were said to take it themselves only if caught poisoning others. Drowning was for criminals and slaves. It could be combined with jumping from a cliff – by women, like Sappho, or, at least in fiction, by men deranged either by love or reading Plato. Although the mythical Hercules climbed onto his own funeral pyre, in reality burning yourself to death was the preserve of weird foreign sages, like the Indian Calanus, or their attention-seeking imitators, like Peregrinus: sometime Christian, sometime philosopher, and, according to his biographer Lucian, full-time charlatan.

The best way for a true Roman man to commit suicide quickly was with a blade. In the free Republic a general facing disaster on the battlefield was expected to literally fall on his sword. This prevented any humiliations the foreign victor might inflict, thus preserving both the general's honour and that of Rome. The civil wars that destroyed the Republic vastly increased the frequency of such suicides: there was always a Roman general, or other high officers, on the losing side. Some military commanders had a member of their entourage tasked with aiding such a death; often these men were gladiators. The civil wars also added another reason for these suicides, a new form of humiliation that ratcheted up the emotional intensity of defeat. Faced with Julius Caesar's overwhelming victory, Cato the Younger decided on death. After high-minded, philosophical conversation with his friends, he stabbed himself. The blow was not fatal and his companions had him patched up. Left alone, Cato tore out the stitches with his bare hands. Cato had disembowelled himself to prevent the ultimate insult to his *dignitas*, or self-esteem – to be shown clemency by another Roman.

Cato's suicide brought together the Roman tradition of falling on one's sword with that of Greek philosophic suicide as epitomised by the death of Socrates. Having been condemned to death in Athens, Socrates refused an offer of escape. On his last day, he calmly discussed philosophy with his friends, before drinking hemlock. Cato's suicide became another model. Under the emperors the Roman elite created a cult of the good suicide.

Calm, rational discussion over dinner with friends on topics such as the potential immortality of the soul. After this a bath, in which the suicide's veins were opened. This could be done by a slave. At some point the veins might be bound up, and the dying man indulge in some more high-minded activities – more elevated conversation, dictating some philosophical reflections, additional setting of his affairs in order, altering his will, freeing some slaves – before removing the bandages and slipping away in the reddened water.

The prevalence of the ideal of the good suicide can be shown in its deliberate parody by Petronius, Nero's sometime 'arbiter of elegance', and almost certainly the author of the novel the *Satyricon*. Having been charged with friendship with a man convicted of treason, Petronius opened his veins. Then, having them bound up, he held a dinner party. There was no conversation about the immortality of the soul or the doctrines of philosophy. In their place came light-hearted songs and frivolous verse. Some of his slaves were given gifts, others whipped. When Petronius' veins were reopened, he seemed to drowse, before dictating his last work, a catalogue of the sexual depravities of the emperor.

Some suicides were enforced. A message came from the emperor granting you the freedom to choose the manner of your death. Others were notionally voluntary. Those on trial for treason – charges of treason were part of most prosecutions of the elite – took their own lives to forestall condemnation, even if innocent. Some took their lives if they merely suspected that they might be charged, some at the first signs of the emperor's disfavour. A senator greeted Augustus, 'Hello, Caesar.' The emperor replied, 'Goodbye, Fulvius.' The senator killed himself.

Interestingly, next to no one tried to run. Where was there to go – Parthia? The few who did almost never seem to have got away. This rich harvest of suicidal death was fuelled partly by the desire to preserve one's own dignity by avoiding execution, and partly by the hope that acquiescence might spare your family and friends persecution, as well as avoiding the confiscation of your estates, which would reduce your family to poverty. The emperor, of course, was above the law, or, as a jurist would put it, the emperor's will *was* law. No matter at what stage the suicide occurred, the emperor could still confiscate the victim's estate. Jurists would then pronounce that the suicide had been caused by a guilty conscience. Conversely, even after condemnation, the emperor could exercise clemency and leave the estate to the family, perhaps even pronouncing a posthumous pardon.

Motives were just as important as methods. Roman attitudes to suicide were very different from Christian attitudes. Suicide was a sin for Christians: both because it damaged God's creation (your body), and because it tried to pre-empt God's decision as to when you should die. Unlike the authors of the Martyr Acts, the majority of the early Church Fathers were not at all keen on voluntary martyrdom; like the pagan governor Arrius Antoninus, they thought it too close to suicide. What troubled Christians did not trouble pagans. In pagan myths the gods had not created man; that had been the work of Prometheus, who defied the gods. Plato and Aristotle had argued you should not die before the gods willed, and were followed in this by some later philosophers, but it was very much a minority view.

A bad Roman suicide was one carried out hastily, without due consideration, caused by panic, fear, grief, madness, a desire for notoriety, or to make a futile political gesture. A good suicide was calm, the result of rational deliberation, a response to intolerable pain, incurable illness, old age, or just the 'tedium of life' (*taedium vitae*). If you had time, starving yourself was quite acceptable, especially for the elderly. But nothing really matched suicide with a blade, not just for your own honour, but for the good of others: Republican generals fell on their swords for the good of Rome; imperial senators opened their veins for the good of their families.

Where did all this leave a gladiator in a gloomy latrine, the dawn of the Games approaching?

Gladiator Suicides

The story of the gladiator in the latrine is in a letter by Seneca. The gladiator is a German, presumably a prisoner of war, who has been condemned to the school that trained beast-fighters. In the same letter Seneca tells of two other gladiatorial suicides. Another beast-fighter, whose origin is not given, is in a cart taking him to the morning spectacle. Despite the presence of guards, he manages to kill himself by pretending to be asleep, and letting his head loll, until it gets caught in the spokes of the wheel, which breaks his neck. The final suicide is another barbarian, who is to fight in the 'second spectacle' (i.e. in the afternoon) in a mass battle on boats (a *Naumachia*). He waits until he is given a spear, which he thrusts into his own throat.

Two other sources tell us about gladiators killing themselves; both are mass suicides. In a letter of AD 393 Symmachus records that on the first day of the Games, twenty-nine of the Saxons, evidently prisoners of war, who were to fight as gladiators, strangled themselves without a rope. In his account of the aftermath of the Second Sicilian Slave War (104–100 BC) Diodorus Siculus says that 1,000 rebel prisoners, who were consigned to fight wild beasts in Rome, instead killed each other at the public altars; after all the others were dead, their leader, Satyrus, took his own life.

We can note that three of the five cases involve beast-fighters, but probably it does not get us very far. Although some individual beast-fighters could become famous, generally they were held in less regard than gladiators who fought human opponents. We have no way of telling if they were more prone to suicide.

Three of the five cases involve barbarians: two are explicitly

Germanic, probably so is the gladiator at the *Naumachia*. This might take us a bit further. Romans usually viewed Germans as violent, irrational and dangerous, especially when fighting them. But from a safe distance they could be seen through a filter of 'soft primitivism' in which they were held up as freedom-loving 'noble savages' to act as a contrast to, and a criticism of, decadent contemporary Roman society. This reached its literary peak in Tacitus' ethnographic treatise the *Germania*. Such 'soft primitivism' was not wholesale invention. Tacitus did not simply take what he saw as the vices of contemporary Rome and foist their opposites on the Germans. Rather, he selected what he knew about the Germans (which, of course, might not be accurate) and nuanced it to fit his Roman-focused moral agenda. Perhaps gladiators of Germanic origins really were more prone to suicide. Certainly, Romans thought they were more likely to kill themselves rather than appear in the arena.

Five cases, from three sources, self-evidently is not enough to draw any confident statistical conclusions. We are better off turning to the attitudes of those writers that talk about the suicides of gladiators.

Symmachus was a pagan traditionalist senator under Christian emperors in the second half of the fourth century AD: a man of enormous wealth, profound self-satisfaction, and many, many words. As part of a high-profile, and mainly successful, career, he gave several Games in Rome on behalf of himself and his son. For all the money he threw at them, Symmachus was unlucky with his shows: the bears and lions arrived in poor condition, the crocodiles would not eat, and (as mentioned already) twenty-nine of the Saxon prisoners of war who were to fight as gladiators strangled each other. Symmachus was furious. 'How could private guards restrain the impious hands of a desperate race?' Impious, presumably because they had broken the gladiatorial oath they had been forced to take– although what it meant to Saxon tribesmen is debatable. No soft primitivism here: these

Saxons were worse than Spartacus! Still, Symmachus tried to console himself. Maybe, with all the other gladiators these twenty-nine might have been too many; perhaps they would have spoiled the show? That said, he slyly suggests he would gladly replace his lost gladiators with some Libyan beasts, if provided by the munificence of the emperor. Symmachus tries to rise above it. He is like Socrates, philosophically accepting the misfortunes of life.

The response of Symmachus – the suicides were caused by the despair and cowardice typical of such scum – was the one we would expect. But it is very much what we do not find in our other two sources.

For a long time, Diodorus Siculus, the Greek historian writing in the second half of the last century BC, was treated with disdain. A cut-and-paste merchant, lacking discrimination, insight or originality, he imported the original authors' views along with the stories he hacked out of his sources. Diodorus was reduced to little more than a quarry for the nuggets he preserved of earlier, and better, writers. A more recent rehabilitation has detected themes that are Diodorus' own running through his work. Now he is considered to have chosen and shaped his material to his own ends; above all a moral purpose about human behaviour and divine retribution. Never more so than with his treatment of the events that led up to the mass gladiatorial suicide.

Despite the very fragmentary nature of his text, Diodorus is our main source for the Second Sicilian Slave War. For Diodorus the revolt was caused by the cruelty of the slaves' owners. Unusually among ancient historians, his narrative is extremely sympathetic to rebellious slaves; an attitude that continues to the suicide. Having defeated the main slave forces, the Roman consul Aquilius determined to finish off the last 1,000 rebels. But the slaves sent envoys and made their submission. Postponing any punishment, Aquilius brought them to Rome, where he consigned them to fight wild beasts. Scorning the arena, the slaves killed each other at the public altars. Last to die was their leader Satyrus.

This is a strange story. It implies that Aquilius acted duplicitously. Would the slaves have surrendered if they had known they would have to appear in the arena? Also, once condemned to fight wild beasts, how were the slaves able to openly kill themselves at the public altars? Despite the unanswered questions, Diodorus is explicit in his judgement – the slaves 'ended their lives with great gallantry and nobleness of spirit'; the death of Satyrus was 'heroic'. Yet there is no discussion of what made the deaths so admirable.

With Seneca we get a complete explanation. Seneca repeatedly denigrates the gladiators. They are the 'vilest sort of men', 'sordid', 'contemptible', the 'lowest class of slaves', and 'wretched and guilty'. Yet their suicides are models of courage. 'How bravely he would have wielded a sword; with what courage he would have hurled himself into the depths of the sea, or down from a precipice!' Seneca is deliberately subverting conventional attitudes. The gladiators have been selected precisely because they are the lowest of the low, who have only degraded ways to kill themselves. They provide the ultimate proof of Stoic philosophy's stance on suicide: motive always transcends methods and backgrounds. Seneca gives the barbarian at the sea fight a dying speech (in Latin!): 'Why, why, have I not escaped from all this torture and all this mockery long ago? Why should I be armed, yet wait for death?' There is no despair or cowardice here, instead the gladiators make a rational and totally commendable decision to end an intolerable life, and to avoid the shame of fighting in the arena. For Seneca they offer a better moral example than Cato and the generals from the civil wars. They provide a model that can be imitated by anyone in any circumstances.

As Seneca put it elsewhere:

Wherever you look is the means to end your woes. See that precipice? That is the way to freedom. The sea, that well? Freedom lies at the bottom. That stunted, blighted barren tree? Freedom hangs from its branches. Your throat, your gullet, your heart? Ways to escape servitude. Are these ways too much trouble, require too much courage or strength? You ask where is the road to freedom? Any vein in your body.

6

Conticinium
(Just Before Dawn)

Conticinium is when the cocks have stopped crowing, but men are still asleep. Except men are not still asleep on the day of the Games. Imagine yourself one of the innumerable gulls that scream and circle above the city of Rome. Even at this hour the gloomy streets down below you are packed. Solid streams of humanity throng the Via Sacra and the Via Labicana, and all the streets heading to the Colosseum. Admission is free, but only by ticket. The Colosseum is always full. Only the elite, with their reserved seats, can afford to arrive late.

Popularity

We think of gladiators when we think of the Roman Games. It is easy to assume that they were the biggest draw in the city. Cold hard numbers show this assumption is wrong in two ways.

The Romans claimed the Colosseum could hold over 80,000 spectators. Modern archaeologists downgrade the number to less than 50,000. This was still more than twice as many as the largest theatre in Rome; the Theatre of Marcellus, which at most could hold 20,500. But it was dwarfed by the 150,000 to 250,000 who could watch chariot racing in the Circus Maximus. If we take the usual estimate that Rome at its height had a population of about a million, only 5 per cent of its residents could fit into the Colosseum, while the Circus Maximus held a staggering 15–25 per cent, perhaps one in four inhabitants of the city.

In a similar vein, regular gladiatorial shows in Rome were very rare compared with other spectacles. Under the Republic there were none. When Augustus set up the principate he decreed there would be just two per year. The number increased over time, but we do not know when. In AD354 there were ten days of gladiatorial combat, all in December, vastly outnumbered by sixty-four days of chariot racing and 102 of theatrical performances, spread throughout the year. Although often taken seriously, the claims in the *Augustan History* that Alexander Severus intended to set up monthly regular Games, and that Gordian I, as an *aedile* (junior magistrate), before he came to the throne (AD238), provided lavish shows every month, are no more than the fiction of a pagan author living under a Christian emperor about AD400, when gladiatorial shows were on their last legs, wistfully imagining how things should have been in a better time.

Things may have been different in some parts of the provinces. In Spain large amphitheatres were built beside rather small towns. In Aquitania, in western Gaul, six huge amphitheatres set in a rural landscape are known. Audiences were prepared to travel long distances for Games. Posters were put up in Pompeii advertising shows at towns that it would take two days to reach, and a character in a novel was robbed when travelling from Macedon to Larissa in Thessaly to see a 'much advertised' gladiatorial display. It might have been somewhat easier to get a ticket to watch gladiators outside Rome, but when we get glimpses of the frequency of performances in the provinces the numbers are still very low. An inscription preserves most of the charter in which Julius Caesar granted the status of Roman colony to the town of Urso in Spain. The two leading magistrates, the *Duumviri*, were to provide four days of *either* gladiatorial Games *or* theatrical shows. Their deputies, the *aediles*, were to provide another four, again *either* gladiators *or* the theatrical performances. It is most improbable that all eight days were ever devoted to gladiators. The gladiatorial troupe owned by the priest of the imperial cult at Pergamon in Asia fought at just one official festival a year.

The infrequency of regular Games explains the existence of small, commercial shows, the itinerant so-called 'penny-shows' (*assiforana*). But both were only part of the story. Under the Republic, as we will see later in this chapter, senators in Rome gave one-off Games, which were never part of the official state calendar, to boost their popularity. Under the principate members of the local elite in the provinces sometimes voluntarily gave gladiatorial shows, unconnected to holding magistracies or priesthoods, for the same reason – to advance their influence in their hometowns. Such shows needed imperial permission. It was not granted in Rome itself. Here, at the latest by the mid-first century AD, only emperors put on exceptional shows. These were held for special occasions: imperial victories, or anniversaries to mark five or ten years on the throne. Each emperor tried to outdo their predecessors. In his *Res Gestae* Augustus wrote that he had funded eight gladiatorial shows at which about 10,000 men fought, and a sea battle involving about 3,000 combatants, as well as twenty-six wild beast hunts where about 3,500 animals were killed. At the Games celebrating the inauguration of the Colosseum under Titus, 9,000 animals died and an unknown number of men fought, some in pairs, others in groups, including two sea battles. When Trajan returned from his victories in Dacia, his Games stretched over 123 days, during which about 11,000 animals were slain, and 10,000 gladiators fought. The numbers are enormous, but by their nature such lavish imperial shows were very rare.

Gladiatorial Games were few and far between, and only a small percentage of the population could see them. Yet frequency and numbers do not equate to significance. Christmas comes but once a year. There is abundant literary evidence for the popularity of gladiators. Marcus Aurelius was grateful that his tutor had taught him not to become a fan of either heavy or light gladiators. The Stoic emperor was not typical. According to Tacitus, gladiators, along with actors and racehorses, dominated the conversation of the young. Not just the young. Maecenas, Augustus' adviser, discussed the form of leading gladiators on a carriage ride with the poet Horace. The playwright Terence complained that a performance had been ruined when a crowd rushed in thinking there were gladiators fighting.

Some of our best evidence for the popularity of gladiators paradoxically comes from Christian writers condemning the institution. Tertullian wrote an entire work damning the spectacles. Not going to the Games marked one out as a Christian, which, of course, indicated that everyone else was keen to attend. Tertullian, somewhat disingenuously, admits that while he used to go, he no longer wanted to remember. Some Christians continued to attend. When rebuked by Tertullian, they replied truculently: where is it forbidden in the Scriptures?

The anecdote that best illustrates the deep-rooted, completely internalised enthusiasm for the arena comes from Jerome's *Life of Saint Hilarion*. The devil repeatedly tempted the saint with three visions: a sumptuous feast, a beautiful naked woman, and gladiators fighting. A handy Satanic index of the pleasures most desired by a Roman man.

Anticipation

The crowd streaming towards the arena is buzzing with excitement. Anticipation was stoked by advance publicity. Pompeii preserves eighty-six painted street posters advertising forthcoming shows. They follow a standard format: the name of the giver of the Games (in big letters), the number of gladiators, the date(s), and the town in which they will be held. Most of the shows are in Pompeii, but several are in other towns in Campania: Capua, Nola, Herculaneum and Cumae. They are held throughout the year, but cluster in the spring, between March and June. Some will only happen if the weather permits, but others will go ahead, rain or shine. With that in mind, some boast there will be an awning, while others offer *sparsiones*: things 'showered' on the audience, which could mean either gifts thrown to the crowds, or perfumed water sprinkled on them. One evocative poster advertises not just the Games, but the sign writer himself: 'Painted by Aemilis Celer, alone, by the light of the moon'; which rather implies that the owner of the house on which the poster was painted had not given his permission.

There were other, more ephemeral, types of pre-publicity. On the day of the show, as well as in the days running up to it, street hawkers sold pamphlets, like race-cards, listing the names and pairings of the gladiators: information not given on the painted posters. Ovid, in the *Art of Love*, advised asking to borrow a copy as a way of picking up a girl at a show. In Lucian's *Toxaris*, as we have seen, Sisinnes decides to sign up to fight when he sees a procession of gladiators in the marketplace of Amastris two days before the show. Finally ,you could go and watch the gladiators eat the night before the fight in the *Cena Libera*. Posters, pamphlets, processions and the 'Last Supper' – all ramped up the anticipation.

Everyone in the crowd is clutching a ticket (a *tessera*). Capacity is limited in these rare events. Demand exceeds supply. Admission is by ticket only. How did you get your hands on one? Obviously for a commercial show, an *assiforana*, you just bought one. The *assiforana* were small, downmarket shows compared with those given by municipal magistrates or Roman senators, let alone those given by the emperor. All these others, we assume, were free. The point was for the giver to win honour by demonstrating his generosity.

How were the tickets distributed? In Republican Rome the senator giving the show probably handed some out to his clients, and others to his friends, who in turn handed them down to their own clients. In the principate, different levels of the stands were designated for different social groups. The lower and nearer to the arena you were, the higher your social class. We also have scattered bits of evidence for reserved seats within these levels. Inscriptions from the amphitheatres in Gaul record blocks of seats reserved at Nemausus (Nîmes) for priests of the imperial cult (*severi Augustales*) and two different associations of merchant shippers (*naviculari* and *nautae*), and at Arelate (Arles) for priests of Isis (*pastophori*) and members of the schools of rhetoric (*scholasticii*). In the Colosseum, the Arval Brethren college of priests, who themselves sat with their own class of senators, had three other spaces set aside at different levels for their families and attendants. Also in the Colosseum, places were designated for two favoured old allies: the citizens of Gades (Cádiz) and Massilia (Marseilles). The Massiliotes (surely only envoys and visiting dignitaries) were allowed to sit with the Roman senators. These are all exceptional cases. We have no evidence for the seating allocation of the vast majority of the audience. The best we can do is assume something similar to the distribution of free grain (the *Annona*): a central list of qualified citizens, who were given *tesserae* (small tokens used as tickets), and assigned distribution points throughout the city.

Each *tessera* had a number which corresponded to one of the seventy-six of the eighty arches of the Colosseum that had inscribed numbers, showing the holder where to enter. No *tesserae* survive from Rome, but a handful have been identified from other amphitheatres. They had numbers to guide people to their allocated block of seating through the labyrinthine staircases and passageways inside. Attendants would have been on hand to ask for directions. Essentially, the lower your class, the more stairs you had to climb; and perhaps the less deferential the attendants would become. Although they would have been wise to be polite to female members of the elite, who, like all women, had to climb right to the top.

At the eastern edge of the piazza around the Colosseum five

stone bollards survive. Originally a ring of bollards ran round the entire area. They are variously interpreted as a religious boundary, anchors for the cables securing the awning, or the basis of an outer ticket barrier. Quite probably they served all three functions. If wooden fences, or chain-link fences, displaying the numbers of the adjacent arches, were erected between the bollards, it would have eased the crush in the piazza as tens of thousands tried to get to the right entry point.

Jostling from the bollards to the arches, many of the crowd would be hoping for a profitable day. Not just those who gambled on the matches. The Games were theatres of generosity. Municipal magistrates and members of local elites often gave out gifts: food and drinks, perhaps small amounts of cash; they might even promise further benefactions. Imperial munificence could be off the charts: perhaps snacks and drinks all day long, maybe a picnic lunch, and at the end of the day seriously valuable gifts. Part of the thrill of anticipation came from the fact that you never knew what you were going to get. The emperor's generosity was closely scrutinised, and frequently criticised by the elite.

As you walk under one of the arches into the Colosseum, the temperature drops, and the dark mass of the building cuts out the light and envelopes you. A certain anxiety was part of the emotion of spectators. This apprehension had several causes.

The 'House of Anicetus' at Pompeii had a unique and fascinating painting on a wall of its garden (**Plate Seven**). Originally protected from the weather by a porch formed by a row of columns (a peristyle), it is now in the Museo Archeologico Nazionale in Naples. The painting depicts the amphitheatre just down the road from the house, with the adjacent palaestra (exercise ground), and the town walls behind. Although instantly recognisable, this is not a faithful architectural depiction. The artist has put eleven, not six, arches beneath the double staircase leading to the upper galleries. Taking an aerial viewpoint from the north, he has omitted the top of the nearer seating, and half the awning, to allow us to look down into the arena itself. In the foreground, at the bottom of the fresco, men in togas are strolling peaceably among trees and stalls. Behind them chaos has erupted. Men, with their tunics cinched up round their waists, are fighting in pairs and groups of three, in the arena and in the stands. The fighting has spread out beyond both sides of the amphitheatre. At least four men are already casualties on the ground.

When the painting was discovered in 1868 it was recognised as a riot described by Tacitus. In AD 59 a man called Livineius Regulus, who had been thrown out of the Roman senate and moved to Pompeii, gave a gladiatorial show. The locals and visitors from the nearby rival town of Nuceria began taunting each other, with 'the typical insolence of country towns'. The situation escalated to abuse, stones were thrown, then steel was drawn. Many were maimed and wounded, a large number were killed. The Nucerians got the worst of it, and complained to the emperor. The result was that Livineius Regulus and the two chief magistrates of Pompeii were exiled, and the town was forbidden to hold gladiatorial shows for ten years.

Why did Anicetus, or whoever owned the house, commission an artist to paint this scene? When found it was flanked by two other, matching paintings. These have not survived but are known from drawings. Both depicted a pair of gladiators at the moment when one was defeated and appealed for mercy. In one of the paintings a third figure (probably a referee but sometimes identified as a woman) restrains the victorious gladiator. The three paintings were executed as a group, designed to be viewed together. One interpretation is that they celebrate the lifting of the ban on gladiatorial shows. Another, not incompatible, is that they are a moral warning: if we behave as we did in the centre, we won't get the pleasure of the gladiators shown at the sides. Where the paintings were sited in the house might be significant. They were not visible from the street, or even from the atrium when you crossed the threshold. To view them you had to walk through the whole house and turn right into the peristyle garden. The house itself is small. Its atrium is tiny and it lacks any large rooms. Guests must have been entertained in the peristyle. So the pictures, screened from passers-by and casual visitors who wouldn't have got past the atrium, were only viewed by those intimate enough to be invited deep into the house. This fits a less creditable interpretation. The frescos were a controversial talking point for the owner and his cronies: remember the day we beat those Nucerians; the gladiators at the sides might be restrained, but look at those bodies on the ground in the centre, we finished the bastards off!

Even when not rioting, large and excited crowds are volatile and dangerous, especially when they are provoked, or aren't carefully controlled. We have already seen that many were trampled to death when Caligula sent troops to disperse a crowd in the Circus Maximus. In 46BC Julius Caesar gave all sorts of entertainments, including gladiators, a massed battle, and a sea fight. Suetonius tells us the result. 'Drawn by all these spectacles, a vast number of people flooded into Rome from every region, so that many of the visitors had to lodge in tents put up in the streets or along the roads. And the crowds were so great on a number of occasions that many people were crushed to death, including two senators.'

The amphitheatre itself could pose a threat. In AD27 an ex-slave called Atilius put on a gladiatorial show for profit at Fidenae, not far from Rome. The wooden amphitheatre he constructed lacked solid foundations and adequate materials. During the show it collapsed, killing 50,000 people, according to Tacitus, both inside and outside the structure. Atilius was banished and the Senate decreed that no one with a fortune of less than 400,000 *sesterces* should give a show (which meant no one below the status of an equestrian), and that no amphitheatre should be erected without the permission of the emperor, and unless the foundations had been inspected. As with all Roman laws, we may wonder how strictly the edict was enacted over time across the empire.

Only once do we hear of a performer – a human, not an animal – harming a member of the audience, and it was an accident. A Roman equestrian called Haterius Rufus had a dream that he was killed by a *retiarius*. The next day, seated in the front row of a gladiatorial show in Syracuse in Sicily, as befitted his status, Haterius looked out onto the sand and recognised the gladiator from his dream. Haterius wanted to leave but his friends talked him into staying. Sure enough, the *retiarius* cornered his opponent, a *murmillo*, in front of Haterius. The killing blow missed and the equestrian was run through and died.

In Rome, after the opening of the Colosseum, these anxieties hardly applied. The building was not going to fall down, the movement of the crowd was well managed, and security was tight. A sheer, marble-faced wall, topped with ivory rollers to prevent climbing, a bronze balustrade and a net, kept dangerous beasts and stray missiles from the audience. Troops were on hand, including archers in crow's nests. Another net was erected some paces in from the wall, both for additional security and to stop any animals, criminals or gladiators cowering against the wall out of sight of some of the crowd. The audience were secure in the knowledge that they would not be trampled, crushed, caught up in a riot, or harmed by the performers. The danger in the Colosseum came not from the arena or the stands, but from the imperial box.

The audience knew the emperor could do anything he wished. There were many stories that told of the remote dangers that could lead to an unfortunate spectator becoming part of the spectacle. When there was a shortage of condemned criminals, it was claimed Caligula had a section of the crowd thrown to the wild beasts. To stop them making an outcry, he had their tongues removed. When stage machinery malfunctioned, Claudius was said to have had its operators thrown into the arena, along with one of his own toga-clad ushers. A man who called out that a *Thraex* was a match for the *murmillo* he was fighting, but not for the giver of the Games, soon regretted the joke. Domitian, who supported the latter type, had the heckler dragged from the audience and thrown to the dogs in the arena, wearing a placard reading: 'A small shield fan with a big mouth'. When Commodus was indulging in his identification with Hercules many of the populace stayed away from the Colosseum. According to Cassius Dio, this was partly out of shame at the spectacle, and partly because of a rumour that the emperor was going to imitate the hero's killing of the Stymphalian birds by shooting some of the audience.

These were all exceptional incidents. Some, or all, of those involving emperors may have been fictitious. But this is rather missing the point. That they were written down demonstrates that they were remembered and believed. These stories were told and retold. A slight frisson of danger added to the audience's excitement at gladiatorial Games.

One autobiographical account of being threatened by an emperor, although later written up to put the author in a good light, cannot be dismissed as merely retrospective fiction. When Commodus was playing at Hercules, only one senator was brave enough to risk death by staying away. Cassius Dio and the rest turned up and discovered they were in just as much danger. Having killed some ostriches the emperor approached the senators, holding the severed head of a bird in his left hand and a sword in his right. Saying nothing, Commodus grinned and shook his own head, 'making it clear he would do the same to us'. Cassius Dio goes on: 'And in fact many would have been put to death on the spot by the sword for laughing at him (for it was laughter rather than distress that took hold of us) if I had not taken some laurel leaves from my garland and chewed on them, and persuaded the others sitting near me to chew on them too – so that, by continually moving our mouths, we might hide the fact we were laughing.'

Origins and History

One thing on which all Romans agreed was that gladiatorial combat was a foreign import. But where it came from was more debateable. Some ancient writers claimed it was Etruria to the north, others Campania to the south. Modern expertise favours one origin or the other, or combines the two: Gladiators came to Rome from Campania via Etruria. In truth, the evidence for pre-Roman gladiators is so thin, and so open to other interpretations – do Etruscan images show gladiators at all? – that there can be no certainty. The important point is that the Romans unanimously believed another people had invented gladiatorial fights. This was not an attempt to shift the blame for a morally questionable institution onto a different culture. The Romans prided themselves on adopting things from others: including Carthaginian farming techniques, Spanish swords, Gallic chainmail, nomad cavalry tactics and Greek philosophy. The Romans liked to believe that they took what was useful from the peoples they conquered then employed these artefacts and practices with maximum efficiency and brought them to perfection. This belief in their own unique but discriminating openness to other cultures was an important part of Roman identity.

The first recorded gladiatorial combat in Rome was at the funeral Games of a senator called Junius Brutus Pera in 264BC. His sons put on three pairs; according to a very late source, each of these gladiators fought as a *Thraex*. Later Romans looked back to this as the first introduction of gladiators into Rome. The highly competitive nature of the senatorial elite rapidly fuelled an inflation in numbers. The next known event featured twenty-two pairs in 216BC. As Rome conquered more and more of the Mediterranean littoral, and wealth flowed into the coffers of the elite, the escalation continued: twenty-five pairs in 200BC, sixty pairs in 183BC, seventy-four pairs in 174BC. By the late Republic the numbers are staggering. In 65BC Julius Caesar exhibited 320 pairs. In 46BC, in addition to an unknown number of pairs fighting 'as was customary', he staged several mass battles – infantry against infantry, cavalry against cavalry, some featuring both, as well as men fighting from forty elephants – and a sea battle on a specially excavated site on the Campus Martius. All these Games were private enterprises, not part of any official, state-run festival. The early contests were held at funerals. Throughout the Republic the link to death remained, but that to funerals became tenuous. Julius Caesar's 'funeral' Games of 65BC and 46BC were respectively for his father and his daughter. Both were long dead: his father for about twenty years, his daughter eight.

The Romans themselves were uncertain about the origins of wild beast hunts (*venationes*). Some animals indigenous to Italy had been hunted, or killed, at a few traditional Roman religious festivals: bulls were hunted, or set on fire, at the *Ludi Taurei*; foxes, with burning torches tied to their backs, were released at the *Cerialia*; and hares and roebucks were hunted at the *Floralia*. The existence of these probably eased the acceptance of *venationes* into official festivals. Elephants were first brought to Rome in 275BC, as part of the plunder taken from Pyrrhus in the south of Italy, but seem to have been displayed in a triumphal parade and not hunted. More elephants, taken from the Carthaginians on Sicily, appeared in a triumph of 252BC. Roman writers were divided on their fate. Some said they were hunted to death in the Circus, others that they were chased by labourers with blunt spears to show contempt for these mighty beasts used in war by Rome's enemies.

In 186BC we have our first unambiguous *venatio* – a hunt of lions and panthers at the *Ludi Magni*. As the empire expanded, so did the numbers and the exotic origins of the animals. Sixty-three African big cats and forty bears and elephant appeared at Games given by the *aediles* in 169BC. To open his theatre in 55BC, Pompey gave Games featuring five or six hundred lions, over four hundred leopards and twenty elephants. Unlike gladiatorial contests, during the Republic *venationes* were frequently part of official Games.

Gladiators and *venationes* were first combined in one event by Julius Caesar, who had become dictator, in his Games of 46BC. Given the brevity, and unique nature, of Caesar's tenure, it is impossible to tell if this was exceptional, or was intended to become the normal arrangement. After Caesar's assassination, gladiators first appeared in an official festival at the *Cerialia* of 42BC. Along with almost everything we think of as 'typically Roman', the reign of Augustus (31BC–AD14) saw the creation of the standard *munera*, with their tripartite division: wild beasts in the morning, executions at midday and gladiators in the afternoon. From now on a show had to feature both wild beasts and gladiators to be a *munus iustum atque legitimum*: a proper and legitimate show.

The Colosseum and Amphitheatres

Gladiators were fighting long before there were amphitheatres. The first purpose-built stone amphitheatres appeared in Campania after the Social War, a revolt against Rome by her Italian allies (91–87BC). As at Pompeii, whose surviving amphitheatre is one of the earliest, they were erected at towns where the dictator Sulla (81–79BC) had confiscated land from the defeated Italians to settle Roman soldiers in colonies. It indicates the popularity of watching gladiators, not just in the army but among wider non-elite circles, as at this time Roman soldiers were not yet professionals. The amphitheatres symbolised Roman military virtues and perhaps served to remind locals who had won the Social War.

The first gladiatorial combat in Rome, in 264BC, took place in the Forum Boarium, the cattle market down by the Tiber. Rome lacked a stone amphitheatre until 29BC, when one was built on the Campus Martius by Statilius Taurus, one of Augustus' most successful generals. Until then, shows were held in temporary wooden arenas in various places across the city: the Roman Forum, the Circus Maximus and the 'Sheep-pen' (*Ovile*), the area for voting which was revamped and extended to become the *Saepta Iulia*. By the time Statilius Taurus built his arena, Campania was studded with some fifteen amphitheatres. Why did the capital lag behind the rest of the empire?

The answer to this, as to so many questions about the Republic, lies in the hyper-competitive nature of the Roman senatorial elite. The senate as an oligarchic group of supposed equals was extremely reluctant to allow one of their number to acquire the lasting glory of erecting a permanent monument dedicated to the pleasures of the people. It was one thing, albeit deplorable, for a senator such as Scribonius Curio in 52BC to build a marvellous 'double theatre': two semi-circular theatres, which somehow revolved – supposedly with the audience still inside! – to form a circular amphitheatre. But it was quite another to build something in stone. Curio's marvel was dismantled after use. It provided a single shot of popularity. A permanent amphitheatre would have carried on winning its builder popular favour every time Games were held. Senatorial reluctance was given an ideological coat of old-fashioned Roman morality: Greeks sat down in stone theatres; if manly Romans did the same, they would become no better than Greeks – soft, effeminate and ineffectual.

The amphitheatre of Statilius burned down in the great fire of AD64. It was not replaced until the Colosseum was opened in AD80. Even when it was standing the amphitheatre of Statilius was seldom used by the emperors. They stuck with the traditional makeshift venues. Perhaps it was too small for imperial Games, perhaps they did not want to put on shows in an arena built by an aristocrat rather than an emperor. Which leaves a question. Why were the emperors so slow in providing Rome with a suitable amphitheatre?

Augustus thought about building one but gave the idea up. Caligula started one but it was cancelled by his successor Claudius. Nero made do with an impressive wooden one on the Campus Martius.

Emperors were above the law, but they were usually bound by convention. An emperor could not tear down the public buildings of his predecessors (as we will see, private imperial buildings were another matter). Nor should they force unwilling private citizens to sell their property. If you walk down the Via Tor de' Conti and look at the rear wall of the Forum of Augustus, you will see it does not run in a straight line, but veers twice, breaking up the regularity of the ground plan. Augustus let it be known that he had been unwilling to dispossess some citizens of their houses. In a masterpiece of image creation, the irregular wall remained as a permanent memorial to his self-proclaimed role as the first citizen in a Republic of free citizens, or, on a more cynical reckoning, the concern of an emperor for the subjects whose freedom he claimed to have restored.

To build an amphitheatre in the centre of Rome, emperors had to wait for opportunity and a pressing motive to come together. The opportunity came indirectly with the great fire of AD64, which also destroyed the amphitheatre of Statilius. Out of the vast swathes of destruction across the city Nero built his Golden House, an enormous assembly of parks and palaces that stretched from the Palatine to the Esquiline. After the suicide of Nero, and the chaos of the 'Year of the Four Emperors', a general called Vespasian came to the throne in AD69. The new emperor came from a relatively humble family and had won power in a civil war in which thousands of Roman citizens had died. He needed to justify his claim to the purple, distance his regime from that of Nero, and create the right image for his new Flavian dynasty. Nero had dug a lake in the middle of the grounds of the Golden House. Vespasian had the waters diverted for public use, filled in the lake, and began the Flavian Amphitheatre (it was not called the Colosseum until the Middle Ages).

Where there had been Nero's lake and the halls of a hateful king now stood the revered Colosseum. As Martial continued, 'Rome has been restored to herself, and what had been the preserve of a master was now a delight for the people.' What the disgraced tyrant had reserved for his own pleasure, the new dynasty opened to the populace. The Flavian dynasty ruled for the people, not for themselves.

In a brilliant intellectual exercise in 'joining the dots', the inscription dedicating the Colosseum has been recreated from the holes where its letters were nailed to the façade: 'Imperator Caesar Vespasian Augustus ordered this new amphitheatre constructed out of plunder'. Its message was clear. The plunder was from Jerusalem, sacked by Vespasian's son Titus (AD 70). The Flavians had shown their fitness to rule, not in the civil war that brought them to power, but in the best way possible: defeating a dangerous foreign enemy of Rome.

The function of the building also conveyed a message. Whereas Nero had wasted his time touring the east, claiming rigged victories in Greek cultural competitions, singing and playing the lyre, Vespasian and his son Titus had gone east to crush the Jewish Revolt. Now the Flavians were back in Rome the entertainments in the Colosseum would not be the effete poetry and music of the Greeks, but the by now traditional exhibitions of Roman martial prowess.

The architecture reinforced the messages. Whichever way you approached the huge, circular structure – down the Via Sacra from the Forum, the Via Labicana past the gladiatorial schools, or any of the many streets that led to the Colosseum – you saw the same thing: three superimposed levels of arches, the second and third containing statues, topped by a fourth storey decorated with shields. It evoked either a *Stoa*, a shaded public place for strolling and leisure, or a series of triumphal arches: victory piled upon victory; the epitome of the martial virtue that secured the Roman *imperium*.

Amphitheatres spread from Italy across the empire in the first two centuries AD. So far, some 280 are known. They were built by the army wherever it was stationed, especially in Britain and along the northern frontiers of the Rhine and the Danube, but also in places such as Lambaesis in Africa. They were built where veteran colonies were settled, from Urso in Spain to Corinth in Greece. Very occasionally they were built in the provinces by the emperors themselves. Gordian III intended the huge, unfinished amphitheatre at Thysdrus (El Djem in Tunisia) to commemorate where his short-lived dynasty was first acclaimed. Many, however, were commissioned, and paid for, by the provincials. It was a staggeringly expensive way for the local elites to demonstrate their commitment to *Romanitas*, the values of Rome.

Yet the building of an amphitheatre by provincials was not the unthinking import of an artefact of the imperial culture. The gladiatorial Games had to fit with pre-existing aspects of the indigenous society and could be adapted to better embody local needs. We know just enough to take Gaul as an example.

The Gauls had a pre-Roman tradition of watching pairs of men fighting ritual duels – both before battles and at feasts – which eased their acceptance of gladiatorial combat. Similarly, the Celtic practice of public human sacrifices – including burning the victims to death in the notorious 'Wicker Man' – meant the spectacular executions at midday in the *munera* were neither unprecedented or grotesque. The Gauls, like every ancient culture, were keen on hunting, so the beast-fights of the morning were not at all outlandish.

The Gauls added their own distinctive twists to the Games. They invented two new types of participants: very heavily armoured gladiators called *Crupellarii*, and the *Trinquii*, 'expected by ancient custom and sacred rites in the most splendid cities of Gaul', who Marcus Aurelius decreed were to cost no more than 2,000 *sesterces*, the same as the most expensive gladiators who fought in groups (*Gregarii*). They may not have been expected to survive, as the text goes on to say that imperial procurators should not sell a man condemned to death for less than six aurei (actually equivalent to 1,800 *sesterces*). There is an irony in the Gauls creating new types of gladiators. Although it had disappeared by the first century AD, when the *munera* spread across Gaul, a popular type of gladiator in Republican Rome had been known as a 'Gaul'.

The Gallic provinces added other distinctive elements to the Games. At Lyons, Christian martyrs destined for death first ran a gauntlet of men wielding whips, 'according to the local custom', which is not recorded elsewhere. Generally, those who took part in beast-hunts were low-status professionals, but several texts from southern Gaul reveal *Ursarii*, bear-hunters, who were young men from local families of good standing.

The Gauls built conventional amphitheatres – such as the famous ones at Arles and Nîmes – but also distinctive structures for gladiatorial shows, virtually unparalleled elsewhere. They are known to archaeologists as 'theatre-amphitheatres', or 'mixed edifices'. These came in two types: the 'semi-amphitheatre', which has a normal elliptical arena, with the addition of a small stage; and the 'theatre-amphitheatre', where the orchestra of a theatre has been replaced by a small arena with a podium wall. As we have seen, in the Gallic provinces structures for gladiatorial Games were often constructed, not in towns, but out in the countryside. Often they were adjacent to a Celtic sanctuary that predated the arrival of the Roman empire.

When you went to watch a day of gladiatorial Games, wherever you were in the empire, you knew what to expect in broad terms, but might be surprised by the specifics. The shows were always the same, but always different.

Justification and Opposition

As a young man, Antiochus IV, the Seleucid king of Syria, spent many years as a diplomatic hostage in Rome. When he returned to the east to take his throne (175 BC), he took with him many Roman customs. Wearing a toga, he would solicit 'votes' in the marketplace of Antioch, and, when 'elected' as *aedile* or 'tribune', would pass judgements seated on the curule chair of a Roman magistrate. Such alien behaviour, along with his unbecoming levity and habit of drinking with the lower classes, as well as sometimes dancing naked at feasts, convinced some of his subjects that he was insane. His official epithet *Epiphanes* ('Manifest god') was transformed into the nickname *Epimanes* ('Madman'). But one of Antiochus' cultural imports was completely successful: gladiatorial combat.

The Roman historian Livy tells the story.

> He staged a gladiatorial exhibition in the Roman style, which was at first received with far more fear than pleasure by men unaccustomed to this kind of show; but later on, by giving more frequent performances, sometimes allowing the combatants only to wound each other, sometimes permitting them to fight without quarter, Antiochus made the sight familiar and even pleasing, and he roused in many young men a joy in arms. So, while at first he had brought gladiators from Rome, purchasing them at high prices, in the end he had a supply at home.

According to Polybius, at one festival Antiochus put on 250 pairs of gladiators and, combined with beast-fights, the show lasted thirty days. This was a scale unknown at the time in Rome itself. But instead of seeing it as a precedent, both in its size and its combination of gladiatorial combat and beast-fights, when the story was retold by Athenaeus, in the early third century AD, it was as an example of the grandiose and vainglorious nature of eastern monarchs.

Similarly, note the slightly patronising tone and the casual racism of Livy – of course these Syrians were initially terrified, every right-thinking Roman knew that all easterners were cowards! Yet, even Livy acknowledged that the innovation worked.

Antiochus had perfectly understood the Roman justification of gladiatorial combat: watching it prepared you for war.

Antiochus ended up using volunteers. In Rome most gladiators were slaves, prisoners of war, or the condemned. Those freemen who volunteered reduced themselves to an almost equally low level. The lowly origins and status of gladiators in Roman combats added an edge to the moral lesson, as set out by Pliny in his *Panegyric* to Trajan, originally delivered in AD 100. 'Next came a public entertainment – nothing lax or dissolute to weaken and destroy the manly spirit of his subjects, but one to inspire them to face honourable wounds and look scorn on death, by exhibiting love of glory and desire for victory even in the persons of criminals and slaves.' If such scum could show courage close to the steel, once the lesson was learned, how much more would be shown by the watching Roman citizens?

The justification always remained the same. Back in the Republic, Cicero was no great fan of the Games, especially when given by political opponents. Writing in the 40 BC, he particularly disapproved of free men fighting. 'But in the days when it was criminals who crossed swords in the death struggle, there could be no better schooling against pain and death.' Almost half a millennium later, about AD 400, the unknown author of the *Augustan History* played with the idea in his pseudo-scholarly fiction. Maximus and Balbinus, the ephemeral emperors acclaimed by the Senate in Rome, gave gladiatorial Games, before Maximus (more usually known as Pupienus) marched off to fight the reigning emperor Maximinus Thrax in AD 238. Whether in reality the Games took place outside this text, they are mentioned to provide an opportunity for a discussion of the origins of the custom. First, the reader is assured that 'many say' that gladiatorial combat began as a sacred ritual offering citizen blood in the form of a battle to Nemesis. All of which is a clever invention – no one else ever said anything of the sort – which seems to be inspired by the concept of *Devotio*, where a general offered himself to the gods of the Underworld to grant victory to Rome. After this we get a denial and a slight twist to make the standard justification the origin of the gladiatorial combat: 'Others have related in books, and this I believe is nearer the truth, that when about to go to war the Romans felt it necessary to behold fighting and wounds and steel and naked men contending among themselves, so that in war they might not fear armed enemies or shudder at wounds and blood.'

The Roman justification of gladiatorial combat was extraordinarily unchanging and long-lived, but not everyone bought into the idea.

In the nineteenth century, and into the twentieth, it was thought that opposition to gladiatorial combat focused in the Greek half of the empire. Gladiators, it was claimed, were never popular among the Greeks: there were far fewer amphitheatres in the east, and some of the most striking literary condemnations were written in Greek. The whole idea, however, was based on little more than a Victorian value judgement: the Greeks, once you left aside the troubling homo-eroticism, and the sometimes tiresome philosophising, were morally better than the Romans. In the mid-twentieth century the great French scholar Louis Robert collated hundreds of inscriptions to prove that the Greeks adopted gladiatorial combat with enthusiasm. Now about three times as many inscriptions as were known to Robert are available, reinforcing his conclusion. Actually, other explanations had always been readily available. Greek cities did not need to build amphitheatres, as they could convert existing stone theatres, or, less often, the curved end of athletic tracks (*stadia*). A great deal of Greek literature survives from the Roman empire – far more than in Latin – but denunciations of gladiators are very few and far between.

The Romans had a unique relationship with the Greeks. Although they prided themselves on adopting specific things from other peoples, it was only the Greeks who were thought to have profoundly altered Roman culture. In our terms, the Romans accepted they had been Hellenised. The process was not without controversy and opposition, but, as Horace famously put it, 'Captive Greece took captive her savage conqueror, and brought the arts into rustic Latium.' Language is a good indicator. From the last century BC Roman schoolchildren learned to read and write in Greek at the same age as they did in Latin. They learned passages of Homer by heart. To be accepted in the Roman elite it was essential not just to know Greek, but to be able to deploy apposite quotes from the Greek classics. Greek was so hardwired into the Roman elite that they might speak in that language at times of extreme stress – when he saw Brutus among the assassins, Julius Caesar exclaimed in Greek, 'You too, my child?'

The Romans and the Greeks not only had a unique relationship, but we know more about it than we do any similar rapport between any other two contemporaneous cultures. Both wrote literature that survives, both had the 'epigraphic habit' (they put up lots of inscriptions, mainly in the first two centuries AD), and both produced artefacts that have left archaeological evidence in many forms. Until fairly recently, this abundant material was interpreted as follows. In the last two centuries BC the Romans (at least the elite) became Hellenised. In the first two centuries AD the Greeks (again, at least the elite) became Romanised. The two processes produced, at some rather unspecified point (maybe by the late first century AD?), an empire-wide unified 'Greco-Roman elite'. Against the background of this scholarly orthodoxy, the Roman origin of gladiators 'seems to lose importance' in the Greek East.

The problem with the concept of a 'Greco-Roman elite' was that it does not fit the evidence, above all the literary evidence on the Greek side, as was pointed out in the 1990s. No one denies that from the Late Republic on, the Roman elite was thoroughly Hellenised. But under the empire the Greek elite stubbornly clung to a distinct Greek identity. This could take strange forms. The historian Herodian, writing in the third century AD, when the Greeks had been ruled by Rome for several hundred years, explained Roman customs to his Greek audience as if they belonged to a new and strange people. Several Greek novels set in the contemporary world failed to mention the Roman empire at all, in effect writing it out of existence. This is not to say the Greeks were not politically reconciled to Roman rule; only a scattering of lunatics advocated rebellion. The Greek elite prospered under *Pax Romana*. They won citizenship in large numbers, many acquired equestrian status, a few became senators, an unknown percentage learned Latin, and some married into families from the Latin West. Rome underwrote the Greek elites' power in their own cities. At times, leading Greeks were proud to flaunt their Roman status. Yet at others they identified as utterly Greek. They moved between Greek and Roman identities, depending on context. But never did their self-fashioning proclaim they were a mixture of the two, that they were 'Greco-Roman'. Caius Julius Antiochus Epiphanes Philopappus is a good example. This grandson of the last reigning king of Commagene, and Roman senator and consul (AD 109), built his tomb on the Hill of the Muses in Athens. Its sculptures proclaimed his two identities: in the upper storey he is seated, wearing the clothes of a member of the Greek elite; in the lower he rides in a chariot, accompanied by twelve lictors, draped in a Roman toga.

Where does the more recent interpretation leave gladiatorial combat in the Greek half of the empire?

A Greek attending the gladiatorial Games in the eastern half of the empire knew he or she was watching a spectacle imported from Rome. The Greeks did not create a terminology in their own language for the types of gladiators. Instead, they transliterated the Roman names (*Retiarius*, *Secutor*, etc) into Greek characters. Artemidorus apologised for using these non-Greek loan words in *The Interpretation of Dreams*. Neither gladiators nor wild-beast fighting were ever incorporated into traditional Greek contests, like the Olympics. Almost all gladiators in the east appeared at festivals of the imperial cult; the cult of the reigning emperors, and of 'good' emperors, who had been deified in Rome after death. The imperial cult was entirely Greek in language, rituals and architecture. Yet it was never forgotten that it was a cult for a non-Greek ruler. No Greek became emperor in the first three centuries AD. Greek intellectuals went to great trouble to talk up the influence of Greek advisers to 'good' Roman emperors, sometimes inventing links. Not ruled by one of their own, it made the Greeks feel better if the foreigner in power could be shown to follow the advice of one of their intellectuals.

Greek audiences viewed gladiators through their own cultural filters. Although the specific types of gladiators were known by Latin loan words, more general descriptions were assimilated to Greek. They called the fighters *momomachoi* (solo-fighters), with connotations of heroic duels in Homer. The combat became a *Pygme* or an *Agon*, the words for a boxing match and a 'contest', as in athletics. The Games themselves (*munera* in Latin) were described either as a 'liturgy' or a 'love of honour' (*philotimia*); traditional Greek expressions for contributions made by the rich to the city. In the Greek East gladiators on their tombstones were assimilated to prestigious athletes. The perception seems to have been shared by a wider Greek audience. From the town of Cibyra in the province of Asia archaeologists have recovered the single largest assemblage of visual images of gladiatorial Games so far known in the Greek East. Several of the sculptural reliefs depict gladiators in unusual ways. In art from the western half of the empire gladiators are normally shown duelling, with some distance between their bodies. Both when in combat, or if one is submitting, the weapons are what matters (See **Plates Two** and **Five**). When we look at one of the reliefs from Cibyra, it is very different (**Plate Eight**). The gladiators are grappling with each other, their bodies close together. The legs of the central pair are entwined. The one on the extreme right has been thrown backwards. Although he has lost his helmet, he is not submitting but still struggling, as is his opponent. These are poses taken from art representing Greek combat sports: wrestling and the *Pankration* (a sort of mixed-martial art). The artist, or the man who commissioned the piece (one of a set) to commemorate on his tomb Games that he had given, viewed gladiatorial combat through a filter of Greek athletics.

A Greek attending the Games did not become Roman, but watching gladiators prompted reflections on the power of the Roman empire, and his or her place within that empire. Gladiators symbolised the Roman martial courage that had won the empire. Before the Roman conquest, war had been an all too frequent close reality for all Greek cities. As Herodian put it, inter-city Greek conflict ultimately had led to enslavement by the Romans. Now the *Pax Romana* had banished all wars to distant frontiers, or confined them to the simulacrum played out in the arena. Only the emperor, or his representatives, such as the governor, could condemn men to the arena. All gladiatorial shows were linked to the emperor. Those not given by priests of the imperial cult legally had to have the emperor's permission. One of a series of inscriptions from the province of Thrace advertising forthcoming Games explicitly locates the Greek audience within the structure of the empire. Minicius, the local priest of the imperial cult, and his daughter Minicia Firmina, invite the citizens of Nicopolis ad Istrum to a gladiatorial show held in honour of the fortitude, safety and eternal life of the emperors Marcus Aurelius and Lucius Verus, also Faustina, Marcus' wife and their children, the Senate and the people of Rome, the governor of the province, as well as the council and the people of the city. Both the council and the citizens of Nicopolis ad Istrum are there – distinct groups, part of the empire, but at the bottom of the chain of power. The Games also reinforced the local power structures within the city. The giver of the show had a link, no matter how tenuous, to the emperor, as his priest or as the recipient of a letter. It was a reminder both that local power depended on the distant emperor, and that the dominance of the civic elite was underwritten by the imperial power. As Plutarch put it, the Greeks should always remember the 'boots above their heads'.

A few Greek philosophers, fewer than usually imagined, reflected on what they saw in the arena, and came to a very negative conclusion – it was a Roman import that should be shunned by the Greeks. When the Athenians were thinking of putting on a gladiatorial show inspired by those in Corinth (a Roman colony), the Cynic Demonax, according to his biographer Lucian, urged them not to pass such a resolution without first pulling down their altar to the goddess Pity (*Eleos*). Demonax's advice was ignored. Upbraiding the moral failings of the people of Rhodes, Dio Chrysostom told them that things were even worse among the Athenians. Emulating Corinth, he said, the Athenians have surpassed all others in mad infatuation with gladiators. While the Corinthians hold the Games in a gorge outside the city – a dirty place where you would not even bury a freeborn citizen – the Athenians stage them in the theatre in the heart of the city, under the walls of the Acropolis, 'so that often a fighter is slaughtered among the very seats in which the Hierophant and other priests must sit'. These two philosophers play it safe – their focus is just on Athens, as the traditional centre of high Greek culture, not the wider Greek world, and their criticism of Rome is indirect: gladiators came via the Roman colony of Corinth.

In the main, Greek intellectuals responded to gladiators by ignoring them. They are hardly ever mentioned in surviving Greek literature. When they are, it is not with any approval. Plutarch thought giving such shows was an ephemeral and expensive way of bribing the people. The philosopher Epictetus saw lavishing attention on them as a sign of ignorance; they were not a fit subject for intelligent conversation. Libanius the orator dismissed them as childish. Exactly the same sorts of comments were made by some Roman authors; although we can wonder if there was more edge when a Roman institution was criticised by a Greek. Marcus Aurelius found gladiators repetitive and boring. In a public speech Cicero proudly reminded his audience that as *aedile* he had given three sets of Games: 'believe me, men do find pleasure in Games, not only those who admit it, but also those who pretend they do not'. As ever, Cicero would say anything that was necessary in a political speech. In a different context, writing advice for his son, he had a very different view: gladiators and wild-beast shows, along with public banquets and gifts of meat, were 'vanities of which only a brief memory will remain, or none at all'. The money was better spent on other benefactions: ransoming those kidnapped by brigands or providing dowries for your friends' daughters. Cicero repurposed words of Aristotle to sum up: 'This sort of amusement gives pleasure to children, silly women, slaves, and free men with the character of slaves; a serious-minded man who weighs such matters with sound judgement cannot possibly approve of them.'

'The philosopher Annaeus Senecas is the only Roman writer to condemn the blood-soaked Games!' This graffito was found in the later gladiatorial barracks at Pompeii. It was scratched on the wall of a large room, identified as the gladiators' dining hall, because of its size and proximity to the kitchen. It is usually read as a poignant *cri de coeur* of a gladiator, unhappy with his fate, bemoaning a cruel world. Almost certainly it was written by a gladiator, but quite possibly, far from being in despair, he was mocking the eccentric stance of the famous philosopher. Whatever his intention, we can assume the author was only vaguely familiar with the ideas of Seneca, whose name he misspells.

The gladiator scribbling on the wall got one thing right – the main criticism of the Games was philosophical. The most prominent schools of philosophy under the principate were Stoicism and Cynicism. Both shared a belief in the brotherhood of man. The concept was underpinned by the idea that everyone has inside themselves a tiny element of the divine reason that rules the cosmos (the *Logos,* in Stoic terms). We might assume that this would account for any hostility to the Games. But we would be wrong. In Stoic philosophy condemnation to a gladiatorial school was unimportant. It was a moral irrelevance. All that counted was your inner virtue. If you had the soul of a free man, you remained free, even if you were a chained slave. Conversely, if you had the soul of a slave, you could be the king of Persia (always a popular example in such moralising), seated on a golden throne, clad in silk, with the adoration of thousands of subjects, but you remained a slave. Slavery, like being a gladiator, was a legal fiction.

The problem with gladiators was that they were too exciting. The best example is a story told by Augustine of a student studying law in Rome called Alypius. He had always detested such shows, but happened to meet some friends and fellow pupils, who pulled him along. Alypius told them, 'You can drag my body there, but don't imagine that you can make me turn my eyes or give my mind to the show.' Although the amphitheatre was 'seething with savage enthusiasm', true to his word, he kept his eyes shut. 'If only he could have blocked up his ears too! For in the course of the fight some man fell; there was a great roar from the mass of spectators, overcome by curiosity, he opened his eyes and received in his soul a worse wound than the man had received in his body – drinking in the madness, delighted with the guilty contest, drunk with the lust for blood, he was no longer the man who had come, but one of the crowd, a true companion to those who had brought him.' From that moment on, Alypius 'shouted and raved with excitement, and took away a madness that would goad him to return'.

Augustine, of course, was a Christian, but his thinking here was shaped by his wide reading of pagan philosophy. Although less evocative, Seneca said much the same. 'Nothing is so damaging to good character than wasting time at the Games; vice steals secretly upon you through the avenue of pleasure . . . I return home more greedy, more ambitious, more voluptuous, even more cruel and inhumane, because I have been among other people.'

Sympathy for those suffering and dying in the arena had no part in philosophical opposition to the Games. Instead, it was all about the threat to the self-control of the elite in the audience. Self-control was an essential element in the identity of the elite. It was what marked them out from everyone else: from barbarians outside the empire, and from the non-elite within the empire. If, caught up in the excitement, you lost your self-control, it made you no better than the plebs in the stands around you, perhaps no better than the slaves, criminals and barbarian captives out on the sand.

7

Prima Lux
(First Light)

The day of the Games begins with a procession at dawn. The gladiators, wearing their best burnished armour, enter the arena. Their appearance is designed to be spectacular. Under the floor of the Colosseum winds a maze of passageways and cells. Sophisticated ramps and lifts lead to trapdoors in the arena. The wild beasts and convicted criminals destined to die during the day remain confined below, for now. An underground walkway runs from the Ludus Magnus *to the Colosseum, perhaps from the other imperial barracks as well. For maximum effect, it is likely the gladiators emerge from the floor of the arena. As if rising up from the underworld, they are led in by attendants dressed as gods from Hades: Pluto, lord of that realm, Mercury, who guides the souls of the dead, and perhaps Charon, who ferries them across the Styx. These deities have a suitably sinister role to play later in the day.*

The Procession

In 1843 a relief sculpture was found in the cemetery outside the Stabian Gate at Pompeii (**Plate One**). The top band is our only visual image of a *Pompa*, the procession that preceded a gladiatorial show. The figures move from the viewer's left to right. Leading the way are two *lictors*, ceremonial attendants of a magistrate, wearing togas and carrying *fasces*, an axe bound in a bundle of rods, symbolising the right to chastise and execute. They are followed by three musicians in tunics and cloaks playing long, straight trumpets. After a small interval four men in belted tunics are bent under the weight of a litter – a kind of wheelless vehicle for transporting people – on which two small figures sit hammering at an anvil. Such litters (*fercula*) are a regular feature of religious processions; usually they carry images of gods. Various unlikely interpretations can be dismissed: the figures are real armourers, rendered diminutive to fit the composition; or are statuettes of the spirits of the deceased. Comparison with a painting of a religious procession from a carpenter's shop in Pompeii indicates that the little men with hammers are light wooden statues representing armourers or blacksmiths. After another short gap come two men in tunics. The first holds an object that looks like a stick, sometimes seen as a tablet used to convey information to the spectators. The second has a palm branch, to be awarded to a victor. The next figure is the giver of the Games. He wears a toga, looks out at the viewer, and makes a gesture with his right hand, in which he has what might be a scroll (always a symbol of intellectuality, and thus elite status). He is followed by six figures, bareheaded and in tunics, each carrying a helmet and shield. The first two shields are small and round, the rest larger and rectangular, while the helmets are all the same. The obvious interpretation is that these are gladiators, but their lack of armour has led some to label them as attendants. Behind them are two men in tunics and cloaks. The first looks back the way they have come, holding something like a cup in his left hand. The other plays a curved musical instrument. Bringing up the rear, two men lead horses, which have elaborate bridles and chest straps but no saddlecloths. Again, the men's lack of combat equipment has led to an identification of them as grooms or arena attendants.

The relief was expensive. It came from an elite tomb and told passers-by that the occupant had been a magistrate and had provided Games for his fellow townsfolk of Pompeii. But we should not assume that the image depicts a specific procession – the deceased may have given more than one show. Nor should we assume that it pictures the entire procession, or that all processions were the same. Instead, the relief poses questions – what route did processions take? Who took part? What did these parades evoke? Why were they held?

The procession on the Pompeii relief is inside the amphitheatre. At the top left and right are swags of patterned material representing the awning over the stands. In a Latin novel a procession makes its way through Corinth to the venue, which, as we have seen, was outside the city. A tomb inscription from Pompeii records that Aulus Clodius Flaccus, three times one of the leading magistrates, gave shows each time he held office. For the first, as well as clowns and mimes, he presented a procession, followed by fighting bulls, bullfighters, boxers and three pairs of gladiators fighting on a raised structure (*pontiarii*, 'bridgemen'), all of which happened in the Forum. For the second, he again staged a procession in the Forum, and bulls, bullfighters and boxers. But this time he added a hunt with wild boars and bears, and replaced the theatrical elements with thirty pairs of wrestlers and forty pairs of gladiators in the amphitheatre. For the latter the procession would have made its way down the street now known as the Via dell'Abbondanza, from the Forum to the amphitheatre.

A modern reconstruction suggests the route of the procession at the amphitheatre in Puteoli: entrance through the eastern gates, either a lap of honour or straight across the arena, out of the opposite gates, counterclockwise round the outside to the southern gates, where it dispersed, the dignitaries climbing a segregated stairway to the box of honour, and the performers and personnel descending via another set of stairs to the murky bowels of the arena. Although quite possible, and extremely evocative, this reconstruction is based entirely on the placement of gates and stairs, and an analogy with the path of the sun.

We don't know where in Puteoli the procession started, but at Pompeii, as at Corinth, the *Pompa* went through the town, drawing crowds. Things may have been very different in Rome. An underground passageway stretches from the *Ludus Magnus* to the huge substructure of the Colosseum. For maximum theatrical effect, here the procession of gladiators need never appear above ground until it dramatically rose up from the floor of the arena.

One way of thinking about who took part is to ask who is not represented on the relief from Pompeii. If we are to believe those who identify the figures with helmets and shields, as well as the men leading the horses, as attendants, then there are no gladiators at all. Even if they are gladiators, four pairs (one on horseback, and three on foot) would not have amounted to much of a show. We know from numerous literary sources that gladiators were the essential element of the *Pompa*. There might be placards identifying them. The subject of a fictitious legal speech was exhibited with a notice explaining that he had sold himself into a gladiatorial school to raise the money to pay for his father's funeral. The audience demanded and won his freedom before he had to fight. This would not have been a bad result for the giver of the show – he had gained the favour of the crowd by granting their request, and in so doing had made a public statement about both his *humanitas* and his munificence.

Others, who were not from the gladiatorial schools, could be part of the parade. Barbarian prisoners of war – destined either to fight beasts or for mass combat – sometimes appeared in imperial processions. Then there were the condemned. A relief from Smyrna depicts two pairs of men: naked, except for loincloths, they are roped together via metal collars round their necks (**Plate Nine**). They are dragged along by two men wearing tunics and helmets. The wild beasts fighting in the bottom register show the prisoners are heading to the arena, and their probable method of execution. That the guards are wearing helmets indicates the scene is part of the spectacle – either their entry onto the sands, or the opening procession. Some especially notorious criminals, destined for particularly spectacular deaths, might have featured in the *Pompa*.

The Latin novel mentioned a moment ago is *The Golden Ass* (also known as *The Metamorphoses*) by Apuleius. The procession at Corinth is the final adventure of the hero Lucius, who had been magically transformed into an ass. In his bestial form he is to feature in a spectacular execution in the arena. On a specially constructed stage set Lucius is to have intercourse with a woman who has been condemned to death for murdering her husband, sister-in-law, two accomplices and her own daughter. The bestial sex is not designed to kill the woman, as Lucius is terrified that whatever wild beast is released will tear him apart too. Although almost incomprehensible to our minds, such displays were not just the products of the imagination of novelists but actually were staged at the Games. The story shows that an animal, not just the horses of mounted gladiators, might be part of the *Pompa*. Not dangerous animals, as Lucius does not know what wild beast will be set loose, but tame ones, at least at provincial shows, where they have top billing.

The relief from Pompeii tells us nothing about one way in which a day at the Games was experienced – the sense of smell. The *munera* involved all the senses and aroma was an important element. Perfume, usually saffron diluted in water or wine, was sprayed in a fine mist on the audience. Such *sparsiones* were important enough to be advertised on posters in Pompeii, and they were standard in the Colosseum. In some amphitheatres the perfume was delivered by ingenious air pumps that shot jets high into the air, to disperse and drift down onto the stands. In the Circus Maximus, too large for pumps, slaves sprayed the perfume by hand. Slaves with sprinklers, and perhaps mobile altars burning incense, would have been used in the procession. Fragrances evoked things for Romans they seldom do for us. Most Romans stank. Yes, there were free public baths, but a day labourer or stevedore at the docks, living on or below the subsistence level, seldom had the leisure for the lengthy process of Roman bathing. The *plebs urbana* could not afford scented oil to anoint themselves with, rub themselves down with, or burn in cheap lamps. For them the smell of perfume summoned up an elite lifestyle. Everyone knew the stories of perfume and flowers released from the false ceiling of Nero's dining room. The nearest the poor would get to experiencing this for themselves would have been the waft of a wonderful scent they might catch in the moments after they had been shouldered aside by burly porters to let a litter carrying a member of the elite pass along the malodorous streets. Fine fragrances also evoked the gods. No religious festival or procession was complete without incense. Smelling good was a sign of divinity. One of the reasons that Alexander the Great was thought divine was that his body naturally gave off a smell like perfume. Incense, along with the blood from animal sacrifices, was the smell of pagan piety.

If we return to those who are depicted on the Pompeiian relief, we see four musicians. The first three play a straight trumpet (the *tuba*), the one at the rear a short trumpet with an upcurved end (the *lituus*). Music was an integral part of the whole day at the Games. Two small orchestras – water organ, *tuba*, and two men playing a curved horn (the *cornu*) – provide a soundtrack to the fighting on the Zliten mosaic (**Plate Five**). In a passage of Petronius' *Satyricon* a carver cuts up meat in time with music, like a 'gladiator in a chariot was fighting to the accompaniment of a water organ'. From this passage it has been suggested that gladiators fought in time to the music, or that the musicians improvised to highlight dramatic moments in the action, like pianists at the screening of a silent movie. But, evidently, this could only work if just one pair was fighting at a time. More likely the orchestra provided background music, drawing attention to when the events changed or paused – the entry of new combatants, the tension when a gladiator submitted and appealed for mercy, the awards to the winners and the very different exits of the victors and the defeated.

Although long neglected, recently there has been much work on the soundscape of the ancient world, especially its music.

From archaeological finds of instruments and texts, including ancient technical treatises and fragments of musical scores, scholars and musicians have made painstaking reconstructions. The resulting music by groups such as Synaulia and the Ensemble Kérylos are widely available on the internet. To my ears it sounds plangent and haunting, alien and exotic; by turns reminiscent of the Near East and Mali. And that is the problem. Even if the reconstructions of instruments, music and technique are totally accurate, we are not acculturated to what we are hearing. It always reminds us of something else – something that would have meant nothing to Roman listeners.

A chance comment by Plutarch gives a hint of the type of music played at a gladiatorial procession. The third day of the triumph of Aemilius Paullus was announced by trumpeters, 'not producing the sound of a procession or ceremony, but the sort of tone that the Romans use to prepare themselves for battle'. A triumph and a gladiatorial *Pompa* had much in common. Both celebrated an individual who orchestrated slaughter: the triumphal general in the recent past; the *editor* of the Games in the imminent future. Martial music was the order of the day at the amphitheatre.

The Romans were very aware of the emotional power of music. It could reveal the listener's inner character. Martial music, according to Dio Chrysostom, made Alexander the Great grab his weapons 'like a man possessed', but caused an effete eastern despot either 'to leap up and dance a fling or else take to his heels'.

The giver of the Games gazes out at us from the relief at Pompeii. It is impossible to say if it was normal for the *editor* to take part in the procession. A relief from Capua shows a procession that has entered an arch, which may be that of the amphitheatre. Two attendants in tunics and two *lictors* carry straight on, while the first of four figures in togas, probably town magistrates, starts to climb some stairs. This might be the moment when the gladiatorial *Pompa* splits up; the magistrates ascending to the *pulvinar* (the box where the giver of the show and his guests sat), and the attendants heading to their less exalted seats. The arch implies that they have come from outside the amphitheatre rather than up from the sands. In the amphitheatre at Puteoli a gate opened from the arena into a shrine under the *pulvinar*, and two sets of stairs led up to a walkway from which the box of the *editor* could be indirectly accessed. Yet if it was normal for the *editor* to enter the arena as part of the procession, rather than have to leave again and then re-enter by another gateway, we would expect to find gates from the arena opening onto monumental staircases up which he could make a stately progress to the *pulvinar*. Such features have not been found in any amphitheatre.

One emperor, we can be sure, took part in the *Pompa*. If he had not been assassinated the previous day, on 1 January AD 193 Commodus was going to become consul dressed as a *Secutor*, having led a procession of gladiators from the *Ludus Magnus* to the senate house. We will see him in a moment on the floor of the arena officiating at the start of the gladiatorial fights. But for all the modern attempts at rehabilitation, Commodus was unique among emperors in his gladiator obsession. A passageway, ironically now often known as the 'Gallery of Commodus', gave private access direct to the imperial box in the Colosseum, presumably from the Palatine. If other emperors usually were part of the *Pompa*, at least one of the hundreds of anecdotes about them – true or fictitious – would be set in the procession to the arena.

A procession with music and fragrances inescapably evoked a religious ceremony. In the provinces, as we have seen, gladiatorial combat was almost always linked to the imperial cult. Yet everywhere other religious elements were in play. All amphitheatres contained statues, and other images, of the traditional gods. The arches of the second and third level of the Colosseum were filled with statues of divinities. As all public occasions began with a sacrifice, we can be sure, despite the absence of evidence, that the same happened at the Games, even if it was just a few pinches of incense sprinkled into the fire on a portable altar. When it comes to which gods were worshipped in the arena, literature and archaeology point in different directions. Ancient writers link Mars, the god of war, and the equally bellicose Hercules to gladiatorial combat, and Diana, the goddess of the hunt, to the *venationes*. Shrines to these deities do not appear in the archaeological remains. Instead, many amphitheatres contain shrines to the goddess Nemesis.

In literature Nemesis, the daughter of Night, was the gods' remorseless punisher of the sins of man, above all of *hubris*, the overweening pride that expressed itself in the humiliation and suffering of others. In cult she had a sometimes gentler, although still inescapable aspect. Equated to Fortune (*Tyche*), she brought whatever good or evil the gods sent. One title of Nemesis was *Ultrix*, the Avenger. On his tombstone one gladiator invoked her against his killer. More generally this dark goddess, who brought triumph or disaster, perfectly fitted the amphitheatre. It was not only the gladiators who needed her kindly aspect. The giver of the Games desperately hoped they would be a success. Just as the army spread eastern cults, like Jupiter Dolichenus, across the empire, the amphitheatres made Nemesis into a major goddess in the religious landscape.

Sinister gods walked in the arena. 'We have laughed, in the midday mixture of cruelty and absurdity, at Mercury using his burning iron to see who was dead; we have seen Jove's brother, too, conducting out the corpses of gladiators, hammer in hand.' Tertullian is talking about attendants dressed as gods. Jove's brother usually is Pluto, lord of the Underworld, but elsewhere Tertullian identifies him as the ancient Italian deity Father Dis (*Dis Pater*). His hammer is to finish off any gladiators who have not been spared and are still alive. In the same passage Tertullian explains that Mercury, in his winged cap, uses his heated metal wand to test if gladiators are dead. Mercury was well known as *Psychopompus*, the conductor of souls to Hades. Commodus, as part of his gladiatorial mania, appeared in the arena dressed as Mercury; both to begin his performance as a wild-beast hunter and to pair off the gladiators.

Charon, another infernal deity, is often thought to have been in the amphitheatre. The evidence here is indirect. In Etruscan art of the fourth century BC, Charon appears as a hawk-nosed executioner wielding a hammer. Some Romans believed gladiatorial combat was an Etruscan import. In Greek and Roman thinking Charon ferried the dead across the Styx to Hades. Although nothing directly places Charon in the arena, he would have fitted into a symbolically coherent triad: Mercury to lead the souls to the Underworld, Charon to ferry them across the Styx, and Pluto/Father Dis to rule over them in the dark meadows of Hades.

A recent trend confines the attentions of the attendants dressed as infernal deities to those condemned to execution, and not to actual gladiators. On the one hand it is pointed out that Tertullian specifically refers to the midday executions, while on the other, the fact that he calls the victims gladiators is dismissed as vague terminology, because Christians viewed the whole day of the Games through the filter of the lunchtime executions when their coreligionists were the victims: all participants were either Christian martyrs or 'gladiators'. This seems to cherry-pick the evidence: the bits that support the argument are accurate, the bits that don't are imprecise. In fact, the argument works just as well the other way round: for Christians all events could be described as the Midday executions. That someone wielding a hammer finished off gladiators finds archaeological support in the gladiators' cemetery at Ephesus – the skulls of four of the dead exhibit fatal wounds consistent with a blow from a hammer.

'The amphitheatre is consecrated to names more numerous and more dreadful than the Capitol, temple of all daemons as it is. There, as many unclean spirits live as the place can seat men.' Tertullian regarded the empire as a dangerous place. He saw pagan daemons everywhere: 'Satan and his angels have filled the whole world.' Tertullian wrote *On the Spectacles* to stop fellow Christians going to the Games. It suited his agenda to play up the religious elements in the *munera*: even to attend was to commit idolatry. His views do not represent those of pagans, any more than his contention that gladiatorial Games were a type of human sacrifice. As far as it is possible to separate religion from any secular institution in the Roman world – and that is not very far – gladiatorial Games had religious connotations for pagans, but were not a specifically religious festival.

The procession was one of the attractions of the Games, but not a headline act. A Pompeiian poster advertises the procession when gladiators were banned in the town. An inscription from Mylasa (modern Milas in Turkey) tells us the desired effect – wonder and amazement, the approving shouts of the crowd. This was achieved by numbers and opulence, but also by novelty. A procession, indeed the whole day at the Games, was like stepping into Heraclitus' river: always different, always the same. Although not if you were Marcus Aurelius, who found the whole thing grindingly repetitive.

Society Stratified in Stone

The gladiator steps out onto the sands of the Colosseum. The air is thick with perfume, the light blinding, the noise deafening – loud music, the roar of the crowd. 'As the trumpets brayed,' a fictitious legal speech said, 'on all sides everything hummed with preparations for death: one man was sharpening a sword, another heating up plates with fire; on this side rods were being brought, on that whips.'

The first thing the gladiator saw was the security net encircling the arena. Some paces beyond that was the unclimbable wall; sheer and faced with smooth marble, topped with rollers, another net, and soldiers – lots of soldiers, some in crow's nests, armed with bows. The same in every direction. No escape, nowhere to hide. Above the defences steep tiers of massed humanity. Near to the sands the throng was gleaming white with flashes of purple, higher up it was darker, more sombre, while at the very top – 'almost beyond the range of human vision', according to Ammianus Marcellinus – there were some blocks of brighter colours.

This was still the parade. There was no imminent danger. The gladiator would do well to study the crowds. His life might depend on them later. There was the imperial box. The emperor resplendent on the curule throne of a senior magistrate, clad in a triumphal toga, either purple and gold, over a tunic embroidered with palms, or white and gold. On his head either a wreath, or later a crown with rays like the sun. With him were his family and friends. Like an imperial council, or a dinner party, the emperor invited whoever he wished to sit with him at the Games. Standing at the back were silent attendants and imposing guards. On the other side of the arena, in another box across from the emperor, were the Vestal Virgins, the aristocratic priestesses who tended the sacred hearth of Rome. They were dressed in the *stola* of a respectable matron, but with the hairstyle of a young bride. Apart from those in the imperial box, the Vestals were the only women anywhere near the sands. With them sat the higher magistrates, also seated on curule thrones, except the tribunes of the plebs, who traditionally were all together on one bench.

On the same level as the boxes, on what was called the *podium*, were the senators, dressed in white togas with a broad purple stripe, special elaborate shoes and either a wreath of laurel or a broad-brimmed hat; all things only they were allowed to wear at the Games. They were seated, between three to nine together, on movable wooden benches without arms or backs. After AD 37 they were allowed cushions to ease their numb buttocks. Here and there among the senators were men with plain togas and ordinary footwear, but with golden crowns. These were military heroes, who had been awarded the *Corona Civica* for saving the life of a citizen in battle, or the *Corona Muralis* for being the first over an enemy fortification. Also here and there on the *podium* were ambassadors from favoured non-Roman peoples, both inside and outside the empire.

Above the senators were the equestrians, distinguished by white togas with a thin purple stripe, and wearing gold rings. In the Colosseum from here upwards all the men sat on fixed marble benches. Some were reserved at this level for military tribunes, equestrian army officers. Next came the plebs who could afford a toga, an impractical and expensive garment, hardly ever worn. Some of the front row was reserved for the citizens who were attendants of the magistrates. Spaces in this section were also set aside for young boys of good families – wearing the specially whitened *toga praetexta* and a golden amulet called a *bulla*, which indicated childhood – as well as their teachers.

Looking upwards, the palate of colours changed. Next were the *pullati*, the poorer plebs clad in dark, undyed, or even dirty clothes. Segregated among these *plebs sordida* were the public slaves. The placement of these *servi publici* was an indication of their importance to the monarchic regime of the emperors, and sartorially suitable, as they were not entitled to the toga of a citizen.

Finally, at the very top, were slaves, foreigners and women. Here the stands and benches were wooden. The women sat on individual chairs with backs. Strict segregation was enforced. It was unthinkable that a sheltered matron might be insulted, or worse, by either a slave, or some hairy barbarian in his native costume. The women themselves were divided. For it was likewise inconceivable that a chaste matron in her *stola* should rub shoulders with a prostitute dressed in the man's toga that advertised her profession.

When the gladiator gazed up at the stands, he saw Roman society: ordered, hierarchical and stratified in stone. It was a society from which, perhaps by his own choice, he was excluded.

The elaborate stratified seating of the amphitheatre did not grow organically. It was imposed by Augustus, drawing on regulations for the theatre, perhaps in stages between 22 and 17BC, as part of the moral reforms of his 'Restoration of the Republic'. Previously, senators had been close to the arena and the rich had better seats; either because they paid for them or because they were allocated to them by the organiser of the Games. Under the Republic men and women sat together. The woman who went on to marry Sulla first attracted his attention by plucking an imaginary bit of fluff from his clothes. We should not assume that Augustus' regulations were always enforced, at least, not at first. After the imposition of segregated seating, the poet Ovid still saw gladiatorial Games as a good place to pick up girls. An inscription from the town of Irni in Spain mentions no fewer than six later emperors (out of ten who had sat on the throne to that point) who had issued decrees concerning seating at the Games. However, these might have been aimed at imposing Roman practice onto the provinces, or were rulings on specific cases, or no more than public statements of each emperor's commitment to upholding established social divisions, rather than responses to actual infringements of the laws.

It is impossible to map the stratified seating arrangements precisely onto the remains of the Colosseum. Most of the seating has gone, and all of the *podium*; the stone robbed in medieval and Renaissance times as building materials, and the marble burned to make lime. If we look at a modern reconstruction (**Plate Ten**), the problem is clear. Looking from the bottom, there are three balustrades, and then two walls with sheer drops, dividing the stands horizontally. Which gives six areas – actually seven, if we include the *podium* closest to the arena – not the five we expect (senators, equestrians, citizens in togas, citizens not in togas, and slaves/foreigners/women). An inscription locates the equestrians in the lowest tiers of benches, and we can place the slaves, foreigners and women at the very top, but the boundaries in between are uncertain. They might have changed over time, or even with each show.

The evidence for arrangements outside Rome is scant. Some things had to be different. There were few, if any, Roman senators to be accommodated, while space had to be allocated to groups not catered for in Rome. We have seen seats reserved for two associations of shippers at Nîmes, and find the same for butchers in the amphitheatre at Lyons and oil merchants in the one at Arles. The foundation charter of the Roman colony of Urso in Spain sets out in exhaustive detail who sat where at *Ludi Scaenici* given by the *Duumviri*, the two chief magistrates. In ascending order: local councillors, priests and any visiting Roman senators; equestrians; colonists; inhabitants of the surrounding areas; resident foreigners; and finally, right at the top, visitors to the town. Astonishingly harsh fines of 50,000 *sesterces* were in place, not only for those who flouted the rules, but even for those who abetted them. *Ludi Scaenici* were theatrical shows (plays, mimes and pantomimes), but, as the *Duumviri* could choose if they gave these or gladiatorial shows, we can assume the same rules applied to both. Specific arrangements will have varied from town to town, but the general principle held – the lower down in the stands, the higher your social status.

This opens up an interesting line of thinking. Compare the modern reconstruction of the seating in the Colosseum with that of the Roman social structure (**Plates Ten** and **Eleven**). They are virtually the same, except for one huge difference. They are inverted: the top of one is the bottom of the other. We think of the Roman elite perched at the top of a steep pyramid. It is impossible not to – every student of the Roman world has seen a similar diagram of Roman society. Maybe we are out of tune with our subject? When the Romans conceptualised the place of the elite, did they picture them lounging, propped on cushions, with plenty of space at the bottom of the stands on the *podium*?

On the day of the Games the stands of the Colosseum gave a snapshot of Roman society, frozen in time. Yet everyone knew that society was not static, that there was the possibility of social mobility. The slave in the top tier dreamed of freedom, and moving down a level to join the dark-clothed plebs. If his ex-master, now his patron, set him up in a business, he might hope to be able to afford a pristine toga and move down another tier. The son of a slave, if born after his father's manumission, and if he acquired the necessary 400,000 *sesterces*, might join the equestrians one level closer to the arena. Theoretically he might go all the way to the imperial box. The emperor Pertinax's father was said to be an ex-slave.

The reintroduction of monarchy with the rule of the emperors increased social mobility in three ways – two upward, and one downward. First, the professional army. After twenty-five years a soldier in the auxiliaries, units recruited from provincials, gained Roman citizenship on discharge. After the edict of Caracalla in AD212, almost every free-born subject of the empire had citizenship. On retirement, after twenty years, a legionary received a bonus equivalent to fourteen years' pay. Enough to set him up as a councillor of a small town or claim a seat among the toga-clad citizens in the Colosseum. Centurions entered the ranks of equestrians. In the military crisis of the second half of the third century AD, a string of soldiers made it from the barracks to the imperial purple.

Then there was the *Familia Caesaris*, the imperial household of slaves and freedmen, who served as a proto-bureaucracy in imperial Rome. Although among the lowest in formal status, the greater their proximity to the emperor, the greater their wealth and power. Horrifying as it was to the traditional elite, some emperors elevated members of the *Familia Caesaris* to the equestrian order, sometimes even to the senatorial.

Finally, the emperors who advanced some groups, downgraded others. The entire estate of a senator condemned for treason was confiscated. His family lost everything. There was no question of them, like those men who resigned from the Senate under Augustus, keeping their places down on the *podium*. In each generation a large percentage of families chose to withdraw from the Senate to the hopefully less dangerous eminence of the equestrians. Such downward mobility eased the acceptance of those travelling upward, although only if such social climbers came from the right sort of background.

Despite everything – the army, the *Familia Caesaris*, the condemnations – social mobility remained very much the exception, not the rule. Apart from imperial service, the only ways to make a lot of money – the sort of fortune that changed your class – were inheritance or marriage. And the wealthy, of course, tended to marry each other and leave their estates to those equally well-off. The vast majority of those in the Colosseum remained at the level in the stands into which they were born.

Attempts at changing one's social status *at* the shows met with very divergent responses. Some German ambassadors were seated at the top of the stands. They noticed envoys from Parthia and Armenia sitting down with the senators. The Germans got up and went to join them, announcing that they were not inferior in virtue and status to any people in the world. Charmed by their simplicity and boldness, the emperor Claudius allowed them to remain there. Compare this with Nanneius in a poem by Martial. Having already been expelled by an usher two or three times from the equestrian seats, Nanneius tried to find a discreet spot at the back of them: 'there, with his head buried in a hood, he peers out, viewing the show indecently with one eye'. Once he had been discovered and ejected once more, he perched in the gangway at the end of a bench: 'with one knee he pretends to the equestrian next to him that he is sitting, and with the other to the attendant that he is standing'. The Germans could be admired and rewarded – they had acted openly and for honest reasons – at the same time as the naiveté of these 'noble savages', who were so completely ignorant of civilised customs, could be a source of gentle laughter. Nanneius, on the other hand, was execrated for furtively breaking the rules he knew all too well, for ignoble and mendacious self-aggrandisement. Martial wrote six poems savaging behaviour like that of Nanneius. Horace and Juvenal also chipped in. These poems, coupled with the enormous fine levied by the town of Urso on those who sat in seats to which they were not entitled, show that the hierarchical seating was taken very seriously indeed.

The great oval sweep of the Colosseum meant that everyone in the stands could, at a glance, see their place in Roman society, and that of everyone else. They had gathered to witness the ritual punishment of dehumanised outsiders in the arena beyond the *podium* wall. For the spectators it was a unifying experience, but one that always contained a visceral warning. If you transgress, rather than sitting in the stands, showered with perfume and gifts, you could find yourself cast out onto the sands: fighting for your life, or, worse, condemned to the flames or the jaws of a wild beast.

The Salute

Hail Emperor, those who are about to die salute you! If you know one thing about gladiators, you know their famous salute. It is shouted in innumerable novels, TV shows and films. But the modern view is to doubt its historical accuracy. It is a scholarly orthodoxy that the salute was no more than a one-off impromptu acclamation that went very wrong.

In AD 54 the emperor Claudius decided to stage a spectacular naval battle on the Fucine Lake before its waters were drained. The battle was to be between the people of Sicily and Rhodes – an alternative history of the pre-Roman past, as in reality the Sicilians and Rhodians had never fought each other. It was a huge event. Numbers vary in our three sources: twelve triremes (a warship rowed on three levels) a side in Suetonius, fifty in Cassius Dio, and an unspecified number of triremes and quadriremes (a larger type of war galley), carrying 19,000 combatants in Tacitus. The Sicilians and Rhodians were to be played by condemned criminals. Security was tight. The lake was ringed by rafts with battlements and torsion artillery manned by the Praetorians, and there were regular marines in decked warships out on the water.

Altogether the combatants bellowed: *Hail emperor, those who are about to die salute you!* And then the ceremony went off the rails. Claudius – a vicious fool in all ancient sources, nothing like the sympathetic character who appears in Robert Graves' novel *I, Claudius*, or its BBC television adaptation – was notorious for his 'feeble and obscure jokes'. He tried one now, replying 'Or not!' Suetonius tells what happened. 'After that pronouncement, none of them was prepared to fight, arguing that he had thereby spared them.' Claudius thought about having them all killed, 'before finally leaping out of his seat and running all round the lake, despite the embarrassment of his limp, and, offering a mixture of threats and encouragement, compelling them to fight'.

The modern consensus among scholars rests on three wobbly legs. This is the only occasion the salute is recorded, so it was the only time it was ever uttered. Everyone in a mass staged-battle, on the water or land, was intended to die. The salute would not have been offered by regular gladiators, most of whom were not going to die. This is unconvincing at every step and needs re-examining, because modern scholarly orthodoxies gain authority the more often they are repeated.

We can, for now, leave aside the idea that all the participants were going to be killed. Although we can note three things here: that it is not the result in any recorded mass combat in the Games; no battle in history has ever achieved 100 per cent fatalities on both sides; and, if the survivors were going to be finished off by soldiers straight after, they would have had no motive to fight. It is true that, on any given day of the Games, most trained gladiators did not die. But to conclude that the salute was in some way unfitting to their position, or beneath them, is to completely ignore the gladiatorial oath: to be burned, bound, beaten, and killed with steel. The gladiators had already sworn that they were prepared to die. Finally, the orthodoxy stems from a misreading of our main source. Suetonius did not record the anecdote because the salute was innovative or novel, but because of Claudius' unique and ill-conceived joke, which threatened to wreck the entire spectacle. There is no reason to think that the salute was not a normal part of the ceremony of a day at the Games.

After the salute came the testing of the weapons, the *probatio armorum*. Things sound more certain if they have a Latin name. The phrase *probatio armorum* was coined in the nineteenth century. Only two ancient writers mention the *editor* of the Games testing the sharpness of the gladiator's weapons. The stories are told of two different 'good' emperors, but worryingly are almost the same. Suetonius says that when two patricians were found guilty of aspiring to the throne, Titus merely warned them to abandon the attempt, saying that imperial power was a gift of fate, and he would give them anything else they desired. Having thoughtfully sent a courier to one of their mothers, informing her that her son was safe, he invited both men to dinner. The next day he seated them near himself at a gladiatorial show, and, when the swords of the combatants were brought to him, handed them over to be inspected by the two erstwhile conspirators. Cassius Dio says that when a patrician called Calpurnius Crassus and some others formed a plot, Nerva had them seated beside him at the Games. Not having told them that their conspiracy had been exposed, Nerva gave them the swords to see if they were sharp; thus demonstrating that he did not care if he died there and then.

The similarities of these stories would be enough to persuade most scholars that they were nothing but literary commonplaces, and that one, or both, were unhistorical. That may well be right, although the possibility should always be allowed that similar emperors did similar things, or that an emperor might copy successful acts of theatre from his predecessors. For our purposes it does not matter if either incident actually happened. The anecdotes show that the testing of the weapons was a common feature of the Games; 'as was often done', according to Dio. Interestingly, both tales are not set down on the sands of the arena, but up in the imperial box. The weapons are brought to the seated emperor, providing additional evidence that emperors usually took no part in the procession.

Warm-Up Acts

When the procession reached the amphitheatre outside Corinth, Lucius was left outside. As an ass, Lucius had a reputation for being docile and biddable. Perhaps too biddable. He had been chosen for his potentially fatal role in the arena as the sexual partner of the condemned murderess because he had already served the bestial desire of a local rich woman: 'She welcomed me in – all of me, and I mean all – every time I pushed my buttocks back to spare her, she violently thrust forward, clutching my back, and fastened herself to me more tightly.'

Eating some sweet grass, Lucius from time to time lifted his eyes to watch the inaugural spectacles through the open gate. First a troupe of boys and girls performed a Pyrrhic dance. Then came a pantomime – nothing like a modern pantomime, much closer to modern ballet crossed with mime – acting out the judgement of Paris. This was a lavish production, boasting a mock-up of Mount Ida, complete with a river and goats peacefully grazing. A shower of saffron diluted in wine perfumed the air and dyed the coats of the goats yellow. Usually such theatrical performances took place at midday, interspersed with executions, and were preceded by wild beast hunts. Here that order is reversed. Lucius, the murderess, and whatever animal was going to be released to kill her, were to provide a link between the dancing and the hunting. The running order of a real day's entertainment was never set in stone. Apuleius, however, may have played with the sequence of events for the benefit of his story. The reader does not need hunting sequences that add nothing to the plot, and also spoil the gathering suspense of the unknown and unseen dangerous animals waiting to be let loose.

A joke tells us about a warm-up act. Seneca's *Apocolocyntosis* is a satire on the posthumous deification of the emperor Claudius. *Apocolocyntosis* means 'transformation into a pumpkin', a play on Apotheosis, transformation into a god. The gods debate, as if they were the Roman Senate, if they should admit Claudius to Olympus. One speaker, Janus, recommends that in future if anyone proposes that a mortal become a god he should be handed over to the *Larvae* (vengeful ghosts) to be beaten with rods along with the new free volunteer gladiators at the next Games. The wording assumes the practice is customary. This beating is symbolic, nothing like a legionary running the gauntlet when a unit was punished with decimation, or the Christian martyrs whipped by ranks of gladiators in Lyons. Even less like the Christian martyr Mappalicus, who was flogged so hard his guts spilled out. The new gladiators had to fight later in the day and needed to be in good condition.

The ceremony enacts a part of the gladiatorial oath: to be bound, burned, killed by steel, and to be beaten. It is significant that Seneca includes only the free men who have volunteered. The beating reminded the volunteers of their new status. It also boosted the attraction of the Games. Audiences particularly wanted to watch free volunteers fight. Unquiet ghosts with an animosity to the living were thought to be dark – brown or black. Arena attendants dressed as *Larvae* combined with those dressed as Pluto, Mercury and perhaps Charon, as well as the trapdoors, lifts and ramps that led to the substructure, to turn the amphitheatre into a portal to the Underworld. Which was where, in reality, many of the participants would be by the end of the day.

Another beating and parade very occasionally featured in gladiatorial Games was the punishment of informers (*Delatores*). Rome could never set up anything like a public prosecutor. To grant such powers to an individual, or small group, would have undermined the oligarchic rule of the senators in the Republic. Equally it would have eroded the power of the emperors under the principate. Roman law always depended on private prosecutions. *Delatores* was a pejorative label given to those who were considered to have made a career of bringing false accusations for their own advancement and financial gain. A successful prosecutor was awarded a proportion of the estate of those convicted. For example, they gained 25 per cent of the wealth of those found guilty of treason (the imperial treasury took the rest).

When a new emperor wanted to distance himself from the reign of a hated predecessor, the most notorious informers were rounded up. First, they were thoroughly beaten with whips and cudgels in the Forum – this was no symbolic punishment. Then they were paraded in the amphitheatre, their heads forced back, so that everyone could see their faces. Remember how Juvenal thought it especially demeaning that the senator Gracchus had chosen to fight as a *Retiarius*, because everyone could see his face. Similarly, when the emperor Vitellius was led to his death, his hair was pulled back and a sword held under his chin so that he could not hide his face. After the humiliation in the arena, some informers were sold into slavery, others sent into exile. Pliny the Younger gleefully hopes that many will be shipwrecked on the way to their inhospitable prison islands.

Although the senatorial historian Tacitus tried to run down the social origins of the *Delatores*, they were an elite phenomenon. Only the affluent had the time and the expertise for recourse to the law, and only the wealthy were worth prosecuting. Watching the humiliation of the informers would have been especially gratifying to those in the lower tiers of seating in the Colosseum; to the senators and equestrians who had been in fear of them. Those in the higher tiers – the slaves at the very top, the plebs in dark clothes just below them, even those citizens in respectable white togas in the middle – might have found it enjoyable for another reason. The Roman lower orders always found it agreeable to see their social betters humiliated.

Pleasing as it was – in different ways to all the audience – the spectacle of punishing *Delatores* was very infrequent. It could only happen at Games given by the emperor, only once in his reign, and only then if he did not care for the previous incumbent on the throne.

Watching the dancing, between mouthfuls of grass, Lucius' shame at having sex in public with a polluted killer gave way to a mounting terror of the unknown wild beast. It would not distinguish between an innocent ass and a guilty woman. The Judgement of Paris was over. The floor of the arena opened and the stage prop Mount Ida vanished. It was replaced with a bed, inlaid with Indian tortoiseshell, plumped with cushions and shining with silk coverlets. At the demand of the crowd, a soldier came out and went off down the street to fetch the woman. Lucius was thought tame. No one was watching him. He took a few furtive steps from the gate. And then he ran for it . . .

8

Matutinus (Morning)

The morning is devoted to venationes *or beast-fights. Originally these were part of shows in the Circus. By the late Republic, although still held in other contexts, they have become an integral part of a gladiatorial show. Some animals are merely exhibited doing tricks; for example, elephants dancing, walking tightropes or writing in the sand with their trunks. Other more fierce beasts are set to fight each other. Often these are unnatural opponents, such as bulls against bears, or tigers against lions. A number of the most ferocious beasts are held back for the midday entertainment. Most of the animals that appear in the morning are pitted against huntsmen. These,* venatores *or* bestiarii, *like gladiators, are either slaves, or in some cases free volunteers. They are unarmoured, instead dressed like the huntsmen of elite households: a smart tunic, with banded leggings. A few use bows and arrows, but most use javelins and spears. In shows given by the emperors the numbers of animals slaughtered, herbivores and carnivores, is staggering. Nine thousand are killed over 100 days at the opening of the Colosseum; 11,000 over 123 days for Trajans's Dacian triumph; both equal an average of about ninety dead animals each morning. A sophisticated system of logistics has been created to trap, transport and feed such large numbers. Inscriptions tell us of* companies (*familiae*) *of hunters and shippers. The meat of the slaughtered animals is either used to feed surviving beasts or distributed to the plebs of Rome. Christians accuse pagans of cannibalism at one remove: they eat the flesh of animals that have consumed humans.*

Attitudes to Animals

When the emperor Septimius Severus disbanded the Praetorian Guard, after they had fought against him in a civil war, one trooper, 'when his horse refused to leave him, but kept following him and neighing, was overcome with grief, and killed both the horse and himself'. Romans loved their pets and animal companions. Catullus wrote a couplet of poems on his mistress Lesbia's pet sparrow and her grief at its death. The later poet Martial riposted: Lesbia might have been forlorn at the loss of her sparrow, how much worse it was for his own mistress having lost a twelve-year-old slave boy whose prick was already a foot and a half long. Affection ran both ways. When a man called Sabinus was executed and thrown into the Tiber, his dog jumped in after his body and was drowned. Sometimes the tombstone of a gladiator depicts him with his dog.

Brought up on Aesop's *Fables*, the Romans anthropomorphised animals. Some of the human characteristics they transferred to animals are familiar: dogs were loyal, foxes were cunning. Others are less common to us: bears were cruel, sparrows were lecherous. Sparrow (*passer*) may have been slang for penis, which opens up all sorts of readings of Catullus' poems. Familiar or strange, the Romans' anthropomorphising went much further than ours. According to the physiognomist Polemo, the lion is 'courageous, bold, mighty, irascible, patient once calm, modest, generous, very ambitious and perfidious'. We can go with the first five, but modesty, generosity, ambition, and perfidy seem a stretch. The Classical world could go further. The mount of another cavalryman was wounded and blinded in one eye. Its owner petitioned the god Serapis: the horse had done no wrong, committed no sacrilege or murder, and never spoken impiously. The mighty deity did not scorn the dumb beast and provided a cure for its eye.

Despite their love and the anthropomorphising, we should

not slip into thinking Roman attitudes to animals were basically the same as ours. For them, the defence of animal rights was an eccentric and unusual stance, entirely confined to certain groups of philosophers. It was espoused by the Pythagoreans, along with their equally strange vegetarianism and odd belief in the transmigration of souls. Influenced by Pythagoreanism, it was adopted by some Platonists, although not by Plato himself. These philosophers knew they were arguing against conventional views. Plutarch employed both an indirect approach and humour. He sets up a debate in *Whether Land or Sea Animals Are Cleverer* that reaches no conclusion; instead, the arguments on both sides are said to prove that animals are rational. In another dialogue, Gryllus, a man that has been turned into a pig (Gryllus means Grunter), tells Odysseus that he has no wish to resume his former condition – animals are more virtuous. For all Plutarch's literary skill, the views of such philosophers remained as alien, and essentially ridiculous, to most Romans as the views of modern philosophers do to most people now. In contrast the views of the two most influential philosophical schools in the late Republic and early empire – the Stoics and the Epicureans – were more in tune with the mainstream in this area. They followed Aristotle: animals were not rational and did not possess a soul. Animals were a lower order of being and thus not entitled to any rights. They existed for the use of humanity. Deeply influenced by Stoicism, Augustine fixed Christian attitudes on the same lines.

'What pleasure can there possibly be for a man of culture to see some pathetic specimen of humanity mangled by a powerful beast, or a splendid animal being run through with a hunting spear? Anyhow, if these sights are worth seeing, you have seen them often, and we spectators saw nothing new.' Very occasionally literary sources, like Cicero here, criticise beast hunts. But never because of any sympathy for the animals. Animal hunts could be seen as a waste of money for the givers, and a waste of time for elite spectators. For the former, because the popularity they gave was fleeting – the money could have been spent on better things: ransoming captives from bandits, underwriting the debts of friends, or helping them acquire or expand their property. As for elite spectators – Cicero's 'man of culture' – they could better spend their time working on their high culture or virtue (which, of course, in elite eyes amounted to much the same, and marked them out from the plebs).

Only once do we ever hear of the crowd expressing sympathy for the animals in the arena. In 55BC Pompey pitted about twenty elephants against Gaetulian javelinmen from North Africa. According to Cicero, who was there, the crowd, although astonished, did not enjoy the spectacle: 'there was even an impulse to compassion, a feeling that the monsters had something human about them'. Writing over a century later, although drawing on earlier sources, Pliny the Elder gives more details. At first all went well. One elephant put up a remarkable fight, crawling on its knees when its feet were pierced, and hurling its attackers' shields high into the air. The spectators marvelled when another elephant was brought down by a single javelin, which penetrated below its eye. Then things went wrong. The entire remaining troupe of elephants attempted to break out through the iron fencing. When this failed, having lost hope of escape, the elephants sought the sympathy of the crowd, adopting a begging posture and wailing a lament. The audience were won over – getting to their feet and weeping and cursing Pompey. Later still, over two and a half centuries after the event, Cassius Dio added yet more detail, although not committing himself to its truth. The elephants had only embarked on the ships that brought them from Africa because their drivers pledged an oath that they would suffer no harm. Now they raised their trunks, lamenting, and 'calling upon heaven to avenge them'.

After defeating those enemies who employed elephants in warfare, most famously Hannibal, the Romans developed a soft spot for them. They nicknamed them 'cows from Lucania', the district of southern Italy where they first encountered them in the army of Pyrrhus of Epirus. As we will see, they frequently exhibited these intelligent animals doing tricks, as in a modern circus. Elephants were believed to understand human language, to hail the rising sun, purify themselves and worship the gods. The unique incident at Pompey's Games was caused because the elephants were thought to be very close to humanity, sharing many of both its good and bad characteristics. According to Polemo, an elephant was 'courageous, feared, strong-willed, dignified, very ambitious, malicious, unfaithful, promiscuous, a lover of depravity, possessing jocularity and cleverness, and peaceable to those who make peace with him' – all in all, much as the Romans saw themselves. Yet it is notable that while the crowd, according to Pliny, wept and cursed Pompey, they did not petition for the surviving elephants to be spared.

Two things in day-to-day life habituated the Romans to the slaughter of animals. First, most butchers practised their trade in the street in front of their shops. In the modern West, supermarket cuts of meat come in cellophane-wrapped trays, completely divorced from slaughter and preparation. When a Roman went to buy meat, he saw the blood and smelled the offal. Animal bones found near the *Meta Sudens*, a water feature outside the Colosseum, indicated public butchery of animals from the shows. Second, animal sacrifice was the central act of pagan religion. The quadruped was stunned with a mallet, its head pulled back and its throat slit. How the blood spurted was carefully noted. For the Underworld deities it should gush downwards to the earth; for the Olympian gods, upwards, ideally splattering the altar. Most sacrifices were followed by a feast. The gods got the bones and fat, the worshippers the roasted meat. The Romans associated the slaughter of animals with piety and a rare culinary treat. They might love individual animals, and credit every species with human characteristics, but they were not in the least squeamish about the beast hunts.

Events

Some traditional Roman religious festivals killed animals in ways other than sacrifice. At the *Floralia*, instituted in 240BC, deer and rabbits were hunted in the Circus. As the name suggests, the *Ludi Taurei* featured the hunting of bulls. The festival, also held in the Circus, was believed to be very ancient, dating from the time of the mythical kings. More alarming to our sensibilities was the festival dedicated to the ancient Italian fertility goddess Ceres. At the *Cerialia* torches were tied to the tails of foxes, then set alight. The tormented animals ran here and there in the Circus in a futile attempt to avoid being burned to death. Given the perpetual fear of fire in Rome, a city largely built of wood, great care would have been taken that none escaped.

As the empire expanded in the third and second centuries BC, and her enemies came from Africa and the eastern Mediterranean, exotic animals were brought back by successful generals to be paraded in their triumphs, along with human prisoners of war. In 275BC the consul Manius Curius Dentatus exhibited four elephants he had taken from Pyrrhus of Epirus in southern Italy. In 252BC no fewer than 140 elephants captured from the Carthaginians were paraded by the proconsul Lucius Caecilius Metellus, who then had them fight against men in the Circus. Pliny the Elder, recording this three centuries later, found his sources differed: one said they were killed with javelins; another that they were merely chased by labourers with blunted spears. Although, as Pliny commented, 'those authors who think they were not put to death do not say what happened to them afterwards'.

The chasing and killing of animals at festivals, and the parading of exotic beasts in triumphs came together to form the distinctive Roman *Venationes* (wild beast hunts). The first unambiguously recorded *Venatio* was staged by Marcus Fulvius Nobilior in 186BC, and starred lions and leopards. The primary venue for wild beast hunts remained the Circus. They rapidly spread from Triumphs to both elite funerals and official festivals. In 169BC the *aediles* had sixty-three African beasts (either lions or leopards), forty bears, and a number of elephants fight in the Circus. There was early, and completely ineffectual, legislation to limit the amount that could be spent on animal shows, and a measure banning the import of African beasts. The latter was soon rescinded, and the numbers of animals expanded, with ever more exotic beasts being added. In 58BC a senator provided 150 leopards, five crocodiles, and a hippopotamus. In 55BC Pompey staged a show with 410 leopards, five or six hundred lions, and various other animals, including the only lynx recorded in the arena, as well as the elephants that excited the sympathy of the crowd. A few years later Julius Caesar produced 400 lions, fighting bulls from Thessaly in Greece, and the first giraffe to be seen in Rome, as well as a set-piece battle featuring infantry, cavalry, and at least forty elephants. This is the first known occasion when beast-fights were held alongside gladiatorial combat. It set the trend. As we have seen, by the reign of Augustus a day at the Games needed both a beast-hunt and gladiators to be 'proper and legitimate' (*iustum atque legitimum*).

Beast shows had three elements: animals doing tricks (or merely being displayed, as at a zoo), animals chasing and fighting other animals, and men hunting and killing animals.

A good way to approach the beast-hunts – for us to get up close to them, be dropped into the middle of the action – is to think about the quite well known 'Magerius Mosaic' (**Plate Twelve**). Found in 1966 close to the insignificant ancient settlement at Smirat in North Africa, in modern Tunisia, it must come from an elite country villa. Its style dates it to the third century AD. Its context within the building is unknown. As it presents two viewpoints – from the top and the bottom of the plate as illustrated here – it was unlikely to have decorated the floor of a dining room, as none of the images or the text would face towards guests reclining on either of the shorter sides.

More likely it was in a room in a private bath house attached to the villa, as these often had two doorways.

There are three registers of images within a patterned border. The top and bottom together contain four leopards and four huntsmen. That all four leopards have a garland round their middles shows the scene is a hunt in the arena, rather than the wild. The four wavy bands of the border might also represent the netting keeping spectators safe. The four leopards are named: Romanus (the Roman), Luxurius (Playful), Crispinus (Curly) and Victor (rather ironically, given the blood gushing from its chest). Likewise, the huntsmen have stage names: Mamertinus (Son of the war god Mars), Hilarinus (Cheerful), Bullarius (perhaps from Bulla Regia, a town in North Africa) and Spittara (a unique name, perhaps hinting at an eastern origin).

The middle register has four unnamed figures. In the centre is a well-dressed herald, identified as such by the inscription which surrounds him. He is holding a big tray on which are four bags of money, each marked with the symbol for a thousand. The herald is flanked by two deities, or arena attendants dressed as gods. The female on his right (the left as we look at them) has been identified as Diana by her costume and the stalk of millet she has in her hands. As the goddess of the hunt, Diana could not be more suitable as a presiding divinity at a *venatio*, especially as she was often conflated with Nemesis, the particular deity of the amphitheatre. The male deity, nude except for high sandals and a cloak, is less certain. Hermes/Mercury, who guided souls to the Underworld, would fit into the context of the arena. But the staff topped with a crescent-shaped prong was an attribute sometimes carried by Dionysus, especially in the art of North Africa. Dionysus, master of the beasts, was quite at home in a *venatio*. Of the final figure (on the right, and upside down, as we look at the plate) only the head and left shoulder are undamaged, apart from the tip of some sort of staff he probably held in his right hand. Elaborately dressed and larger in scale than the others, this is the giver of the Games.

Dionysus gestures towards him with a circular object; it looks as if the god is about to crown him. We might be surprised this local dignitary is not wearing a toga. Yet after AD212 all free men were entitled to the dress of a Roman citizen. Maybe he thought a more elaborate costume would better point up his wealth and status.

It is the inscription that brings this unique mosaic to life. MAGERI, MAGERI – at each end of the middle register, one facing each way – a man's name in the vocative. These are the acclamations of the crowd, calling out to the giver of the show: 'Oh, Magerius!' The one above Magerius' head has an unidentifiable symbol after it, pointing down like an arrow, just in case you have not worked out the main man.

The two long inscriptions take us directly into a moment in the day. They are a dialogue between the crowd and Magerius, who is speaking through the herald. Quite deliberately like an emperor at the Games, he is far too grand to talk to the masses himself.

On our left it reads.

> *Said by the herald. 'My Lords, that the* Telegenii *for each leopard deserve your favour, give them 500 denarii.'*

On our right the crowd reply.

> *It is acclaimed. 'By your example may the Games be understood by those in the future! May those of the past hear of it! Whence such a show? When such a show? On the example of the Quaestors you give a show! At your own expense you give a show! It is your day!'*
>
> *Magerius gives.*
>
> *'This is wealth! This is power! This is now! Night is now! From your Games let them be dismissed with the money bags!'*

We have met the *Telegenii* before, at the last supper with the sleeping bulls on the El Djem mosaic (**Plate Three**). They were one of the organisations (*familiae*) of *venatores* from North Africa that trapped, shipped and then hunted animals in the

1. A day at the Games depicted in a first-century marble relief at Pompeii.

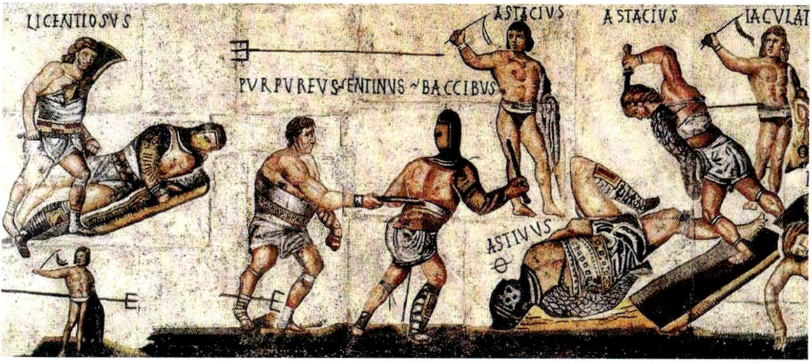

2. Gladiators fighting – a scene from the fourth-century Borghese mosaic.

3. The *cena libra* as depicted in the third-century El Djem mosaic.

5. The Zliten mosaic, found in Libya, depicting gladiatorial contests and animal hunts.

4. A funerary relief showing two gladiators – the victor on the left, the loser on the right.

6. A terracotta lamp from Arles showing a woman and man making love.

7. A wall painting depicting the amphitheatre at Pompeii.

8. Gladiators seen grappling in combat.

9. A relief from Smyrna showing two pairs of condemned men being dragged along by men in tunics and helmets.

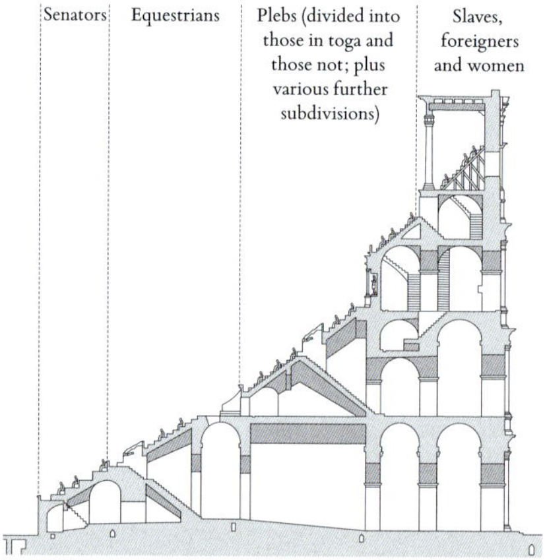

10. A cross-section of the seating in the Colosseum.

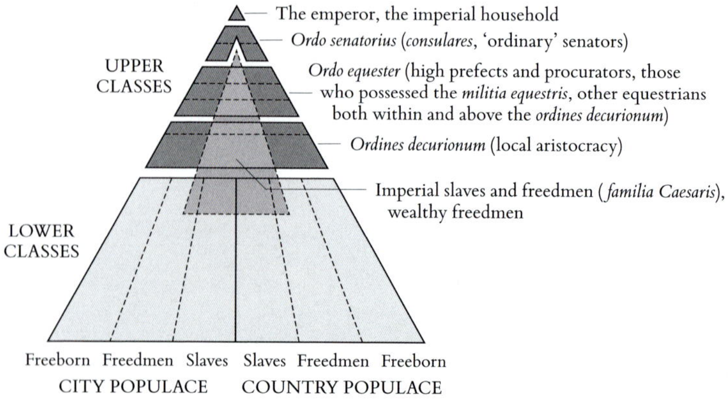

11. The social structure of the Roman Empire.

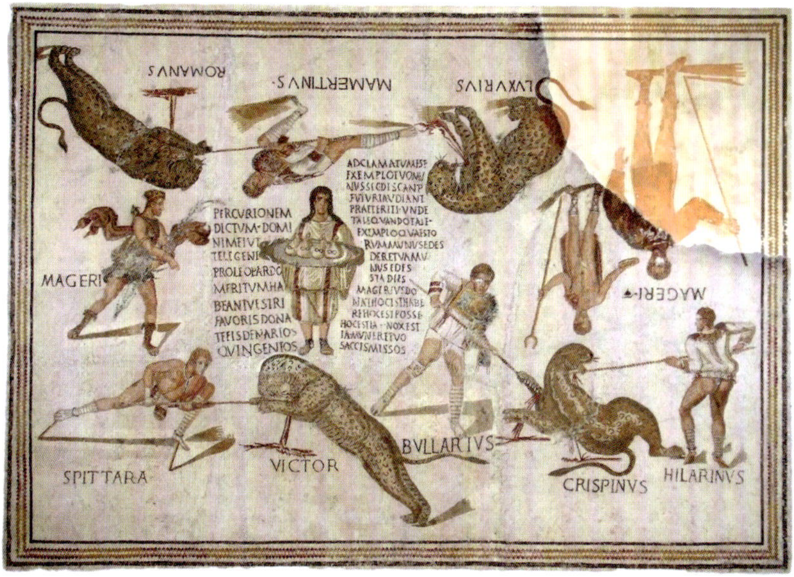

12. The third-century Magerius mosaic, found in Tunisia, depicting a beast hunt.

13. A terracotta relief showing beast hunters.

14. A detail from the Great Hunt mosaic showing animals being transported. The mosaic is on the floor of a palatial fourth-century villa near Piazza Armerina in Sicily.

15. Another detail from the Great Hunt mosaic, depicting a huntsman on horseback.

16. A detail from the Great Hunt mosaic showing a woman, thought to represent Aethiopia, next to a frankincense tree.

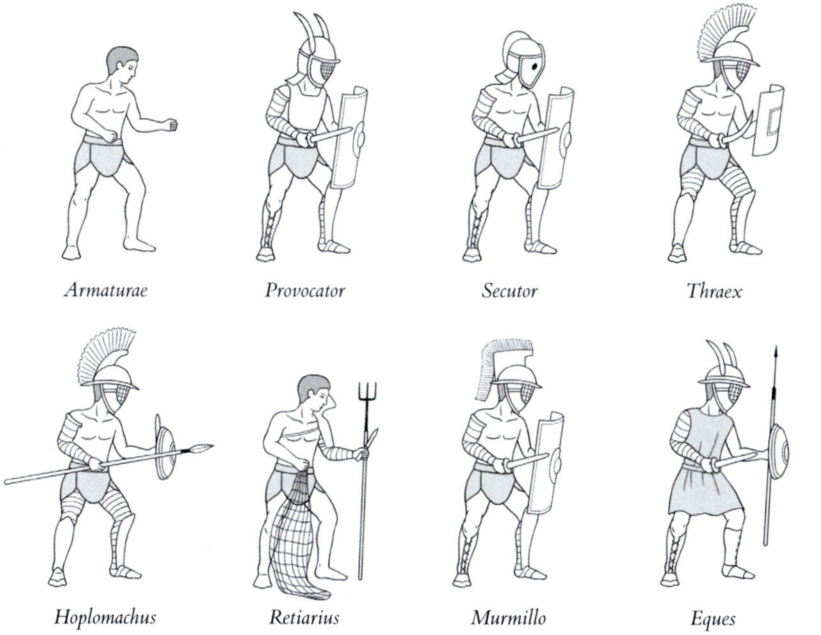

17. The different types of gladiators.

18. Two gladiators receiving the decision of the *editor*.

19. (*Above*) A relief from Halicarnassus, Turkey, showing two female gladiators.

20. (*Left*) A gladiator armed with shield and sword stands in the 'first position'.

arena. When you hired the *Telegenii*, as did Magerius, you got the whole package. Dionysus and Diana were patron deities of the *Telegenii*; the staff with a curved prong and a stalk of millet were two of their symbols. They might have taken their name from Telegonos, the son of Odysseus and Circe, the witch who transformed men into animals. Notice that the shadows cast by Spittara end in what seem to be the claws of a fierce beast.

There is a twist in the story. The herald asks the crowd to give the *Telegenii* 500 *denarii* per leopard, even though everyone knew it was Magerius who would actually pay. Although unmentioned in the dialogue, the symbol on the moneybags shows Magerius demonstrated his generosity by giving twice that amount. One thousand *denarii* was 4,000 *sesterces* – a reasonable payday for one fight.

The mosaic, like much Roman art, plays with and conflates time. The mosaicist has depicted everything happening at once. But the conversation between the herald and the crowd in the middle took place after the action in the other two registers, after the leopards have been killed. In what order should we read the events at the top and bottom? Sequentially, it has been suggested, clockwise from the top left: so Mamertinus faced Romanus first, and Spittara fought Victor last. But Bullarius, having mortally wounded Luxurius, goes to help Hilarinus against his leopard. All the combatants were in the arena together. *Night is now!* The inscription says it is time the hunters are dismissed. Long shadows, all pointing in the same direction, stretch out from huntsmen, beasts and gods. The fight took place late in the day. Should we assume what we see was all of the show? Or have we just been given the highlight? As the climax of his Games Magerius sent into the arena four stars of the renowned *Telegenii* to face four leopards, whose fame from previous exploits in the arena had made them household names.

As with the mosaic of the last supper from El Djem, this was a unique work of art, specially commissioned by a local magnate hoping to immortalise his munificence. By the chance of its survival, against all the odds, Magerius' ploy worked – we are still talking about him now.

One of the most fascinating things about this mosaic is the role of the crowd. They are far from passive. When they chant that those in both the future and the past will hear of Magerius' Games, they are exerting pressure on other members of the local elite to give similar lavish displays, not only when they hold office (as quaestors), but at other times and at their own expense. The herald treats the crowd as if it is their show. He asks them to approve the money to be handed to the huntsmen, and he addresses them as 'My Lords' (*domini mei*). The poor and oppressed in the stands are 'Lords' for a day.

Three of the hunters on the mosaic are equipped as typical *venatores*. They wear embroidered tunics and banded leggings – Bullarius also has banded protection on his left forearm – and all wield a spear, just like the huntsmen employed by an aristocratic household. Spittara is different. Half-naked, with an amulet round his neck, he appears to fight from a pair of stilts (unless these are intended to be part of his shadow). Such an extraordinary display of dexterity would be a fitting addition to the climax of a beast-hunt. Novelty always had an attraction at the Games. Occasionally *venatores* used bows and arrows. Archers from Parthia (modern Iraq and Iran) trained Commodus to shoot ostriches in the arena. The emperor used special crescent-shaped arrowheads so that the birds carried on running after they had been decapitated. Archery was rare in the arena because bows have an effective range of over 150 yards, and the safety nets were not guaranteed to stop an arrow. Cassius Dio tells us that the audience once stayed away from the Colosseum because of a rumour that Commodus, playing the role of Hercules killing the Stymphalian birds, was intending to shoot some of the spectators.

Despite the appeal of novelty, *venatores* were not divided into subgroups with distinctive equipment and costume, as were gladiators. An exception to the uniformity of equipment among hunters is found on relief sculptures from the reign of Augustus, as well as terracotta reliefs that copy them in the first, and possibly into the second centuries AD (**Plate Thirteen**). The egg-shaped spheres on top of the arch through which the lion charges are there to count the laps in chariot races in the Circus Maximus. The huntsman on the right is a normal *venator*. The one on the left, who has not noticed the lioness about to attack him from behind, is kitted out much like a gladiator. He has a plumed legionary helmet and a large oval shield, and is armed with a sword. Unlike a legionary, he has no tunic or body armour, being clad in a kilt and protected by boots and banded material on his right arm. A modern suggestion is that he is not a *venator*, but a different type of animal fighter called a *bestiarius* (plural, *bestiarii*). It is an appealing theory, but no ancient evidence applies the label *bestiarius* to these depictions, and such a clear distinction may demand too much precision of how language was used by the Romans. *Bestiarii* were first and foremost arena attendants who handled the animals. The term also came to be used for all those who faced animals on the sands, both professional huntsmen (*venatores*), and those condemned to death by the animals (*damnatio ad bestias*). By similar extensions, Christians applied the terms *noxii*, technically meaning those condemned to death, and even *gladiator* to everyone involved in the arena. The bare-chested man about to be mauled by the lioness was a *venator*, who, like any hunter in the arena, could also be referred to as a *bestiarius*. His style of fighting with shield and sword seems to have been an innovation of the reign of Augustus, which disappeared in subsequent generations.

A huntsmen of the arena could achieve fame. Martial composed three poems praising Carpophorus. He talks of how, by throwing his spear with unerring aim, the young *venator* outdid the twelve labours of Hercules, vanquishing 'twice ten beasts at one time'. If Carpophorus had been born in a barbarous land in ages past, Hercules was not the only hero he would have surpassed. Theseus, Bellerophon, Jason and Perseus – all would have been left in the shade. One blow would have finished off the hydra. In the Colosseum Carpophorus slew an arctic bear, a lion and a panther.

Outside the spotlight of Martial's poetry, however, we know little about *venatores*. Unlike gladiators, they did not leave tombstones. Many, unlike Carpophorus, were born in 'barbarous' lands, on the borders of the empire or beyond. The king of Mauretania (roughly modern Morocco) sent Sulla a hundred lions and a hundred native spearmen to fight them. Lucius Domitius Ahenobarbus imported a hundred Aethiopians to hunt a hundred Numidian bears. As we saw, Pompey's unfortunate elephants were killed by Gaetulian tribesmen from North Africa. Commodus was trained for the arena by Mauretanian spearmen, as well as Parthian archers. These 'un-Romanised' immigrants did not have the 'epigraphic habit' of setting up inscriptions. Most of them would have not had the money to pay for even a small commemoration.

Venatores were less glamorous than gladiators but they attracted less social opprobrium. This was in large part because many were barbarians, which meant that they would never attract the same adulation. Conversely, though, their low initial status meant that appearing in the arena was not seen as such a disgrace. Youthful members of the elite fought bulls in Ephesus (incidentally the only type of arena hunting usually done on horseback). Young men from good families fought bears in Gaul. We have seen that in Rome itself fighting beasts in the arena brought no shame, if it was done to prove courage rather than for sordid gain. Both Claudius and Nero employed regular officers and troopers of the imperial horse guards (the *equites singulares*) in arena hunts. These were admittedly unusual events but there was never any suggestion that the guardsmen might fight as gladiators. In a sense free men, such as soldiers, or even members of the elite, participating in a *venatio* were just hunting in an arena, rather than in the wild.

The beast shows themselves were undoubtedly popular. In the fourth century AD Libanius says people queued all night for tickets in Antioch. Some individuals were more interested in them than in gladiatorial combat. In *On the Spectacles*, celebrating the opening of the Colosseum, Martial devotes some sixteen poems to beast-fights, but only four to gladiators. In North Africa mosaic representations of *venationes* vastly outnumber those of gladiators. Yet beast-fights were subordinate to gladiatorial combat from the reign of Augustus. In a 'proper and legitimate' show the *venationes* in the morning were a warm-up for the main attraction of the gladiatorial combat in the afternoon.

Imperial shows were huge and exotic, as each emperor sought to outdo his predecessors. In the potted autobiography set up in front of his mausoleum, Augustus said he had given beast-hunts on twenty-six occasions, during which some 3,500 African beasts were destroyed. In the Games held by Titus at the opening of the Colosseum, 9,000 animals, both wild and tame, were killed over 100 days. In 123 days of Games to celebrate the Dacian triumph of Trajan, 11,000 beasts, again both wild and tame, met their end. The theme appealed to the author of the *Augustan History*, who enjoyed making up lists in his fiction. On one day the emperor Probus slaughtered 1,000 ostriches, 1,000 stags, 1,000 wild boars, then deer, ibexes, wild sheep and other herbivores. On another it was the turn of 100 lions, 100 Libyan leopards, 100 Syrian leopards, 100 lionesses and 300 bears – a total of 700 wild beasts, which trumped the average of ninety animals of all kinds a day of Titus and Trajan.

Lavish imperial extravaganzas were very much the exception. Outside Rome things were on a vastly smaller scale. Inscriptions tell of shows in Italy. At Miturnae one featured just four grass-eating animals on each of its four days, and ten 'cruel bears' in total. One at Beneventum boasted only sixteen bears and four other 'fierce' beasts. Although another, unnamed, town had to make do with ten herbivores and a mere four 'fierce, toothed' animals, it was still considered worth immortalising it in stone. Perhaps Margerius and his mosaicist were showing us the entirety of his Games after all?

Hunting

Hunting and warfare were at the centre of the Roman mind. Romulus and Remus became leaders because of their prowess in fighting and the chase. (So later Romans implicitly believed.) The battlefield and the hunting field remained at the heart of Roman self-identity long after the realities of both had vanished from the experience of the vast majority of the inhabitants of the city of Rome.

Roman hunting began as a simple, low cost, and egalitarian activity: a few men on foot, maybe with a couple of dogs and some nets and spears, usually hunting rabbits and hares. It was much like that of Classical Greece. With the conquest of the eastern Mediterranean in the last two centuries BC, the Roman elite adopted new ways of hunting from the Hellenistic royal courts – the traditional Macedonian style of mounted hunting supercharged by the wealth of the Persian empire. The quarry now regularly included big game, and the pursuit involved expensive imported hounds, well-bred hunting horses, fine equipment and many liveried huntsmen. The elite established hunting parks on their landed estates.

Almost everyone thought hunting was good for you. The embittered politician-turned-historian Sallust was a rare dissenting voice, claiming the revolutionary Catiline had corrupted young men: some with hounds and hunters, others with whores. Sallust also made the extraordinary claim that both hunting and farming were servile occupations. Next to no one would have agreed. Just like farming, out in all weathers, often in unforgiving terrain, hunting toughened up the body. It required endurance as well as strength and skill. Hunting was good for the soul too. Dio Chrysostom told the emperor Trajan, who was a keen huntsman, that it amounted to a philosophical education. The hunter glimpsed his prey, then lost it. The experience trained the soul to deal with the outrageous swings of fortune; taught it how to handle triumph and disaster. Facing fierce beasts demanded courage. Hunting was the ideal preparation for warfare. The gods, as well as the hunter's expertise, determined the result. Success in the chase showed the piety of the huntsman, because it demonstrated the favour of the gods.

Hunting in the right style was a mark of elevated status. Trajan was not the only devotee. His successor Hadrian's love of the chase can be seen in the relief sculptures on the tondos incorporated into the Arch of Constantine outside the Colosseum. That of the consul and historian Arrian shines through his surviving *Cynegeticus*, a manual on hunting. Members of the elite were expected to go hunting. Even Pliny the Younger, far from an outdoors man, felt obliged to go, although he expected ridicule for his efforts, and took his notebooks with him to while away the time. At the close of the day, after a successful hunt, offerings were made to appropriate deities and everyone settled down to a feast, either in the field or back home.

Hunting could be used to attempt to advance social status. Horace mocked a man who had a boar brought back from the market by servants equipped with spears and nets, as if it had been caught out hunting. In Petronius' *Satyricon*, the ghastly social-climbing freedman Trimalchio staged an elaborate sort of double hunt plus alfresco feast in his dining room. The couches were spread with coverlets embroidered with nets and spears. Hounds imported from Sparta were slipped among the guests. A huge boar, wearing a cap of liberty, was carried in, accompanied by a man wearing the leggings and decorated coat of a huntsman. The latter turned out to be a carver and the boar turned out to be cooked. When the boar's flank was cut with a hunting knife, thrushes flew out. Fowlers caught the edible birds with twigs sticky with lime. Trimalchio explained the porcine cap of liberty – the boar had been sent away untouched by his guests the night before.

The urban plebs of Rome had no part in hunting. They were too poor and they lived in a huge city. Likewise, they had no part in the leisured and civilised life of elite rural villas, of which the chase was an integral part. When Augustus redesigned the northern part of the Campus Martius into a *rus in urbe* pleasure park, his intention was to give the *plebs urbana* access to an aspect of the life of the elite on their private estates: plants and animals, open space, picnics, and shaded walks. Equally when an emperor gave a beast-hunt in the Amphitheatre he gave them a temporary and vicarious taste of the pleasures of elite hunting. For a morning the plebs in the stands became 'Lords' of the hunting field. As the meat of the slaughtered animals was butchered and distributed at the end of the day, some of the plebs later enjoyed an elite feast of a haunch of venison, or some more exotic beast.

Universal Empire: Geography

Most of the animals in any arena were local. In Rome, Italy and across the provinces, the standard fare was bulls and bears, wild boars and deer, with hounds in pursuit. Far more prestige attached to exotic beasts from distant lands: elephants and ostriches from Africa, crocodiles and tigers from the east. Africa was the great source. So much so that 'African beasts' came to be synonymous with fierce animals.

Under the Republic supply was ad hoc, relying on local contacts. As we have seen, King Bocchus of Mauretania sent Sulla a hundred lions; Caelius pestered Cicero for panthers. Under the emperors, more regular logistics were needed. It gave the professional army a role in peacetime. Sometimes their efforts to secure sufficient numbers of wild animals resembled a large-scale military manoeuvre. At Montana, in Moesia, on the northern frontier, Tiberius Claudius Ulpianus, the commander of the First Cohort of Cilicians, set up a votive altar for the successful capture of bears and bisons for an imperial show. The hunt had involved not just Ulpianus' auxiliaries but detachments from the First Legion Italica, the Eleventh Legion Claudia and the fleet on the Danube (the *Classis Flavia*). Usually, activity was on a smaller scale. We hear of individual soldiers released from other duties because they were hunters (*venatores immunes*), or specialist bear-hunters (*ursarii*). At Dura-Europos on the Euphrates the troop roster of the Twentieth Cohort of Palmyrenes records soldiers assigned 'to the lions' (*ad leones*): five infantrymen, and two cavalrymen in AD219; just three on foot, and a single mounted man in AD222. An inscription from Germany commemorates a centurion who captured fifty bears in six months. In Africa the high demand for animals, and the relatively low number of troops stationed there – just one legion, although there were auxiliary units – opened the way for the *familiae* of professional hunters, like the *Telegenii*. Some historians, making comparisons with more recent times, have suggested that much of the dangerous work was foisted onto indigenous hunters and trappers. Little ancient evidence, however, supports the theory, while much points to the army and professional *venatores*.

As far as possible, animals, like all bulk goods, were transported by water – down rivers and across the sea. There would have been much suffering, and many deaths – remember the problems Symmachus had getting animals alive, or in any state to fight in his shows. Yet, unless conditions were adverse, the transit time would have been quicker and the survival rate higher. On land, convoys of animals were a drain on the resources of the communities through which they passed. In AD417 the civic officials of Hierapolis near the Euphrates complained to Theodosius II that a caravan had stayed for three or four months and made illegal requisitions. The emperor decreed that henceforth no convoy should linger longer than seven days in any place. Wild beasts in transit also posed a threat to humans. A sculptor called Pasiteles went down to the docks at Ostia when a shipment of animals came in from Africa. He was making a relief of a lion, peering into its cage, 'when it so happened that a leopard broke out of another cage, and caused serious danger to this most conscientious of artists'.

The most remarkable evidence for the capture and movement of beasts destined for the shows is the Great Hunt Mosaic from the palatial, fourth century AD, rural villa near Piazza Armerina in Sicily (**Plate Fourteen**). Part of the greatest surviving assemblage of ancient mosaics surviving in situ, at over 65 yards long, and five and a half wide, the Great Hunt Mosaic is the largest in the villa and also occupies the most important position. You had to cross the Great Hunt to enter the main reception hall of the villa. To make sure your eye was drawn to the mosaic under your feet, the floor of the main hall was one of the few without elaborate decoration. Set in the countryside, the mosaic depicts animals fighting animals, and men hunting with a view to a kill. But mostly it shows animals being trapped and transported for the shows.

Soldiers, or huntsmen dressed in the military style fashionable in the fourth century, drive animals into nets. A horseman, clutching a tiger cub, desperately rides up the gangplank of a ship. The pursuing tigress has stopped, distracted by a mirror, in which she sees a diminutive reflection of herself, which she mistakes for her cub (**Plate Fifteen**). Although this is not depicted, the tigress will be captured while she is preoccupied. Unlike modern zookeepers, those running the Games were not in it for the long term. They had little interest in rearing or breeding animals. Mature adults were wanted for immediate display or slaughter. Some captured animals are transported in cages on carts, others are trussed up and carried suspended from poles or manhandled with ropes. In the centre of the mosaic two ships cleverly represent a sea voyage. From left and right animals are dragged, with more or less reluctance, up gangplanks on board. Sailors on deck haul ropes to unfurl the sails. Then, in the middle of the mosaic, animals disembark from the other end of the same vessels. Presumably they have arrived on Italian soil, where a distinguished group of men awaits them.

If the centre of the mosaic is Italy, attempts to identify specific areas of the empire in the rest of the action are unconvincing. African animals – lions, African elephants, ostriches – are mixed with eastern – tigers, an Indian rhinoceros with one horn – and a mythological beast: a griffon. The message that animals for the Games are gathered from across the empire is reinforced by the mosaics in the apses at either end. In each sat a female personification of a region. The one on the left is heavily damaged, but enough remains – curly hair, a tiger cub tucked under her arm – to suggest she is Mauretania, Rome's most westerly African province. The one to the right has been argued – mainly on the basis that she is black and sits next to a frankincense tree – to be Aethiopia; the kingdom south of Egypt (**Plate Sixteen**). From the far west to the distant (south-) east animals are captured for the Roman Games.

Aethiopia was a rare personification in Roman art. Only one other image has been identified; in a painting from Pompeii. Contemporary viewers, like many modern scholars, might have just identified her vaguely as 'eastern'. While the three animals around her were at times linked to Aethiopia, they were not most associated with there. The tiger on her left was quintessentially eastern: from Armenia, Persia and India. The elephant on her right, with its big ears and concave back, is North African. Above the elephant is a mythical phoenix, flames licking up from its nest, which was usually placed in Arabia or Egypt (we will look at what the mythical phoenix and griffon are doing here in the next section). Even within the Aethiopian apse, fourth-century viewers might have concluded that animals were collected from across the entire wide geographic spread of the empire.

Except that some animals exhibited in the Games at Rome came from regions objectively outside the empire: rhinos from sub-Saharan Africa, a giant snake from India, polar bears (if 'Arctic bears' did not just mean 'very northern'; maybe they were the same as 'Caledonian bears'; either way, north of Hadrian's Wall was outside the province of Britannia). *Objectively outside the empire* to our mind, but not necessarily in Roman thinking.

The Romans thought the world was much smaller than it really is. Obviously, they did not know the Americas or Antipodes. The world they did know, the 'inhabited world' (*oikoumene* in Greek, *orbis terrarium* in Latin) was believed to be an oval, about 8,046 miles 'long' (east to west), and half as 'wide' (north to south). This vastly compresses northern Europe and misses out the majority of Africa. They also conceptualised geography in a different way from us. Armed with NASA images and accurate atlases, we think in terms of blocks of territory: so-called 'cartographic thinking'. Attempts at accurate topographical maps existed in the Classical period, but were extremely theoretical and confined to the ancient equivalents of ivory towers. Most Romans instead thought in terms of lines – of rivers, coasts, mountain ranges and roads – along which various peoples were situated. Maps produced for practical use were itineraries – lists of stopping places along roads – or *periploi* – lists of ports along coasts: the products of so-called 'odological thinking'. Roman concepts of geography influenced their views of the place of their empire in the world. For the Romans the world was smaller, and their empire bigger, than they are for us.

When we think of the Roman empire, we think of directly administered Roman provinces. Open any atlas of ancient history, and that is the sort of map you will find. The Romans, however, considered that their empire extended wherever Roman power ran, which in practice meant wherever their orders were obeyed. Client kingdoms and peoples were judged an integral part of the empire. Tacitus included them when surveying the empire in his *Annals*. A modern map drawn on those lines would considerably expand Roman territory. Yet the Romans went further. From the early second century BC, the Romans, like the later imperial Chinese, formed the extraordinary view that any diplomatic approach by another people, no matter the intentions of the senders, amounted to submission to Rome. In 20BC, on the island of Samos, Augustus received an embassy from an Indian ruler bearing gifts. In AD14 Augustus' potted autobiography (the *Res Gestae*) was set up in bronze at the entrance to his Mausoleum and copied in stone throughout the empire. In a lengthy list of peoples who he had made submit by warfare or diplomacy, Augustus included 'frequent embassies from Indian kings'. Exhibiting animals from beyond the frontiers in the arena, like Augustus receiving Indian ambassadors, was a strong ideological claim to universal rule.

Universal Empire: Nature

When Lucius the ass peered through the gate of the arena outside Corinth he saw a wooden mountain, complete with grass, trees, a stream tumbling down from the top, she-goats cropping the grass – Homer's Mount Ida, the setting for the judgement of Paris. When the pantomime was over – Venus, the winner of the beauty contest, dancing off in delight, the losers, Juno and Minerva, leaving with gestures of indignation, sorrow and rage – 'a fountain of wine, mixed with saffron, broke out from a concealed pipe at the mountain top, and its many jets sprinkled the pasturing goats with a scented shower, so that their white hair was stained a rich yellow. The scent filled the whole amphitheatre; and then the stage machinery was set in motion, the earth opened, and the mountain disappeared from view.' Impressive for a provincial show.

At Rome, sophisticated technology at the Games frequently not only replicated but also subverted nature – the solid fell to bits, the immobile moved, and time speeded up. Under Augustus a model of Etna broke apart, throwing a notorious bandit to his death among the wild beasts released from their cages by the collapse. In Nero's amphitheatre a forest grew up in moments from the ground. At the opening of the Colosseum the crags of the Rhodope Mountains moved slowly towards Orpheus, drawn by the power of his music; the forests, like Dunsinane Wood, approached rather faster. A huge boat, which Septimius Severus had built on the floor of the Circus, was shipwrecked, releasing 700 animals at the same time. The author of the *Augustan History* played with such ideas in his fiction – the emperor Probus had the army pull up an entire forest, roots and all, for an improbable beast-hunt. Imperial shows made the natural landscape uncertain and paradoxical: land and sea existing in the same place. Martial has the gods of the sea disconcerted by land animals hunted in the water. Venues were flooded for a naval battle, then drained in no time for an engagement on land.

The arena played with the senses of smell and sight through which the world was observed. Nero's trees, like Apuleius' Mount Ida, jetted forth a spray of saffron-scented mist. The quality of light was changed. The awnings overhead were coloured. The effect was that of stained glass in a cathedral, casting shifting blocks of colour over the stands. The awning did not cover all the arena. The oval gap in the middle concentrated the sunlight out on the sands, acting as a spotlight. The sands themselves could be stained: red, white, or a green-blue copper colour. Mosaics from North Africa show the floor of the arena strewn with rose petals.

It was not just the landscape that was changed in the arena, so too was the nature of animals. The Romans divided animals into two types: either wild (*ferae*) and toothed (*dentatae*), or domesticated (*pecudes* or *mansuetae*) and herbivores (*herbariae*). Both might be dyed unnatural colours for the Games: bulls painted white, with gilded horns; sheep stained scarlet or purple, ostriches vermillion. Both types might be trained to do unnatural tricks. If we look again at the Zliten mosaic (**Plate Five**), in the middle of the hunting scene is a misshapen man, perhaps a dwarf. Holding what look like apples in his hands, he is directing a wild boar to dance on its back legs. The man wears his hair in the topknot of an athlete. The latter was ironic in Roman eyes, and, like lion trainers being depicted as old men, emphasised the domination of the animal kingdom by humanity: even the aged and deformed can master fierce beasts. Elephants were best at performing tricks. They danced and mimed gladiatorial combat. Reclining on enormous couches, they had dinner parties at which they displayed impeccable manners. One wrote Greek in the sand with his trunk. Others walked tightropes, even from the top of the theatre to the ground – which would have added another element of exciting apprehension for those in the seats under the tightrope. Equally alarming would have been a bull that was snatched from the arena up into the heavens.

When it came to the beast-hunt, herbivores presented no problem. They were expected to flee. Fierce beasts were trickier. The first reaction of a predator released into the blinding light and deafening noise of the unfamiliar arena was to find somewhere to cower. This was overcome by mistreatment and starvation in the run-up to the show, which made them more savage. Most likely they were also denied much water, although this was mostly so the thirst of those that survived could be used to aid their recapture. Even so, they could be reluctant to leave their cages. Whips and burning torches were used to drive them out. Once on the sands they might be taunted to increase their aggression. Bulls were goaded into tossing straw toys, before moving on to their real opponents. A stone block with an inset iron ring found in situ in the amphitheatre at Chester suggests that some animals were tethered in the middle of the arena.

Nature was further altered. Animals were matched against species that they did not fight in the wild. On the Zliten mosaic (**Plate Five**) a bull and a bear are chained together. A popular combination, but not the only one. An otherwise tame tigress from the shores of the distant Caspian Sea gored a lion; 'a new thing, unknown in any age'. A reluctant rhino, once it got its blood up, tossed a bull like a toy. In another poem the rhino dispatched a bear, two bullocks, aurochs and bisons, and drove a lion onto the spears of the hunters. Strangest of all is a report of cranes battling elephants; no idea how that worked.

Some animals exhibited in the arena were so rare and odd that they were unnatural in themselves. At the Games of Septimius Severus the first corocotta seen at Rome was killed. According to Cassius Dio, who was an eyewitness, it came from India and had 'the colour of a lioness and tiger combined, and the general appearance of these animals combined, as well as that of a dog and a fox, all curiously blended'. Other writers claimed it could mimic human speech. It is alongside fantastical beasts like the corocotta that the mythical creatures on the Great Hunt Mosaic at Piazza Armerina belong (**Plate Fourteen**). The phoenix sits on its burning nest next to the personification of Aethiopia, or somewhere else hot and dark, in the allegorical south apse. But the griffon is out in the main action, where perfectly normal animals are captured. The method of trapping a griffon is engagingly practical. You use a man as bait, as a kid nailed to a board is used to lure a leopard at the other end of the mosaic. You put the man in a box and the griffin tangles its claws in the wood trying to get at him. We regard these creatures as fictional. The Romans were not so certain. It is easy to smile at their naiveté. But they believed they *had* seen such beasts, albeit only their corpses. A phoenix, discovered in Egypt in AD 36, was exhibited in Rome by Claudius. Pausanias, the Greek travel writer, saw the remains of a triton, a sort of merman, among the wonders of Rome. These fabulous creatures were preserved in the imperial palace along with living oddities, including an Indian boy with no arms and a ten-foot-tall Jew. After Augustus usurped the highest religious authority from the Senate, the emperors were the ultimate mediator between man and the gods. Things that confounded nature were sent to them. The imperial palace was not only the centre of political power and the ultimate source of social patronage, it was also part-natural history museum, part-freak show.

Cliffs and woods that appeared and disappeared, that moved and collapsed; unnaturally coloured animals that behaved in unnatural ways; the light strangely tinged, and the air spiced with saffron – all symbolised the emperor's (and thus Rome's) control over nature. Sometimes the message was very straightforward. In one of Martial's poems, an elephant, having defeated a bull in the Colosseum, performed adoration (*adorat*) to the emperor. Adoration (*proskynesis* in Greek) was usually reserved for the gods. It consisted of bowing slightly and blowing a kiss with your fingertips. Easy enough for an elephant with its trunk. But, as the elephant is characterised as 'supple', maybe it went for full grovelling, flat out on its face. In another poem, a doe hunted by hounds cast herself in front of the emperor as a suppliant, and the dogs did not touch her. The poet assures us these were not tricks they had been taught – these animals innately recognised the sacred power of the emperor. Did Martial believe his flatteries? In a culture where the power of the emperor could only be comprehended by comparison with that of the gods, maybe it is the wrong question to ask.

The Games changed the natural world outside the arena. A minor Greek poet composing under the empire wrote: 'Libya, your plains are no longer impassible with beasts of prey, you no longer tremble at the roaring of lions, for the young Caesar [emperor] has caught a vast number, and made them face his fighters; the mountains, the former lairs of wild beast are now pastures for cattle.'

Similar sentiments were expressed from the reign of Augustus to the fifth century AD. Modern archaeozoology agrees that a range of species in North Africa, and elsewhere, were pushed to the verge of extinction, or eradicated. The difference is that the ancient poet sees it as a thoroughly good thing.

9

Tempus Meridianum
(Midday)

Midday is lunchtime. Many of the audience have left the cramped seating for the cool passageways and arches of the Colosseum, or the shade cast by the enormous edifice outside. There are vendors selling food and drink; wine and roasted chickpeas and sausages and pies; the scene is oddly reminiscent of Shakespeare's Globe. There is entertainment for those who picnic in the stands in the form of the Pyrrhic Dance. Acrobats and jugglers and animals doing tricks also appear on the sands. But the distinctive lunchtime entertainment is the public execution of those convicted of serious crimes, such as murder, treason, sacrilege and arson. Those condemned ad flammas *are burned alive. Those condemned* ad bestias *might be unshackled so that they can be chased round the ring, their futile scurrying here and there intended to amuse the crowd. They might also be driven with whips towards the beasts or tied to a stake. These latter punishments can be combined; the prisoner is bound to a stake mounted on a small chariot that is pushed towards his fate. Sometimes the convicts must act out scenes from myths. The animals – big cats, bears and bulls – unlike those in the morning, have obviously survived the encounter. Some are seasoned man-killers who have acquired names and a public reputation. Others have to be goaded. The story of Androcles spared by the lion, from whose paw he had removed a thorn, is well-known, probably because such an outcome is so very rare and unlikely.*

Half-Empty Stands

Seneca says that the stands emptied at midday. Domitian once provided not just snacks, but lunch for everyone in the Colosseum. This exceptional generosity elicited gushing praise from the poet Statius: ages past knew nothing like it; the waiters were as handsome as Ganymede, the wine flowed freer than in the Golden Age. Usually, unless they had brought a picnic, the spectators went outside to buy food from street vendors in the great piazza round the arena. They needed to stretch their legs. Although ancient Romans were smaller than modern Westerners, seating was cramped; much the same as a budget airline. Senators were allowed cushions. In the hierarchic society of Rome, with its lingering feeling that sitting down in comfort to watch entertainment might make you soft – perhaps no better than a Greek! – the privilege was not extended to the lower orders. Cushions or not, after hours on a stone or wooden bench, everyone's arse was numb. They drifted off to talk to their friends. An arena, with continuing events and music, was a poor place for conversation. If there was no awning, they retreated into the passageways and under the arches to get out of the weather: the burning Mediterranean sun in summer, the cold and rain in winter. Ironically, if there was an awning, it was the elite, down in the ringside seats, that were exposed. Senators were permitted broad-brimmed hats. Given the laws governing the dress code at the Games, again it is unlikely those further up the stands shared this concession.

A popular modern idea, which occasionally makes its way into scholarship, holds that the spectators had sex with prostitutes at the Games. Dogging was very much not a Roman thing. In their view, coupling outside, in the view of others, was a mark of ultimate and bestial barbarity. The salacious modern misapprehension stems from prostitutes working out of the shadowed arches of the deserted Colosseum when the Games were not being held.

The crowd emptied out because the midday entertainments, centred on executions, were the bottom of the bill. As a character says in *The Golden Ass*, gladiators bring famous courage to a show, beast-hunters proven agility, and condemned criminals a banquet of themselves for the animals. Some inscriptions from backwater towns in Italy advertise executions. At Puteoli a four-day show featured four unnamed fierce beasts, sixteen bears, an unspecified number of herbivores and four *noxii* destined for execution. A one-day event at Paestum exhibited 'noble' gladiators, 'big' bears and a single *noxius*. It sounds like scraping the barrel.

Seneca found the executions distasteful, and others may have felt the same. However, the views of a multi-millionaire, imperial councillor and hard-line Stoic philosopher should not be assumed to represent those of the majority. On the other hand, elite writers accused some emperors, such as Caligula, Claudius and Heliogabalus, of taking too keen a pleasure in watching executions. Their prurient gaze revealed their tyrannical cruelty. It was ironic that as a child Caracalla burst into tears at such sights – he turned out to be one of the cruellest of all.

Entertainments

One day Seneca went to the Games at noon. He was expecting 'playful, diverting, and relaxing' entertainments. Presumably risqué mime shows, balletic pantomimes, acrobats and jugglers, animals doing tricks or dancing. Or maybe *paegniarii*, 'play-gladiators', who fought burlesque duels with wooden weapons or whips. Incidentally, if *paegniarii* were not all volunteers, how did those condemned to a gladiatorial school land this non-fatal role: could an affinity for slapstick, or natural comic timing, save your life?

A distinctive element of the midday entertainments was the Pyrrhic Dance. Originally this was a formal armed dance from the Greek world. Under Rome, young boys of good families were brought from the east to perform the original display. But the Pyrrhic Dance diversified. The label was also applied to animals dancing. Performed by humans it acquired a plot and became a type of pantomime. But it also took other, darker turns. Condemned criminals, exotically dressed, engaged in real combat. More startling to us, it could also turn into execution. Plutarch tells us that,

> there are some people, no different from little children, who see criminals in the arena often dressed in tunics of golden cloth with purple cloaks, wearing crowns and doing the Pyrrhic Dance, who, struck with awe and astonishment, suppose that they are supremely happy, until the moment, before their eyes, the criminals are stabbed and flogged, and their gaudy and sumptuous costume bursts into flames.

Whatever relaxing entertainments Seneca was hoping for, he says he got something else, something he described as 'pure murder'. Pairs of condemned men were set to fight with swords, but without any defensive equipment or training. The fights were to the death. Each victor was immediately pitted against a new combatant, until only one man survived, and he was reserved for another butchering.

This is a tricky passage to interpret. First, we should clear up some misconceptions. When Seneca writes, 'in the morning they throw men to the lions and bears; at noon they throw them to the spectators', he does not mean it literally. The condemned were not torn apart by the audience, as asserted, with unshakable confidence, by writers on the internet. Instead, they were sacrificed to the desires of the crowd: 'Kill him! Flog him! Burn him! Why is he so timid close to the steel? Why does he strike so feebly? Why doesn't he die bravely? Whip him forward to meet his wounds! Blow for blow with chests naked and exposed!' Nor does it show, as some will assure you, that Seneca was necessarily opposed to gladiatorial combat. Seneca is clear that these men are criminals, not gladiators. He objects to the lack of art, skill and the defensive equipment that gives a combatant a fighting chance. Again, it has nothing to do with massed battles occasionally put on in the arena – this time the false link is made by scholars – as Seneca is explicitly talking about an ever diminishing number of individual duels.

Seneca maintains that he was surprised by what he witnessed. Executions were a mainstay of midday entertainment. Therefore, what startled Seneca was this *specific* type of killing. Which implies that it was highly unusual. A cynic might go further. We know of nothing else quite like this. Seneca cheerfully contradicts himself. He says the arena was empty, having told us a few lines earlier that most people prefer this slaughter to ordinary gladiatorial duels. The work this comes from, the *Seventh Letter, To Lucilius*, is a short tract of philosophy for a public readership cast in the form of a private letter. Its argument is that one should avoid crowds: bad people have a bad effect on you, an effect that is multiplied by a crowd. This is not the place to look for clear-eyed, unbiased and accurate recording of facts. Perhaps Seneca exaggerated both the bloodshed and the reaction of the crowd – They all die! The crowd loses all control! – to give emphasis to his philosophical point that crowds should be avoided.

Executions

The Romans were good at killing people. They were both ingenious, and, for a pre-industrial culture, remarkably efficient. A parricide was tied in a sack with a snake, cockerel and a dog, and drowned in the Tiber. A Vestal Virgin who had broken her vows was walled-up alive in an underground chamber.

Deserters and enemies of the state might be tied to a wooden fork and flogged to death. These were exceptional punishments for exceptional crimes. The usual means of execution were crucifixion or beheading. None of these were much use for the Games.

Crucifixion was too slow; a man might linger for days on the cross. At Pompeii an advertisement for a gladiatorial show at Cumae included *cruciarii*, individuals to be crucified. As there would be only twenty pairs of gladiators spread over four days, the unique reference to *cruciarii* again sounds like scraping the bottom of the barrel. In order for crucifixion to work in the arena it needed added elements. At Lyons the Christian Blandina was hung on a cross and wild animals were released. In the Colosseum a criminal playing the part of a mythical bandit called Laureolus was crucified and attacked by a bear. The paradoxical spectacle delighted Martial – Laureolus' limbs lived, while his body was consumed! At Smyrna, in Asia, the Christian Pionius was nailed to a cross and burned to death. In AD64 Nero deployed both additions. Christians, whom he blamed for the great fire of Rome, were fastened to crosses. Some were burned to death, serving as torches to illuminate the night; others were dressed in animal skins and torn apart by dogs.

If crucifixion was too slow, beheading was too quick; not just too quick but too honourable. In the early empire this relatively painless and un-humiliating death was reserved for Roman citizens, as opposed to slaves and foreigners. At some uncertain point – maybe by the late second century AD, certainly after AD212, when Caracalla granted citizenship to free inhabitants of the empire – it became restricted to the elite: to the *honestiores*, the 'honest', rather than the *humiliores*, the 'humble', as the upper and lower classes were known. As we will see, defeated gladiators who were not spared were seldom accorded the dignity of decapitation.

In the arena the normal methods of executing condemned criminals were to expose them to wild beasts or to burn them alive. Both could be made more spectacular by elaboration. On the Zliten mosaic (**Plate Five**) a naked man throws up his hands in horror as he is gripped by the hair and driven with a whip towards a springing lion. Two others are bound to stakes on small chariots. One is pushed towards a leopard, while the other has already been seized by a leopard, which claws his body and bites his face. On a terracotta from North Africa a woman, naked apart from a loincloth, is bound astride the back of a bull. A leopard has driven the bull to its knees and is now savaging the woman. For us it is an odd household ornament, but for a Roman master presumably a useful deterrent, reminding his slaves of the punishments awaiting the disobedient.

At the foot of the terracotta, a man, crouched on his knees, peers out from behind a large shield as the leopard strikes. Such executions brought danger to the beast-handlers. On the Zliten mosaic, the *bestiarius* with the whip leans back from the prisoner and the onrushing lion. Those manhandling the chariot also try to keep their distance. The authors of Christian Martyr Acts liked nothing better than a story of a beast ignoring the Christian and instead turning on its handler. In Carthage, when Saturus was tied to a wild boar, the beast merely dragged him about. But it had already gored the *bestiarius*, who died some days later.

Some of the condemned were not killed by the beasts. Everyone knew the story of Androcles and the lion. As a runaway slave in North Africa, Androcles had pulled a thorn out of a lion's paw. Recaptured, and condemned to the beasts in Rome, Androcles encountered the same lion, which fawned on him like a dog. When the backstory was explained, both man and beast were spared. After their reprieve, Androcles was in the habit of visiting inns, a collecting box in one hand, the lion's lead in the other; alarming for the other drinkers, but a good way of encouraging generosity. Such a happy ending was incredibly rare. If the condemned were not in too bad a condition, they were taken away to reappear later. When the beasts ignored Blandina, hanging on her cross in Lyons, she was taken out for another event: 'After the scourges, the animals, and the hot griddle, she was at last tossed into a net and exposed to a bull . . . thus she was offered in sacrifice.' Saturus in Carthage, having been dragged about by the boar, was later returned to the arena to be the victim of a bear. When the bear would not come out of its cage, Saturus had another stay of execution. At the third attempt, a leopard took a big bite out of Saturus but still failed to kill him. Those too mauled for further appearances, like Saturus, were finished off by *confectores*, low-status novice gladiators. Having had time to convert one of the soldiers guarding him, Saturus met his end without moving, in silence. His fellow martyr Perpetua, who had survived being tossed by a mad cow, was killed right after him. She screamed when the first blow struck bone, but then 'she took the trembling hand of the young gladiator and guided it to her throat.'

A supposed elaboration of condemnation to the flames was to build the pyre out of damp wood, so that the victim did not burn to death but was suffocated by the smoke. Apart from one incident, however, this seems to have been confined to executions in literature. According to his prosecutor Cicero, it is one of the novel cruelties inflicted by Verres, the corrupt governor of Sicily – too easy a charge to refute, if it were not true. Much later, about AD400, the author of the *Augustan History*, who had read Cicero, played with the idea. There was a colloquial expression in the late Empire for financial corruption in government: 'selling smoke'. To illustrate his entirely fictional creation of the *severity* of the emperor Alexander *Severus* (he loved puns!), the author brought together the contemporary phrase with what he had read in Cicero: a venal official was tied to a stake and suffocated while a herald proclaimed, 'the seller of smoke is punished by smoke'. That did not exhaust the novelist's invention. In an anecdote in Suetonius, a man about to be crucified protested that he was a Roman citizen; Galba, then governor of Nearer Spain, ordered him to be hung on a particularly tall cross that had been painted white. The inventive author of the *Augustan History* knew Suetonius, as well as Cicero, and merged them in his life of the pretender Avidius Cassius. 'He was the first to invent the following method of punishment: after erecting a tall post, 180 feet high, he bound condemned criminals on it from top to bottom, he built a fire at its base, and so killed some by the flames, others by the smoke, the pain and even by sheer fear.'

A horribly real elaboration of the immolation of the condemned in the arena was the gaudy and sumptuous costumes of Plutarch's Pyrrhic dancers, which we have seen suddenly bursting into flames. The punishment of torching clothes treated with inflammable materials was so common it gained its own name; the *tunica molesta*, the tunic of torment. It was a staple of spectacular executions.

Spectacular Executions

The condemned sometimes were complicit in their own executions. They acted out scenes from the past: overwhelmingly from what we would categorise as myth; very occasionally from an event we might believe was history. It raises any number of questions: about Roman power and the past; about the expectations of organisers and audience at the Games; and, to me most intriguing of all, why did the condemned play along in their own deaths in these 'fatal charades', or 'snuff plays'? Let's first see some examples.

A condemned man wearing the burning 'tunic of torment' was playing the role of Hercules. The wife of the hero was tricked into giving him a poisoned tunic. The pain was so intolerable that Hercules built a pyre and burned himself to death. Self-immolation was a rare and extraordinary event in the Roman world. It had been done by Indian mystics a long way from home, and, according to a hostile biography, a notoriety-loving charlatan philosopher, and sometime Christian, called Peregrinus. The arena conflated the poisoned tunic and the pyre and made the whole thing more mobile, with the victim not lying down motionless but running about in agony.

The criminal taking on the role of the bandit Laureolus, in the view of Martial, was also playing Prometheus. The Titan Prometheus was punished by Zeus. Chained-up in the Caucasus Mountains, every day an eagle feasted on his liver, which miraculously regrew overnight, so the torment could begin again the next day. Yet Prometheus survived. Eventually, after eons of torture, he was freed by Hercules. In the arena Prometheus-Laureolus was eaten by a bear: a quickish end, at least.

On wings of his own invention, Daedalus famously escaped from the Labyrinth of King Minos on Crete; first to Cumae in Campania, then to Sicily, where he killed the pursuing Cretan king. Things did not work out so well in the Colosseum, where Daedalus was killed by an Italian bear (from Lucania, not Campania). In a story more familiar to contemporary readers, Daedalus also made wings for his son Icarus, who flew too near the sun. When the wax holding his wings together melted he fell to his death in the Aegean Sea. As Icarus flew into a show, the stage machinery failed and he crashed into the sand close to the imperial box, splattering Nero with blood.

Orpheus, whose impatience had condemned his wife Eurydice to return to the Underworld, moved animals, trees and rocks with his music, but not some Thracian women, who tore him limb from limb, and threw his still-singing head into the River Hebrus. In the arena, trees and rocks moved towards Orpheus, birds flew above his head and animals gathered round his feet. But here his wife released an 'ungrateful bear' from a trapdoor, which enacted a fatal revenge on the husband who had failed her.

Very occasionally, things turned out better in the arena than in the myth. The hero Leander drowned in a storm swimming the Hellespont to visit his lover Hero. When recreated in the Colosseum, Leander was spared.

These myths were common currency for rich and poor, educated and uneducated, alike in ancient Rome. Despite the unexpected survival of the condemned man playing Leander, these spectacular executions reinforced the gulf between the spectators, sitting in their hierarchic social order, in the dress appropriate to their rank, and the bizarrely clad outsiders being subjected to extraordinary suffering and death down in the ring. They were a visceral warning against transgression: 'If you break the law and are cast out of society, you will find yourself out there on the other side of the podium wall, experiencing terror and pain comparable to – perhaps exceeding – that of characters from myth.'

An anecdote from fiction opens other avenues of interpretation. A man sold the wife of the emperor Gallienus fake jewels. The emperor discovered the fraud and had the jeweller condemned to the beasts. A cage, like that containing a lion, was brought out. The cage was opened . . . and a capon emerged. Gallienus had a herald announce, 'He practised deceit, then had it practised on him', and sent the man home.

Of course, it is all made up; a product of the inventive stylus of the author of the *Augustan History*. But it points to an often overlooked element of the arena. Spectacular executions were meant to be funny. Men running here and there, rolling on the sands, trying to put out the flames of the 'tunic of torment' were a cause for laughter, according to the Christian Tertullian. What good did Icarus' wings do as he crashed to his death? Watching Icarus' father mangled by a bear amused Martial – how Daedalus wished he still had wings! Then there was the myth of Leander. How was it staged? Let's leave aside the irreconcilable differences between ancient writers, who said that the Colosseum could be filled with water, then drained, and modern engineers, who say that both actions were impossible. Even if all the floor of the Colosseum could be flooded (highly likely before the sub-structure was dug?), it is less than eighty-four yards long (76.96 metres to be exact). It would take an average swimmer a lot of laps to be in any danger of drowning – a tedious spectacle. Something was needed to add jeopardy. Maybe some hydrological device to simulate a storm? Martial says Leander was spared by 'Caesar's wave'. Modern thinking has other suggestions. Leander was burdened with weights, or crocodiles were released into the water. Everyone to whom I have mentioned the last possibility has laughed.

Very few of the enactments of myths end like the originals. Orpheus is killed by a bear, not ecstatic women. Prometheus is attacked by a bear, not an eagle. It created an air of uncertainty and suspense. What wild beast is going to be released into the arena? Lucius the ass had no idea. How is the condemned going to die? Indeed, are they going to die at all? Or will they, too, be saved by Caesar's wave? Some reenactments of the past were about mutilation, but not necessarily death. Like the god Attis, a man in the arena castrated himself; Tertullian found this funny too. Another played the unique role of a famous figure from Roman history. Captured by the Etruscans, Mucius Scaevola demonstrated his indifference to torture by voluntarily thrusting his right hand into a fire. There was even a chance of surviving the 'tunic of torment'. Tertullian tells us that a volunteer took money to wear it for a certain distance.

The past was summoned up in the arena. As Martial put it, fables were made real. They were not just given flesh and blood – lots of blood – they were altered. The 'fatal charades' not only combined humour with graphic warnings against social deviancy, they demonstrated the god-like power of the emperor and the empire. Just as the exotic animals in the morning beast-hunts signified Rome's power over geography, the mythical executions at midday symbolised its mastery over time itself: the emperor, and those he allowed to hold Games, could rewrite the past.

The uncertain outcomes of the 'fatal charades' suggest an explanation of why the condemned played along. Certainly, there was coercion, although it is sometimes hard to think of a worse fate with which they could have been threatened. Equally, there would be the fatalism that stops the victims of mass executions running or fighting back. But there was also Pandora's terrible gift to humanity – when she opened the jar, all the evils flew into the world, but hope remained.

Picture Orpheus in the arena. Trees and rocks move towards him. Birds fly above his head. A throng of animals gathers at his feet. As he plays the lyre and sings, he does not know what will happen. He looks round wildly. Which of these beasts are fierce, which tame? He knows he has not pulled a thorn out of a lion's paw, like Androcles. Perhaps, like Gallienus' capon, they are all harmless. Even if they do have sharp teeth and claws, maybe the savage beasts will not attack. Maybe they will just maul him. If he plays his part well enough, he might be pardoned.

Then a trapdoor yawns open. He sees a woman dressed as Eurydice, and something else . . .

Christians to the Lion!

For Christians the Colosseum is where thousands died for their faith. Modern archaeologists have stripped out most of the memorials later erected by the church, but if you look carefully you can still spot the odd crucifix. No genuine evidence locates a single martyr in the Colosseum. This does not mean it did not happen. We know about plenty of Christians killed in other arenas. It is merely a salutary reminder of the patchiness of our evidence. When it comes to the numbers of Christians executed, as with the number of common or garden criminals, or the total number of gladiators in the empire, we do not have the materials to form trustworthy estimates. It was certainly in the interests of Christian writers to inflate the numbers. In AD212 Tertullian tried to persuade the governor of Africa not to persecute Christians with the highly unlikely claim that when Arrius Antoninus had done the same, some twenty years earlier in Asia, his court had been overwhelmed by their numbers. In another work, the *Apologia*, Tertullian mocked the traditional shout of the pagan crowd, 'Christians to the lion!' – 'What, all of them to one lion?'

Christians, as we have seen, were regarded as atheists because they denied the existence of the pagan gods, and thus posed an existential threat to the very safety of the empire. Also, their attention-seeking intransigence was infuriating. After his arrest in Lyons the Christian Sanctus was asked the standard questions, 'but would not tell them his name, race, place of origin, whether he was a slave or free'. Always the same maddening answer: 'I am a Christian!'

Yet Christians were different from others executed at the Games in two ways. First, as an identifiable and loathed group, their identity was clearly proclaimed. In Lyons, Attalus was led round the arena behind a placard reading, 'This is Attalus, the Christian'. At Catania in Sicily another martyr had the Gospels fastened round his neck, while a herald announced, 'Behold Euplius the Christian, an enemy of our emperors, and your gods!' The same was not always the case with run-of-the mill executions, where the crimes might not be so well advertised. In Lucian's *Toxaris*, when men in chains had dogs loosed on them, the heroes 'conjectured they were criminals'. Likewise, when the body of the convict playing Laureolus/Prometheus was mangled by a bear, Martial considered it a 'deserved punishment; doubtless he was a slave who had killed his master, or temple robber, or an arsonist'.

The thing that really made Christians stand out from murders, arsonists and the like, was that they did not have to be there. Christianity was a deniable crime. In Martyr Act after Martyr Act the put-upon Roman governor alternately threatens and pleads with the defendant to show some token acknowledgment of the pagan gods; saying something like: 'Have pity on yourself; just offer a pinch of incense; just say the words, you don't have to mean them, just say them with your lips, not in your heart.' Again and again the governor grants them days to consider their response. But, in the Martyr Acts, if not always in reality, the answer was always the same: 'I am a Christian!'

Sexual Executions

In Apuleius' *The Golden Ass,* the murderess was to be subjected to bestial rape, before being mauled to death by a wild animal in the arena. The scene is so ghastly and shocking we are tempted to ascribe it to the overheated imagination of the novelist. But that might be a mistake. At a show in the reign of Nero, many of the spectators believed that a woman playing the role of Pasiphaë, hidden in a wooden replica of a heifer, was penetrated by a bull. Suetonius, who records the incident, was unsure. Things had got more certain by the reign of Titus. The audience saw the bull mount Pasiphaë. Martial was an eyewitness: the fable had become real. A series of cheap clay lamps discovered in Athens, depicting women being penetrated or mauled by an ass, have been interpreted as souvenirs of the Games. Above anything, we are reminded that the Romans were not, as they are in so many bad historical novels, 'just like us'.

The hideous, sexual executions of these women, it has been suggested, were designed to re-establish gender boundaries: the woman had transgressed her role as a female by committing murder, or whatever crime, and so was put back in her place by suffering such degradation. But this might be to import a modern concept into an ancient culture. Both men and women were usually executed either naked or semi-naked, or sometimes in fancy dress. Men were subjected to sexual punishment: Attis had to castrate himself in the arena. According to rumour, Nero observed gender equality in his private versions of sexual executions. Dressed in the skins of wild beasts, he would savage the genitals of both men and women who had been tied to posts.

10

Tempus Postmeridianum (Afternoon)

The afternoon is the highlight of the day. It is the time of the gladiator. Where has he been waiting since the Pompa *at first light? Most probably he has seen nothing, just heard the yells of the crowd, the roar of wild beasts and snatches of music, all of which have echoed down to the secure cell in which he has been held underground. Finally, he is led out into the blinding light of the arena. Combat is not a savage free-for-all. He has no choice who he fights. A pair of gladiators are matched against each other. Before the contest a branch of palm is set up to await the victor. Given the numbers involved in imperial Games, and the sheer size of the Colosseum, it is likely that more than one pair fight at once. The trumpets blare. Time for a few last words . . .*

Last Words and Arrangements

'If I win, Toxaris, we shall go away together, with all that we need; but if I fall, bury me and go back to Scythia.' These were the last words of Sisinnes in the arena at Amastris. 'I have lived long enough,' a poor young volunteer in another arena said to the friend he had replaced on the sand. Just two words in Latin (*satis vixi*), concise and powerful, but there was time for more: an explanation of why he was there, a last kiss through his visor, and a second valedictory. 'By this my last glimpse of the light, by the celebrated sincerity of our love, do not let my father have to beg; sustain him, help him, give him your affection; if I merit it, be my substitute in caring for him.'

Of course, none of these words were actually spoken by gladiators. They were imagined by elite writers. Yet Rome was a culture that put a high value on last words, as well as brief, well-turned phrases delivered at moments of crisis. Julius Caesar was the master: 'The die is cast', when crossing the Rubicon; 'And you, my child', at seeing Brutus among the assassins. Gladiators were part of this culture, as we will see; they spoke laconic words, freighted with meaning, from beyond the grave.

Gladiatorial combat was not a wild scrum, like the mêlée in a medieval tourney. Two gladiators were matched in a duel. The pairings could be advertised in advance. At Pompeii the poster for the forthcoming show of Marcus Mesonius listed the names of each pair, their type of equipment, their victories, and noted those that came from one of the prestigious schools owned by the emperor. After the event, another hand added the results; a sign of the popularity of the Games. Other posters at Pompeii just give the number of different pairs that would be fighting. The match-ups might be made on the day. We find Commodus making matches out on the sand, and Titus in the imperial box responding to the demands of the crowd. We have a hint that the crowd were often active in this regard. When Commodus himself fought, sometimes it was an opponent he had challenged, sometimes one chosen by the spectators; 'for in this', Cassius Dio says, 'he put himself on an equal footing with other gladiators.' Sometimes the pairings were decided by lot, although we imagine the biggest names would be held back for the finale. The emperor, or the giver of the Games with imperial permission, was in control of the day. Novelty was as appreciated in the running order and the pairings, as in every other aspect of the show.

The narrator in Pseudo-Quintilian's fiction complains of the unfairness of the bout. The crowd pitied him. As a novice pitched against a veteran, there could be only one outcome – his death. Normally the *palus* ranking system prevented such mismatches. Seneca claims a gladiator thought it ignominious to be set against an inferior, 'as he knows it is without glory to defeat an opponent without danger'. Although the observation of an outsider, it reflects a reality. Fighting those of a comparable or higher status brought greater prizes, advancement in the rankings, and more glory, perhaps even discharge from the gladiatorial school. If, of course, you won . . .

Types of Gladiators

Gladiators, unlike beast-fighters, were divided into very different types. There were those with 'big shields' (*scutarii*), and those with small (*parmularii*). Joyless as ever, Marcus Aurelius was glad he had never been a fan of either. Within these broad categories there was a bewildering array of specific armaments. Painstaking modern research has identified the main types. The results are tabulated in **Plate Seventeen**. Some are well known today: the *murmillo* with his big, crested and visored helmet, large rectangular shield and short sword, wearing a greave on his left leg; the *Thraex*, again with a visored and crested helmet (the latter often featuring a griffon), but carrying a small shield, curved sword, and with greaves on both legs; above all the *Retiarius*, without helmet or shield, wearing armour only on his left arm, and using a trident and net. Others are more obscure: the *Hoplomachus*, with a large, visored helmet, greaves on both legs, fighting with a spear and small, round shield; or the *Eques*, fighting on horseback, at least initially, wielding one or more javelins and a small, round shield.

The research proceeds by matching literary descriptions, less often archaeological artefacts, with visual images. Those images that have an inscription naming the type provide the starting point. Where there is no inscription, however, the methodology can lead to misplaced certainty. For instance, an image of a gladiator with a short, curved sword is always identified as a *Thraex*. But this assumes that all Thracian gladiators always used such a sword, and that it was never used by any other type. Again, the *Laquerarius*, who was equipped with a lasso, is thought to have been identical to a *Retarius*, except the latter had a net. Yet it is estimated that 90 per cent of images identified as *Retiarii* do not depict a net. Some types mentioned in literary sources, such as the *Dimachaerus*, who fought with no shield and a sword in each hand, or the *Manii*, mentioned by a character in Petronius, have yet to be identified in the visual material. On the other hand, some images cannot be matched to descriptions in written sources. If we look at **Plate One**, we do not know what type is represented by the three figures, one group in from the right in the central register, who are taking a break. Equally, we have no idea about the two gladiators receiving the decision of the *editor* in **Plate Eighteen**.

The types of gladiators were not unchanging. The Samnites and Gauls of the Republic disappear from view under the principate, when the *Retiarius* emerges, along with the *Murmillo* and the *Secutor*. There is little to distinguish the last two; the only significant difference is the *Secutor*'s helmet, which had no plumed crest, and a visor with eye holes, not a grille. Both might be descended from the Samnite. Gladiators varied across the empire. The *Crupellarii*, so encased in armour that they were almost invulnerable, were a specialty of the Gallic provinces, as were the mysterious *Trinqui* mentioned in the attempt of Marcus Aurelius to fix the price of gladiators.

To add to the difficulties of interpretation, equipment could vary within a type of gladiator. The *Provocator*, to us a lesser-known type, differed from a *Murmillo* mainly in having an armoured plate that covered the upper part of his chest and a greave that extended up to the knee, which might imply a somewhat smaller shield. An inscription from Rome records a *Provocator* who fought with a *spatha*, a long cavalry sword, not the standard short *gladius*. Likewise diverging from the norm, a

Retiarius on a pottery relief from Gaul, instead of being almost naked, wears a helmet, body armour and greaves.

Finally, there is the issue of names of gladiators shifting from one type to another. A *Secutor* or *Murmillo* who fought a *Retiarius* was called a *Contraretiarius*. Perhaps the *Manii* in Petronius was a fan name for a type usually known by another designation?

While the broad outlines are fairly clear, dogma should be avoided when dealing with the various types of gladiators. The man giving the Games could alter the equipment of the combatants for a specific occasion. Julius Caesar kitted out those appearing in his Games with silver weapons. Caligula, out of preference for their opponents the Thracians, made the fight more dangerous for the *Murmillones* by making their armour lighter.

One type of gladiator, distinguished not by equipment but by sex, has attracted a lot of recent attention: women. Mainly the interpretations are up-beat: although rare, they were not a novelty act, but a serious contest; there was no prejudice against women fighting, just a social one against elite women in the arena; they were there to prove their courage (*virtus*); at the extreme, it is claimed some women entered the Games as an act of defiance, flouting gender expectations, to win 'fame and glory'. Most of this sits rather uneasily with the evidence.

Only one visual image of female gladiators survives, a relief sculpture from Halicarnassus (modern Bodrum in Turkey, **Plate Nineteen**). The two participants are named as Amazon and Achillia, the female form of Achilles; both are obviously stage names, and so neither are from an elite background (elites tended to use their real name; their status was part of the attraction). They are depicted fighting with the same equipment: large shields and short swords, their right arms protected by banded armour. Yet, as often in Roman art, time is elided – the fight continues but it is also over. They have taken off their helmets and put them on the ground (these have no crests; are the women *Provocatores*, *Secutores*, or something else?). Above them the inscription records that the contest was a draw; both have been granted a reprieve. We do not know who commissioned the relief, or where it was displayed. It is not a tombstone. There are two plausible suggestions. Either it was part of a larger, public monument, erected by the giver of a show, recording a remarkable moment in his Games, or it was put up in the gladiatorial school to which Amazon and Achillia belonged, commemorating a remarkable event in the history of the *familia*. Whichever, it was remarkable in two ways. First, it was rare for both fighters to be released from the sands, *stans missus*. Second – remember that this monument is unique – it was remarkable that the combatants were female.

There are a few, scattered references to female gladiators. In AD 19 a law banned females of senatorial and equestrian families from appearing in the arena, which implies some had done so previously. We hear of women fighting as gladiators or beast-hunters at imperial shows in Rome during the reigns of Nero, Titus and Domitian. The historian Cassius Dio heaved a sigh of relief that those women who entered the arena under Titus were not from the elite. Similarly, he approved when Septimius Severus forbade any woman, no matter what her origin, from fighting as a gladiator. As with many imperial laws, compliance may not have been absolute. On an inscription from Ostia, the port of Rome, that might postdate Severus' enactment, a local magnate called Hostilianus boasted that he was the first to exhibit women fighting 'since the founding of the city'. Given there had been half a millennium of gladiatorial combat, the proud boast – *Ab Urbe Condita!* – clearly indicates the extreme rarity of female gladiators.

Combat was highly gendered in Classical antiquity. Homer set the tone. In the *Iliad* Hector told his wife, 'let war be the care of man'. Part of the appeal of female gladiators was their very paradoxical nature. For the poet Statius they illustrated the emperor's command over human nature, geography and the past: 'The sex that is inexperienced and ignorant of steel stands like men in wicked combat; you would think them troupes of Thermodon in battle heat by the River Tanais or wild Phasis'; in other words, Amazons from the distant past who came from along the far shores of the Black Sea. For Martial they showed that the goddess Venus had joined the god Mars in serving Caesar.

There were other, less elevated, reasons to watch women on the sands. One was male titillation. Amazons traditionally went into battle with at least one breast exposed. Amazon and Achillia in Halicarnassus are topless, wearing only a loincloth. Christian moralists thundered against the sinful pleasures of watching naked female flesh at the Spectacles. For Saint John Chrysostom, it was the 'shipwreck of the soul'. The pagan Martial enjoyed the sight.

A final, equally lowbrow, motive comes into view if we think about others with body shapes unusual in the arena. Dwarfs occasionally fought in the arena. It is a popular misconception that dwarfs fought women. Although the two were sometimes on the same bill, dwarfs took on each other or animals. In Statius a 'bold string of midgets' appears after the Amazon-like women. First, they dealt each other wounds and threatened death – mock- gladiatorial combat or boxing? – then they were attacked by cranes, thus acting out the mythical battle between the birds and pygmies. How the audience laughed, the poet assures us. In paintings, pygmies fight hippos and crocodiles in the Nile; some are shown being eaten. Not recreated in the arena – presumably too one-sided. Once in a while, a very bad emperor was said to have rounded up the disabled. Caligula selected respectable family men of good reputation, who were conspicuous for some physical disability, for a mock fight. The result was far worse in the story we have already encountered of Commodus personally clubbing to death disabled men sewn into fish tails and armed with sponges. In art we find children, or *Erotes*, chubby toddlers with wings, fighting as gladiators or hunters in the arena, once even as condemned to the beasts. All were intended to be amusing.

A key attraction of watching female gladiators was the paradoxical spectacle of women displaying *virtus*, fighting with the courage of men. For some spectators, like Statius and Martial, it evoked the power of the emperor, and the empire, over nature, as well as over geography and time (Look at those Amazons from a farflung place in the distant past!). But there were baser attractions: the pleasure of viewing half-naked women, sweating and panting, and the licence for ribald humour and coarse laughter. The Romans did not share our sensibilities about gender or deformity. Like dwarfs and the disabled, female gladiators were considered funny. But, unlike the disabled, they were transgressively sexy. Look again at the girl with gladiatorial kit in **Plate Six**. Think about the responses of a Roman man viewing her – 'She is really fucking him [in both English senses: literal and metaphorical]! Imagine her riding you like that! Imagine "conquering" her; taking her in a more dominant position!' Unsurprisingly, there was a current of disapproval, a compound of the moral, political and social. The higher the status of the women the stronger it ran. Eventually the disapproval won. Septimius Severus banned women from the arena. We hear of no more female gladiators after Hostilius' show: perhaps Ostia only saw women in the arena once?

Female gladiators were so rare there was no name for them in Latin or Greek. *Gladiatrix* is a modern invention. In the Roman empire they were a novelty act that provoked a wide range of responses.

The Laws of the Fight

In a lawcourt a speaker lamented the death of his friend: if only his courage had been exhibited on the battlefield, not in the arena, where it was constrained by the 'laws of the fight' (*leges pugnandi*). We can find glimpses of these 'laws'.

On the Zliten mosaic (**Plate Five**) two men wear white tunics with purple stripes. One of them wields a long stick. These are the referees. There were two grades: the *Summa Rudis* and the *Secunda Rudis* (the 'chief' and 'second' stick). Usually only one is depicted officiating at each fight, as here. They were ex-gladiators. Almost always they are shown at the climax of the fight. They restrain the victor when his opponent has submitted and everyone waits for the life-or-death decision of the giver of the Games. On the Zliten mosaic one referee grabs the sword arm of the victor with both hands; the other shields the defeated with his stick. While this was the most dramatic function of the referees, there were others. They might use their sticks to drive forward reluctant fighters. They enforced the enigmatic 'laws' and perhaps coached the combatants during the duel. The sticks were wielded again if the combatants had not shown enough spirit. In the *Satyricon* a character recounts a disappointing show: 'they were all flogged afterwards; there were so many shouts from the crowd of *Give them what for!*'

Gladiators usually fought 'to the finger' (*ad digitum*). One combatant raised a finger to indicate defeat and to appeal for mercy, for the giver of the Games to release them from the fight (*missio*). There were other rituals indicating submission, which could be combined: dropping your weapon; taking off your helmet and placing it on the ground; putting down your shield; getting on your knees; perhaps clasping the knees of your opponent. Clear and obvious gestures were needed in the heat of the action. They were not always permitted. Some inscriptions explicitly record that gladiators fought 'for their life'. At the other extreme, Marcus Aurelius would only issue blunted weapons in the Games he gave in Rome. His reluctance was unusual, and it is a modern misunderstanding that he banned sharp weapons in shows given by others outside Rome. Those inscriptions that mention 'fights with sharp weapons' do not indicate that most were fought with blunted weapons; rather they boast that these Games were the 'real thing'. Some fights were advertised as *sine missione* ('without release'). It has been argued that this meant until one fighter was wounded, or incapacitated, but it is more likely that it meant to the death. If that was the case, when Augustus banned people from giving Games where combat was *sine missione*, his ruling did not outlast his reign. As we have seen with Amazon and Achillia, very occasionally both gladiators were granted *missio*.

Certain types of gladiators were customarily matched against certain other types. *Thraex* against *Murmillo* or *Hoplomachus*, and *Secutor* against *Retiarius*, were particularly popular pairings. Yet a gladiator might be called upon to fight any type, including his own. *Provocatores* usually fought other *provocatores*. The nature of their equipment meant that some types always had to take on their own sort. An *Essedarius*, who fought from a chariot, or an *Eques* on horseback would be at too great an advantage if he took on a pedestrian opponent. Modern commentators believe *Equites* dismounted at some point to finish their fight on foot, as that is how they are almost always depicted in art. A fresco from Pompeii depicts two mounted *Equites* in mid-fight. One is getting the worst of it; wounded in the thigh, he flees. His name is above his head: Spartaks. The language of the inscription is not Latin but the local Oscan; which suggests the painting may be early, perhaps before the great slave revolt of 73–1BC. But if it was produced afterwards, Spartaks was an ominous, and unique, stage name. Isidore of Seville, writing in the seventh century AD, long after gladiatorial combat was defunct but drawing on earlier authors, says the *Equites* were the opening combat – they entered the arena from opposite gates, preceded by military standards, wearing gilded helmets, carrying light weapons and mounted on white horses.

Certainly the *Anabata*, who fought blindfolded, or with a fully enclosed helmet, would have had no chance unless matched against someone equally handicapped. They were equipped with bells – how else would they have located each other over the noise of the crowd? A letter of Cicero shows this vicious version of blind man's buff was particularly funny: 'but enough of this joking'.

Each type of gladiator had a well-known and distinctive style of fighting. In *The Interpretation of Dreams*, Artemidorus expected his readers to accept that the *Thraex* always advances to attack, the gladiator in 'silver armour' gives ground, and the *Secutor* goes after his opponent. Dream of one of those, and that is the type of wife you will marry: respectively domineering, faithful and obedient, or a cause of no end of trouble. He thought his readers would find the fighting techniques of the other six types mentioned so obvious that there was no need to explain why a dream of a *Retiarius* meant your wife would be promiscuous, an *Eques* devoid of any sense, an *Essedarius* stupid, a *Provocator* flirtatious and randy, and either a *Dimaecherus* or an *Arbelas* a malicious witch.

Combat between trained gladiators was thought to have an expected rhythm, like music. The predictable thrust and parry were like the argument and counter-argument of schooled orators. The crowd knew the drills and could shout out advice. When done well, Cicero thought that the execution of the basic moves was graceful; 'whatever is useful for the combat is attractive to look upon'. When done badly, it degenerated into fighting by rote. In the story in the *Satyricon*, only one of the disappointing gladiators, a *Thraex*, fought with any spirit, but he too displayed no initiative. The *Thraex* was flogged along with the others.

What were the moves that the crowd knew? The 'first position' of a fight, for a gladiator armed with shield and sword, has been identified in a pose often repeated in art (**Plate Twenty**). The gladiator stands with his body half-turned to the left, feet well apart, left foot forward, looking over his left shoulder. His shield is tucked close into his body, his sword held underarm, low and well back, near to his side. He is braced against an attack, and protected by helmet, shield and the greave on his left leg. Equally, he is balanced, ready to transfer his weight and step off either foot in any direction, either to avoid or strike a blow, like a boxer.

What happened after the opening move, in the thrust and parry of the fight? Experimental archaeology, where modern reconstructions of original equipment are used to recreate combat, offers some answers. Most interestingly the shield can be used in a range of offensive moves: to open an enemy up for a blow by feinting or sweeping his weapons aside; to shove an opponent to the ground, or off-balance; to jab at the face with the front or edge. The sword is not employed as in fencing, to turn incoming blades, but reserved for attack. Following the theory of Vegetius, the thrust, which exposes less of the attacker, is preferred over the slash or cut. It is the work of a moment to shift from an underhand to an overhand grip to vary the angle of the thrust.

Although experimental archaeology makes much of its 'scientific' methods and 'unequivocal' results, such recreations actually tell us only what *could* have been done. There is no certainty. Those recreating the combats have not been trained in a Roman *Ludus* and are not fighting for their lives. It is a truism of studies of modern battle that equipment is not always used in the optimal way. Culture always trumps efficiency. In Papua New Guinea in the 1960s an anthropologist faced a moral dilemma. In the highly ritualised battles of the highland peoples some warriors used a bow and arrow. An individual ran forward, took a shot, and retreated. Few people got hit. It occurred to the anthropologist that bowmen are far more effective shooting a volley in a group. It is relatively easy to avoid a tennis ball that has been thrown at you, much harder to get out of the way of half a dozen. Humanely, and sticking to the principle of observing, not altering, the anthropologist kept his lethal advice to himself.

The Mind of the Gladiator

Polemo was a Sophist, and, like all such public display orators, he had an overwhelmingly high regard for himself and his art. When he encountered a gladiator sweating with terror before a fight to the death, Polemo heartlessly quipped, 'You are in as great an agony as though you were going to declaim.' A speaker in a fictional courtroom recounted waiting for his first fight. 'I thought of my ancestry, the brilliance of my fortune – once so illustrious – my liberal education, everything in the past that had been more honourable than that of the giver of the Games: house, family, friends, all the rest I would never see again.' He wondered what his nearest and dearest were doing, in complete ignorance of his fate. When a friend suddenly appeared, his senses failed him completely. It took some time before his vision returned and he could speak. Placidianus, the greatest gladiator ever according to the poet Lucilius, suffered from no flashbacks, or maudlin and debilitating thoughts. Instead, he visualised the course of the coming fight. 'This is the way I think it will happen – I will take his blows head on, before I thrust my sword in the stomach and lungs of that swine.' Placidianus did not intend to delay, he was: 'transported with anger, fed by my passion and hatred of him'. Yet the danger of fighting angry was widely recognised. As Seneca put it, 'skill protects gladiators, anger strips them naked'. The ideal was to be calm and controlled, to shut out all distraction, as the adage ran, 'the gladiator takes counsel in the sand'.

These emotions were imagined by elite writers who were never in any danger of appearing in the arena. We get closer to the mind of the gladiator if we turn to the epitaphs on their gravestones.

A tombstone, even if small, with poorly cut inscription and no visual image, costs money. It also implies buying in to Roman and Greek ways of thinking and doing things. And it shows the deceased is sufficiently embedded in society that there are those who would memorialise him. Tombstones represent gladiators with a certain level of integration and success, at least within their gladiatorial *familia*.

Gladiators were buried with their own kind at Ephesus, Nîmes and Salona. It may not have been their choice. Horatius Balbus, paying for a communal cemetery in his hometown of Sassina, specified certain undesirables were not to be buried there, among them volunteer gladiators. Yet even if enforced, gladiatorial cemeteries fostered a group identity among the living.

The primary identity displayed on tombstones was *gladiator*. Not just any gladiator, but a specific type. In Gaul and Spain, where tombstones tended not to display a visual image, an abbreviation of the gladiatorial type – for example TR for *Thraex* – was placed at the top of the stone in bigger letters than the rest of the inscription. The armature of a style became a key marker of identity. Take the opening words of a gladiator's epitaph from Rome:

M(arcus) Antonius Exochus
Thraex
Marcus Antonius
Exochus Nat(ione)
Alexandrinus

It is as if *Thraex* has become part of his name, an additional cognomen. Certainly, it is listed before his nationality – he was from Alexandria in Egypt.

The proclaimed identity was not just *Thraex*, or whatever type, it was 'skilled and successful fighter'. Tombstones listed the victories of the deceased, less often the times they had been spared, having received *missio*, either after a draw, or following a defeat. Sculptural reliefs of the palms and crowns they had won served the same function. Status within the *Ludus* – *primus* and *secundus palus* – was proudly flaunted. If the age at death was included, a high number also pointed to a skilled survivor. On the other hand, a low number evoked pathos – a cruel fate had cut short youthful potential.

The terrible irony of these portrayals of successful gladiators is that almost without exception they had been killed fighting in the arena. The two halves of the empire dealt with this differently. In the Latin West the final fight usually was ignored, edited out of the account. In the Greek East it was acknowledged. Yet the given cause was never lack of skill. Blame was always shifted to something else: illness, old age, tiredness, fate, a daemon, Nemesis, trickery, or just the sheer brute force of his opponent.

Gladiator was not the only identity carved in stone for eternity. The deceased often appear as husbands. The majority of tombstones were set up by women claiming to be the wives of the gladiators. Because they ranked as slaves, gladiators could not legally marry. This does not mean these memorialised fighters had been either free volunteers or freedmen. Instead, the tombstone was an attempt to claim a higher status than they were entitled in law. Other identities appear – the gladiator as son, brother, father and friend. The friendship was usually with other gladiators. But that is not always specified. Some gladiators had friends in the wider community beyond the *Ludus*. Inscriptions tell us about a *Collegium*, a club – partly to ensure burial of its members – dedicated to the god Silvanus. Its members included twenty-three gladiators, a maker of arm protection and a masseur. All these were part of the *Ludus*, but there were also seven *pagani*, best translated here as 'civilians', men from outside the arena. The two men who ran the club were a freedman of the emperor and a *Cryptiarius*, who looked after the *Crypt*, maybe the clubroom or the communal grave. The latter may have been part of the *Ludus*, the former was not. Gladiators are shown as the owners of pets; always dogs. Less endearing to us, they are also recorded as the owners of slaves.

The self-fashioning as a type of gladiator did not totally erase previous identities. Take the tombstone of a gladiator buried in Edessa (modern Urfa, in Turkey).

> I was called Meilesis, my civilian [paganos] name was Mestrianos. I fought five times and hurt no one. Now I have been hurt. And from her own funds . . . Alexandra erected this in memory of her husband. Farewell, all you who pass by.

Meilesis/Mestrianos was far from alone in continuing to use his original name in certain contexts. Likewise, Marcus Antonius Exochus – who came from Alexandria in Egypt, and who we recently met dead in Rome – was not in the least unusual in continuing to define himself throughout his life by his hometown. Fourteen tombstones of gladiators are known from Nîmes. Seven of them give the origins of the deceased. Three are local boys, from Gaul. The remaining four identify themselves as a Spaniard, a Greek, an Arab and another Alexandrian from Egypt. Gladiators were far better travelled than the vast majority of the inhabitants of the Roman empire.

Still, they were near the bottom of the social hierarchy, and they tried to identify themselves with groups higher up the pyramid. Again, there was a difference between the two halves of the empire. In the Latin West gladiators wanted to see themselves as soldiers. The larger barracks at Pompeii was decorated with paintings of traditional military-style trophies (captured arms and armour nailed to a post), but modified to include gladiatorial equipment. They called each other 'tentmates' (*contubernales*), or 'comrades-in-arms' (*coarmiones*), like soldiers. The man they fought (*pugnare*) was an 'enemy' (*hostis*). Their tombstones, with their bare enumeration of name, 'unit' and career, and their weapons and awards sculpted alongside or above them, were modelled on those of soldiers. Interestingly, outside the city of Rome, gladiatorial tombstones in this style are extremely rare in areas where large numbers of troops were stationed. It suggests that real soldiers – although they enjoyed watching contests in military amphitheatres, indeed some legions owned troupes of gladiators – were not receptive to these social inferiors appropriating their persona.

In the Greek East gladiators assimilated themselves to athletes.

> . . . you see me dead, traveller. My *paganos* name was Apollonius, my homeland was Apamea, but now in the lands of Nicomedia the threads and strings of Fate hold me down in the ground. Having won the contest [*agon*] in the stadia eight times, during the ninth fight [*pygme*] he gave up his fate. Joke and laugh, traveller, and know that you also must die.

We do not know what name Apollonius used as a gladiator; the beginning of the inscription is damaged. He says his victories were in the stadia. Some stadia were converted for gladiatorial fights, but its primary connotation was a venue for athletics. Likewise, he describes his combats as an *agon* or a *pygme*. The former was the standard word for an athletic contest, the latter for a boxing match. Greek gladiators referred to the man they were matched against as an *antipalos*, the term for an opponent in wrestling. Some called themselves 'Athletes of Ares [the god of war]', some went all the way, straightforwardly styling themselves as athletes.

Athletes in the Greek world were free young men from good families. They were far above the status of professional soldiers in the empire. Yet, unlike in the west, the gladiators' assimilation sometimes worked. A gladiator claims on his tombstone from Thessalonica, 'Conquering six times, I gained honour for my fatherland'. Sometimes, like athletes, they were honoured in cities other than their hometown.

> To the gods below. Aelia to Publius Aelius, the illustrious *Summa Rudis* from Pergamon, a member of the *Collegium* of *Summae Rudes* in Rome, to my own husband, happily joined to me in life, having lived thirty seven years, Aelia

> set this up in his memory; and he was a citizen of these cities in order: Thessalonica, Nicomedia, Larissa, Philippopolis, Apros, Berga, Thasos.

Nothing like this is found in the Latin West.

Gladiators in the east wanted to see themselves as athletes, and, like athletes, they went much further, attempting to equate themselves to the famous heroes of myth.

> Look at beautiful Miletus, beautiful to look at,
> The fighter who won eight times in the stadia,
> As beautiful as Adonis, son of Cinyras, when he was once out hunting,
> Or as the beautiful boy Hyacinthus, who was once struck by a discus.
> Now Fate has taken me by force from the ring
> And laid my body in the dear earth of Pamphylia.
> This marker my good friend Odysseus has set up here for me to be my tomb,
> In loving memory, to preserve my name.

That is one hell of an epitaph for a lowly *Retiarius*; a net and trident are depicted on the stone. Crafty Odysseus of Homer's epic poetry needed no introduction. The story of Miletus, who founded the city in Asia that carried his name, was more obscure. But it was a fitting stage name. In one version of the myth Miletus did not found the city, but re-founded it after sacking the settlement and putting all the men to the sword. Obscurity was not a problem for this text, which moves easily in the world of myth. Everyone had heard of Adonis and Hyacinthus; this text not only knew their stories, but even their genealogy: 'Adonis, son of Cinyras'. The crafty gladiator Odysseus, composing the epitaph in the hexameters of Epic, situated his friend and himself in the world of heroes, and staked a claim to high culture.

Miletus was 'beautiful' (*Kalos*, always an epithet of an athlete), as 'beautiful' as the desirable youths Adonis and Hyacinthus.

Together they formed a trinity: Adonis the most beautiful youth in the hunting field; Hyacinthus on the athletics track; and Miletus in the arena (although here he fights in the *stadia*). The repetitions of 'beautiful', the choice of comparisons with 'passive' lovers, and the 'yielding' nature of the *Retiarius*, together convey an erotic charge. It suggests that Odysseus was the older lover (the *erastes*), and Miletus the younger object of desire (the *eromenos*), an arrangement commendable in traditional Greek thought. The inscription can be read as documenting the tragic end of a love affair between two male gladiators.

Gladiators did not just equate themselves to the heroes of old, sometimes they claimed to have surpassed them. As on this tombstone from Alexandria Troas in Asia Minor:

> Traveller, you see me, Melanippus from Tarsis, who was bold in the stadia, a Retiarius of the second rank, dead. No longer do I hear the voice of the brazen trumpet, nor when competing do I raise the shrill of the unequal pipes. They say that Heracles completed twelve contests [*athla*], but I completed the same and finished with thirteen. Thallus and Zoe made this for Melanippus from their own funds in remembrance.

Again, this is a big claim for a second-rate *Retiarius*. But such hyperbole was accepted outside the gladiatorial *Ludus*. We have already seen the poet Martial in Rome comparing the beast-fighter Carpophorus to Theseus, Bellerophon, Jason, Perseus and Heracles. The latter only had twelve labours, Carpophorus vanquished twenty beasts at one time.

Gladiators presented themselves as men of traditional religious beliefs. Most of their tombstones begin 'To the Gods Below', *Dis Manibus*, often abbreviated to *DM*, or the Greek equivalents. This was completely formulaic. Almost everyone's tombstone, no matter who they were, started that way. Yet some argue that ritual formulas were the heart of Classical paganism. Public adherence to the traditional gods might have had an added point in the arena, where Christians and other religious deviants were executed for atheism and sacrilege. A gladiator might have been especially keen to publicise the soundness of his religious views, as sacrilege, in the form of tomb-robbing, was one of the crimes that might get a man convicted to fight in the arena.

Gladiators liked to see themselves as morally good. Often their tombstones say they were 'worthy', or 'well deserving' (*bene merenti*). This is a cliché, often cut down to *BM*, but who is to say that a cliché has less meaning than an original line. A far more arresting statement of goodness was that they were merciful. Marcus Antonius Exochus, *Thraex*, who we met a few moments ago, stated that he caused Fimbria, an opponent, to be spared (*missum fecit*). The life-or-death decision was the prerogative of the giver of the Games. Only once do we hear of it being delegated to a gladiator. The emperor Caracalla said to a defeated gladiator, 'I have no power to spare you', and handed the decision to the victor. Even in this unique example, the decision was not really that of the gladiator; for the victor, who was inclined to mercy, 'did not dare release him, fearing to appear more humane than the emperor'. What Exochus meant, when he claimed to have spared Fimbia, was that he could have killed him, but instead let him submit, and thus be granted a reprieve by the giver of the Games. This fits with tombstones on which gladiators claim to have 'saved' their opponents. An extreme form was Meilesis/Mestrianos (above), who fought five times, but stated that he 'hurt no one'. This was an ideal of Classical combat sports. The philosopher Dio Chrysostom wrote two works praising a young boxer who won every fight without ever hitting anyone. The floating like a butterfly apparently wore down his opponents without ever needing to sting like a bee! That many gladiators wanted to 'save' their opponents shows that for most of them the arena was about skilful victory, not mere slaughter.

Gladiators frequently spoke in the first person from beyond

the grave. Meilesis/Mestrianos, Apollonius and Melanippus, above all, talk directly to the viewers of their tombs. This was quite normal in funerary commemoration. It is usually thought that they were not composed by the deceased but by those left behind who erected the memorial. Yet perhaps we should not be so certain. Gladiators lived in a culture which put a high value on last words, and their profession meant they might be needed at any moment. Quite likely some gladiators left instructions about what they wanted on their tombs. Either way, the tombstones were put up in the vast majority of cases by the widows or gladiator friends of the dead. Both lived within the *Ludus*. Here we are as close as we can get to the mind of the gladiator.

The very quality of mercy on which gladiators prided themselves sometimes caused their death. Take the tombstone of the gladiator Diodorus. On the marble relief, Diodorus stands over his opponent, who has dropped his shield and helmet and raises a hand in submission. Diodorus holds a sword in each hand; his own, and that taken from his foe. He has also discarded his shield and helmet. There is a palm branch behind Diodorus. They were set up in the arena; perhaps Diodorus has already claimed it. He believes he has won. But that is not what happened.

> Here I lie victorious, Diodorus the wretched. After breaking my opponent Demetrius, I did not kill him immediately. But murderous Fate and the cunning treachery of the referee [*Summa Rudis*] killed me, and, leaving the light, I have gone to Hades. I lie in the land of the original inhabitants. A good friend buried me here because of his piety.

The referee, not accepting the submission, ordered Diodorus to give back Demetrius' sword. The fight resumed and Diodorus was killed.

Something similar lies behind the rare murderous last words of the *Secutor* Urbicus: 'I advise that he who defeats a man should kill him.' In a previous bout, Urbicus could have killed his opponent, but let him submit and be granted mercy. In a rematch the same opponent killed Urbicus.

Another gladiator sought and gained revenge from beyond the grave (obviously he did not compose his own epitaph).

> Victor, a left-handed gladiator, lies here, though my fatherland is Thessalonica. A daemon killed me, not perjured Pinnas, who boasts no longer. My companion-in-arms Polynices avenged me by killing Pinnas. Claudius Thallus built this memorial from the estate of Victor.

Some gladiators broke the 'laws of the fight'. Even in a contest 'to the finger', they fought to kill, like the great Placidianus in the poem of Lucilius ('I will take his blows head on, before I thrust my sword in the stomach and lungs of that swine').

The gladiator talks to us directly, sometimes with an enigmatic, haunting beauty – 'Find your own star, I advise you all; don't put your trust in Nemesis, that is how I was deceived' – and we feel we know the mind of the gladiator.

Mass Combat

The gladiator takes counsel in the sand – he had no choice, because almost always he fought on his own. First and foremost, gladiatorial combat was a duel between two men. Usually only one pair at a time appeared in the arena. In a show put on at Pompeii by a father and son, thirty pairs fought over five days: an average of six matches a day. That was quite a large show for most towns. In Games given by the emperor the numbers of gladiators involved, and the limited time available, meant that more were on the sand at once. At Trajan's Games celebrating the conquest of Dacia, 10,000 gladiators fought over 123 days. If each gladiator fought only once, that would have been 5,000 matches at an average of over forty fights a day. Actually, we know of a gladiator who fought at least three times in Trajan's Games, so the daily number was even higher.

A bout lasted no longer than ten minutes to quarter of an hour, perhaps twenty minutes at the very outside. Modern studies show that is the maximum time a man in combat can maintain the necessary level of intense physical activity. Ancient battles had a rhythm: brief bursts of fighting interspersed with pauses while the combatants got their breath back and somehow steeled themselves to resume the fight. Each duel in the arena might have been quite short, but several pairs would have had to fight at once to get through the numbers at Trajan's show. Anyway, a single pair might have seemed rather lost in the sheer expanse of the Colosseum.

Some emperors staged mass combats between groups of fighters. They could be on land or water. The latter, known as *Naumchiae*, were held on lakes, as we have already seen. These lakes were manmade or natural, or even in amphitheatres flooded for the occasion, and featured scaled-down warships. Land battles and *Naumachiae* could be part of the same show and are best treated together. These vastly expensive entertainments, involving hundreds, sometimes thousands, of participants were very rare. They were only ever held for a special occasion; as part of a triumph, like that of Julius Caesar in 46BC, or Domitian over the Dacians, or to celebrate the dedication of a major building or engineering project, such as Augustus' Temple of Mars Ultor, Claudius' draining of the Fucine Lake, or the Flavians' Colosseum. In AD248 Philip the Arab is said to have held a naval battle to commemorate the thousandth anniversary of the founding of Rome.

Although often repeated, the modern assertion that these events were mass executions where everyone was killed is misconceived. As we have seen, no battle in history ever achieved, or could have achieved, 100 per cent casualties on both sides. The participants were criminals and prisoners of war, but so were ordinary gladiators. No ancient writer states that everyone died, and their narratives demonstrate the opposite. At Claudius' *Naumachia* on the Fucine Lake, after the combatants were prompted to fight with spirit, the survivors were spared. When a storm hit, Domitian insisted his *Naumachia* continue, which resulted in 'practically all the participants, and many of the spectators' perishing. Evidently not the expected outcome.

The mass combats were set in the distant past, before the rise of the Roman empire. Some were historical battles. Augustus and Nero exhibited Athenians against Persians, probably refighting the Battle of Salamis (480BC). Titus staged Corinth against Corcyra (433BC) and Athens against Syracuse (414–413BC); both famous from Thucydides' *History of the Peloponnesian War*. Other mass combats were alternative history, pitching against each other ancient peoples who never fought in reality. Julius Caesar displayed Tyre against Egypt, and Claudius Sicily against Rhodes.

The creative reworking of history in the arena was paralleled by depictions of battles in Greek novels written under the Roman empire. These were either set in the Classical Greek past, before the conquest by Rome (such as Longus' *Daphnis and Chloe*), or in an alternative history (such as the anonymously authored *The Story of Apollonius King of Tyre*). The latter could include an alternative contemporary Greek world where the Roman empire did not exist (Achilles Tatius, *Leucippe and Clitophon*). As in the arena, the battle scenes in the novels might feature genuine historical opponents (Persians and Egyptians in Chariton's *Chareas and Callirhoe*), or peoples who did not fight in history (Aethiopians against Persians in Heliodorus' *Aethiopika*, and Greeks in Egyptian service against Tyre in Chariton). The Greek novels ignoring, or writing out of existence, the Roman empire had an ideological point. It both recreated the ancient glories of Greece and paraded supposed eternal Greek virtues, which allowed contemporary Greek elite readers to feel better about their lack of political autonomy under Roman rule.

The battles in the arena likewise had an ideological point. All those mighty peoples of the past (Athenians, Egyptians, Tyrians, and so on, even, at a pinch in Roman eyes, Persians) had been conquered by Rome. Now, no longer a threat, their martial qualities were summoned up for the amusement and edification of the Roman crowd. Rome not only ruled the present, it controlled the past.

The outcome of arena battles was not scripted. Sometimes they followed history – the Athenians defeated the Persians – sometimes the result was reversed – the Athenians were victorious at Syracuse. Far from posing a problem, it illustrated how Rome could even alter history.

The uncertain result of an arena mass combat – either side could win – explains the extreme rarity of anyone playing the Romans. On the few occasions Romans did appear the event was different from normal in one of two ways. They were either harmless or fixed.

In the late fourth century AD, Ausonius, an intellectual and politician from Gaul, wrote a poem in which he compared a spectacle he had seen on the River Moselle to two *Naumachiae* staged in Italy. In the Bay of Cumae the famous Battle of Actium, in which the future emperor Augustus defeated Antony and Cleopatra in 31BC, was enacted. On Lake Avernus the less well-known Battle of Mylae, where Agrippa, Augustus' general, was victorious over Demochares, the admiral of Sextus Pompey, in 36BC, was recreated. Ausonius makes it clear that these 'harmless clashes between ships' were 'playful engagements' in which no one was hurt and the right side won. Ausonius' poem helps us understand one written centuries earlier by Horace. 'Although careful to avoid anything tasteless or foolish', according to Horace, the recipient of the poem, a man called Lollius, and his brother, used their slaves to stage Actium on a lake on their father's estate. While fought with 'appropriate hostility', it was just 'having some fun'. Again, a scripted battle, without casualties, and an outcome that matched historical reality. For Lollius and his brother, a result where Augustus lost Actium would not have been just 'tasteless and foolish', it would have been exceedingly dangerous.

Only twice do we hear of Romans represented in mass gladiatorial combat that featured real fighting. Both occasions are extraordinary. In 40BC, during a civil war, Sextus Pompey was camped at Messana in the north-eastern tip of Sicily. On the Italian mainland opposite, Salvidienus Rufus, commanding the troops of Augustus, had been building a makeshift fleet of leather boats for an invasion of the island. Using prisoners captured from the other side, Sextus Pompey staged a *Naumachia* on the straits in full view of both forces. Those fighting as the Pompeians were equipped with small wooden warships; their opponents were given leather boats. Cassius Dio, who records the incident, does not need to tell his readers the result.

After the invasion of Britain (AD43), Claudius, in military costume, presided over the storming of a native town (possibly Colchester) on the Campus Martius in Rome. The sack was partly choreographed. Some kings who had surrendered in Britain were kept out of harm's way so that they could surrender all over again in Rome when the model town representing their home fell. But the fighting was real. British prisoners played themselves as the defenders, looking suitably hairy and barbaric. The 'Roman' attackers were probably professional gladiators. British tribesmen were too hairy and barbaric for the role, and any casualties among genuine Roman soldiers would have been unacceptable. Obviously, the right result was essential. The Romans might have vastly outnumbered the Britons. Not very heroic to our mind, but to a contemporary audience this would symbolise the overwhelming might of Rome. Or, as in Sextus Pompey's *Naumachia*, the side destined to lose had inferior weaponry: the Britons perhaps armed with wooden swords, the Romans with steel. Again, not at all 'fair' to our way of thinking, but, as mentioned previously, an audience in the Colosseum watched Commodus club to death disabled victims who were armed with 'rocks' made of sponge.

The arena had been a different theatre of history before the introduction of mass battles, probably by Julius Caesar in 46 BC. Under the Republic some types of gladiators were named after the defeated foes of Rome: the Samnite, Gaul and Thracian, perhaps also the *Hoplomachus*, a loan word from the Greeks. By the first century AD we no longer hear of the Samnite and Gaul. It has been suggested that they were no longer suitable names for gladiators, as the inhabitants of Samnium and Gaul had become integrated into the empire. Yet this does not explain the persistence of the *Thraex* and *Hoplomachus*, when Thracians and Greeks were also integrated, the Greeks perhaps more than any other people. Some changes in the fashions of the Amphitheatre defy easy explanation.

The first emperor Augustus professionalised the Roman army. No longer a citizen militia, theoretically called up for the duration of one campaign (although some campaigns stretched over years), soldiers now signed on for a fixed term of long service with the eagles. Over the first century AD the vast majority of army units were stationed in permanent camps along the frontiers. These developments inspired a new conception of the shape and nature of the empire, mainly expressed by Greek intellectuals like the sophist Aelius Aristides and the historian Herodian. The empire was imagined as an armed camp, ringed by walls and soldiers. Outside was barbarity, inside civilisation. The Colosseum offered the same image, but reversed. In the middle of the circle, down on the sands, were barbarians, or those reduced to the same outsider status. They were ringed by walls and Roman soldiers. Encircling them was civilisation: Roman society in formal attire and seated in order.

This powerful new image was not just for Roman consumption. Numerous anecdotes attest the presence at the Spectacles of delegations, not just from provincials, but from peoples outside the empire. We have seen the naïve envoys of the Frisians moving down the theatre to take more honourable seats. What race was so distant, or so barbarous, Martial asked, that it did not have spectators in the Colosseum? They came from everywhere, from within and beyond the frontiers: Thracians, Sarmatians, Egyptians, Britons, Arabs, Sabaeans (a sub-group of Arabs), Cilicians, Sygambrians (Germans) and Aethiopians. Martial assures us they spoke different languages, but all hailed the emperor as Father. Seated in areas of the stands designated by the Romans, these barbarians could not have avoided the message that their current place in the order of the world was contingent, and that the alternative to obedience was being demonstrated out in the middle. On one occasion the message was made explicit. The Dacians, who lived by the Danube, sent envoys to Augustus but sided with Antony in the civil war. Subsequently some of them were captured. In 29BC they were exhibited in the arena, fighting a mass battle against another enemy of Rome, the Suebi, whose territories were beyond the Rhine. With such distant homelands, they could never have fought each other when free. But such was the power of Rome that they could be enslaved, brought to the centre of the empire, and made to kill each other for the enjoyment and instruction of the crowd.

Which leaves the gladiators called *Gregarii*, who Marcus Aurelius in his edict fixing the prices of gladiators decreed should henceforth make up half the number of combatants in all Games. They were low-price gladiators, costing between 1,000 and 2,000 sesterces; the highest limit in the edict was 15,000 sesterces. Their name, which means belonging to a herd (from which derives the English adjective gregarious), implies they fought in a group. This is confirmed in the edict, where they are defined as fighting under a standard (*sub signo*). The problem is that they are hardly ever mentioned anywhere else.

We might imagine that members of the local elites, who copied the emperor's hairstyle, manner of speaking and way of walking, also imitated him by staging cut-down versions of mass combats. These, it would be necessary to assume, were beneath the notice of historians and also not worth commemorating on inscriptions honouring local dignitaries who had given Games. None of which is very convincing.

Another explanation can be offered. In the AD 160s, Rome suffered a double blow: the Marcomannic Wars against a dangerous coalition of tribes on the northern frontier (AD 165–180), and the roughly contemporaneous Antonine plague, which ravaged the whole empire. Short of manpower, Marcus Aurelius conscripted gladiators into the Roman army. This led to a rise in the cost of gladiators, which prompted the price-fix legislation. To take this argument further, not only would the Marcomannic Wars curtail the supply of regular gladiators, they would also provide a potential source of replacements. Were the mysterious *Gregarii* of the edict tribesmen captured in the northern wars?

Conscripting gladiators into the army was always going to be a temporary measure. Although they liked to see themselves as soldiers, there was a paradox about gladiators and the army. It was commonly thought that a gladiator possessed more individual skill at arms than a legionary. In 105 BC the consul Publius Rutilius summoned trainers from a gladiatorial school to instruct his troops. But on the few occasions gladiators were drafted into a real battle, their performance was unimpressive. The heavily armoured Gallic gladiators called *Crupellarii*, fighting for the rebel Sacrovir in AD 21, only briefly delayed the Roman troops, who soon hacked them down with axes and picks, or knocked them over with poles and pitchforks, 'leaving them lying like the dead, without any attempt to get up again'. After an initial success in a surprise raid in the civil wars of AD 69, the gladiators fighting on the side of Otho lost their next fight because of ill-discipline and fear. They then mutinied and tried to murder their commander.

The paradox – gladiators' individually skilful, but ineffective in groups – is more apparent to us than it would have been to the Romans. It was accepted that some barbarians, such as Gauls, were bigger and stronger, and better at one-to-one combat, than Roman soldiers. Yet it was always thought that they would be defeated by Romans in an open pitched battle, because as a group they lacked the essential Roman virtue of *Disciplina*. It was the same with gladiators.

Commodus, the son who succeeded Marcus Aurelius, ended the Marcomannic Wars. Gladiators ceased to be drafted into the army. Equally the large-scale supply of prisoners of war ended. *Gregarii* probably reverted to their original status as B-list gladiators who fought in a group because of lack of individual skill, and who were occasionally deployed to bulk up a show. They became again what they had been when glimpsed earlier, in the reign of Caligula. Once five *Retiarii*, fighting as a group, as *Gregarii*, submitted to five *Secutores* without putting up any resistance. When they were ordered to be killed, one of the *Retiarii* snatched up his trident and slaughtered all the *Secutores*. Rather than praising the feat of arms, Caligula condemned the 'cruellest murder' and denounced those who could watch such a spectacle. The *Retiarius* had breached the conventions of defeat and death in the arena.

Defeat, Death and Victory

The defeated gladiator awaits the decision on the sand. Helmet, shield and sword lie around him. He has discarded those parts of his identity, but there is one thing he must cling to – his courage.

The man giving the Games will decide the gladiator's fate: life or death. The *editor* is pulled in different ways. If his decision is death, and he owns the gladiator, it will be a financial loss. Even if he has hired him, the loss is the same, as he will have to pay fifty times the cost of renting him. It makes economic sense to spare the gladiator, to grant him *missio*. On the other hand, deciding on death might win the favour of the spectators, as it will show his open-handed generosity.

The *editor* has the final decision, but he is expected to heed the opinion of the crowd. He can ignore its wishes, although that would undercut the purpose of giving Games – winning popular acclaim. The spectators make their opinion known. They wave handkerchiefs, and shake the folds of their togas if they want the defeated gladiator spared. If they want him killed, they gesture with their thumbs (we will come back to this gesture in a moment). The crowd chant: 'Spare them! Spare them!' (*Missos! Missos!*), or 'Throat! Throat!' (*Iugula! Iugula!*). The *editor* has more room for manoeuvre, or perhaps a trickier choice, if the opinion of the crowd is divided. A character in Petronius predicts a quarrel over a man condemned to the beasts. Sometimes the same must have been the case over gladiators.

The gladiator has known from the start the importance of getting the crowd on his side. Courage and skill are essential. A star of the arena, maybe also a journeyman veteran who has survived a few fights, has some residual goodwill. Showmanship helps – stylish interaction with both his opponent, and those in the stands. A *Retiarius*, with his fisherman's net and trident, taunted his opponent: 'I do not attack you, I attack a fish. Why do you flee from me, Gaul?' Sheer endurance has a high value: 'Among the most courageous gladiators, one suppresses any sign of his wounds and stands his ground; another, addressing the clamouring crowd, signifies it is nothing and permits no intercession.' Perhaps it is not too late, even after submitting, to make a good impression. Some gladiators plead for their lives, with tears, prayers and protestations. It is counterproductive, provoking disgust. As Cicero explained, 'we are accustomed to dislike those who are timid and suppliant, and who pray to be allowed to live'. Far better to remain quiet, stay where you are and send an attendant to wait below the box of the *editor* for the verdict. Calm fortitude in the face of death may yet win a reprieve. 'In the savage arena, although the crowd threatens with a hostile thumb, the defeated gladiator has hope.'

All eyes are on the box of the giver of the Games. Music

heightens the drama, adds to the reverberating noise. The sign needs to be clear and unambiguous. Everyone waits on a hand gesture. Among scholars it is almost an orthodoxy that the modern popular belief that thumb down meant death, and up meant life, is the wrong way round. The certainty is misplaced. Ancient sources tell us the thumb turned, but not which way. Sometimes the assertion that up meant death is supported by a claim that this was the direction of the killing blow: up into the throat. But, as we will see in a moment, this appears to be totally wrong. There is no good reason to believe that thumb down did not mean death. The gesture to grant life was more complex than a simple thumbs-up. On the gladiator relief from Munich (**Plate Eighteen**) a hand emerges from the musicians. It is either the disembodied hand of the *editor* (usually he is off screen in visual images), or his gesture repeated by one of the trumpeters. The thumb is turned upwards, the first two fingers extended straight out. We recognise it as the Christian sign of benediction. That might be hugely important, and we will return to it in the last Chapter. Here it signifies *missio*, life.

The thumb turns: *missio*. The reprieved gladiator collects his equipment, probably attendants help. He leaves by whichever entrance was designated the Gate of Life. He goes out on his own feet if he is able, if not on a stretcher, like those depicted beside the musicians, and between the gladiators and those condemned to the beasts on the Zliten mosaic (**Plate Five**). The gladiator lives another day.

The thumb turns: *Iugula,* death. Condemned criminals were dragged from the arena and had their throats cut out of sight. We know this because the crowd so greatly loathed the Christians martyred in Carthage with Perpetua that it demanded they were brought back so that their death could be witnessed. Gladiators were different. They died in the middle. It was part of the spectacle.

The gladiator was expected to die well. As Cicero put it: 'What mediocre gladiator has ever groaned, or changed countenance? Who of them has ever disgraced himself, not on their feet, but in their fall? Who among the fallen has drawn in their neck when ordered to receive the steel?' Recollection of his own words could have steeled Cicero's resolve at the end of his life. When the executioners sent by Mark Antony caught up with him, he calmly extended his neck. Although the lowest of the low socially, a gladiator who showed courage could at least die like a good Roman, and win some sort of redemption. The death of the gladiator was a popular metaphor with moral philosophers. The virtuous man should face the vicissitudes of life, and his own mortality, as a gladiator faced the steel. Seneca particularly favoured the image: 'Even the gladiator who has been very timid throughout the fight offers his throat to his adversary and guides the wavering blade to the vital place.'

The method of killing varied – perhaps over time, across regions, or from one school or Games to another. If the skeletons unearthed in York are from a gladiatorial cemetery, the method there was decapitation. Various poses are depicted in art, often the blow comes from above and behind, sometimes into the back. The victims that are shown lying facedown are either incapacitated or are not meeting death in the right way. In the gladiatorial graveyard at Ephesus those killed were kneeling, and the fatal blows were struck from above to their heads. Like the full-face helmets, which depersonalised the wearer during the fight, the lack of eye contact at the moment of execution made it easier to kill someone who might be a member of the same *familia*, a 'cell-mate' and friend. In the powerful phrase of Seneca, 'gladiators fight those with whom they drink'. On a moving tombstone from Pamphylia in Asia Minor, Polynices, 'who won a great reputation' in the arena, says he inflicted the fatal blow on 'his dear friend Tachinus'.

At least it was meant to be quick; just one blow. There was none of the frenzied hacking and mutilation found in mass burials at medieval battle sites, such as Visby in Sweden or Towton in North Yorkshire. But the first blow was not always clean. At

Ephesus it took two blows to finish off one of those interred in the gladiatorial cemetery. At Carthage the novice gladiator's first thrust struck bone. The Christian martyr Perpetua screamed but then guided his trembling hands to the fatal place.

After the victor had struck the blow, it was time for the sinister attendants dressed as the gods of the Underworld to make sure the fallen were dead. Mercury pressed his heated metal wand into their flesh. If there was a sign of life, Pluto/*Dis Pater* swung his hammer down onto their heads. The skulls of four of the gladiators from Ephesus have square traumas consistent with an unsurvivable blow from a hammer. Finally, perhaps, Charon the Ferryman dragged their corpses out of the Gate of Death.

A palm branch was set up on the floor of the arena before each fight. The victor either took it or was handed it, sometimes as soon as his opponent submitted. Think again of Diodorus the wretched. He already had the palm branch, before the treacherous cunning of the referee made him resume the fight and lose his life. There could be further rewards. The *editor* might award a crown, probably of laurel leaves or similar, as if to an athlete. More substantial in material terms, he might grant the victor a dish or plate, possibly itself of precious metal, containing coins, as we saw Magerius give the *Telegenii* beast-fighters (**Plate Twelve**). After a stupendous performance, very exceptionally, an *editor* might award the *Rudis*. This was not a wooden sword like those used in training, as is often thought, but the stick or rod of a *lanista* or referee. It symbolised discharge from the gladiatorial school, and thus freedom. Like ordering the death of a gladiator, this represented a substantial financial loss. The *editor* could only give the *Rudis* to a gladiator he owned, not to one he had rented. You could not give away someone else's property!

The victor took in the applause of the crowd. On many tombstones the gladiator stands square on, looking out at the viewer. He holds the palm branch in one hand, often his weapon in the other, and is surrounded by his equipment, along with crowns and more palms symbolising his victories. The pose is nicely called in French *le gladiateur dans sa gloire*. Like Caligula, after one of his fixed fights, the gladiator could make a lap of honour round the arena. Of course, the victor himself might be badly wounded. In which case the best he could manage perhaps was to wave as he was taken out on one of the wheeled stretchers. Either way – prone, or on his own feet – he left through the Gate of Life.

11

Solis Occasus
(Sunset)

The final act of the Games is keenly anticipated by many of the spectators. If they are lucky and fast and resolute, they might go home rich, or at least with some gift from the emperor. The senators in the days of the Republic spend fortunes on the plebs: holding gladiatorial contests, handing out wine and food and clothes. Such euergetism*, along with conspicuous consumption – flamboyant houses in Rome, trains of attendants, villas on the Bay of Naples – is necessary to maintain their position at the top of the social pyramid. Senators specifically hope it will encourage the people to vote them into magistracies. It is impossible to overstate the importance to senators of climbing the* cursus honorum *(the 'ladder of offices'). It is central to the construction of their identity. The glittering prize at the summit is to become one of the two consuls elected each year. This both ennobles a man's family for ever, and confers a form of immortality, as the year is named after the two consuls. Elite families mortgage their estates, and some incur bankruptcy, in the fierce struggle for office. Under the rule of the emperors after the fall of the Republic, gift-giving at the Games becomes both institutionalised and a focus of ideological tension between emperors and the elite.*

Gifts

At the Saturnalia one year Domitian showered the crowd in the Colosseum with gifts at first light. Statius wrote a poem commemorating the day. Domitian's Games were exceptional. Not just edible gifts at dawn, but later a full meal with copious wine. Everyone – children, women, plebs, equites, senators, even the emperor himself – as Statius put it, 'ate at one table'. The show featured novelty acts: women fought women, and dwarfs against dwarfs. As evening drew in, the scattering of more gifts was accompanied by female dancers from across the empire: girls from Lydia in Asia Minor, Syria and Gades in Spain (the latter especially known for their lascivious routines). That was not the end. When night fell, the Colosseum was illuminated, the entertainment continued and the food and wine flowed freely. Statius could not take any more. He went home, tipsy and happy, and by the next day had knocked off his poem of praise.

As we can infer from Statius, the usual time for gifts was the end of the day. Seneca advised leaving beforehand to avoid the scuffles. An easier decision for a multi-millionaire senator than for others of lesser means, but, as we will see in a moment, Seneca both had a deeper reason for leaving and was taking a calculated risk.

Domitian's early morning gifts were fruit, nuts and pastries. Statius enthuses about their distant origins: the shores of the Black Sea, the fertile hills of Judea, Damascus, the Balearics and Asia Minor, as well as Gaul. Those in the evening featured vast clouds of edible birds, released from above. Again, Statius itemises their exotic habitats: the Nile, the far end of the Black Sea and North Africa (probably flamingos, certainly pheasants and maybe guinea fowl). In the arena, food, and dancing girls, like exotic animals, served to emphasise the geographic sweep of the empire.

In other shows coins were thrown to the audience. They, and the birds, could be replaced with tokens (*missilia*) to claim the largesse later. This was known as the *sparsio missilium* (literally the *sprinkling of things thrown*). Tokens were used to represent all sorts of other gifts: gold and silver, precious stones, paintings, clothes, slaves, houses, lands, boats, food and live animals, both domestic and wild. You never knew what you were going to get. It might be really valuable, or it might just be a snack. That was part of the fun. Gamblers were prepared to take a punt and buy the tokens. There must also have been a lively resale market after the goods had been claimed – a wild beast or a boat was of limited appeal to a dweller in a tenement block.

Just as the giver of the Games 'killed' gladiators without wielding a sword, so he 'threw' gifts without lifting a finger. Indeed, it would have taken a strong throwing arm to get any tokens from the imperial box down by the sand up to the plebs seated beyond the fourteen rows reserved for the elite. Domitian's meal in Statius' poem was the simplest way to distribute gifts. Attendants – handsome and smartly dressed, like so many Ganymedes, according to the poet – passed along the gangways handing out or throwing the presents. There was a more high-tech delivery method, the *linea dives*, the 'line of wealth'. Two visual images have been identified. They are an arrangement of ropes and hammocks strung high above the stands, up near the awning. They were opened to tip gifts onto the audience, and could be hauled in to be refilled and then run out again. In a painting from Pompeii, down shower nuts and fruit, turtle doves, guinea fowls, domestic pigeons and ducks.

Such munificence was expected from emperors and hoped for from other givers of Games in the provinces. An advertisement for Games hosted by a member of the local elite in North Africa boasts it will be complete 'with things thrown' (*cum missilibus*). This was not just naked greed on one side and cynical favour-buying on the other. Such gift-giving had deep ideological roots. The essence of Greek and Roman political philosophy was simple. Only three types of political system were possible. If 'good', they were kingship, aristocracy (in the original sense of 'rule by the best') and democracy. If 'bad', they became tyranny, oligarchy ('rule by the few') and ochlocracy ('rule by the mob'). What made them 'good' or 'bad' was whether those in charge ruled for everyone, or for themselves. The most prestigious philosophers (men such as Dio Chrysostom, and Plutarch) argued that the only justification for any political regime was to give benefits to its subjects. Debates on which constitution was best continued under the emperors, although the answer was always kingship. The king was a king because he had virtue (*arete*), specifically the virtue of love of mankind (*philanthropia*), which manifested itself in giving benefits to his subjects. These could be abstractions, such as justice and peace, or could be very material: new roads and bridges, or bags of coins and *missilia* that might make you rich.

Despite an underlying ideology that argued that giving benefits justified a regime, throwing gifts to the crowds at the Spectacles became a stick with which 'bad' emperors were beaten by the elite. They did it for the wrong reasons: not love of mankind, but for their own selfish and cruel pleasure. They liked to watch the crowd fight over the tokens. This was taken to an extreme in literary condemnations of the emperor Heliogabalus. According to the contemporary historian Herodian, he had high towers specially constructed from which he threw down gold and silver cups, all kinds of clothing, including fine linen garments, and every kind of domestic animal, except pigs. In the ensuing scramble many were killed; either trampled to death or impaled on the spears of soldiers. The much later author of the *Augustan History* pushed the chance of the tokens to absurdity. The audience might get ten bears, or ten dormice, or ten lettuces, or ten pounds of gold. While the prizes for the performers might be a hundred gold pieces, a thousand silver pieces, a hundred copper coins, a pound of beef, or a dead dog.

Did the senators catch gifts? The philosopher Epictetus claimed that dignified men do not scramble for such small stakes as figs and nuts. The reality was rather different. When most of the tokens had fallen among the plebs, Domitian ordered another 500 thrown to each of the sections occupied by the senators and equites. Late sources claim that rich senators complained if they did not get their share. Not to catch the emperor's gifts was tantamount to renouncing his friendship, and such a course was fraught with danger. Imperial gifts scattered on senators at the Spectacles publicly reinforced the emperor's dominance over the elite. The enforced levity – senators in white togas stained yellow from the sprays of saffron in wine, scrabbling for tokens – reduced them to the level of the plebs. No doubt that humiliation brought much pleasure to the real plebs looking down from the rows above.

Seneca had good reason to leave before the *sprinkling of things thrown*, but an ostentatious exit might also be interpreted as spurning the emperor.

Politics and the Crowd

The extraordinary growth of gladiatorial Games in the last two and a half centuries BC was fuelled by the politics of the Roman Republic. Senators expended much time, ingenuity and money putting on shows to try and win popular acclaim. It could be a risky strategy. At the Games the people were free to express their views. To understand gladiatorial Games, we need to think about the role of the people in the Republican constitution. A good place to start is the views of a contemporary senator, Cicero: 'For the opinion and feeling of the Roman People in public affairs can be most clearly expressed on three occasions, at a meeting, at an Assembly and at a gathering for the Games and gladiatorial shows.'

Later in the same speech, Cicero privileges the latter two.

> Expressions of public opinion at Assemblies and at meetings are sometimes the voice of truth, but sometimes they are falsified and corrupt: at theatrical and gladiatorial shows it is said to be common for some feeble and scanty applause to be started by a hired and unprincipled claque, and yet,

when that happens, it is easy to see how and by whom it is started and what the honest part of the audience does.

In his letters, as well as in this speech, Cicero gives examples of politicians being hissed or cheered by the crowd. Of course, Cicero was not in the least impartial. In his writings – public and private – politicians he liked are applauded, while those he disliked are jeered. Yet the essential truth is clear. Crowds at the Spectacles acted as a sort of barometer of public opinion.

No politician of any shade ever denied that the people were sovereign in the Roman Republic. Only they, gathered in formal assemblies, could pass laws or vote men into office. Less formal meetings (*Contiones*) were held in advance to gauge the mood of the populace. But how active the people were in their sovereignty, indeed how active in politics at all, has always been a matter of debate.

Polybius, a member of the Greek elite held as a diplomatic hostage in Rome for several years, paused the narrative of his *Histories* to discuss the constitution of the Roman Republic. It was, in his view, a mixed constitution, combining the three good types of regime. The consuls were the kingly element, the Senate the aristocratic, and the Assemblies the democratic. It was unchanging, perfect and eternal (at least until the cyclic destruction of the world, which Polybius, following Stoic cosmology, thought would reset mankind to a primitive level). It would be naïve to read this as dispassionate analysis. Polybius had two main intentions in his *Histories*. The first was to explain to his Greek readers how, in the short space of about half a century, they had been conquered by Rome. His answer was somewhat comforting. The Romans had taken the best of Greek political philosophy out of the treatises of intellectuals and put it into practice. His other aim was to reassure his Roman senatorial friends. At the time Polybius was writing, in the 140sBC, traditional elite dominance of the Republic was coming under threat from renegade members of the nobility who espoused popular politics. The fears of conservative-minded senators were allayed by Polybius. The Republic was so robust that even if some minor changes were made, its fundamental nature would remain. In other words, concessions were possible, but essentially the Republic would be unaltered and elite control would continue.

For most of the twentieth century, few agreed with Polybius' argument that the Republic was a mixed constitution. Instead, the Republic was seen as an oligarchy, where a small number of the great senatorial families manoeuvred against each other in factions. The key was the Roman social institution of patronage. As clients of senatorial houses, the plebs voted for their patrons. The plebs had no agency of their own. The Republic was reduced to a rather arid boardgame. With no real issues or even policies at stake, the faction with the greatest number of clients won.

The oligarchic interpretation of the Republic was overturned in the 1980s. First, it was pointed out that while there was evidence for many temporary political alliances (called *amicitia* to those who favoured them; to those who disapproved they were *factiones*, whence our faction), there was none for stable, long-lasting groupings, let alone ones that had previously been considered to last over several generations. Indeed, senators, brought up from earliest childhood to believe in their own individual *virtus* and *dignitas*, were unlikely to tolerate simply being foot soldiers following the line of a faction boss. Second, if the plebs just voted as instructed by their patrons, why did the elite invest so much time and effort in seeking to persuade them by public face-to-face oratory in *contiones* and assemblies, and squander so much money attempting to gain their approval providing gladiatorial Games? Third, some of the plebs had more than one patron – who did they vote for? Finally, and rather less convincingly, it was noted that neither Polybius nor any other contemporary source, stated that a client had to vote for his patron. In this new way of thinking, the Roman Republic becomes surprisingly 'democratic': the plebs were active in politics because that is what they wanted; the senate could not exclude them.

The 'democratic' Roman Republic is now largely accepted. Yet there are uncertainties and problems. Polybius had good reason to write patron-client links out of his account of Roman politics. Its inclusion would have fatally undermined his elaborate edifice of the Republic as a mixed constitution. More generally it could be that patronage was one of the great unspoken truths of Roman politics. No senator was ever going to stand up and say: 'Vote for this law/this man because it is what I want as your patron.' Better to dilate on how it was good for Rome, the empire and the people, and fitted the will of the gods and ancestral tradition (the *mos maiorum*). Above all, the 'democratic' consensus stumbles over the end of the Republic. When Augustus effectively removed the people from the political process – the formal assemblies downgraded to purely symbolic occasions, with few present, which merely rubber-stamped decisions made elsewhere, and the rowdier preliminary debates (the *contiones*) abolished – far from protesting at the loss of their rights, the plebs urged their new ruler to take more overt power.

Another explanation can be offered. It was always in the interest of the senators to have the plebs involved in the political working of the Republic. They functioned as a safety valve. If they had not legislated and chosen who held high office, these decisions would have had to be made within the senate house itself. This would have increased the already intense competition among senators and rapidly torn apart their oligarchy (or, rather, accelerated this process, because senatorial competition eventually did destroy the Republic). The people remained in Republican politics because the senators wanted them there, and gladiatorial Games were a crucial element of their role.

The Emperor and the Crowd

'Long ago, with no votes to sell any more, the people cast off their cares; those who once gave military commands, magistracies, legions and everything, have narrowed their scope to anxious hope for two things – bread and circuses.' Everyone has heard of Juvenal's cynical phrase 'bread and circuses'; less attention is paid to the 'military commands, magistracies, legions and everything'. Which rather obscures the essential truth of his comment – the people, who had been a central element of Republican politics, had lost this role under the emperors. Once the elections were removed to the senate, the assemblies reduced to ceremonial occasions, and the preliminary *contiones* abolished, the only place where the people could interact with their rulers, could have any voice in politics, was the Spectacles.

The emperor was expected to attend. Augustus was assiduous, sending his apologies, and someone to represent him, if he was unable to go because of illness or other duties. Tiberius increased his unpopularity by staying away in order to avoid the requests made by the crowds. The emperor's first duty was to be visible. Both Nero and Domitian damaged their public image by screening off the imperial box with curtains. The emperor was expected to pay attention. Both Julius Caesar and Marcus Aurelius were criticised for catching up on their paperwork at the Games. In fact, emperors needed to do more than simply pay attention, they had to enter into the spirit of the occasion. This was tricky for the emperor, as different parts of the audience wanted different behaviour. The Senate looked for him to display dignity (*dignitas*), while the plebs enjoyed levity (*levitas*). Claudius, like the North African Magerius on his mosaic, called the crowd 'Lords' (*domini*), and counted out the cash prizes he awarded on the fingers of his left hand (the *vulgar* hand, which the elite usually kept out of sight). Such pandering to the masses was frowned upon by the elite. Titus, however, managed the balancing act better. According to Suetonius' positive biography, he 'often engaged with the crowd in lively interchange with words and gestures like a real partisan, but without any loss of dignity or fairness'.

The crowd made their wishes known by rhythmic chants. These were ubiquitous at public occasions in the Roman world. Sometimes they were started by a claque. Yet at other times the crowd seem to have displayed a facility for improvising new chants on the spot, like English cricket and football fans. Cassius Dio, who was an eyewitness to one example of these feats of invention, put it down to divine inspiration.

Many chants were specific to the show being watched. In the Colosseum, when some asked for one famous gladiator and others wanted a different fighter, Titus, 'with either hand raised', brought out both. At Smyrna the mob shouted, 'Go and get Polycarp!', and the governor had the Christian brought out. The man giving the Games did not always bow to popular demand. When the crowd called for a brigand called Tetrinius, Caligula said they were 'Tetriniuses' too. Despite persistent calls for him to grant freedom to a man who had trained a man-eating lion, Marcus Aurelius ordered that a proclamation be made saying the man had done nothing to deserve it. Yet it was hard to go against the desires of the audience. Marcus felt the need to issue an imperial pronouncement forbidding presiding magistrates across the empire from freeing condemned slaves when demanded by the crowd, at least without the permission of the owner.

Some demands were more general but still motivated by self-interest. For several days in the reign of Tiberius demands were made in the theatre for a reduction in the price of grain. The emperor upbraided the Senate, which issued a stern decree. In the Circus the spectators entreated Caligula for a reduction of taxes. That emperor's response was to send agents into the crowd, the most vociferous were arrested, and summarily executed.

Other demands were more altruistic. Suetonius claims Tiberius stopped going to the Spectacles after being forced in the theatre to buy the freedom of a comic actor. The same emperor had removed a statue called the Apoxyomenos ('Man using a Body-scraper'), which stood outside the public baths, to his own bedroom. It was returned when the crowd in the theatre chanted, 'Give us back the Apoxyomenos'.

At times the demands of the people moved into the realm of politics. They might demonstrate in favour of members of the imperial family who they considered were being badly treated by the emperor. Although we are not told in what venue, the people urged Augustus to restore his daughter Julia, who had been exiled for alleged immorality. When he said that fire would mix with water before that happened, they threw lit torches into the Tiber. Later, according to Cassius Dio, 'they brought such pressure to bear that she was at least brought from the island [of Pandateria] to the mainland'. When crowds took to the streets to celebrate the false rumour that Nero had recalled Octavia, the popular wife he had divorced, the emperor had them dispersed by troops. Conversely, they might raise an outcry against an unpopular imperial favourite. A crowd of children, led by a tall maiden, ran into the Circus, and began to chant against Cleander, the loathed Praetorian prefect of Commodus. The crowd took up the chants, 'bawling out every conceivable insult', then set off to the suburban villa where the emperor was staying. To restore order, Commodus had Cleander killed.

On a few, rare occasions the crowd made clear their opposition to the policies of the emperor, or even to the emperor himself. When Septimius Severus was away fighting a civil war in Gaul against Albinus, the former ally he had appointed his caesar, the throng in the Circus Maximus shouted out as one, 'How long are we to suffer such things?', and 'How long are we to be at war?', before chanting 'So much for that', and turning their attention back to the chariot racing.

During the brief reign of Macrinus (AD217–8), who never

made it to Rome after taking the purple, the crowd went further – symbolically renouncing their allegiance to the emperor altogether. In the Circus, where races were being held to celebrate the birthday of Macrinus' young son, the senators and equestrians dutifully chanted, 'What a glorious day! What noble rulers!' The crowd, however, 'emboldened by their numbers', were having none of it and refused to join the chorus. Instead, they raised their hands to Jupiter in heaven and chanted: 'There is the Augustus of the Romans; having him, we have everything!'

The most extraordinary act of dissent is said to have occurred in AD 312. The emperor Maxentius was in Rome, about to march out to face Constantine at the Battle of the Milvian Bridge, which would decide the civil war. The crowd in the Circus Maximus shouted out with one voice, 'Constantine the Invincible!' The historical truth of the acclamation can be doubted. Lactantius, the Christian apologist who recorded the incident a few years later, could not have been more biased. Yet he hoped his readers would find his account plausible.

The conversation was not one way. The emperor was expected to 'talk' to the crowd. He communicated with them, in ascending order of civility, via placards, heralds, or his own gestures and voice. Cassius Dio tells a revealing story about Hadrian.

> Once at a gladiatorial contest, when the crowd was demanding something very urgently, he would not only not grant it but further bade the herald proclaim Domitian's command, 'Silence.' The word was not uttered, however, for the herald raised his hand and by that very gesture quieted the people, as heralds are accustomed to do (for crowds are never silenced by proclamation), and then, when they had become quiet, he said: 'That is what he wishes.'

Later Hadrian rewarded the herald, whose initiative had turned what would have been a rude command, reminiscent of a tyrant, into a cause for laughter.

The crowd could turn nasty. They might hiss and jeer. Cicero said the noise made both the gladiators and their horses take fright. In the Late Republic the *aediles* issued an edict that the spectators could only throw fruit, not stones. Such hostility was reserved for unpopular members of the audience, or unsatisfactory performers. Except for one occasion, when soldiers in the Circus attacked the future emperor Augustus, the giver of the Games was not the target. To do so would have ensured that no gifts would be forthcoming.

At the worst, a full-scale riot might erupt. Although Clement of Alexandria included the arena as a place that Christians should avoid, because you might get caught up in violent public disorder, only one riot is known to have taken place at a gladiatorial show. It was not in Rome, but the notorious outbreak at Pompeii (which we looked at in Chapter Six, Anticipation). They feature more frequently in stories set in the Circus and the theatre. The crowd appears to have been generally more quiescent at the amphitheatre. Most of the examples of strident demands and politically dissident outbursts mentioned in this section are drawn from the Circus and theatre, not the amphitheatre. This apparent docility seems to have been real, not just an impression caused by the chance survival of evidence. Philostratus, in his *Life of Apollonius of Tyana*, has those rioting in the theatres and circuses of various cities blush and check themselves at the mere sight of the real man. It is significant that he does not make his wonder-working hero perform the same function in an amphitheatre.

Why were the spectators at gladiatorial contests better behaved than at the other popular shows? It was nothing to do with sheer numbers. Many more attended the Circus, and fewer could fit into the theatre. Likewise, it was unconnected to the social mix imposed by stratified seating. The theatre was subject to the same arrangements as the amphitheatre. Arguments based on the supposed relative intrinsic interest in the entertainments on offer, or their frequency, seem highly subjective. To someone brought up in Newmarket racing stables, the suggestion that horseracing is not 'inherently fascinating' is inexplicable. Likewise, the idea that gladiators did not fight for long enough, or often enough to rouse intense emotions, is dubious. In rugby, the British and Irish Lions only play a handful of matches every fourth year but inspire a passionate following. The leading modern boxers have huge fanbases but their bouts, separated by many months, sometimes years, can be over in moments.

A very prosaic reason can be advanced for the crowd being more dormant at the amphitheatre than in the Circus or the theatre. Soldiers acted as security at all three venues. The Praetorians were stationed inside while the urban cohorts patrolled the deserted streets outside. For Claudius' naval battle the Fucine Lake was ringed with Praetorian cohorts on rafts equipped with palisades and torsion artillery, while marines in decked warships were on the waters. This *Naumachia* was an exceptional event with 19,000 combatants. Yet its high level of security points to a general rule – gladiators, and wild beasts, posed a far greater threat than chariots and actors or dancers. There were more troops on duty in the amphitheatre.

12

VESPER
(Evening)

In the gloom a gull circles above the Colosseum. Below, crowds stream out of the eighty arches. They throng the streets in all directions. There are scuffles in which anyone can get caught up. Although the rich tend to have their homes on high ground to catch the breeze, and the poor occupy the lower places – as Cicero put it, this is the 'dung heap of Romulus', and shit flows downhill – and although some districts like the Subura are considered déclasseé, ancient Rome is not 'zoned' like modern Western cities: elite and non-elite live in surprising proximity. The gull knows that soon they will all be gone, leaving behind rich pickings of discarded scraps.

Magic and Medicine

The gladiators have long since left the arena. The dead have been dragged by Father Dis, Mercury, or Charon through the Gate of Death. Fresh sand has been scattered and raked, obliterating all trace of their passage. The dead are taken to the *Spoliarium*. This place takes its name from the *Spolia*, the 'spoils' taken from the body of a defeated warrior. In the *Spoliarium* the corpses are stripped of their equipment. Wiped clean of blood, dents knocked out, broken straps and buckles replaced, later it will be altered to fit a new gladiator. (One of the problems faced by the unexpected volunteer gladiator in a fictitious legal speech preserved under the name of Quintilian is that his hastily provided equipment was ill-fitting.)

Attempts to identify the *Spoliarium* at the archaeological site of any amphitheatre run into two problems. We ascribe a single function to rooms: an office, or a living room, and so on. The rooms and spaces of Roman public buildings, as well as houses, tended to be used for different things at different times. Then again, the *Spoliarium* was not always in the amphitheatre at all. It might be back in the gladiatorial school. An inscription from Rome records a man who had been a *Retiarius*, before becoming a trainer in the School of the Beast Fighters, as well as the curator of the *Spoliarium*; probably indicating they were housed in the same complex. The *Spoliarium* might be in another building somewhere nearby. Another inscription, from Praeneste, honours a man who had both given a gladiatorial show, showing the amphitheatre already existed, then purchased land for the construction of a *Spoliarium*, which must have been elsewhere.

The bodies of gladiators who had a wife, family or friends to claim them were handed over for burial. These are the gladiators we have met on their tombstones. Men such as Diodorus the wretched, killed by the cunning treachery of the referee, or the beautiful *Retiarius* Miletus, mourned by his probable lover Odysseus.

Not all were so lucky. The corpses of the unclaimed gladiators, like all who had died by violence, were thought to possess power, and might be harvested for magic and medicine.

But first two strange modern fantasies need to be dispelled. The claim that the sweat of gladiators was collected and sold to rich women as an aphrodisiac goes back no further than an article in *Sports Illustrated* in 2001. The origin of the often-repeated assertion that Roman women dipped their hairpins in the blood of gladiators, for no very obvious reason, appears to be an invention based on a real practice, to which we can now turn.

In a traditional Roman wedding ceremony, the bride had her hair parted by a spear. Plutarch, a Greek commenting on

Roman customs, offered a wide range of possible reasons, none particularly credible. The Roman Ovid merely said that the spearhead was bent. Festus, a Latin scholar, specified that the spear had to have been previously thrust into the corpse of a gladiator. He speculated that just as the spear had clung to the body of the gladiator, so the bride would cling to her husband.

To us this looks like superstition and magic. To a participating Roman it was a religious rite whose origin and meaning had been lost in the mists of time. Superstition and magic were always, for Romans, things that others believed or did. Superstition was the province of women, slaves, the lower classes, and foreigners. Magic, again, was practised by women. If it was done by men, they were either foreigners, almost always easterners, or they were Pythagorean philosophers. As the mythical figure of Pythagoras was believed to have been instructed by easterners, the circle was closed. *You* practised religion, *others* indulged in superstition and dabbled in the occult.

Two things emerge from the odd marriage custom with the spear. As almost all gladiators fought with a sword, the spear thrusts were administered post-mortem, as Festus implies. It happened in the *Spoliarium* and the weapons were taken away and stored for later use at weddings. The spearhead would be crusted with dried blood but not dripping in the fresh gore of some modern imaginings.

Another story involved the blood of a gladiator and the (in) fidelity of a wife. In the *Augustan History* Faustina, the wife of Marcus Aurelius, fell in love with a gladiator. She became ill; frustrated love often had this effect in the ancient world. Eventually, she confessed her feelings to her husband. On the advice of Chaldeans (note they were *eastern* magicians), Marcus had the gladiator killed, and Faustina 'wash herself from beneath in his blood'. The wording seems to imply a sacrifice like that of a bull over a grating in a taurobolium, so the blood splashed on those below. Still covered in gore, Faustina then had sex with her husband. This had the beneficial effect of curing her passion for the gladiator, but the unintended consequence was that Commodus, the result of the imperial coupling, had the character of a gladiator.

The moment of conception was always tricky. It was believed that the child could take on not just the character but the physical form of whatever the mother viewed at the crucial moment. In Heliodorus' *Aethiopica*, the queen of Aethiopia, while having sex with her husband one hot summer afternoon, happened to look at a painting depicting the mythical heroine Andromeda as a white woman (conventional in Classical art, but odd, as Andromeda was Aethiopian too). When the royal couple's daughter was born white, not black, the infant was exposed to die. Of course, as this was a novel, the child was saved.

Not too much faith should be put into the historical reality of Faustina's blood bath. The *Augustan History* says that 'many writers' had another story – Commodus simply was the product of the empress' adultery with a gladiator. The unknown author also distances himself from his own version – which he may well have made up – saying that some have embroidered it from a 'tale current among the common people'. In reality, of course, all of this talk about infidelity and sacrifice was arguing backwards from the adult Commodus' very real obsession with gladiators.

The corpse of a gladiator had a very specific use in 'alternative' medicine. It was believed to cure epilepsy. Scribonius Largus, a medical writer of the first century AD, gave many prescriptions; some easily obtained (thyme, vinegar and honey), others less so (crocodile testicle). He was very fond of treatments spread over time. One was to 'devour some little bit, given nine times, of the liver of a gladiator whose throat has been cut'. The association of gladiators and epilepsy was so strong that it was important at second hand: an extended treatment of swallowing rennet extracted from a fawn worked best if the animal had been killed with a weapon that had cut a gladiator's throat. As with the spear for the wedding ceremonies, the 'operation' was performed in the *Spoliarium*, and the liver taken away for subsequent use.

The blood of a gladiator, not his liver, was more often a cure for epilepsy. Tertullian turned an accusation against Christians on its head – it is not us, but you pagans that are cannibals. Not only do pagans eat the flesh of beasts that have consumed men in the arena, there are those who catch the fresh blood of gladiators and 'carry it off as a cure for their epilepsy'. It would be tempting to dismiss this as baseless religious invective, if it was not confirmed in pagan sources. Pliny the Elder wrote that epileptic patients were 'in the habit of drinking the blood of gladiators'. Celsus, a medical writer of the first century AD, said that 'some have freed themselves from such a disease by drinking the hot blood from the cut throat of a gladiator'.

Although the Christian Tertullian says the blood was taken away for later use, as were the liver and the bloodied spear, the pagans have it consumed there and then in the *Spoliarium*. Pliny even claims that the epileptics 'drink the warm, breathing blood from the man himself, and put their mouth to the wound, to draw out his very life'. Aretaeus of Cappadocia, another medical writer of the first century AD, was not quite as graphic, but claimed autopsy: 'I have seen people holding a cup below the wound of a man recently killed and drinking a draught of blood.'

Magic and medicine overlapped in the Roman world. Yet harvesting the corpses of gladiators to cure epilepsy went too far for our sources. Scribonius Largus held that such things 'lay outside professional medicine'. Celsus thought they were not the real concern of the practitioner, who should turn instead to letting blood from the victim. In Pliny, not himself a medical man, they inspired horror: 'Far from us, far also from our writing, be such prescriptions! It is right for us only to describe remedies, not abominations!'

The problem was that such *abominations* might work. The jury was out. Pliny implied they did not. No one could tell Aretaeus if they did. Yet according to Scribonius Largus they 'apparently worked in some cases'. Celsus was more certain: 'some have freed themselves'. It was, in his words, 'a miserable aid made tolerable by a malady still more miserable'.

Wounded gladiators left the arena – on their feet, or on a stretcher – via the Gate of Life. Trained gladiators, even novices, were an expensive investment. They received the best medical treatment their school could afford. At the top end this was very good. Galen, who went on to be a physician to the emperor Marcus Aurelius and his son Commodus, served at the start of his career for four years in the gladiatorial school in Pergamum owned by the high priests of the imperial cult. Galen won the post after proving his surgical skill with many public anatomical demonstrations. One of these was a vivisection in which he first disembowelled a live monkey, then replaced its intestines, before severing its large arteries and stopping the blood with a ligature. The monkey survived.

Galen learned much about human anatomy and surgery treating the gladiators at Pergamum. The dissection of human corpses, let alone vivisection, was frowned upon, and very rare in the ancient world. As Celsus noted, the wounds of gladiators offered doctors the opportunity to observe the internal structures of the human body. Galen was proud of his work in Pergamum, which he recalled in references scattered throughout his later literary works. Not all of his patients made it. Those gladiators who took a wound to the heart always died; if one of the ventricles was perforated they bled to death straight away; if not they might live through the night and perhaps the following day. Evidently, Galen stayed with them, as he noted they remained lucid to the end. Others he saved, later boasting of his innovative techniques in suturing muscles and ligating veins and arteries. His experiences vivisecting monkeys stood him in good stead when he operated on a gladiator who had been nearly disembowelled. Galen removed almost all the protective membrane and replaced the small intestines. The gladiator survived, but ever afterwards had to wrap wool round his abdomen as he was constantly cold.

Almost everything we know about gladiatorial medicine comes from Galen, which gives an inflated impression of its efficacy. Not all treatment would have been so good. Before Galen's sole tenure, the gladiators at Pergamum had been tended by a board of two or three older doctors. Under their care, Galen is happy to say, many more gladiators died. Owned by a succession of fabulously rich high priests, Pergamum was a top school, as, of course, were those owned by the emperors. Things got worse as you went down the scale. In those *familiae* that provided the low grade commercial 'penny shows', the wounded gladiators would have had to rely on a local quack hired for the occasion, or whatever medical knowledge the *lanista* himself had picked up.

Roman medicine in general was good at stitching up cuts and setting broken bones. In the cemetery at Ephesus eleven gladiators had well-healed cranial injuries; five of them had suffered two or more injuries. One of them had survived a large blade injury to the front of his skull, which would have required extensive stitching. Fifteen individuals had healed injuries to other parts of their bodies, including three broken forearms. One gladiator had even survived the amputation of his right leg.

Yet there was always the danger of infection. Although only intending to keep the wound 'moist', Galen actually reduced the chances of infection by placing on the wounds linen cloths soaked in wine, and covering these dressings with sponges to which more wine was added day and night. Unfortunately, he also came up with a way of catching the excess wine in skins and reusing it, thus most likely adding to the risk posed by pathogenic microbes. Infection, rather than sustaining a mortal wound, might lie behind the tombstones of those gladiators who won their fight but died later: men like Vitalis, the unbeaten *Retiarius*, who 'fought it out to the end on an equal footing with his opponent', but died anyway.

The Future of the Games

In AD 325, only a year after seizing control of the whole empire, Constantine, the first Christian emperor, ruled that criminals were no longer to be condemned to the gladiatorial schools; instead, they were to go to the mines. As convicts were a main source of gladiators, probably *the* main source, that should have been the end of the Games. That was how Eusebius, a contemporary Christian and committed supporter of Constantine, took it: the emperor had forbidden the pollution of cities 'with the bloodshed of gladiators'. It made, and still makes, a neat and satisfying story: a Christian came to the throne and straightaway abolished gladiatorial Games. Except that was not what happened.

Gladiatorial Games continued: testimony to both their popularity and to the limits of the power of any emperor. Three years after Constantine's ruling, the orator Libanius tells us of a gladiatorial show in Antioch. In the last year of his life, Constantine himself permitted the northern Italian town of Hispellum to hold a gladiatorial show, to spare the inhabitants a tough trip through the Apennines to the shows in the town of Volsinii. They were going strong at Carthage in the 360s and Rome in the 380s. Saint Augustine's younger friend Alypius got bitten by the bug in both places. In AD 365 the emperor Valentinian ruled that no Christian was to be condemned to a gladiatorial school. He followed this up in 367 with a letter to the prefect of the city of Rome ordering that no one who had been a member of the palatine bureaucracy should suffer the same fate. Both are evidence that Constantine's rescript, like so many imperial pronouncements, had been widely ignored. In the last quarter of the fourth century there were enough gladiators in Apamea in Syria for the local bishop, a zealot called Marcellus, to hire a gang of thugs to desecrate pagan temples. At the turn of the fifth century the Christian poet Prudentius beseeched the emperor Honorius to abolish the Games. Between AD429 and 438 the *Theodosian Code* was published. This was an enormous collection of some 2,500 imperial laws. Among them was Constantine's ruling of AD325. Although Theodosius, the emperor who had commissioned the collection, was a fanatical Christian, gladiatorial combat was still regulated rather than outlawed. In the 430s and 440s medallions depicting gladiators were minted at Rome, celebrating the Games held at the inauguration of new consuls.

Christians' relationship with the gladiatorial Games was complex. In every Christian text where they are mentioned, they are condemned. We have seen Tertullian in *On the Spectacles* trying to convince Christians not to attend; which, of course, shows that enough did to make the attack worthwhile. There is a paradox that those who most deplored gladiatorial shows – men like Tertullian and the authors of the fictionalised Martyr Acts – and thus their readers, whether or not they physically went to the amphitheatre, actually spent a lot of conceptual time at the Games.

There was another paradox. As a strategy of persuading their co-religionist not to go to the Games, Christian authors invested the arena with more religious significance than it actually held for followers of the traditional gods. Tertullian points to the religious aspects of the opening procession and, also with some justification, talks of Mars and Diana, the deities of war and the hunt, as patrons of the Games. But he goes much further: 'For the amphitheatre is consecrated to names more numerous and more dire than the Capitol itself, that temple of all demons, it holds as many unclean spirits as it does men.' That was a lot of demons, by ancient counts about 80,000 in the Colosseum.

Christians, unlike pagans, were quite certain about the origins of gladiatorial contests – human sacrifice. The distant past was not enough. The contemporary arena had to feature human sacrifice. To further this assertion Christian apologists claimed that at the festival of Jupiter Latiaris (of Latium) blood from victims of the Games was poured onto the cult statue, or even that one individual was sacrificed. Christians – drinking the blood and eating the body of Christ – were accused by pagans of human sacrifice. With the supposed rites of Jupiter Latiaris, they turned the accusation back on their pagan detractors; probably with no more historical justification.

Under the pagan empire Christians developed an aggressive ideology to deal with the Games. They colonised them, taking them over, and, at least in their own minds, turned them into a Christian event. Martyrs were often seen as athletes. Sometimes this blurred into seeing them as gladiators. Perpetua in one of her dreams fought a devil in the arena at Carthage. The combat was imagined as a mixture of *pancration*, a type of all-in fighting, and a gladiatorial bout. Martyrs displayed the virtues of a gladiator: courage and endurance in the face of death. The martyrs seized the initiative. Rather than passively waiting, they goaded the wild beasts to attack. For those condemned to the flames, the smoke of their burning became the perfume of the arena. They took control of the whole event. The actual giver of the Games was not in charge, it was Christ or God. Above all, the Christians had a trump card up their sleeve – a forthcoming Games like no other. The Day of Judgement would be a show where the roles were reversed. The pagan organisers and spectators of today would become the participants of tomorrow. Christians gloated: 'You might burn us now, but you will burn for ever in hellfire.' Tertullian exulted in a vision of emperors 'groaning in the depths of darkness' and governors 'melting in flames fiercer than those they themselves kindled in their rage against Christians'. The arena – with its fires, whips, weapons, tortures and devils, like Charon – shaped the enduring Christian vision of Hell.

Yet the gladiatorial Games eventually came to an end. Our last evidence is the medallions from the consular Games in the 440s. Almost a century later, in AD 529, the *Codex Iustinianus*, was published. The emperor Justinian's huge compilation, amounting to some 5,000 laws in its second edition, included

Constantine's ruling of 325. The earlier emperor's words were rewritten to reflect contemporary realities: 'We altogether forbid the existence of gladiators.' At some point in the ninety or so years between the minting of the medallions and the accession of Justinian, gladiatorial combat had ceased, and the first Christian emperor was retrospectively, and wrongly, credited with its abolition.

By the reign of Justinian gladiatorial Games had stopped, but wild-beast shows continued; so too did spectacular public executions, both of which had far stronger associations with Christian martyrs. Although crucifixions were banned, men and women were still condemned to be burned alive and savaged to death by fierce animals. Indeed, the range of methods was increased, such as pouring molten metal down the throat of the condemned, as was the range of crimes which brought the death penalty. Some explanation is needed.

But providing answers turns out to be far from easy. From the second quarter of the third century our evidence becomes very thin. After the end of Herodian's *History* in AD238, apart from twenty-five years illuminated by the surviving books of Ammianus Marcellinus (AD353–78), we are thrown back on three brief and inaccurate late fourth-century epitomes of history in Latin, the creative inventions of the *Augustan History*, and two much later and error strewn Greek overviews of history. At about the same time the number of inscriptions dwindles to next to nothing, as – for reasons also hard to define – the 'epigraphic habit' dies. Archaeology can only tell us so much about the end of the gladiatorial Games. It can date when an amphitheatre was in use, but not what for; when it ceased to be used, but not why. When an amphitheatre was incorporated into defensive walls, or simply abandoned, it does not prove the end of gladiators in that town – as in Republican Rome, they could have fought in temporary arenas in other public spaces.

Amateur historians, and the media, like single, big explanations. They are always finding *the cause* of the Fall of the Roman

Empire, or whatever, when they are not discovering *the real* King Arthur. Scholars, rightly, are dubious about monocausal explanations. They prefer multi-layered and interlocking answers.

For the decline of gladiatorial Games many look to the 'third century crisis' of the Roman empire. Between the conventional dates of AD238 and 284 the empire suffered barbarian invasions, endless civil wars, a bewildering succession of very short-lived emperors and pretenders, and a staggering rate of inflation. Although perhaps not the 'total crisis' sometimes claimed, there can be no doubt that it was a time of political, military and economic turmoil. The latter has been seen to hold the key to the end of the Games – a straightforward lack of money, or, more elaborately, rampant inflation leading to a lack of available credit. It is an appealing explanation, except beast-fights and chariot racing also cost a great deal of money and they both continued to thrive. Another answer might be sought in the changing social and geographic origins of the Roman emperors. In the second half of the third century they no longer came from the traditional senatorial, or even equestrian elite of Italy and the central provinces. Instead, they had risen from the ranks of common soldiers enlisted mainly from along the Danube frontier. Except the 'barracks emperors' appear to have had an ultra-traditional attitude, and, at least according to the *Historia Augusta*, were devoted to Games in the arena.

A better approach is to look at changes in the composition and mentalities of the local elites. This takes us into the fourth century. In the provinces the numbers of those in the local elites were shrinking. A few families got much richer, while most became poorer and dropped out of the elite. The handful of families remaining, more securely in control in each town, might no longer have felt the need to compete with each other by funding gladiatorial Games to win popular favour.

A more important change in the fourth century was in elite attitudes to munificence, of the gifts they gave to the community. When Constantine had his soldiers paint the Chi-Ro symbol on their shields, before the Battle of the Milvian Bridge in AD312, and later fought his way to dominance over the whole empire in AD324, Christianity was very much a minority religion. No one would have thought that Constantine's dynasty would last, or that, with the brief interlude of Julian the Apostate (AD360–3), every emperor for the rest of the century and beyond would follow Constantine's eccentric choice of religion. Political advancement, and tax breaks, combined with the traditional habit of copying the interests of the reigning emperor to produce widespread, if not necessarily profound, conversion among the elite. Christian munificence was aimed at building churches and giving alms to widows, orphans and the poor, not funding gladiatorial shows. So, although not by imperial decree, Christianity caused the end of combat in the arena after all.

Certainly, Christians later claimed the credit. Not just Justinian's lawyers putting a decree of abolition into the mouth of the long dead Constantine. In AD404 a monk called Telemachus leaped out onto the sands of the Colosseum during a show and demanded an end to the slaughter. The irate crowd stoned him to death. Telemachus' death prompted the emperor Honorius to ban gladiatorial combat. A neat and, if you were Christian, edifying story. And a complete invention. But it shows later Christian views, and, maybe, points to a wider truth: Christianity killed the Games.

The Future of the Gladiator

The unwounded gladiators – the victors, and those granted *missio* – have left by the Gate of Life and returned to their *Ludus*. Their arms and armour have been removed and stored in the school's armoury. The gladiators have had a restorative drink of ash dissolved in wine. If it is an upmarket school, they will have had a massage, perhaps a bath. What does their future hold?

Every gladiator fantasises about turning in a superb performance – winning a crown, a fat purse of prize money, and the ultimate accolade: the *Rudis*, the wooden stick that symbolised freedom and release from the *Ludus*. But the award of the *Rudis* was very rare. The sort of gladiator who might win a *Rudis* was a valuable commodity. Even if he were a free volunteer, presumably the man giving the Games would have to pay the outstanding stipend for the remainder of his contract. Another reason for its extreme rarity was to preserve the prestige of the award.

A more realistic hope was to survive the rest of your time in the *Ludus*. What were the gladiator's chances? The modern, popular image of the gladiatorial Games – seen in innumerable novels and films – is a bloodbath. Every fight ends with at least one of the two combatants dead. This is a misconception. A careful study conducted in the twentieth century, looking at a hundred inscriptions, estimated that the chance of death in a fight was one in ten in the first century AD, rising to one in four in the second and third centuries. These figures are often followed. Some, however, implicitly doubting the increase in lethality, prefer to average out the numbers; to, say, one in six. There is also a tendency to downgrade the fatalities, sometimes even as far as one in twenty.

The evidence consists of graffiti and advertisement posters, with the results added later, from Pompeii and tombstones from across the empire. They need to be compared with the total number of gladiators at any one time in the empire, and that is unknowable. Modern guesses fall in the range of 16,000 to 20,000. If an average of 18,000 is vaguely in the right order of magnitude, and we arbitrarily assign twenty-five years to each generation, it gives twenty-eight generations of 18,000 in the 700 or so years gladiatorial combat existed: resulting in a total number of gladiators of well over half a million. Although new tombstones continue to be discovered, it is obvious that our evidence, which will never amount to more than a few hundred inscriptions, represents an infinitesimally small sample – far too small to have any statistical validity.

Another problem is that the tombstones do not represent a random cross-section of all gladiators. They were more likely to be set up for the successful than the unsuccessful, for free volunteers than those condemned to the schools, for those from within the empire than prisoners of war from beyond the frontiers, and for those from the more 'Romanised' provinces (and thus for gladiators rather than beast-fighters). Finally, they might be unrepresentative in yet another way. Did some gladiators who survived their time in the *Ludus* merge back into the population? Would their tombstones, erected perhaps years or decades later, still identify them all as gladiators, or would they boast some new identity, one untouched by *infamia*, the prejudice that clung to their former profession? If this idea has any merit, then the epitaphs of gladiators favour those successful enough to have made some sort of career on the sand, but not successful enough to escape the arena altogether.

The chances of survival in a fight were contingent on time and place. At one extreme, we are told, Nero once put on a gladiatorial show in which no one, not even criminals, died. At the other an inscription boasts of a show at the town of Minturnae in Italy in AD249 in which all eleven matches ended with the death of one of the pair. More representative of a normal show is a largely undamaged column, which can be clearly read, from an inscription of the Games given by Marcus Mesonius at Pompeii. It records eight fights. Of the sixteen combatants two had died: one in eight.

Another crucial factor in a gladiator's chances of survival was how often he fought. Modern estimates are low but vary widely: from just once a year to two or three times. Again, lacking the data for any realistic statistical analysis, we have to create a pattern from isolated flashes of illumination. Caracalla forced a gladiator called Bato to fight three men in a row. When Bato was killed by the third, the emperor honoured him with a funeral. Cassius Dio, however, gives this as an example of the capricious bloodthirstiness of Caracalla. Yet men might fight more than once in a show. We have already met the *Thraex* Marcus Antonius Exochus from Alexandria. His epitaph tells us that he fought at least three times in the Games for Trajan's triumph; *at least* three times, because the inscription breaks off as it begins to recount the result of the third match, and there may have been more. Trajan's Games were exceptional, lasting 123 days, but the existence of the word *Suppositicus* (Substitute) on inscriptions, with no need for any explanation, indicates that it was not completely unusual for a gladiator to fight more than once. Presumably the *Suppositicii* came out if a gladiator was injured or killed in his first match, or if his initial opponent was not thought to have put up enough of a contest, or even to test his endurance, as Caracalla did with Bato. Martial claimed that the outstanding gladiator Hermes, who could fight in every style, was his own substitute – meaning either he never needed a *Suppositicus*, because he was never defeated, or that no one could replace him. At the other end of the spectrum of frequency is the tombstone put up by Purricina for her 'well-deserving husband', Iuvenus the *Provocator*, who died aged twenty-one. Uniquely it tells us how long he had been in a gladiatorial school, as well as the number of his fights: five in four years. It is an average of just over one a year, or one and a half, if a discreet veil has been drawn over the final fight in which he was killed, as is often the case in gladiatorial epitaphs from the western half of the empire.

What does all this mean for the chances of survival for a Spanish cattle-rustler condemned to five years in a *Ludus*, three of them in the arena, by the rescript of Hadrian (which we looked at in Chapter Two)? If we take the higher modern estimates – nine fights, at three a year, each with a one in four chance of dying – things are not too good. On the lower figures – just three fights, one a year, with a one in ten chance of being killed – the future looks more hopeful.

The temptation to generalise from Hadrian's ruling – 'all gladiators fought in the arena for three years' – should be resisted. We just saw that young Iuvenus was still fighting after four years, and those rare gladiators who built up dozens of victories did not do so in just three years. In the arbitrary way of Roman government each judge could condemn a man to the gladiatorial schools for as long as he liked, or 'as long as his crime deserved', as the judge would have put it. Similarly, we can safely assume that every free volunteer negotiated exactly how long he would serve, perhaps even precisely how many times he would fight.

Constantine, always a savage-minded man, expressed the hope that free men condemned to the gladiatorial schools for kidnapping would perish by the sword before they had time to learn how to defend themselves. It points to the truth that novice gladiators – not just *tirones*, but those in their first few fights – were far more likely to be killed. For reasons explored already, novices seldom had individual tombstones. On a communal grave for a gladiatorial troupe from Venusia, in Italy, the number jumps up: out of twenty men, five are described as *tirones*, and another six died in their second or third fight. Although, it must be noted, we do not know the percentage of novices in the whole school.

An apt comparison is with new pilots over the Western Front in World War One, where life expectancy could fall as low as ninety-two hours of flying time. As a contemporary officer wrote: 'The majority of the casualties occurred amongst pilots newly out from England and were the result of inexperience combined with inferior aircraft. Once past a certain point pilots rarely became casualties.' In this world, evocatively recreated in Cecil Lewis' autobiography *Sagittarius Rising*, and V. M. Yeates' largely autobiographical novel *Winged Victory*, the deaths of friends were profoundly felt, but those of novices might be barely noticed.

To put it the other way round, a veteran gladiator was far more likely to survive. Not only did he have more experience – probably to the disappointment of Constantine – but he had a reserve of goodwill from the spectators. The latter, coupled with his cost, made him more likely to be granted *missio* by the giver of the Games. As a gladiator progressed up the *Palus* system of ranking, the numbers thinned out at every level. As gladiators usually were matched against those of the same level, or a level up or down, the higher you went, the fewer men there were to fight. Not only was the veteran more likely to survive, he stepped out onto the sand less often than the novice.

Whatever his status, whatever the odds, every gladiator lived with the very real prospect of his own violent death. The pagan afterlife was not promising. There were the Isles of the Blessed, situated somewhere in the distant west, where the souls of a select body of heroes enjoyed a good afterlife. Gladiators in the eastern half of the empire liked to see themselves as heroes, but imagining gaining access to the Isles of the Blessed seems a stretch. Conversely there was Tartarus, a region of the Underworld, three times as dark as the darkest night, where the most impious and guilty were tortured. But few men see themselves as utterly evil, and gladiators' tombstones express conventional piety. For most of the departed, the afterlife was flitting like a bat over the gloomy asphodel meadows of Hades. At least they might drink from the pool of Lethe, which brought forgetfulness. For most sentience only made a brief return when the living made an offering of blood. This was always done for the sake of the living, usually to learn something. Those summoned back were not happy. The ghost of Achilles told Odysseus that he would rather be a poor landless labourer than rule over all the dead.

Just as philosophers could see themselves as gladiators, so gladiators might draw some consolation from popular philosophy. As we saw, a gladiator in the barracks at Pompeii scrawled a graffito about Seneca, even if he could not spell his name. You did not need to read works of philosophy to have some idea of its basic tenets. For the Stoics, in the formulation of Seneca, if you felt no pain before you were born, why should you expect to after death? The Epicurean Lucretius had the best line: 'If in the end all returns to sleep and rest, why worry?'

If the gladiator sat in the courtyard of the *Ludus Magnus* and looked up beyond the looming bulk of the Colosseum at the night sky, the stars enjoined fatalism. Astrology was pervasive in all levels of Roman society. Not everyone believed, but everyone took it seriously. Although marginalised by modern scholarship, because of its subject and difficulty, about as much astrological literature as historical survives from the Roman empire.

Firmicus Maternus, a fourth-century senator from Sicily, wrote a long and complex book on the subject. Despite its almost impenetrable technical virtuosity, Maternus claims to be no more than an amateur. That he could strike such a pose says something about the widespread diffusion of astronomical knowledge. Incidentally, Lollianus Mavortius, the high imperial official to whom the book was dedicated, was also no astrologer. Originally, he had asked Maternus for a work on the natural curiosities of Sicily. Amidst a vast range of horoscopes – from emperor and governor down to water carrier and sewer cleaner – Maternus told those of gladiators.

No matter how you became a gladiator – as free volunteer or condemned to the schools – it was predetermined by the alignment of the stars at your birth. Although likely to die a brutal death in public, a gladiator might win victories and fame. That was some consolation. As was the certainty that the time and manner of every man's death was preordained. Why worry, if it was written in the stars?

Ave atque vale

It is time for dinner. There are empty places at the table. Tonight there are none of the delicacies of the cena libera. *It is back to barley and bean stew, and wine gritty with ash. Tonight no one comes to the school to watch the surviving gladiators eat.*

Demetrius does not look at where Diodorus used to eat. When the Summa Rudis *ordered the fight resumed, Diodorus had not been himself; slow and tired, as if his spirit had deserted him. In no time Demetrius forced him to submit. Alienated by the brevity of the second combat, perhaps by Diodorus' weaker performance, the crowd had bayed for blood. The emperor had turned his thumb towards the sands. It was not the first time Demetrius had killed a man refused* missio, *but it was the first time he had executed a friend.*

Diodorus had met his end well, offering his neck without flinching. Demetrius had given him the kindness of a quick death; one clean thrust down into the back of the neck. At least he had not had to look into his friend's eyes.

Diodorus had no wife or children. Demetrius had claimed the body. From his prize money he would commission a tombstone. Perhaps one day, if Fate decreed it was his turn to leave the light and go down to Hades, another pious friend would do the same for him.

Further Reading

This section is designed for those readers who want to dig a little deeper, but do not want to engage with the scholarly Endnotes and Bibliography that follow. I list, sometimes with a few words of commentary, some books and articles that I have found especially useful, or are often cited.

Two short books offer enjoyable introductions to gladiators, each viewed from a very specific angle: K. Hopkins, and M. Beard, *The Colosseum* (London, 2005); and J. Toner, *The Day Commodus Killed a Rhino: Understanding the Roman Games* (Baltimore, 2014). A more traditional overview, stressing the importance of beast-fights, is C. Epplett, *Gladiators and Beast Hunts: Arena Sports of Ancient Rome* (Barnsley, 2016). Gladiators are put into context of Roman entertainments in general by H. Dodge, *Spectacle in the Roman World* (Bristol, 2011).

A great deal of the evidence was collected by two French scholars: L. Robert, *Les gladiateurs dans l'Orient grec* (Paris, 1940); and G. Ville, *La Gladiature en occident des origines à la mort de Domitien* (Rome, 1981). Much of it is translated into English by A. Futrell, *The Roman Games: Historical Sources in Translation* (Malden, MA, 2006). A wealth of visual material can be found in E. Köhne, and C. Ewigleben (eds.), *Gladiators and Caesars: The Power of Spectacle in Ancient Rome* (English tr., London, 2000).

The articles in two handbooks are essential for getting to grips with the Games: P. Christesen, and D.G. Kyle (eds.), *A Companion to Sport and Spectacle in Greek and Roman Antiquity* (Malden, MA, Oxford, and Chichester, 2014); and T.F. Scanlon, and A. Futrell (eds.), *The Oxford Handbook of Sport and Spectacle in the Ancient World* (Oxford, 2021). Likewise invaluable is a commentary on Martial's book of arena poems, K.M. Coleman, *M. Valerii Martialis Liber Spectaculorum* (Oxford, 2006).

Among the many books that talk about gladiators are: J.P.V.D. Balsdon, *Life and Leisure in Ancient Rome* (London, 1969), contains a most enjoyable section; T. Wiedemann, *Emperors and Gladiators* (London, and New York, 1992), one of the very best studies; C.A. Barton, *The Sorrows of the Ancient Romans: The Gladiator and the Monster* (Princeton, 1993), imaginative, and thought-provoking; P. Plass, *The Game of Death in Ancient Rome: Arena Sport and Political Suicide* (Madison, Wisc., 1995), using game theory; A. Futrell, *Blood in the Arena: The Spectacle of Roman Power* (Austin, 1997), useful on religion and the provinces; D.G. Kyle, *Spectacles of Death in Ancient Rome* (London, and New York, 1998), with a concentration on the disposal of corpses; D.L. Bomgardner, *The Story of the Roman Amphitheatre* (London, and New York, 2000), good on archaeology, especially of North Africa; L. Jacobelli, *Gladiators at Pompeii* (Los Angeles, 2003), focused on visual culture; F. Meijer, *The Gladiators: History's Most Deadly Sport* (London, 2004), short on references, long on odd assertions; R. Dunkle, *Gladiators: Violence and Spectacle in Ancient Rome* (Harlow, 2008), a fine survey; T. Wilmott, *The Roman Amphitheatre in Britain* (Stroud, 2008), of wider importance than just Britain; D.S. Potter, 'Entertainers in the Roman Empire', in: D.S. Potter, and D.J. Mattingly (eds.), *Life, Death, and Entertainment in the Roman Empire* (2nd ed., Ann Arbor, 2010), 280–349; and D.S. Potter, *The Victor's Crown: A History of Ancient Sport from Homer to Byzantium* (London, 2011), both provocative and lively; and G.G. Fagan, *The Lure of the Arena: Social Psychology and the Crowd at the Roman Games* (Cambridge, 2011), using social psychology.

Some important articles are: K. Hopkins, 'Murderous Games', in: K. Hopkins, *Death and Renewal: Sociological Studies in Roman History 2* (Cambridge, 1983), 1–30; K.M. Coleman, 'Fatal Charades: Roman Executions Staged as Mythological Enactments', *JRS* 80 (1990), 44–73; K.M. Coleman, 'Launching into History:

Aquatic Displays in the Early Empire', *JRS* 83 (1993), 48–74; J.C. Edmondson, 'Dynamic Arenas: Gladiatorial Presentations in the City of Rome and the Construction of Roman Society during the Early Empire', in: W.J. Slater (ed.), *Roman Theatre and Society: E. Togo Salmon Papers I* (Ann Arbor, 1996), 69–112; and K.M. Coleman, 'Defeat in the Arena', *GR* 66.1 (2019), 1–36.

Acknowledgements

Writing a book is a solitary occupation, but it could never get finished or published without the help of many other people. All the following have my thanks.

First the professionals. James Gill, my literary agent at Felicity Bryan Associates, turned my chaotic initial idea into the most detailed outline we have ever submitted. Anna Argenio, then at Hutchinson Heinemann, and Todd Portnowitz, at Alfred A. Knopf, commissioned the book. For the edit, Todd in New York was joined by James Pulford at Hutchinson Heinemann in London. I have never worked with more thoughtful and helpful editors.

Once again, I have been struck by the kindness of other scholars. Ken Dowden, Ted Lendon, Simone Rendina and Glen Storey took the trouble to send me work of theirs that I was struggling to find. Ted Lendon went further; sending me back a piece of my own work that I had lost in moving office and changing computers. Tony Wilmott was good enough to read through the whole book. Needless to say, Tony is not to be blamed for any errors of fact, or unlikely interpretations – those are down to my own ignorance, arrogance and perversity.

Finally, my family: my wife Lisa, eldest son Tom and his girlfriend Charlie Wombwell, my younger son Jack, my aunt Terry, who sadly died before the writing was finished, and my mother Frances, to whom the book is dedicated.

Endnotes

I have tried to avoid unnecessary multiplication of references, and where possible have given modern scholarship in English. Abbreviations mainly follow *The Oxford Classical Dictionary* (4th ed., Oxford, 2012).

Introduction: Twenty-Four Hours in the Colosseum

1 ***The gladiator takes counsel in*:** Following Cat Jarman's brilliant Viking history *River Kings* (2021), each chapter opens with an imagined reconstruction in italics. The evidence for these pieces of historical fiction follows in the main text. Only if it does not are references given in these Endnotes. This gladiatorial match is taken from a tombstone discussed in Ch.10, *The Mind of the Gladiator*. I have made Diodorus and Demetrius members of the same school and friends, as well as moving the location from Amisus, in Asia Minor, to the Colosseum in Rome; hence the reference to the emperor's box.

3 **They were *munera*, from:** Definition at Dunkle (2008), 6.

4 **This book was inspired:** Jones (2021); also Crane (2015) on Waterloo; and Willis (2008), who builds a composite picture of a sea battle in the eighteenth century; interestingly Jones (2021), ix, was inspired to 'add a further level of complexity and challenge', beyond the constraints imposed on a historian by the evidence, by two French novelists 'writing under constraint' (in their cases not using the letter 'e', and describing the same incident from ninety-nine angles, using ninety-nine different styles); I have already employed the twenty-four hour structure in my novel *The Last Hour* (2018).

4 **The Latin poet Martial:** reflected running order, Coleman (1993), 61; problems with idea, Coleman (2006), commentary on *De Spect*, 10.

5 **A sculptural relief:** Below, Chapter 7, *The Procession*; **Latin novel**: Apul. *Met*. 17; **Commodus**: Below, Chapter 1, *Disgrace and the Elite*.

5 **We know from a philosophical**: Sen. *Ep*. 7; **dialogue in a novel,** Petr. *Sat*. 9.
Greek novella: Luc. *Tox*. 60; Below, Chapter 1, *Backgrounds*; **Christians at Lyons,** Eus. *HE* 1.36 (Musurillo [1972], 72–3).

6 **Our day is a composite**: Ville (1981), 129–73: a modern construction for Hopkins, and Beard (2005), 70–2.

1. *Vesper* (Evening)

The Cena Libera

7 **Fragments of evidence: Latin novel**: Petronius, *Satyricon* 26.7; **Greek philosophy**, Plutarch, *Epicurus Makes a Pleasant Life Impossible*, *mor*. 1099B; **Christian propaganda**, *The Passion of Perpetua and Felicitas* 17 (Musurillo [1972], 124–5); and Tertullian, *Apology* 42.4; **Humorous mosaic**, El Djem Mosaic, Dunbabin (1978), 78–85; plate 69; Tuck (2021), 535–6; figure 41.2. **In the *cena libera*:** Some modern reconstructions: Ville (1981), 365-6; Futrell (2006), 86; Dunkle (2008), 74–6.

Diet and Body Shape

8 **A vegetarian diet:** Dalby (2003), 340–1.**For the Pythagoreans**: F. Graf, in: *OCD* (4th ed., Oxford, 2012), *s.v. Pythagoras (1), Pythagoreanism*, 1245–6; **Seneca**, *Ep*. 110.17–23.

8 **The social pyramid:** Alföldy (1985); MacMullen (1974); **Religious festivals**, Plut. *mor*. 1099B.

9 **Gladiators were also usually vegetarian:** Curry (2008), 28–30; **Pliny**, *NH* 18.72; **Punishment rations in army**, Polyb. 6.38; **Vitellius**, Suet., *Vit*. 12; Futrell (2006), 132; **Elite commentator**, (Ps-) Quint. *Major Declamations* 9.5.6.

9 **Gladiators not only ate:** Pl. *NH* 36.203; **Ephesus cemetery, calcium**, Kanz, and Grossschmidt (2009), 218.

9 **Gladiators were fattened up:** Borghese Mosaic: https://www.collezionegalleriaborghese.it/en/opere/floor-mosaic-with-gladiators-and-hunters-4; **Cyprian**, *Letter to Donatus*, 7.

Food and Participants

10 **Translates as the 'free dinner':** Balsdon (1969), 32–53, is an enjoyable introduction to dining in general.

11 **Apart from gladiators:** ***Bestiarii***, Tert., *Apol.* 42.5; **Lion,** Tert., *Spec.* 2.1 .

11 **Alongside the gladiators: condemned at *cena libera***, Ville (1981), 363–4; Potter (2010), 337.

11 ***The Passion of Perpetua and Felicitas*:** the translation of Musurillo (1972) is now joined by Heffernan (2012), who also provides text and commentary. This text has generated a vast amount of scholarship, which I have only sampled. Shaw (1993) is a classic study; Hunink (2010) a typical example of wanting Perpetua's words to be her own; Vierow (1999) and Rea (2016) are particularly thought-provoking on the text as literature.

12 **The anonymous narrator claims: Christians sat, rather than reclined**, Tert., *Apol.* 39.16–19.

Backgrounds

12 **Barbarian prisoners of war: Jews,** Jos., *JW* 6.424; 7.37–40; 96.

13 **The greater the number: Barbarian prisoners of war in fiction**, HA, *Prob.* 19.7-8; *Aur.* 33.4–34.2.

14 **Condemned to the arena: Roman prisoners as gladiators, Spartacus,** Florus 2.8.9; App. *BC* 1.14.117; **Jews,** CD 68.32.1–2.

14 **After the battle of Cannae: Hannibal**, App. *Han.* 28; Pl. *NH* 8.7; cf. Polyb. 3.62–3; with Rawlings (2007/9), 22–4; **Not hear of symbol turned back on Rome:** Diodorus Siculus, 33.21a, says that in 139BC 200 pairs of *momomachoi* fought at the funeral of Viriathus, the Lusitanian chieftain, but not that they were prisoners of war; rather than an emulation of Rome, probably this was an indigenous Celtiberian practice, Wiedemann (1992), 42.

14 **Only once, in the aftermath: Cornelius Balbus and Fadius**, Cic., *Fam.* 10.32.

15 **Criminals convicted of heinous crimes:** (Ps-)Quint. *Major Declamations* 9.21.4; Phil. *VA* 4.22; **Legal texts edit out gladiators**, Wiedemann (1992), 29; 105–6.

16 **Numbers of criminals varied**: Pl. *Ep.*10.31–2; *Digest* 48.19.31.

16 **When the guilty are punished:** Tert. *De spect.* 19; Varro in Sosipater Charisius 1.133; with Futrell (2006), 122–5; Toner (2014), 55.

17 **Slaves were the third:** Suet. *Vit.* 12; I have slightly altered the translation of Catherine Edwards (Oxford, 2000); see Adams (1982), 200-201, on sexual 'disgrace'.

18 **Owning a slave: Slavery unnatural,** Arist. *Pol.* 1.3; 1.2.4–5; *Digest* 1.5; **Lack of abolitionism in slave revolts**: See Bradley (1989); but cf. Urbainczyk (2008), 75–80.

18 **Owner could sell a slave: 19BC,** *Digest* 48.11.1–2; **Hadrian,** HA *Had.* 12.

18 **Running away and selling themselves:** *Digest* 11.4.5, where gladiators have been edited out, leaving the still relevant arena and fighting beasts.

19 **The final source of gladiators:** ***Infamia***, overviews focused on gladiators, Wiedemann (1992), 28–30; Dunkle (2008), 35–6.

19 **We have an eyewitness:** Sisinnes, Luc. *Tox.* 57–60; Bosporan Kings, Luc. *Tox.* 44; 51; with Jones (1986), 56–8; 'earlier Toxaris', Luc. *Scyth.* 1–8; **Poverty:** Hor. *Epist.* 1.18.36; (Ps-)Quint. *Major Declamations* 9.23.7; Sen. *Ep.*37.

21 **Descent into poverty: Caused by moral badness; Extravagance,** Sen. *Ep.* 99.13; **Gluttony,** Juv. 11.1–20; (Ps-)Quint. *Minor Declamations* 302.4; **Tatian,** *To the Greeks* 23; **Goodness,** (Ps-)Quint, *Major Declamations* 9.22.8.

21 **Modern historian's analysis:** Ville (1981), 227, love of glory, predisposition to violence, sadism, a taste for killing, and death wish; **Love of adventure**: Meijer (2004), 43.

22 **A great deal of money: Legionary pay,** Le Bohec, (1994), 210; **Another 10,000 drachmas,** Luc. *Tox.* 33.

22 **Away from the fiction: Marcus Aurelius price fix**: Oliver, and Palmer (1955), 320–49; Carter (2003), 83-114; Potter (2010)A, 363–71; Potter (2011), 261–2; 297–9; **Interpreting this text**: The argument of Oliver, and Palmer (1955), 324–7, that the imperial proposal was connected to a specific persecution of Christians in Gaul is unconvincing. Gaul, mentioned twice, seems to be introduced by the senator, who claims special knowledge of the province. Likewise, the elaborate, and to my mind quite unenforceable, price bands might be an addition on the part of the senator. If so, it might have several implications. His

speech focuses on limiting the expense of Games given for the imperial cult. This could well account for the erection of the two inscriptions in Italica in Spain and Sardis in Asia, where documentary proof would help provincial priests wishing to control their costs when negotiating with *lanistae*. More importantly, it is often overlooked that the start of the text, as we have it, sets out the moral and religious imperative behind the legislation, which is nothing to do with helping the finances of the provincial elite. The emperors renounce taxes on the provision of gladiators, which are 'contaminated with the shedding of human blood', and have caused what we know as the Antonine plague. The abolition of these 'foul and shameful' taxes will restore 'complete health'. Is it possible that the imperial initiative went no further, that the senator has not elaborated but created the price fix, and that the law only applied to Games held as part of the imperial cult, and not to others given by municipal magistrates and private individuals?; **Cost of keeping family**, Potter (2011), 261; massively higher after inflation in third century AD, Toner (2009), 19–20.

23 **If the gladiator was: Deductions from soldiers' pay**, Campbell (2002), 84.

23 **Yet three factors suggest: Antoninus Pius Price Fix**, HA, *Ant. Pius* 12.3.

24 **So far we have been: *Gregarii***, Below, Chapter 10, *Mass Combat*; **Highest fees**, Suet., *Tib*. 7.1; **Country estate**, Hor. *Epistles* 1.1.4.

24 **These figures, however, illustrate: Gaius**, *Inst*. 3.146; Carter (2003), 102–3, who thinks the Marcus decree, like Gaius, concerned hiring, not purchasing; but see Potter (2010)A, 371, n.44; **Gaius continued to be used**, T. Honoré, in: *OCD* (4th ed., Oxford, 2012), *s.v. Gaius (2)*, 599; **Marcus decree not stand test of time**, See further, below, Chapter 10, *Mass Combat*.

25 **The acclaim of the crowd: Increase in numbers of free volunteers**, Argued by Ville (1981), 252–5; followers include Barton (1993), 14; and Meijer (2004), 44; others are more cautious, among them Potter (2011), 259–60, who sets out the numbers given here; **Epigraphic habit**, MacMullen (1982), 233–46; **'Skewed' evidence of inscriptions**, See further, below, Chapter 12, *The Future of the Gladiator*.

26 **Increasing numbers of free men: *Gloria***, Brunt (1990), 288–323; **Horatius**, *OCD*, 4th ed., s.v. Horatius Cocles, p.707; **Manlius**

Torquatus, Oakley (1985), 393–4; **Professionalised army**, Keppie (1984), 145–54, is a good introduction; **Septimius Severus**, CD 75.2.5–6.

27 **Substitute for war: Manilius**, *Astronomica* 4.224–6; **Tertullian**, *Ad Mart.* 4–5.

27 **Literary commonplaces:** Wiedemann (1992), 109; **Ulpian**, *Digest* 3.1.1.6.

Disgrace and the Elite

28 **Mark of disgrace: *Dignitas***, Sidebottom (2022), 24; **Julius Caesar**, *BC* 1.9.2.

28 **Shady characters:** Toner (2014), 56, raising the possible problems of re-integration; but see below, Chapter Twelve, *The Future of the Gladiator*; **Freedmen**, Petronius, *Sat.* 45.

29 **Major problem for the elite: Bad emperors force, Caligula**, CD 59.10.1–2; **Nero**, Suet. *Ner.* 12; cf. Tac. *Ann.* 15.32

29 **Man of abominable reputation:** HA *Mar.* 12.2; **Children play**, Epict. 29.3; **Baby's bottle**, Hopkins (1983), 7; **Julius Caesar**, CD 43.23.5; **38BC**, CD 48.43.2; **Augustus, 22BC**, CD 54.5; Suet. *Aug.* 43; **Augustus, AD 11**, CD 56.25.7–8; **Tiberius**, Suet. *Tib.*35; Futrell (2006), 157; **Vitellius**, CD 64.6.3; Tac. *Hist.* 2.62; **Great uncle**, Stothard (2023), 14; **Septimius Severus**, CD 76.8.3.

31 **Desire of their social inferiors:** Tac. *Hist.* 2.62; Her. 7.3.4–6.

31 **Sliding scale of degradation: Watching training**, Balsdon (1969), 295; Apul. *Apol.* 98.

31 **Watching the training was bad: Military training**, Cic. *Cael.* 4.11; **Marcus Aurelius**, CD 73.4.4; **Gladiatorial training**, Futrell (2006), 157.

32 **Fighting in private: Consul and prostitute**, CD 76.8.2.

32 **Fight in public:** Gracchus, Juv. 8.199-210; ***Retarius* effeminate**, Juv. 6. Fr.7–13.

Emperors: Uninterested, Dunkle (2008), 178; **Caracalla and Geta**, CD 77.7.1; ***Augustan History***, *Had.* 14.11; *Mar.* 8.12; *Did. Iul.* 9.1; *Mac.* 4.1–8; with Sidebottom (2022), 68–9; **Suetonius**, *Ner.* 53.1; *Cal.* 32.2.

33 **In the early autumn: Commodus in the Colosseum**, CD 73.18.1–21.3; Her. 1.15.1–9; the details given by the two vary, and the claim of the latter to be an eyewitness can be doubted, Sidebottom (1998), 2782;

Hekster (2002), 137–62, for a modern discussion; **Private/public**, CD 73.17.1–2; **Mercury/Hercules**, CD 73.17.3–4; **Statue/victories**, CD 22.3; Her. 1.15.9; HA *Com.* 15.8; **Deformed**, CD 73.20.3; the *Augustan History*, *Com.* 9.4–9, uses the passage in Cassius Dio to create further elaborate fictional killings.

34 **The rehabilitation of 'bad' emperors:** Hekster (2002) is a thoroughgoing example; Smith, and Niederhuber (2023), 43–62, is more nuanced.

35 **In many ways fundamentally flawed:** Sidebottom (2022), 256–7; 319–20.

36 **On New Year's Eve: Killing of Commodus**, the accounts of Cassius Dio, 73.22.1–6, and Herodian, 1.16.1–17.11, which vary on timing and detail, have been combined; Smith, and Niederhuber (2023), 60–2, stress Commodus in the arena as the cause.

36 **His last *cena libera*: *Pentepharmacum***, HA, *Ael.* 5.4-5; cf. *Had.* 21.4; **Heliogabalus' food and drink**, HA *Hel.* 19.4–6; 20.5; **Caracalla as common soldier**, Her. 4.7.4–7; CD 78.13.1–2.

Privacy

37 **Take the public baths:** There is an enormous amount of scholarship, which I have only sampled; Balsdon (1969), 26–32, is an enjoyable introduction; Toner (1995), 53–64, provides an insightful cultural history; **Hadrian and the veteran**, HA *Had.* 17.6–7; **Mixed bathing**, HA *Hel.* 31.7; *Alex. Sev.* 24.2; **Prostitutes**, Beard (2008), 247; **Fathers and sons**, Plut. *Mor.* 274A; August. *Conf.* 2.3.6; the language of the latter is ambiguous, perhaps only the physical evidence of puberty, cf. Lane Fox (2015), 41; **Penises in the baths**, Celsus, *De Med.* 7.25.1; Martial 1.96; 9.33; Sen. *Nat.* 1.16.1–9.

39 **Communal latrines:** Jansen (2003), 137–52; Koloski-Ostrow (2015), esp. 84–122; two illuminating studies, from which almost everything in this section is drawn; **Tertullian**, *Spec.* 21.2; **Lucan**, Suet. *Vita Luc.* 17–20; **'Tavern of the Seven Sages'**, the room was later part of a bath complex, with the paintings covered, and so now is usually known as the 'Baths of the Seven Sages'; Clarke (2007), 125–31; Koloski-Ostrow (2015), 115–7.

40 **Privacy and sex: Erotic art, Villa Farnesina**, Clarke (1998), 93–107, with the most convincing interpretation, and good illustrations;

House of Caecilius Iucundus, Clarke (1998), 153–61; and Plate 5; ***Cubiculae***, Riggsby (1997), 36–56; Plutarch, *mor.* 140B; **Petronius**, *Sat.* 45; **Other works of art**, I am thinking of the famous Warren Cup; Clarke (1998), 61–72, see figure 21.

42 **The boundaries of Roman privacy: Pliny**, *Pan.* 83.1; *Ep.* 2.17. 20–24; Dunn (2019), 72–8, is a wonderful evocation of Pliny's villa; **Domitian**, Suet. *Dom.* 3; **Caracalla**, Her. 4.13.4–5; different versions in CD 79.5.4; and HA *Carac.* 7.1–2; with Sidebottom (2022), 17–8.

43 **Privacy was culturally coded:** Herodotus 3.38; Amm. 23.6.76–84.

Reasons

44 **Various explanations: Compensation/thanks**, Ville (1981), 365–6; **Raise status**, Brettler, and Poliakov (1990), 93–8; **Mediation**, Plass (1995), 52.

44 **All these operate: Origins (and human sacrifice)**, See below, Ch. 6, *Origins and History*; **Christians (and human sacrifice)**, see below, Ch.s 9, *Christians to the Lion!*; and 12, *The Future of the Games*.

45 **Another proposal: Advertisement**, Dunkle (2008), 75.

45 **Far odder to our mind: Philosophical inquiry**, The passage of Plutarch is in *Epicurus Makes a Pleasant Life Impossible* at *mor.* 1099B; the linked treatise is *Reply to Colotes in Defence of the Other Philosophers*.

46 **No doubt more common, motive: *Schadenfreude*, One in eight**: See below, Chapter 12, *The Future of the Gladiator*; **Viewer not going to die**, But see below, Ch. 6, *Anticipation,* for perceived dangers to spectators; **Afterlife**, See below, Ch. 12, *The Future of the Gladiator*; **Fascination with death/*momento mori***, Hope (2009), 25–7; **Petronius**, *Sat.* 34, tr. J.P. Sullivan; **Horace**, *Odes* 1.11.

47 **There was another: Gambling**, Toner (1995), 89–101; **Scholars divided, Accept**, Hopkins (1983), 26; Toner (1995), 99; Edmondson (1996), 99; **Reject**, Beard (2023), 271; oddly Hopkins, and Beard (2005) accept betting at p.56, but reject it at p.72; presumably the result of joint authorship; **Gaming boards, Aphrodisias**, Toner (2014), 115; **Colosseum**, Toner (1995), 90; **Cock fighting**, Toner (1995), 91; **Chariot racing**, Ovid, *Ars. am.* 1.163–76; which can be read as including betting at the arena as well as the circus; Tert. *De spect.* 16.1; **Laws**, *Digest*, 11.5.2.1; 11.5.3.

A Mosaic and Conversations

48 **One visual representation: El Djem mosaic**, Dunbabin (1978), 78–85; plate 69; Tuck (2021), 535–6; figure 41.2.

48 **After some debate:** Balsdon (1969), 351–2, gives a brief overview; **Symbols**, Dunbabin (1978), 79; **Patron deities**, Dunbabin (1978), 83.

49 **Location of the *cena libera*:** Unless the mosaic depicts a gladiatorial school that, like the *Ludus Maximus*, had a miniature arena for training.

Revenge

51 **The Jews: First Jewish Revolt**, See above, *Backgrounds*; **Diaspora Revolt**, Birley (1997), 72–3; **Bar Kokhba**, Birley (1997), 268–78; **Jews spectators, not participants at the Games**, Olshanetsky (2023), 119–48

51 **The *Babylonian Talmud*: Reish Lakish**, Brettler, and Poliakoff (1990), 93–8; Olshanetsky (2023), 129–33, the latter arguing against the translation that puts him in a gladiatorial school.

52 **A good one-liner:** Brettler, and Poliakoff (1997), 96, have a gladiator gnashing his teeth; Olshanetsky (2023), 130, has Reish Lakish himself.

2. *Prima Vigilia* (The First Watch of the Night)

The cena libera is over . . .

53 **Slaves eat leftovers:** Apul. *Met.* 10.14; Balsdon (1969), 52; Thébert (1987), 369.

The Schools

53 **Spartacus was owned**: **Batiatus**, Plut. *Cras.* 8; evidence for the revolt is collected and translated by Shaw (2001), 130–65; and discussed by Bradley (1989), 83–101; ***Lanistae* contaminated by blood/necessary evil**, From the speech in the Senate on fixing gladiatorial prices; *CIL*. 2.6278, lines 7–12.

54 **A troupe of gladiators: Individual owners under the Republic**, Dunkle (2008), 163–5; **Atticus**, Cic. *Ad Att.* 4.4a.2; 4.8.2.

55 **5,000 in *ludus*:** Cic. *Ad Att.* 7.14.2; commentators often emend the text to 1,000 to bring down the incredibly high number; the passage says 5,000 'shields' (*scutorum*), probably slang for gladiators, although some interpret it as a reference to equipment; see Dunkle (2008), 39, n.47; **320 pairs of Julius Caesar**, Plut. *Caes.* 5.9.

55 **Objects of suspicion: Praeneste**, Tac. *Ann.* 15.46.1; **Violence,** Dunkle (2008), 164–7; **Faustus Sulla**, Asconius, *Scaur.* 18; **Metellus Nepos**, Plut. *Cato min.* 27–9.

55 **Extremist senators: *Populares* and *optimates***, Wirszubski (1950), 31–65, is still the best place to start; **Clodius and Milo**, Asconius, *Mil.* 26.

56 **Forestall gladiatorial violence: Expelled from Rome**, Sal. *Cat.* 30.7; **Expelled from Capua**, Cic. *Pro Sest.* 9; **Capua in 49BC**, Caes. *BC* 1.14.4–5; Cic. *Ad Att.* 7.14.2.

57 **Death knell for private schools:** Edmondson (1996), 80–1, reads a difficult passage of Cassius Dio, 54.2.4, as Augustus restricting private *munera* in Rome in 22BC; interpreted here as restricting *munera* given by magistrates; **Ludus Aemilius**, Hor. *AP* 32; **Statilius Taurus**, Richardson (1992), 11, s.v. *Amphitheatrum Statilli Tauri*; **Publius Servilius**, CD 53.27.6.

57 **Combats in private: Gladiators at dinner parties, Nicolaus,** Athen. *Deip.* 4.153; **Caligula's auction**, Suet. *Cal.* 38; CD 59.14.1–5; **Strabo**, 5.4.13.

58 **Imperial schools: In Rome**, Dunkle (2008), 51–4; **Mesonius graffito**, *CIL* IV.2508; Jacobelli (2003), 45–6; ***Ludus Magnus*, *Matutinus*, *Dacicus*, *Gallicus***, Richardson (1992), 236–8; Coarelli (2007), 170–2; ***Ludus bestiarius*,** Sen. *Ep.* 70.20; **Dacian and Gallic prisoners of war**, e.g. Meijer (2004), 55; **Domitian's Dacian wars**, Sidebottom (2017), 1017–8; **Gallic revolt AD68–70**, Wellesley (2000), 169–83.

59 **Imperial schools: Across the empire**, Wiedemann (1992), 170–1; **Ravenna,** Str. 5.1.7.

60 **The greatest owner of gladiators: Imperial procurators in Italy and provinces**, Evidence, mostly epigraphic, assembled by Edmondson (1996), 81, n.47; and Dunkle (2008), 52–3.

61 **Below the level of the elite: Three *lanistae* at Pompeii**, Numerius Festius Ampliatus, Marcus Mesonius, and Pomponius Faustinus; identification as *lanistae*, rather than civic dignitaries, is uncertain, as the word *lanista* is avoided, Jacobelli (2003), 45–7; a fragmentary

inscription from Venusia on the communal tomb of the *familia* of Gaius Salvius Capito lists at least twenty-nine gladiators, and likewise avoids the word *lanista*, *ILS* 5083; **Marcus Aurelius price fix**, Above, Ch.1, *Backgrounds*; **Seneca**, *Ben*. 87.15–6; ***Negotiator familiae gladiatoriae***, *CIL* XII.727.

The Oath

62 **The midwinter: *Saturnalia***: Balsdon (1969), 124-5; **Suckling pig**, *CDCC*, 683–4; **Sing stark naked**, Lucian, *Sat*. 2.

62 **Davus:** Hor. *Sat*. 2.7; gladiatorial oath at 2.7.58–9; **satire not autobiography**, Sharland (2005), 109–10; **modern discussions of the gladiatorial oath** include Robert (1940), 32–3; Ville (1981), 246-–9; Wiedemann (1992), 106–9.

62 **Not have an ancient discussion: Seneca**, *Ep*. 37.1–2; **Petronius**, Sat. 117; with Schmeling (2011), 446.

63 **Slight variations in these oaths:** Wiedemann (1992), 107, sees a 'standard formula'.

63 **Time limit on the oath: Cattle rustlers in Spain**, Futrell (2006), 123.

63 **Who took the terrible oath: *Lex Aelia Sentia***, Gaius, *Inst*. 1.18.

63 **A free volunteer: Theft of free people**, Gaius, *Inst*. 3.199; Carter (2003), 105; **Sister buys out brother**, Quint., *Inst*. 8.5.12.

64 **No more than empty ceremonial: Study of modern combat**, Holmes (1985), 31–4; **Fadius**, Cic., *Fam*. 10.32; above Ch.1, Backgrounds.

Training

65 **The sources for the training:** Fagan (2015), 122–44; and Carter (2018), 119–31 are useful modern studies.

65 **Juvenal was a man:** *Satire* 6; with the commentary of Watson, and Watson (2014); gladiatorial training at lines 246–67.

66 **Vegetius, a bureaucrat:** Milner (1996) provides an excellent translation of the *Epitoma Rei Militaris*, with illuminating introduction and notes; **Ailments of horses**, Vegetius is generally accepted as the author of *Digesta Artis Mulomedicinae*.

66 **Recruits set up: Vegetius on training**, Veg. *Mil*. 1.11–12; 2.23; Vegetius' stress on thrusting, not cutting was anachronistic for

contemporary troops. When he was writing, Roman soldiers used the *spatha*, primarily a slashing sword. The earlier *gladius* was designed for both, and there is evidence of it being used as a cutting weapon, e.g. Polyb. 18.30.7, at 2.23 Vegetius has them using the edge as well as the point; Vegetius' martial arts movie-style jumping in the air to strike seems to be a generalisation from a technique sometimes used against an enemy that had locked their shields together to form a 'shieldwall'.

67 Tentative programme of gladiatorial training: Seneca, *Dec.* 9. 8–9; Carter (2006), 157, citing Cic. *Att.* 1.16, suggests heavy practice swords could have been made of iron; **Ephesus cemetery**, Kanz, and Grossschmidt (2006), 207–16; **Commodus**, CD 7317.2; **Trainee orator/gladiator**, Quint. *Inst.* 10.5.20.

67 A *doctor* or a *magister*: Hermes, Martial 5.24; ***Doctores myrmillonum* etc**, Fagan (2015), 130.

68 Very different training: 'Snatching feathers', Levick (1983), 99; **Feathers on helmets**, Junkelmann (2000), 37; **'Feather-wearers'**, Juv. *Sat.* 3.152–8.

68 Who decided what sort: Cicero on Vatinius, *Pro Sest.* 132–5; **Gracchus**, Juv. *Sat.* 8.199–210.

Sex

69 A good time for sex: Vespasian, Suet. *Vesp.* 21; **Caligula**, Suet. *Cal.* 36; cf. 25; and Suet. *Aug.* 69.

69 Cresces the net-fighter: written by the gladiator himself, Jacobelli (2003), 48–9; contra the 'breathless groupies' of Carter (2008), 114; or the 'innocent girls' of Meijer (2004), 70.

69 The remains of a woman: Beard (2008), 5; visiting her lover, e.g. Ewigleben (2000), 133; and Bomgardner (2000), 54.

70 Sexual charge: Martial 5.24.10; Tert. *De spect.* 22.2; **No erotic appeal for men**, Vout (2022), 146–7; but see 136–7; **Effeminate *retiarii***, Above Ch.1, *Disgrace and the Elite*; and below, Ch.3, *Security*; and Futrell (2021), 676-9; ***Softy* and *Depilated***, Carter (2008), 119–20; **Stage names**, Dunkle (2008), 124–6; and see below Chapter 10, *The Mind of the Gladiator*.

70 Roman sexuality: Clarke (1998) is a wonderful introduction via art; Sidebottom (2022) more briefly, focusing on Heliogabalus; **Maastricht**

gladiator and Aphrodite of Knidos, A brilliant observation by Wiedemann (1992), 38–9; **Sex as fighting and other metaphors**, Adams (1982), 138–70.

71 **Gladiators their erotic appeal: Ideal male beauty**, Vout (2022), 4–5; **Fat**, Above, Chapter 1, *Diet and Body Shape*; **Bad teeth**: Kanz, and Grossschmidt (2009), 218; also broken teeth, if the cemetery from York is that of gladiators, Hunter-Mann (2015), 9; **Bad breath**, Toner (2009), 133–4; **Scars and bites**, Tert. *Ad mart*. 4–5; **Tattoos**, Gustafson (2000), 21; **Short haircut**, Toner (2014), 29–30; **Topknot**, Dunbabin (1978), 66; Plate XX, on Zliten mosaic; **Sergius**, Juv. *Sat*. 6.107–9; **Almost deformed**, Pl. *NH* 11.99; **York cemetery**, Toner (2014), 64; as the burials were deposited between the late first and late fourth centuries AD, not a result of executions in AD211, as Sidebottom (2022), 110; although decapitation is relatively common in cemeteries in Roman Britain, and otherwise unattested as a method of execution in the arena, various factors point to a gladiatorial cemetery; the percentage of those decapitated is far higher than normal (71 per cent cf. 5 per cent); the percentage of young men (98.5 per cent); is comparable to that in the epigraphically identified gladiatorial cemetery at Ephesus; as are the many healed injuries; the deformations caused by training are comparable to those of modern athletes; and one skeleton has bite marks from a large carnivore; (Hunter-Mann (2015), 6–10.

72 **Often described as beautiful**: **Irony**, Cic. *Pro Sest*. 133-5; **No irony**, Sen. *Controv.* 10.4.18; the inscribed speech of the senator replying to the proposal of Marcus Aurelius and Commodus to fix the price of gladiators has been read as referring to the highest category of gladiators as the 'best and most beautiful', e.g. Barton (1993), 80; the text is damaged, and most modern editors restore not 'beautiful' (*formonso*) but 'famous' (*postremo*), Oliver, and Palmer (1955), 336, but, if *formonso* was not in the speech, it could have been a telling slip on the part of the stonemason: being a top gladiator, in a strange way, made you 'beautiful'.

73 **Sexual appeal: Violence**, Juv. *Sat*. 6.110–2; with Watson, and Watson (2014), ad loc.; ***Gladius***, Adams (1982), 20–1; **Briseis**, Ovid, *Ars Am*. 2. 711-5; **Transgression**, Pet. *Sat*. 126.

73 **Also very funny: Lamp**, Clarke (2003), 151, interpreting her as working out with weights; **Catalogue** at 137; **see also** 147–8, fig. 101, on a

medallion, made to be applied to a drinking vessel, which is now lost, and known via a drawing and photograph, which has a similar image of a woman riding a man while wielding a large shield (*scutum*) and short sword (*gladius*) – the kit of either a legionary or a 'big shield' type of gladiator – here the humour is more obvious; the man, whose penis has slipped out of her, and who is losing his erection, shouts 'Look out! That's a shield!' (*ORTE SCUTUS EST*).

3. *Secunda Vigilia* (The Second Watch of the Night)

The gladiators are snoring . . .

There is a surprising amount of high-quality recent scholarship on **the Roman night and sleeping**; this chapter draws heavily on Dowden (2003), 141–63; Linn (2014); Nissin (2015), 95–133; Storey (2017), 307–31; and Wilson (2018), 59–89.

75 ***Snoring***: Could be, not just irritating for others, but, as it was seen as caused by a lack of self-control, interpreted as a sign of moral badness, Linn (2014), 16–8; ***they sleep on***, Camp beds and straw pallets are unlikely to leave any archaeological traces; Nissin (2015), 101–2; cf. Davison (1989), 238–9, on the furniture of soldiers' barracks, noting lack of evidence for bunk beds.

The Measure of Time

75 **The Romans had more time: Counting the days**: Balsdon (1969), 56–7.

75 **Twenty-four hours:** Laurence (1994), 123; Linn (2014), 3, n.3, has a useful table; **Four watches**, Nissin (2015), 119.

76 **Segmented sleep:** Argued to be common in premodern societies by Ekirch (2005), 300–1; enthusiastically followed by Sticka (2017), who surveys the evidence at 19–33; its existence in Rome cautiously accepted by Storey (2017), 327–9, who, however, raises the absence of words to describe the getting up and the second sleep; and persuasively rejected by Nissin (2015), 118–9 .

76 **Difficult to tell the time: Sundials and water clocks**, Wilson (2018), 60; Jones (2019), 125–57; **Lupins**, Pl. *NH* 18.133; 252; **Candles**,

Wilson (2018), 66; **Military trumpets**, Poly. 6.24; ***Vigiles***, Webster (1985), 99–101; ***Nyktophylakes*** *and* ***Praefectus nocturnae custodiae***, Chaniotis (2018), 12; ***Eirenarch***, Fuhrmann (2012), 71–3.

77 **'Truly, I say to you':** Matthew 26.34; **Vague conceptualisations**, Nissin (2015), 118–9; Balsdon (1969), 18, provides the exegesis of *conticinium*; Now see Ker (2023), which I obtained too late to use in this section.

The Difficulties of Sleeping

77 **'Now the rest of the gods':** Hom. *Il.* 2.1–2; there is a lot of insomnia in Greek epic poetry, Gibson (1996), 457–9; **Bedbugs**, Linn (2014), 122–4; **Vinegar,** Varro 1.2.25; **Seneca**, *Ep.*124.

78 **The main barrier to sleep: Dogs, shouts**, Nissin (2015), 105-6; **Laughter**, Mar. 12.57; **Singing**, Sen. *Ep.* 51.12 (actually, at Baiae); **Music**, Plut. *Ant.* 75.3–4 (actually, supernatural music in Alexandria); **Snoring neighbour**, Cic. *Ad Att.* 4.3.4.

78 **After Julius Caesar:** Laurence (2013), 253–5; **Children buried at night**, Ker (2004), 219, n.43; **Millers**, Wilson (2018), 76–7; **Bakers**, Mar. 12.57; **Stevedores**, extrapolated from Alexandria in Egypt, Wilson (2018), 78; **Baths at Vipasca**, Wilson (2018), 72–3; ***Augustan History***, *Alex. Sev.* 24.6; *Tac.* 10; **Bars**, Laurence (1994), 126; **Messalina**, Dunn (2024), 355; **Clitoris**, Juv. 6.129.

79 **Sleeping draught:** Nissin (2015), 123.

79 **Leave the city:** Nissin (2015), 106, with many references; **Juvenal**, *Sat.* 3.232–41, is the classic account of disturbed nights in Rome.

79 **The main thoroughfares:** ***Vivarium***: Balsdon (1969), 313; Richardson (1992), 431–2.

The Cult of Sleeplessness

79 **Cicero was disturbed:** *Ad Att.* 4.3.4; **Lack of zoning**, MacMullen (1974), 57–87; **Renting out shops**, Wallace-Hadrill (1994), 118–42.

80 **Obtain nocturnal silence: Pliny**, *Ep.* 2.17.20–4; ***Silentarii***, Jones (1964), 571–2; **Caligula**, Suet. *Cal.* 26.

80 **Cultivated a cult of sleeplessness:** ***Lucubratio***, Like cigarettes and alcohol for some modern novelists, *lucubratio* became a part of the creative process for Latin poets; there are many studies, particularly

illuminating are Dowden (2003), 150–4; and Ker (2004), 209–42; **Quintilian,** *Inst.* 10.3.22–5; **Health,** Ker (2004), 218.

81 Military service: Sleepless Generals, Dowden (2003), 153–4; Chaniotis (2018), 8, n.23; **Ulpius Marcellus,** CD 73.8.1–6.

81 The role of the emperor: Emperors and Military, Campbell (1984); **Day in the Life of the Emperor,** Suet. *Vesp.* 21; CD 77.17.1; HA *Alex.* 29.1; 21.6.

82 Civic Officials: Smith (1999), 182–8.

82 Out in the country: Rural Slaves, Cato, *Agr.* 5.5; Colum. 12.1.1–3; **Martyrdom of Perpetua and Felicitas,** 16.11–3 (Musurillo [1972], 124–5).

Sleeping as Weakness and Wickedness

83 Greek poetry: Magowan (2017), 34; **Homer,** *Od.* 23.386–8; **Necessity,** Nissin (2015), 121–2; **Latin poets,** Martial 1.71; Statius, *Silv.* 5.4.

83 Sleep had a dark side: Undermine spirit, Ovid, *Rem. Am.* 145–8; **Antony,** Cic. *Ad Att.* 10.13; **Night into day,** Plut. *Ant.* 9.3–4; HA, *Hel.* 28.6; **Seneca,** *Ep.* 122; discussed by Ker (2019), 184–213.

83 Summertime siesta: Nissin (2015), 115-6; **Litany of vices,** Nissin (2015), 121, n.203.

83 Criminals: Ker (2004), 219; **Crimes worse at night than day,** Chaniotis (2018), 11.

84 The Roman authorities: Bacchanalian suppression, Gruen (1990), 34–78.

84 Catiline was the archetype: Rives (1995), 72–3.

84 Christians, who met before dawn: Enjoyable ways into this huge subject are MacMullen (1984), and Lane Fox (1986).

85 Christians posed an existential threat: *Pax Deorum*, Sidebottom (2022), 230–1; **Rise of Christianity as series of chance events,** Argument sketched in a couple of pieces for a general readership, Sidebottom (2014), 24–8; and (2024).

86 Adherence to the traditional gods: Below, Ch.10, *The Mind of the Gladiator*.

Sleep and Darkness as Fear and Death

86 Alexander the Great: Plut. *Alex.* 22; **Gods sleep in Epic,** Dowden (2003), 144–5; **'Lord of mortal men and all the gods',** Hom. *Il.* 232–3.

86 **Hypnos:** Stafford (2003), 71–106.

86 **Romans were afraid of the dark: Street lighting**, Wilson (2018), 65–6; 85; **Chamber pot**, Juv. *Sat.* 3.268–78; **Drunken waggoneer**, Wilson (2018), 78.

87 **Not all the dangers: Assaulted**, Juv. *Sat.* 3.278–301; **Robbed or murdered,** Prop. 3.16; **Arrested**, Wilson (2018), 63; **Supernatural countryside**, Sidebottom (2022), 14–6.

87 **More terrors than the dark streets: Tenements**, Scobie (1986), 399–33; **Collapse and fire**, Juv. *Sat.* 3.190–202; **Dionysius**, Eus. *HE* 6.40.

87 **Places of supernatural anxiety: Ghosts and *daemons***, E. Eidinow, 'Ghosts', in: *OCD* (4th ed., Oxford, 2012), 615–6; **Clanking chains**, Pl.7.27.5–6; **Dark and embodied**, CD 67.9.1–4; Edwards (2007), 162–3; **Plotinus**, Porphyry, *Plot.* 8–9; **Brutus**, Plut. *Brut.* 36–7; 48.

88 **Darkness and night intensify emotion: Witches**, Spaeth (2010), 231–35; Storey (2017), 310–1; **Christians fear of supernatural sex**, Nissin (2015), 125; pagans seem to have been more relaxed about daemonic figures visiting for sex; a dream of intercourse with Ephialtes (in Latin *Incubus*) foretold great benefits, Artem. *Oneir.* 2.37.3; and the shepherd being mounted by a winged female on a relief, probably from the Bay of Naples, which dated to the second century AD, but likely reworks a Hellenistic image, looks unalarmed and sports a fine erection, Harris (2009), 35, plate 5, who, to fit his theory that no one much believed in dreams, unconvincingly dismisses it as a 'parody'; Christians also worried about their souls leaving their sleeping bodies, Tert. *De anim.* 44.

88 **Precautions were advisable: Offerings**, Hel. *Aeth.* 3.4; **Arbutus etc**, Spaeth (2010), 231–2.

88 **Sleep was too close to death:** Nissin (2015), 126, n.252; Apul. *Met.* 2.25; **Darkness and death**, Hom. *Il.* 5.47; **Nightlights**, I have not found a scholarly study. Clearly the practice was not universal. In Tacitus, *Ann.* 14.44, a senator claims all the slaves in a household must have realised that one of their number intended to kill their master, because, among other reasons, the murderer must have taken a lamp into the bedroom. In Heliodorus' novel *An Ethiopian Story* a character calls for a lamp at bedtime, although he intends to pass the time telling stories, as well as sleeping (3.4); another has a lamp brought in to where he was sleeping in order to read (8.12); **Lamps for lovers,** Martial 14.39; **Agrippina**, Tac. *Hist.* 14.8; **Lucian**, *Greek Anth.* 11.432.

89 **Gladiators were the second most:** Clarke (2003), 137; Above, Ch.2, *Sex*.

4. *Tertia Vigilia* (The Third Watch of the Night)

The gladiator turns in his sleep . . .

90 **Dreams:** In the last thirty or forty years there has been a lot of scholarly work on Classical dreams and dreaming; including two important books in English: Harris (2009); and Harrisson (2013); it is still well worth reading Dodds (1951), 102–34; and (1965), 38–53; characteristically insightful is Pelling (1997), 197–212.

90 ***The gladiator . . . had dreamed*:** From Artemidorus, *Oneirocritica* 5.58; on the text see below, *How to be a Dream Diviner*; ***What it all means***, because the meaning of the dream was not fully worked out until after he had retired from the arena, see below, *The Dreams of Gladiators*.

The Importance of Dreams

90 **Septimius Severus dreamed:** CD 75.3.3; 73.23.1–5; 80.5.3; Her. 2.9. 5–6 also records Severus' dream, and adds the equestrian statue, the precise location of which within the Forum is uncertain, Richardson (1992), 'Equus Severi', 145; on dreams and the writing of history in the Roman empire, see Sidebottom (2007), 73–4.

91 **Dreams were meaningless:** Harris (2009) argues for widespread disbelief, at least until c.AD 100, but can be thought to privilege evidence that fits his contention; Walde (2011), 208; the supposed increase in credulity in the second century AD might amount to no more than the survival of the works of Aelius Aristides and Artemidorus; cf. Harrisson (2013), 75–124; **Epicureans**, Harris (2009), 261–5; **Sextus Empiricus**, *Ad Math.* 9; **Incubation**, F. Graf, 'Incubation', in: *OCD* (4th ed., Oxford), 731–2; **Dozens of inscriptions**, the line of Harrisson (2013) that many inscriptions were put up either by priests to promote their sanctuary, or by dreamers to 'reintegrate' themselves into society, and thus do not reflect real dreams, is unconvincing, as a dream and self-interest do not have to be mutually exclusive; **Aelius Aristides**, Downie (2014), 105–13.

91 **Some specialists:** Cic. *De Div.* 1.30.64; Artem. *Oneir.* 4.59.3.

91 **Not all dreams were significant: Food and drink**, Pl. *NH* 10.98; **Gates of Horn and Ivory**, Hom. *Od.* 19.630–40; Vir. *Aen.* 6.893–6; **Later in the night**, Hor. *Sat.* 1.10.33 (after midnight); Artemidorus (*Oneir.* 1.7) thought the time made no difference; **Hangovers**, e.g. Pl. *NH* 17.37; 20.21; 20.34; 32.49.

92 **Some true dreams: Javelin dream**, Artem. *Oneir.* 5.59; **3,800 coins dream**, Artem. *Oneir.* 2.59.3.

How to be a Dream Diviner

92 **The whole spectrum of society: *Oneirocritica***, A game-changer for the study of Artemidorus was the publication of the excellent translation by Martin Hammond (2020), with Introduction and Notes by Peter Thonemann (2020)A, and the accompanying study by Thonemann (2020); an earlier ground-breaking study was Price (1986), 3–37; **Flourishing genre**, Artemidorus refers to about eighteen literary predecessors, Thonemann (2020), 22; such books were not popular, according to Harris (2009), 134–5, because no papyri of Artemidorus have been found; on this logic no literature was really popular except Homer.

93 **Artemidorus was born: Ephesus/Daldis**, *Oneir.* 3.66.7; Thonemann (2020), 7–8.

93 **Artemidorus was writing: Coins**, Thonemann (2020)A, xv–xvi, points out, on the one hand, the coins feature the local deity Apollo Mystes, who was the writer's patron (*Oneir.* 2.70.13), but, on the other, Artemidorus is not a rare name; **Paulus the lawyer**, *Oneir.* 4.80.2; **Iulius Paulus the jurist**, Mennen (2011), 151–2.

93 **Complex structure:** Thonemann (2020)A, xvi–xviii.

94 **Artemidorus' methods:** Thonemann (2020)B, xviii–xxii; Thonemann (2020), 36–7; **Numerology**, Thonemann (2020)A, 231–2; **Advice to son**, *Oneir.* 4.20.1.

94 **Freud read Artemidorus:** Price (1986), 3–37; Thonemann (2020), 35; **Illustrate character**, Pelling (1997), 197–212.

94 **Artemidorus implicitly aligns himself:** Thonemann (2020), 7–12; Thonemann (2020)A, xv–xviii.

95 ***Rich* and *poor*:** Thonemann (2020), 178–81; **Marketplace diviners**, *Oneir. Praef.* 4.

95 ***The Cheese and the Worms*: Subordinate counter-culture**, Ginzburg (1980), esp. xiii–xxvi; 154–5; the existence of this counter-culture can be doubted, as the odd views of the miller can be interpreted as distorted reflections of elite views, Price (1984), 107–8; Sidebottom (1990), 298–300.

96 **Autobiographical dreams:** *Oneir.* 1.19; 2.48.3; 2.59.2; **Previous writers**, Fifteen predecessors named by Artemidorus are listed in the index of Hammond (2020), 328; **Same sorts of dreams**, An exception is that 'insignificant' men do not dream about momentous public events, unless – and it is a significant *unless* – lots of them do, *Oneir.* 1.2.11–12; **If a rich man dreams**, 2.53.1.

96 **The evidence of Artemidorus: Inhabit the same culture**, Toner (1995), esp. 65–88; the existence of a counter-culture in Rome already questioned by Momigliano (1971), 1–18; **If a poor friend shits on your head**, *Oneir.* 2.26.2.

96 **Viewed from the city: Gentleman farmer**, *Oneir.* 2.31.1; **Outlying farm**, 5.84; **Full of bandits**, Fourteen references in the index of Hammond (2020), 317; **Countryside and roads**, 2.68.4; 2.28-1–2.

97 **A dangerous place:** All are in the index of Hammond (2020); **Slaves**, Thonemann (2020), 178, more dream meanings apply to slaves (89), than any other categories (poor = 72; rich = 53).

97 **You need to be alert: Physically impossible**, *Oneir.* 5.69; 5.62; **Supernatural**, 4.69; 1.80.3; **Socially taboo**, 4.44.2; 1.79.1–7; **Mundane**, 4.41; 1.223; 2.2.1.

97 **Fatalistic world: Rare advice**, *Oneir.* 2.2.2; 2.33.2; 4.8; 5.66; **Paws of a bear**, *Oneir.* 5.49.

98 **Unique, and very strange, window: Many new paths**: Cf. Thonemann (2020)A, xxv.

Dreams about Gladiators

98 **Gladiators in Artemidorus:** Carter (2001), 109–15; Carter (2008), 114–35; Carter (2015), 39–52; Thonemann (2020), 174–6.

98 **A poor man dreams . . . :** *Oneir.* 1.5.5; with Thonemann (2020)A, 237; it is interesting that serving in the army and being a passenger on a ship are naturally thought of as bad things; presumably the former because of a mixture of the hard terms of service and the danger, the

latter not just because of the danger, but also the proverbial bad characters on ships.

98 **The type of gladiator . . . :** *Oneir.* 2.32.1–4; drawing on the translation of Hammond (2020), and the notes of Thonemann (2020)A, 263–4.

99 **Artemidorus tops and tails:** Doubted by Thonemann (2020), 39–40; possibly the stupidity of the ***Essedarius*** stemmed from an ethnic cliché about the inhabitants of Britain, if the type was thought of as inspired by the chariots encountered by Julius Caesar; on the ***Dimachaerus*** and ***Arbelas*** Thonemann (2020)A, 264, suggests daggers evoke deceit and assassination, both of which were associated with witches, who were seen as malicious and ugly.

100 **Associated with marriage:** Thonemann (2020)A, 237, highlights the **sexual**; on the **close bonds** of marriage see below; **spear ritual,** Balsdon (1962), 182–3, n.39 collects the references; and see below, Chapter 12, *Magic and Medicine*.

100 **Predicts a bad wife: Tied to the cross**, *Oneir.* 2.53.2.

100 **Before launching into: Foretold generally**, *Oneir.* 2.23.1; **Decapitation**, *Oneir.* 1.35.1–8.

101 **Fighting wild beasts:** *Oneir.* 2.54; perhaps here, as in other texts, the line between those who fought beasts, and those who were executed by them, both of whom could be called *Bestiarii*, has blurred.

101 **The background of the dreamer: Ethnic customs**: *Oneir.* 1.8.2.

The Dreams of Gladiators

102 **Athletes:** Filling an entire column of the index in Hammond (2020), 316; **Not rule out gladiators as clients**, Thonemann (2020), 174–5, does not agree; **Galen,** Mattern (2013), 81–97.

102 **Destined for the arena: Sex with a lump of iron**: *Oneir.* 4.65.2.

102 **Possibly Artemidorus: Self-castration in the arena**: below Chapter 9, *Spectacular Executions*.

102 **Paws of a bear:** *Oneir.* 5.49; with Thonemann (2020)A, 300.

102 **Gladiators already enrolled: Terror and Fear**, *Oneir.* 2.39.5; **Inn of Salvius**, Beard (2008), 230–1; illustrated at plate 13.

103 **The other dream of gladiators: Milk in their breasts**: *Oneir.* 1.16.2.

103 **Sarcophagus full of blood:** *Oneir.* 5.58; with Thonemann (2020), 175; Thonemann (2020)A, 300; the argument of Carter (2015), 39–52,

that the volunteer was a special type of gladiator who only 'fought' criminals executed at the midday spectacle, rests on no more than the dreamer's long career, a thing that can be paralleled in inscriptions.

5. *Quarta Vigilia* (The Fourth Watch of the Night)

The gladiator chokes himself to death

104 ***In the dark, damp room***: Sen. *Ep*. 70.20; in the anecdote the gladiator is a German in the *Ludus* of beast-fighters.

Security

104 **The effeminacy of contemporary men: Obscene part of gladiatorial school**, Sen. *QNat* 7.31.3; **Remotest part,** Juv. *Sat*. 6. O 7–12; on both passages, Carter (2008), 122–6.

105 **Bunked with their own sort: Gladiators' tombstones**: See below, Chapter 10, *The Mind of the Gladiator*.

105 **Mapped onto the archaeological evidence: Barracks, Rome, *Ludus Magnus***: Richardson (1992), 236–8; Coarelli (2007), 170–2; ***Ludus Matutinus***, Richardson (1992), 238.

106 **Two of the other: Pompeii**, Jacobelli (2003), 65–7; Beard (2008), 271–2; collapse of V 3.5 Fagan (2015), 126, n.10.

106 **The fifth and final barracks: Carnuntum**: Neubauer et al (2014), 173–90.

107 **The gladiator choked himself: Security**: Fagan (2015), 125–6.

109 **Who were the guards?: Soldiers provide security at Games**, See below, Chapter 6, *Anticipation*, and Chapter Eleven, *The Emperor and the Crowd*; **Detached as guards**, Fuhrmann (2012), 212; **Private *Ludi*, *Palus* ranking system**, Carter (2003), 89–98; **Aelius Marcion**, *CIL* 6.10183; **Spanish cattle rustlers**, Futrell (2006), 123.

Roman Suicides

This section draws heavily on the classic article 'Philosophy, Cato, and Roman Suicide' (1986) by my much-missed friend Miriam Griffin; also on van Hooff (1990), and Edwards (2007); as well as Plass (1995); Hill (2004); and Hope (2009).

110 **'I am a Christian, and I want to die':** *The Acts of Euplus* 1 (Musurillo [1972], 314–5).

110 **Voluntary martyrs:** de Ste Croix (1974), 234–8; **Arrius Antoninus**, Tert. *Ad Scapulam*, 5; Arrius, governor of Asia in AD184/5, Tertullian wrote in AD212, Rendina (2022), 209, n.1.

110 **Easy for a modern reader: Black humour**, Rendina (2022), 209–16; **Aemilianus**, *The Martyrdom of Bishop Fructosus and his Deacons, Augurius and Eulogius*, 2 (Musurillo [1972]), 178–9.

111 **Arrius Antoninus suggested: Jumping and hanging**, Griffin (1986), 192; van Hooff (1990), 64–77; Edwards (2007), 204; **Sappho**, Dunn (2024), 81; **Bad slave**, *Dig.* 21.1.23.3; **Heliogabalus**, HA *Hel.* 33.2–7; **Out of window**, Tac. *Ann.* 6.49.1; **Gordian I**, Her. 7.9.9; HA *Gord.* 16.3; *Max. et Bal.* 4.3; **Public cemetery**, *CIL* 11.6528; Edwards (2007), 107–8.

111 **Disreputable ways to kill yourself: Poison**, van Hooff (1990), 59–62; **Drowning**, van Hooff (1990), 72–4; **Criminal/slave**, van Hooff (1990), 151; **Love**, van Hooff (1990), 100; **Plato**, Edwards (2007), 105; **Burning**, van Hooff (1990), 57–9; **Peregrinus**, Luc. *Per.* 20–45.

112 **With a blade:** van Hooff (1990), 47–54; **Civil wars**, good accounts by Philip Matyszak, 870–6; 890–5; 896–903; Richard Marshall, 911–2; and Stephen Matthews, 940–60; 963–82; all in Whitby, and Sidebottom (2017); **Often gladiators**, Turns out to be harder to prove than I thought; the Eros of Mark Antony has a name popular with gladiators, Pl. *Ant.* 76.7; Pelling (1988), 306; a study of the origins of these suicide enablers – friends, freedmen, slaves, gladiators – would be illuminating; **Cato's suicide**, Osgood (2022), 233–52.

112 **Socrates:** As written up in the *Phaedo* of Plato; **Cato as model**, Edwards (2007), 113–43.

113 **Parody by Petronius:** Tac. *Hist.* 16.18–19; Hill (2004), 237–52; Edwards (2007), 158–9; 176–8.

113 **Some suicides were enforced:** Plass (1995), 81–134, is interesting, if hard going; Edwards (2007), 144–60, is equally illuminating, and more enjoyable; MacMullen (1966), 46–94, provided a characteristically evocative background; **'Goodbye, Fulvius'**, Plut. *mor.* 508A; **Next to no one tried to run**, An unexplored topic that, along with attempts to hide and live incognito, would repay study.

114 **Motives were just as important:** van Hooff (1990), 79–132; Edwards (2007), 98–107; motive could trump method, e.g. Pl. *Ep.* 1.12; and see

next section; **Church Fathers**, Griffin (1986), 69; Edwards (2007), 210, n.16.

114 **A bad Roman suicide: Starvation**: Griffin (1986), 66; **Especially for elderly**: Edwards (2007), 107.

Gladiator Suicides

115 **Seneca:** *Ep.* 70.19–24.

115 **Two other sources: Symmachus**, *Ep.* 2.46; **Diodorus Siculus**, 36.10.

115 **Two are explicitly Germanic: Romans on Germans**, Sherwin-White (1967), 1–32; Balsdon (1979), *passim*; Isaac (2004), 427–39; **Tacitus, *Germania***, Sherwin-White (1967), 33–40; Rives (1999).

116 **Symmachus was a pagan traditionalist:** Salzman provides a useful introduction to his life in Salzman, and Roberts (2011), xiii–xliv; although not without some errors and inconsistencies Kelly (2015), 161–3; for his letters Sogno (2016), 175–89, gives an overview; there is no translation into English of Books Two to Ten; there is an Italian commentary on Book Two by Cecconi (2002), which, unfortunately, I have not been able to access; **Saxons**, Mitchell (2012); **Symmachus was furious**, Stothard (2010), 3–10, imagines his response.

Diodorus Siculus: **Rehabilitation**: Sacks (1990); **Sympathy for slaves**, Urbainczyk (2008), 81–90.

118 **This is a strange story: No discussion**, This can be explained by the fragmentary nature of the text, but a cynic might wonder if Diodorus has just lifted the passage from a text where the reasoning was explained.

118 **With Seneca we get:** The best way into his life and works are two hugely enjoyable biographies: Griffin (1976); and Romm (2014).

118 **As Seneca put it elsewhere:** Sen. De *ira* 3.15.4.

6. *Conticinium* (Just Before Dawn)

Popularity

120 **The Romans claimed: Audience numbers**: Figures for Colosseum, Theatre of Marcellus, and Circus Maximus taken from Richardson (1992).

121 **In a similar vein: Frequency of shows, Augustus**, CD 54.2; **AD354**, The Calendar of Filocalus, Futrell (2006), 30, n.62; December 2,4–6, 8, 19–21, 23–4; ***Augustan History***, *Alex*. 43.4; *Gord*. 3.5–8.

121 **Parts of the provinces: Spain/Gaul**, Futrell (1997), 55–8; 66–76; **Travel, Posters at Pompeii**, Coleman (2006), *s.v.* commentary, *Spect*. 3, although her placing Cales and Forum Popilii, which are both in Campania, c.80 kilometres away from Pompeii must be a confusion with towns of the same names near the Adriatic, Talbert (2000), index; **Character in novel**, Apul. *Met*. 1.7.5–6; **Urso**, *CIL* 2. 5.1022; Chamberland (2021), 380; **Pergamum**, Mattern (2013), 86.

122 **The infrequency of regular Games: Augustus**, *RG* 22-3; **Titus**, CD 66.25; **Trajan**, CD 68.15; Kyle (1998), 76–7, suspects inflation of numbers by ancient authors; certainly the author of the ***Augustan History*** has fun making up lists of exotic animals and gladiators exhibited by various third-century emperors; *Gord*. 3.5–8; 33.1–2; *Aur*. 33. 1–35.6; *Prob*. 19.2–4.

122 **Few and far between: Frequency and numbers not equal significance**, Hopkins (1983), 6–7; **Marcus Aurelius**, *Med*. 1.5; **Tacitus**, *Dial*. 29.3; **Maecenas**, Hor. *Sat*. 2.6.44; **Terence**, *Hecyra*, prologue 33–42.

123 **Some of our best evidence: Tertullian**, *De spect*. 24.3; 19.5; 3.1.

123 **The anecdote that best illustrates:** Jerome, *Life of Hilarion* 7.

Anticipation

123 **The crowd streaming towards: Pompeii street posters**, Jacobelli (2021), 490–1; Jacobelli (2003), 39–42, with good illustrations; Beard (2008), 264–6; **By the light of the moon**, *CIL* 4.3884; the paintings of gladiators in Pliny, *NH* 35.52, seem to commemorate shows, rather than advertise them; see also the inscriptions from Thrace advertising forthcoming Games, discussed below, *Justification and Opposition*.

124 **There were other, more ephemeral: Pamphlets**, Cic. *Phil*. 2.97; *Ad Fam*. 2.8.1; HA *Claud*. 5.5; **Ovid**, *Ars am*. 1.167; **Parade**, Luc. *Tox*. 58; ***Cena Libera***, Above, Chapter One.

124 **Everyone in the crowd: Tickets, We assume were free**, A few isolated pieces of evidence might indicate the opposite; see Futrell (1997), 164–6; but Gaius Gracchus tearing down barriers in the Forum, so

that the plebs could watch for free, Plut. *G. Gracc.* 12.3–4, probably does not mean there was a general admission charge, but that previously you had to pay for certain upmarket viewing points; a similar explanation might lie behind a magistrate from Cirta in Numidia who erected a statue of himself with the profits from his *munera*, *CIL* 8.6995; but we might be wrong to assume one practice prevailed across the entire empire for centuries.

124 **How were the tickets distributed?: Republican senators and clients**, Futrell (1997), 163; **Reserved seats**, **Gaul**, Futrell (1997), 165; Bomgardner (2000), 114; **Colosseum**, Dunkle (2008), 269–70; ***Annona***, D.W. Rathbone, in: *OCD*, 4th ed. (Oxford, 2012), *s.v. Food Supply* (Roman), 584; the *Praefectus Annonae* guaranteed the seating of the Arval Brethren, and perhaps oversaw seating arrangements in general; most likely there was a black market in reselling free tickets, Futrell (1997), 165–6.**Arches of the Colosseum**: Claridge (2010), 318; ***Tesserae***, Fagan (2011), 100–1; **Labyrinthine staircases and passageways**, Bomgardner (2000), 9–17, tries to make them comprehensible; **Attendants**, Mart. 5.14.

125 **Five stone bollards:** Claridge (2010), 319; Rose (2005), 103–5.

126 **'House of Anicetus':** 1.3.23; Often discussed, recently by Bomgardner (2000), 50–3; Clarke (2003)A, 152–8; Jacobelli (2003), 71–3, with photograph reversed; and Fagan (2011), 93–6; the dwelling is sometimes referred to as the 'House of the gladiators', as the attribution to Anicetus rests on three bits of graffiti on the façade facing the street; similarly, the modern idea that Anicetus, who was a pantomime artist, had previously been a gladiator relies on the frescos in the house, and on identifying him with an 'Anicetus Castre[n]sis' ('Anicetus of the Camp'), from other graffiti, and assuming that Castrensis indicated that he was a gladiator.

127 **Riot described by Tacitus:** Tac. *Ann.* 14.17; The outbreak at Pompeii is often described as unique, but in the late second century AD, Clement of Alexandria warned that you might get caught up in a riot at the arena, *Paedagogus* 3.11.77.

127 **Why did Anicetus: Drawings**, illustrated at Jacobelli (2003), 74; **Interpretations**, mine is not incompatible with that of Clarke (2003) A, 155–6: that the owner, 'and his buddies . . . delighted in seeing Roman social order turned upside down'.

128 Even when not rioting: Crowds trample and crush, Caligula, Suet. *Cal.* 26; **Julius Caesar**, Suet. *Jul.* 39, translated by Catherine Edwards (2000).

128 The Amphitheatre itself: Collapse, Tac. *Ann.* 4.62–3; Suetonius, *Tib.* 40, put the death toll at more than 20,000; Cassius Dio, 58.1a, generalises, 'when some persons put on shows outside Rome, they died in the ruins of their own theatres'; **Imperial permission**, *Dig.* 50.10.3.

129 Only once do we hear: *Retiarius* kills equestrian, VM 1.7.8; an odd story, as the *retiarius* runs Haterius through with a sword, which that type of gladiator did not use; it would have been more likely that a badly aimed throw of a trident had killed the equestrian; the anecdote is undated; evidently it is not set in the surviving amphitheatre at Syracuse, (which was built under Augustus, Valerius Maximus wrote under Tiberius), perhaps it should be located in the famous theatre, which had not had adequate safety features installed for the show?

129 In Rome, after the: Security, Bomgardner (2000), 21, gives a concise survey; Scobie (1988), 191–243, an extended discussion; Bingham (1999), 369–79, argues that the Praetorian Guards were stationed inside, while the urban cohorts patrolled the streets during the shows; we actually have very little direct evidence for security in the Colosseum, scholars transfer state-of-the-art measures known from other venues, principally Nero's wooden amphitheatre, but it seems sensible.

129 The emperor could do anything: Stories of danger from imperial box, Caligula: CD 59.10.3; a different version at Suet. Cal. 27, with elite men condemned to the mines, road-building or the beasts for either not liking his shows, or not swearing by his *Genius*; **Claudius**, Suet. *Claud.* 32.2; **Domitian**, Suet. *Dom.* 10.1; **Commodus**, CD 73.20.2.

130 All exceptional incidents: Added to the excitement: Hopkins (1983), 10–11.

130 Autobiographical account: CD 73.20.1–21.2; discussed by Beard (2014), 1–8, whose translation is quoted here.

Origins and History

131 **One thing on which: Origins**: Modern discussions well surveyed by Futrell (1997), 11–21; Campania to Etruria to Rome, Ville (1981), 1–56.

131 **The first recorded: 264BC,** Futrell (1997), 20–2; **Inflation in numbers**, Hopkins (1983), 4, n.3, with references.

132 **Wild beast hunts**: **Origins**, Futrell (1997), 24–8.

132 **Unambiguous *venatio*: Pompey**, Balsdon (1969), 306–7.

133 **Gladiators and *venationes*:** CD 43.22.3; ***Cerialia* of 42BC**, Futrell (1997), 44; ***iustum atque legitimum***, Kyle (1998), 51, n.105.

The Colosseum and Amphitheatres

133 **Gladiators were fighting: Early amphitheatres**, Bomgardner (2000), 40–1; 58–60, provides an introduction; Welch (1994), 59–80, and Welch (2007), extended studies.

133 **Forum Boarium:** Later Romans believed it had started life as a cattle market; although this is doubted by Richardson (1992), 162–4; **Amphitheatre of Statilius Taurus**, Richardson (1992), 11; **Various places across the city**, Edmondson (1996), 78; ***Ovile/Saepta Iulia***, Richardson (1992), 278; 340–1; **Campania**, Welch (2007), 189–92.

134 **The answer to this:** Hopkins, and Beard (2005), 38, suggest the senate was reluctant to allow a venue where the plebs might express themselves; not entirely convincing given that the plebs gathered in very large numbers in the Circus Maximus; **'Double theatre' of Scribonius Curio**, Bomgardner (2000), 36–7.

135 **Augustus thought about: Abandoned projects**, Edmondson (1996), 78.

135 **Emperors were above the law: Forum of Augustus**, Beard, and Henderson (2001), 165–75, is a wonderful introduction.

135 **To build an amphitheatre: Colosseum**, Dodge (2021), 412–25, for a lively and up-to-date overview; Hopkins, and Beard (2005) for an enjoyable, longer introduction.

136 **Where there had been: Martial**, *Spect*. 2.

136 **'Joining the dots': Dedicatory inscription**, Alföldy (1995), 195–226; reconstruction doubted by Hopkins, and Beard (2005), 32–4.

136 **The function of the building: Jewish Revolt**, Above, Chapter 1, *Backgrounds*.

136 **The architecture reinforced the messages:** ***Stoa***, Futrell (1997), 8; **Triumphal arches**, Toner (2014), 11; **Statues**, although coins and a relief sculpture show statues in the arches, Richardson (1992), 9, doubts their existence, because these images do not show the parapets in the actual arches.

136 **Amphitheatres spread from Italy: Military amphitheatres**, Futrell (1997), 147–52; **Thysdrus**, Bomgardner (2000), 146–51.

137 **The Gauls: Duels**, Cunliffe (1988), 87–92, a vivid overview of pre-Roman Gaulish society; **Human sacrifice**, Rives (1995), 68, n.21; **Hunting**, Woolf (1998), 165.

137 **The Gauls added:** ***Crupellarii***, Tac. *Ann.* 3.43; ***Trinquii***, Oliver, and Palmer (1955), 333 (text), 343 (translation).

Other distinctive elements: **Run gauntlet of whips**, Eus. *HE* 5.1.38; ***Ursarii***, Potter (2011), 271.

138 **The Gauls built conventional: 'Mixed edifices'**, Futrell (1997), 70–4; **Celtic cult**, Futrell (1997), 93–110.

Justification and Opposition

138 **Antiochus IV:** Livy 41.21; Polyb. 26.1; 30.25–26 (= Athen. 14.615); DS 29.32; Antiochus' gladiators are discussed by Carter (2001)A, 45–62.

140 **Antiochus ended up using volunteers: Roman justification**, Wiedemann (1992), 35–40

140 **Pliny:** *Pan.* 33.1; translation B. Radice (Cambridge, Mass., and London, 1969).

140 **Justification always remained the same:** Cic. *Tusc.* 2.17.41; *HA*, *Max. et Bal.* 8.5–7; As the *HA* was written under a Christian emperor, Ville (1960), 304–5, suggested that this was a piece of pagan propaganda urging the restoration of gladiatorial combat, but this might be to credit too serious a purpose to the playful author.

141 **Opposition to gladiatorial combat: Idea Greeks not keen on gladiators**, Mann (2009), 273; **Louis Robert**: (1940), and subsequent articles; **Three times as many inscriptions**, Mann (2009), 273, n.6.

141 **Unique relationship with the Greeks: Hellenisation**, Beard, and Crawford (1985), 12–24, is a splendid introduction; Gruen (1993), is a typically, and engagingly, idiosyncratic read; **Horace**, *Ep.* 2.1.156–7;

Assassination of Caesar, Woolf (2006), 7–8; although Suetonius says in other accounts Caesar said nothing.

142 **The Romans and the Greeks: 'Greco-Roman elite'**, Bowersock (1969) was an important milestone in this line of thinking; **Gladiators Roman origin 'seems to lose importance'**, Price (1984), 89.

142 **Literary evidence on the Greek side: Not fit 'Greco-Roman elite' concept**, Argued in two seminal, and independent, works, Swain (1996); and Schmitz (1997); **Strange forms**, Sidebottom (1998), 2823–6; **Philopappus**, Smith (1998), 70–3.

143 **A spectacle imported from Rome: Transliteration**, Mann (2009), 282; **Artemidorus**, *Oneir*. 2.32; Cassius Dio also distances himself from such words, 72.19.2; **Not in Greek *Agones***, Mann (2009), 279; **Imperial Cult**, Price (1984) on Greek nature of cult; Futrell (1997), 79–93, on gladiators and imperial cult; Carter (2004), 44, points out that in the province of Asia, twenty-two of the twenty-five known gladiatorial *familiae* were owned by priests of the imperial cult; **Greek intellectuals as advisers of emperors**, Rawson (1989), 233–57; Sidebottom (1996), 453–6.

144 **Through their own cultural filters: *Monomachoi***, Mann (2009), 282; ***Pygme***, Carter 2009), 310; **Liturgy**, Carter (2004), 55–6; ***Philotimia***, Mann (2009), 282; **Cibyra**, Berns and Ekinci (2015), 143–79; Plate Eight: Berns and Ekinci (2015), 161–2, Figs. 14 and 15 (Block B 4); interestingly it can be read as either three separate pairs fighting, or as a narrative from left to right of one fight.

145 **A Greek attending the Games: Reflections on power, Herodian**: 3.2.8; **Banished wars**, Sidebottom (1993), 241–64; **Only the emperor**, Carter (2014), 626; **Minicius inscription**, *IGBulg*. II 660; discussed by Streinu (2018), 359–60; other similar inscriptions from Thrace add the Roman army; **Plutarch**, *mor*. 813E; Swain (1996), 166.

146 **A few Greek philosophers**: the usual list comprises Musonius Rufus, Apollonius of Tyana, Dio Chrysostom and Demonax, Carter (2009), 298–9; Musonius should be removed, when Dio Chrysostom refers to a philosopher 'inferior in birth to no Roman', *Or*. 31.122, he does not mean the Italian equestrian Musonius, but a Greek, quite likely himself; likewise, the criticism by Apollonius of the Athenians for holding gladiatorial shows is invented by his biographer Philostratus, *VA* 4.22, from that of Dio Chrysostom; **Dio Chrysostom**, *Or*. 31. 121–2; **Lucian**, *Dem*. 57.

147 **The philosopher Annaeus Seneca: Greek intellectuals on gladiators,** Plut. *mor.* 802D; 822F; Epic. 2.24.23; *Ench.* 32; Lib. *Or.* 1.5; **Roman authors, Marcus Aurelius,** *Med. 6.46;* **Cicero,** *Pro Mur.* 40; *De off.* : *CIL* 4.4418; Bomgardner (2000), 55, who reads it as a protest.

148 **Too exciting: Alypius,** Augustine, *Confessions* 7.8, translation Warner (Ontario, 1963), slightly altered and abridged; Lane Fox (2015), 166, draws a comparison with the effects on Lord Byron when he witnessed the public execution of three robbers in Rome; actually, Alypius had fallen for the Games before in Carthage, below, Chapter 12, *The Future of the Games.*

148 **Wide reading of pagan philosophy: Seneca**: *Ep.* 7.3.

7. *Prima Lux* (First Light)

The Procession

150 **In 1843 a relief sculpture:** Jacobelli (2003), 95; **Often discussed,** Wiedemann (1998), 93–5; Junkelmann (2000), 65; Dunkle (2008), 75–8; Jacobelli (2021), 494; **Real armourers,** Dunkle (2008), 77; **Spirits of the deceased,** Wiedemann (1992), 94; **Carpenter's shop,** VI.7. 8–12; Clarke (2003)A, 85–7; **Tablet,** Dunkle (2008), 77; **Attendants,** Junkelmann (2000), 65; Dunkle (2008), 77.

152 **Inside the amphitheatre: Route of processions – to the amphitheatre, Corinth**: Apul. *Met.* 10.29; **Pompeii tomb inscription,** *CIL* 10.1074d; the relief of the *Pompa* is sometimes thought to have come from the tomb of Aulus Clodius Flaccus, noted by Jacobelli (2021), 494.

152 **A modern reconstruction: Route of processions – at the amphitheatre, Puteoli reconstruction,** Bomgardner (2000), 82.

153 **Who is not represented: Fictitious legal speech,** Quint., *Minor Declamations* 302.

153 **Others in the parade: Barbarian prisoners of war,** *Pan. Lat.* 12.23.3; **The condemned, Relief from Smyrna,** Meijer (2004), 149–50.

154 **The Latin novel mentioned: Others in the parade, Animals,** Apul. *Met.* 10.23–35; See below, Chapter 9, *Sexual Executions.*

154 **The sense of smell:** Day (2017), 176–92; **Malodorous streets,** Aldrete (2014), 51–3; **Scent of the gods,** Belayche (2021), 374.

155 **We see four musicians: Petronius,** *Sat.* 36.6.

155 **Soundscape of the ancient world:** The literature is fast-expanding; illuminating among the works sampled were: Simpson (2000), 633–9; Laurence (2017), 13–22; D'Angour (2018), 31–43; Belayche (2021), 366–88; Bradley (2021), 125–40.

156 **A chance comment by Plutarch:** *Aem.* 33.1.

156 **Emotional power of music: Reveals character**, Dio, *Or.* 1.1–3.

156 **The giver of the Games: Relief from Capua**, Bomgardner (2000), 99; **Shrine at Puteoli**, Bomgardner (2000), 77.

157 **One emperor: Commodus**, CD 73.22.1-6, and Her. 1.16.1–17.11 **'Gallery of Commodus'**, Bomgardner (2000), 9.

157 **Evoked a religious ceremony: Imperial Cult**, Above, Chapter 6: *Justification and Opposition*; **Mars and Hercules**, Futrell (1997), 110; **Diana**, Tert., *Spect.* 12. **Nemesis**: Futrell (1997), 110–119.

158 **Sinister gods: Pluto/*Dis Pater* and Mercury**, Tert. *Apol.* 15.5; *Ad Nat.* 1.10.47; **Commodus**, CD 73.17.3–4; 19.4; the argument that the infernal gods were a comic act, Dunkle (2008), 93, rests on Tertullian laughing at their cruelty and absurdity, but his Christian reaction should not be transferred to pagan viewers.

159 **Charon, another infernal deity:** Kyle (1998), 44; 157, sets out the evidence, but concludes that 'Etruscan Charon should not be forced into the amphitheatre'; **Coherent triad**, Charon's hammer might suggest that sometimes he replaced Pluto/Father Dis.

159 **A recent trend confines:** e.g. Kyle (1998), 157–8; **Ephesus cemetery**, Kanz, and Grossschmidt (2006), 212–4.

159 **The amphitheatre is consecrated:** Tert. *Spect.* 12.7; **Whole world**, Tert. *Spect.* 8.9.

160 **Not a headline act: Pompeiian poster**, *CIL* 4.7993; **Wonder and amazement**, Robert (1940), 174.171; **Marcus Aurelius**, *Med.* 6.46.

Society Stratified in Stone

This section, ultimately inspired by Hopkins (1983), esp. 17–18; draws heavily on Edmondson (1996), 69–112, where most of the references to what follows can be found, but reaches somewhat different conclusions; Edmondson sees the seating of the Games as not 'reflecting' or 'mirroring' social structures, but contributing to their creation; to me this seems too 'dynamic'; the amphitheatre changed nothing;

that subgroups were seated within the main groups in the stands reinforced, rather than challenged, social cohesion – the more addresses you have, the more you belong, the more you are fixed in place; the segregation only contributed to the creation of the social structure by making it visible, and allowing its clear visualisation; Fagan (2011), 96–120, is another very useful study; Suet. *Aug.* 44 is the key text, which also says that soldiers were separated from civilians, and married men from bachelors, although not if this affected all levels of the audience; **Fictitious legal speech**, (Ps.-)Quint., *Major Declamations* 9.6.3.

160 **Security net encircling the arena:** Above, Chapter Five, *Security*: **Ammianus**, 16.10.13.

161 **This was still the parade: Vestals**, Beard (1980), 12–27; some females of the imperial family were given the right to sit with the Vestals, Fagan (2011), 107, n.75.

161 **On the same level: Military heroes**, Maxfield (1981), 67–100.

162 **The elaborate stratified seating: Sulla's wife**, Plut. *Sulla* 35; **Ovid,** *Ars Am.* 1.163–76; **Irni**, *Lex Irnitana* Ch.81; text, translation, commentary, and discussion, Gonzales (1986), 147–243.

163 **Impossible to map: Stone reused from Colosseum**, Hopkins, and Beard (2005), 160–4; **Modern reconstruction**, Edmondson (2002), 17, Fig. 5; **Five we expect**, Or six, if the equestrians were divided into *seniores* and *iuniores*, Rawson (1987), 105–6; **Equestrian inscription,** *CIL* 6.32098b.

164 **Outside Rome: Nîmes, Lyons, and Arles**, Edmondson (1996), 101; **Urso**, *CIL* 2.5439; discussed by Futrell (1997), 164–5; and Fagan (2011), 103–4.

164 **This opens up: Roman Social Structure**, Alföldy, (1985), 146, Fig. 1.

164 **On the day of the Games: Roman society and social mobility**, MacMullen (1974) is far away the most imaginative and enjoyable book on the subject; Alföldy (1985) is more conventional, and thus duller; **Slaves' dreams of freedom**, Artemidorus recounts many, Hammond (2020), 335, Index, *s.v.* FREEDOM for slaves; **Pertinax**, Birley (1988), 63–4, n.2.

165 **The reintroduction of monarchy: Emperors and army**: Campbell (1984).

165 ***Familia Caesaris***: Weaver (1972).

165 **Downgraded others: Condemnation of elite**, Sidebottom (2005), 320–9; **Senatorial withdrawal**, Hopkins, and Burton (1983), 120–200.

166 **Despite everything: Social mobility remains the exception**, MacMullen (1974), *passim*.

166 **Changing one's social status: At the Games, Germans**, Suet. *Claud*. 25.4; Tacitus, *Ann*. 13.54.1–4, has an almost identical story, set in the Theatre of Pompey, about a German tribe called the Frisii under Nero; **Nanneius**, Martial, 5.14; **Martial**, 3.95; 5.8; 5.14; 5.23; 5.35; 6.9; **Horace**, *Epod*. 4.15–6; **Juvenal**, 3.153–9.

The Salute

167 ***Hail emperor*: Scholarly orthodoxy**, Grabbing the three books nearest to my desk (a completely unscientific sampling) yields unanimity that the salute was unique to the Fucine Lake: Kyle (1988), 93–4; Futrell (2006), 88; Dunkle (2008), 195–6.

167 **In AD54: Alternative history**, See below, Chapter 10, *Mass Combat*; **Three Sources**, Suet. *Claud*. 21.6; CD 61.33.3–4; Tac. *Ann*. 12.56; **Numbers**, If we assume about 200 per trireme, as in Classical Athens, this gives c.4,800 combatants in Suetonius, and 10,000 in Cassius Dio.

168 **Altogether the combatants bellowed:** Suetonius is the best source, here in the translation of Catharine Edwards (2000); Cassius Dio, who was drawing on Suetonius, omits Claudius' joke, replacing it with the combatants avoiding hurting each other until compelled to fight; Tacitus has neither the salute nor the joke, but has the criminals fighting with the spirit of free men.

168 **We can for now leave: Gladiator survival rates**, Below, Chapter 12, *The Future of the Gladiator*; **Oath**, Above, Chapter 2, *The Oath*.

169 ***Probatio armorum*:** Phrase coined by G. Lafaye in 1896, Carter (2008), 318, n.17; **The two stories**, Suet. *Titus* 9.1–3; CD 68.3.2.

Warm-Up Acts

170 **Lucius was left outside:** Apul. *Met*. 10.18–35; quote at 10.22.

170 **Eating some sweet grass: Pyrrhic dance etc**, Below, Chapter 9, *Entertainments*.

171 **A joke tells us: New volunteers beaten by *Larvae***, Sen. *Apoc*. 9; **Mappalicus**, Cyp. *Ep*. 7.2–3.9.

172 **Punishment of informers:** ***Delatores***, Defined by Rutledge (2001), 9–16.

172 **The most notorious informers: Beaten and paraded**, Pliny, *Pan.* 33–5; Suet. *Tit.* 8; Martial, *Spec.* 4–5; **Gracchus**, Above, Chapter One, *Disgrace and the Elite*; **Vitellius**, Suet. *Vit.* 17.

173 **Watching the dancing:** Millar (1981), 63–75, is the classic article on social history in Apuleius' *Metamorphoses*.

8. *Matutinus* (Morning)

The day of the Games begins . . .

174 ***Venationes***: Epplett (2014), 505–19, and Kyle (2021), 254–65, are useful recent introductions; see also Dunkle (2008), 207–44; two hugely enjoyable overviews of animals in the Roman world, written for the non-specialist, are Jennison (1937); and Toynbee (1973).

Attitudes to Animals

175 **When the emperor Septimius Severus:** CD 75.1.1; **Catullus**, 2;3; **Martial**, 7.14; **Sabinus**, Pl. *NH* 8.145; **Gladiator tombstone**, Coleman (2019), 16, n.43.

175 **Aesop's *Fables***: Accessibly and enjoyably translated in Penguin Classics by Temple, and Temple (1998); ***Passer* as penis**, Adams, (1982), 32–3, doubts this interpretation. **Anthropomorphised,** Polemo, *Physiognomy*, text and translation in Swain (2007), 385–91, provides a lengthy list; **Innocent cavalry horse**, Ael. *NA* 11.31.

176 **Roman attitudes to animals: Animal rights**: Concise overview by R. Sorabji, in: *OCD*, 4th. ed., (Oxford, 2012), 87, *s.v. animals, attitudes to*; important studies by Sorabji (1993); and Gilhus (2006); other scholarship in this fast-growing field listed by Gordon (2009), 639, n.13; **Plutarch**, *mor.* 959B–985C; 985C–992E.

176 **What pleasure?**: Cic. *Ad Fam.* 7.1; Cicero here is consoling a friend on missing the show, his was not the general view, he has just described these *venationes* as 'magnificent – nobody says otherwise'; **Waste of money/time**, Cic. *De Off.* 2.55–6.

177 **Only once: Pompey's elephants**: Cic. *Ad fam.* 7.1; Pl. *NH* 8.20.1; CD 39.38.2–3; often discussed, e.g. Fagan (2011), 249–52; Line (2022), 6–31.

177 **After defeating those enemies: Elephants**, Toynbee (1973), 32–54; **As we will see**, Below, *Universal Empire: Nature*; **Polemo**, Swain (2007), 386–7; **Not petition**, Fagan (2011), 250.

178 **Two things in day-to-day life: Butchers**, Frayn (1995), 107–14; ***Meta Sudens***, MacKinnon (2021), 553; **Animal sacrifice**, J. Scheld, in: *OCD*, 4th ed., (Oxford, 2012), 1307–8, *s.v. sacrifice Roman*.

Events

179 **Some traditional Roman religious festivals:** Futrell (1997), 24–6; Kyle (1998), 42-3; possibly the bulls at the *Ludi Taurei* were also set on fire, Futrell (1997), 25, n.65.

179 **Paraded in their triumphs:** Futrell (1997), 26–8; Epplett (2014), 505–7; **Pliny**: *NH* 8.6.16–17

179 **the distinctive Roman *Venationes*: Fulvius Nobilior**, Livy 39.22.2; **Aediles**, Livy 44.14.8; **Ineffectual legislation**, Kyle (2021), 257; **Numbers expanded**, Epplett (2014), 507–9; **As we have seen**, Above, Chapter 6, *Origins and History*.

180 **Animals doing tricks:** Below, *Universal Empire: Nature*.

180 **Magerius Mosaic:** Often discussed, Dunbabin (1978), 67–9; Futrell (2006), 49–51; Fagan (2011), 128–32; a recent and particularly thought-provoking analysis by Bomgardner (2009), 165–77; **Date**, second quarter of third century, Bomgardner (2009), 166; mid to late third century, Fagan (2011), 129; **Bath House**, Bomgardner (2009), 166–7.

181 **There are three registers: Names**, Cf. Bomgardner (2009), 168; and Coleman (2012), 14; **Spittara eastern?**, Greek and Roman names do not start Spit . . . , but some Persian ones did.

181 **The middle register: Gods**: Futrell (2006), 50, Hermes/Mercury and Nemesis; Bomgardner (2009), 173, Dionysus and Diana.

182 **It is the inscription:** Bomgardner (2009), 168–9, has the text and a translation slightly different from mine; acclamations are difficult to translate; they are rhythmic and often terse, so need expansion to make sense; contemporaries knew what they meant, we do not.

182 **Magerius speaking through the herald:** Dunbabin (1978), 67, suggests the speaker is the herald of the *Telegenii*, not Magerius, which would alter our understanding of the exchange.

182 ***Magerius gives*:** Is it possible that the last piece of dialogue was spoken by Magerius? The speaker(s) refers to 'your Games', but the herald had called the spectators 'My Lords', and implies it was their show.

182 **Met *Telegenii* before:** Above, Chapter 1: *A Mosaic and Conversations*.

183 **A twist in the story: Per leopard**, It is interesting that the *Telegenii* are paid by animal, not by human participant, obviously unlike gladiators. Is this a 'match fee', or prize money on top of a fee, or instead of a fee?

183 **Plays with and conflates time: After the action**, Actually, there is another time shift in the middle register; the 1,000 *denarii* moneybags appeared after the 500 *denarii* conversation.

183 **Sequentially, it has been suggested:** Bomgardner (2009), 174–5; **Just highlight?**, If this is correct, we have no way of knowing the total cost of Magerius' Games; which undermines the clever and painstaking attempt by Bomgardner (2009), 170–2, to determine at which local town the show was held.

184 **Equipped as typical *Venatores*:** Junkelmann (2000), 70–4, who detects subtle changes in reality, which might instead be explained by changing artistic conventions; **Parthian bowmen**, Her. 1.15.5; **Stymphalian birds**, CD 73.20.2–3.

185 **An exception to the uniformity:** Junkelmann (2000), 71; **Modern suggestion**, Dunkle (2008), 78–82.

185 **Could achieve fame: Carpophorus**, Martial, *de Spect*. 17; 26; 32; all with commentary by Coleman (2006).

186 **Outside the spotlight: Imported huntsmen**: Dunkle (2008), 79–80, for Sulla, and Ahenobarbus.

186 ***Venatores* were less glamorous: *Equites singulares*: Claudius**: CD 60.17.9; Suet. *Claud*. 21.3–4; **Nero**: CD 61.9.1.

187 **Undoubtedly popular: Libanius** 199.9, although by then, under Christian emperors, gladiatorial shows were in decline; **Martial**, *de Spec*. 8;11–22; 26; 32–3, on beast-fights, 23;27; 31; 34, on gladiators; **North Africa**, Dunbabin (1978), 65–87; *venationes* also comprise well over half of all representations on African Red Slip Wares of the third century AD, Bomgardner (1992), 163; although mosaics and pottery

could be an artistic style, perhaps reflecting pride in the animals which were Africa's contribution to the Games,

187 **Imperial shows were huge: Augustus**, *RG* 22.3; **Titus**, CD 66.25.1; **Trajan**, CD 68.15.1; although Cassius Dio, writing about Julius Caesar's show in 46BC, says that numbers were regularly exaggerated, 43.22.4, the argument of Mackinnon (2006), 153–5, that the low number of animal bones, especially exotic species, recorded in the archaeological context of amphitheatres means we should doubt the high numbers in literary sources, is unconvincing, given (a) the chance of survival, (b) that some earlier archaeologists would have been uninterested and not recorded them, (c) that Mackinnon discounts those that did record such bones, because they then discarded them, and (d) that pre-industrial societies had various uses for animal bones; **Probus**, HA *Prob.* 19.1–8; **Average a day**, But Suetonius claims, *Tit.* 7.3, that 5,000, out of 9,000 animals killed at Titus' show, died in a single day.

187 **Imperial extravaganzas the exception**, Lindberg (2019), 260–2; **Italian inscriptions**, Toynbee (1973), 19–20.

Hunting

188 **Roman hunting began:** Two venerable works of scholarship, Aymard (1951); and Anderson (1985), have been joined by two excellent, more recent articles, Green (1996), 222–60; and Lane Fox (1996), 119–53; although the former concentrates on just early Roman hunting, and the latter only looks at Rome in passing; the subject is overdue an up-to-date, full-length study of all its practical and ideological aspects.

188 **Hunting was good for you: Dissenting voice,** Sallust, *Cat.* 4.1; 14.6; **Body and soul**, Sidebottom (1990), 156–66; **Dio Chrysostom**, *Or.* 3.133–8.

189 **Mark of elevated status:** This section is inspired by two works on other periods of history, Carr (1976); and Saul (1986); **Hadrian tondos**, Hannestad (1988), 204–6; **Pliny**, *Ep.* 1.6; cf. 5.18; and Martial, 12.1.

189 **Advance social status:** Cf. Carr (1976), 2; **Horace**, *Epist.* 1.6.56–61; **Petronius,** *Sat.* 40–1

190 **The urban plebs:** ***Rus in urbe*** **lifestyle**: Clarke (2003)A, 19–28.

Universal Empire: Geography

190 **Under the Republic supply:** MacKinnon (2006), 137–61; Epplett (2014), 512–4; Lindberg (2019), 251–63; Mackinnon (2021), 545–56; **Army**, Epplett (2001), 210–22; **First Cohort of Cilicians**, *AE* 1987 867; ***Familiae* of *Venatores***, Tuck (2021), 535–7; ***Immunes/ursarii/ad leones*/centurion**, Epplett (2001), 212–16; **Indigenous hunters and trappers theory**, Mackinnon (2006), 144–5; Epplett (2014), 8–9.

191 **Transported by water:** MacKinnon (2021), 449–52; **Hierapolis**, Bomgardner (2000), 213; **Sculptor**, Pl. *NH* 36.40.

192 **Great Hunt Mosaic:** Wilson (1993); Dunbabin (1999), 138–9; **Largest,** 59.63m by 5m.

192 **Soldiers or huntsmen: Distracted by mirror**, The Romans thought a tigress saw her cub in a reflection, modern experience believes she saw the threat of another tigress, Jennison (1937), 147.

192 **Unlike modern zookeepers:** *pace* MacKinnon (2006), 146.

193 **Attempts to identify specific areas:** Wilson (2020) on Steger (2017); **Aethiopia**, Wilson (2004), 153–70.

194 **Outside the empire: Rhinos**: Toynbee (1973), 125–4; **Giant snake**: Str. 15.1.73; **Arctic bears**, Toynbee (1973), 93–4.

194 **The Romans thought the world: Geography**, Mattern (1999), 41–66; ***Oikoumene***, Sidebottom (2004), 68–9; **Odological thinking**, Janni (1984).

194 **Directly administered Roman provinces: Client states**, Lintott (1993), 22–44; **Tacitus**, *Ann.* 4.4–5; **Embassy as submission**, Sidebottom (2007)A, 4–5; **Chinese**, Peyrefitte (1989); **Augustus and India**, CD 54.9.7–10; Str. 15.1.73; Aug. *RG* 31.

Universal Empire: Nature

195 **Lucius the Ass:** Apul. *Met.* 10.30–4; translation by M. Grant (1950), 180, who, however, eccentrically re-numbers the text.

196 **Sophisticated technology:** Hammer (2010), 63–86, a theoretical work, to which this section is much indebted; **Etna**, Str. 6.273; **Nero's forest**, Çalp. Sic. *Ecl.* 7.69–72; **Rhodope Mountains**, Mart. *De Spec.* 24; **Septimius Severus' boat**, CD 77.1.4–5; ***Augustan History***, *Prob.* 19.2–3; **Land and sea**, Mart. *De Spec.* 27; 34; the paradox of a land battle at sea, and vice versa, appeared in Greek novels, Ach. Tat. 4.

13–4; Hel. *Aeth.* 1.30; the practicalities of such hydraulic engineering is much discussed, Coleman (1993), 58–60; Epplett (2016), 53–5.

196 Senses of smell and sight: See above, Chapter 7, *The Procession*; **Sight**, Toner (2014), 11; only 'bad' emperors staged events at night, the condemnation of those who turned night into day (above, Chapter 3, *Sleeping as Weakness and Wickedness*) made nocturnal shows proof of 'badness' of an emperor; was there a covert criticism when Statius, *Silv.* 1.6, went home drunk and happy while Domitian's show continued into the night? Below, Chapter 11, *Gifts*.

196 The nature of animals: Wild/Domesticated, Balsdon (1969), 308; **Dyed animals**, Toner (2014), 9; **Old tamers of lions**, Coleman (2006), comm., *s.v. De Spec.* 12; **Elephant tricks**, Balsdon (1969), 305; **Flying bull**, Mart. *De Spec.* 18–19.

197 Herbivores presented no problem: Predators seek somewhere to cower, Jennison (1937), 86; Toner (2014), 61; **Thirst**, Balsdon (1969), 313; **Whips, torches, and toys**, Coleman (2006), comm., *s.v. De Spec.* 22; **Tethering ring**, Wilmott (2008), 162–3; such a block also depicted on gladiatorial mosaic from Bignor.

198 Nature was further altered: Tame tigress, Mart. *De Spec.* 21; **Reluctant rhino**, Mart. *De Spec.* 11; 26; Coleman (2012), 15, showing it is the same rhino; **Cranes versus elephants**, CD 66.25.1, the passage can also be translated as the cranes and elephants fighting their own species; a marble relief shows a crocodile fighting a bear in an amphitheatre, Jennison (1937), Plate 1, following p.98.

198 Unnatural in themselves: Corocotta, CD 77.1.4; Jennison (1937), 84–5; **Mimic human speech**, Ael. *NA* 7.22; Porphyry, *Abst.* 3.4; cf. Pl. *NH* 8.72–3; **Kid nailed to board**, Holloway (1991), 173; **Phoenix**, Pl. *NH* 10.2.3–5, who judges it a fabrication; **Triton**, Paus. 9.21.1; **Living oddities**, CD 54.9.8.

199 Control over nature: Animal *proskynesis*, Mart., *De Spec.* 20; 33.

199 Changed the natural world: Minor poet, *Anth. Pal.* 7.626; **Similar sentiments**, expressed by Strabo, 2.5.33, under Augustus and Luxurius, 60, 146–7, 223–24, in the fifth century AD; conversely Themistius, in the fourth century AD, 10.140.2–4, asked if people did not feel regret when species were eradicated from their habitat, like hippos from the Nile, but he had the invidious task of praising the emperor's humiliating peace with the Goths – was it not sad if a race of barbarians was exterminated, usually a highly desirable aim, just like a species of animals? – politicians, like Themistius, will say anything that suits the need of the moment; **Modern archaeozoology**, Bomgardner (1992), 161–6; the idea that fewer dangerous animals appeared in shows in the third century AD, e.g. Jennison (1937), 83, and Epplett (2016), 161–2, partly as a result of scarcity, may well be correct, but needs re-examining, as it seems to rest on fiction from the *Historia Augusta*.

9. *Tempus Meridianum* (Midday)

Midday is lunchtime

201 **Midday entertainments:** Meijer (2004), 147–59; and Dunkle (2008), 90–4, are useful introductions to the *meridianum spectaculum*; this chapter draws heavily on Coleman (1990), 44–73; also Epplett (2014)A, 520–32; and Carucci (2019), 212–34.

Half-Empty Stands

202 **Seneca says:** *Ep.* 7.5; **Statius**, *Silv.* 1.6; **Street vendors**, Dalby (2000), 218–9; no evidence explicitly places them outside the Colosseum, but their presence can be inferred, as the crowd went out to get refreshments at midday, Suet. *Claud.* 34.2; and Wilmott (2008), 178, collects the (admittedly scanty) archaeological finds putting them outside amphitheatres in Britain; **Cramped seating**, Edmondson (1996), 101, n.145; **Senators' cushions**, Edmondson (1996), 92–3 **Senators' hats**, Edmondson (1996), 85.

202 **Sex with prostitutes:** e.g. Lindström (2010), 315, admittedly not a work of history, but psychology, which, having paid lip service to treating the Romans on 'their own terms', proceeds to apply supposedly universal truths of human nature; Statius, *Silv.* 1.6.65–74, merely makes the standard Roman equation of female dancers at Domitian's show to prostitutes.

203 **Bottom of the bill:** Thompson (2002), 34, an 'interval', or 'time-out'; **Apuleius**, *Met.* 4.13; **Puteoli inscription**, *ILS* 5063a; Epplett (2014) A, 523, who, however, sees such inscriptions as a sign of the popularity of executions; **Paestum inscription**, *AE* 1975, 256; Cook (2012), 34.

203 **Seneca found the executions distasteful: Cruel emperors enjoying executions**, Suet. *Cal.* 32.1; *Claud.* 34.2; HA, *Helio.* 25.7–8; **Caracalla crying**, HA, *Carac.* 1.5, perhaps invented precisely to create the irony?

Entertainments

203 **One day Seneca:** *Ep.* 7.3–6; ***Paegniarii***, Junkelmann (2000), 63; they may be depicted in the middle band of the Pompeian relief (**Plate One**), the second group in from the right.

204 **A distinctive element of the midday:** Balsdon (1969), 327; Coleman (1990), 56, n.109; 68–70; **Plutarch**, *mor.* 554b.

204 **A tricky passage: Torn apart by audience/opposition to gladiators**, Not worth dignifying with references; **Mass battles**, See, below, Chapter 10, *Mass Combat.*

Executions

205 **Good at killing people: Ingenious methods**: MacMullen (1990)A, 204–17, is the best way to first approach the subject.

206 **Crucifixion was too slow:** Coleman (1990), 56; ***Cruciarii* advertised**, Cook (2012), 69–82; **Blandina**, Musurillo (1972), 74–5; **Laureolus**, Martial, *de Spec.* 9, with commentary by Coleman (2006); **Pionius**, Musurillo (1972), 162-5; **Nero**, Tac. *Ann.* 15.44; discussed by Barrett (2020), 143–74.

206 **Beheading was too quick: Defeated gladiators**, below, Chapter 10, *Defeat, Death and Victory*.

206 **The normal methods: Zliten mosaic**: Above, Chapter 2, *Sex*; **Terracotta**, Wiedemann (1992), 82.

207 **In Carthage, when Saturus:** Musurillo (1972), 127–8.

207 **Some of the condemned: Androcles**, AG 5.14.29; Seneca has a similar story, where a lion recognises a *bestiarius* as its former master and defends him against other beasts in the arena, *de Ben.* 2.19.1, maybe a Senecan elaboration on Androcles?; **Blandina**, Musurillo (1972), 78-81; **Saturus and Perpetua**, Musurillo (1972), 127–31.

208 **A supposed elaboration:** Cook (2012), 84, 'fictional or not'; **Verres**, Cic. *Ver.* 2.45; ***Augustan History***, HA, *Alex.* 37.2; *Avid. Cass.* 4.3; **Suetonius**, *Galba* 9.1.

Spectacular Executions

209 Complicit in their own executions: 'Fatal charades', Coleman (1990), 44–73, coined the term in her essential article; **'Snuff plays'**, Barton (1993), 61.

209 A condemned man: References can be found in Coleman (1990), 60–6; **Indian mystics**, Jones (1986), 126; **Hostile biography**, Lucian, *On the Death of Peregrinus*.

210 On wings of his own: Icarus, was the malfunction that he was dropped in the wrong place, or that he was dropped at all, as Coleman (1990), 68, thinks?

210 Orpheus: I link Martial's *de Spect*. 24 and 25 to make one story.

211 An anecdote from fiction: HA *Gall*. 12.4.

212 Very few of the enactments: Volunteer for *tunica molesta*, Tert. *ad Nat*. 1.18.10; Cook (2012), 88, n.70.

212 Summoned up in the arena: Fables made real, Martial, *de Spect*. 6.

Christians to the Lion!

213 For Christians: Hopkins, and Beard (2005), 5–7; 103; **No genuine evidence**, For ancient Christian fiction about Telemachus the monk in the Colosseum, see below, Ch.12, *The Future of the Games*, **Numbers of gladiators**, See below, Chapter 12, *The Future of the Gladiator*, for modern speculation; **Arrius Antoninus**, Tert. *Ad Scapulam*, 5; see above, Chapter 5, *Roman Suicides*; **One lion**, Tert. *Apol*. 40.

214 Christians, as we have seen: Above, Ch.3, *Sleeping as Weakness and Death*; **Sanctus**, Musurillo (1972), 68-9; see also Conon, Musurillo (1972), 188–9.

214 Christians were different: Identity proclaimed, **Attalus**, Musurillo (1972), 74–5; **Euplius**, Musurillo (1972), 318–9; a note of caution, all the evidence for such proclamations are from Christian sources; a literary martyr act would not work, if the spectators did not know who the victims were; **Lucian**, *Tox*. 59; **Martial**, *de Spect*. 9; but cf. Petronius, *Sat*. 45, where a character predicts all the audience will know the identity of a man who will be executed, and will be divided in their sympathies.

214 Not have to be there: Christianity deniable crime, **Governor pleading**, Some examples, Musurillo (1972), 8–9; 30–1; 86–7; 90–1;

102–3; 114–5; 'lips, not heart', adopted by a Christian sect, Eus. *HE* 6.38; Generally, see Lane Fox (1986), 421–3.

Sexual Executions

215 **Apuleius' *Golden Ass*:** *Met.* 12.23–34; **Nero**, 12.2; **Titus**, Mart. *de Spect.* 6, with commentary by Coleman (2006); **Clay lamps**, Epplett (2014), 527.

215 **Re-establish gender boundaries:** Epplett (2014), 526–7; **Naked/ fancy dress**, Thompson (2002), 47; **Attis**, Tert. *Apol.* 15.4–5; **Nero**, Suet. *Ner.* 29.1; CD 62.13.2.

10. *Tempus Postmeridianum* (Afternoon)

Last Words and Arrangements

217 **'If I win': Last words**, Luc. *Tox.* 59; (Ps.-)Quint. *Major Declamations*, 9.7.6–9.3, translated by M. Winterbottom (2021).

218 **Actually spoken by gladiators: Words from beyond the grave**, Below, *The Mind of the Gladiator*.

218 **Medieval tourney:** Which actually had certain rules, Crouch (2005); **Marcus Mesonius**, *CIL* 4.2508; text and translation, Fagan (2011), 318–21; **Commodus**, CD 73.19.4; **Titus**, Mart. *De Spect.* 23; **By lot**, Toner (2014), 12.

218 **Unfairness of the bout:** (Ps.-)Quintilian, *Major Declamations*, 9.6.3; **Seneca**: *de Prov.* 3.4.

Types of Gladiators

219 **Divided into very different types: *Scutarii and parmularii***, Balsdon (1969), 299, n.296; Martial turned the contrast into a joke,14.23; **Marcus Aurelius**, *Med.* 1.5; **Modern research**, Junkelmann (2000), in German, is the seminal work; see Junkelmann (2000)A, 45–64, for a summary in English.

219 **The research proceeds: Images of *Retiarii***, Junkelmann (2010), 515; ***Dimachaerus***, Carter (2011), 65, n.9; ***Manii***, Petr. *Sat.* 45.7.

220 **Gladiators were not unchanging: Changes over time**, Wiedemann (1992), 41; Junkelmann (2000)A, 35–7; ***Crupellarii***, Tac. *Hist*. 3.43; ***Trinqui***, Above, Chapter 1, *Backgrounds*.

220 ***Provocator*****:** Junkelmann (2000)A, 37–8; 57–8; ***Spatha* inscription**, *CIL* 6 10183; translated and discussed by Carter (2018), 127-8; **Armoured *Retiarius***, Junkelmann (2010), 524.

221 ***Contraretiarius*****:** Junkelmann (2000)A, 61; ***Manii***, Pet. *Sat*. 45.7; Brunet (2004), 157–8.

221 **The man giving the Games could:** Pl. *NH* 33.53; **Caligula**, Suet. *Cal*. 55.

221 **distinguished not by equipment but by sex:** A sample includes, Vessey (1998), 85–93; Brunet (2004), 145–70; McCullough (2008), 197–209; Kocjan (2018), 49–56; Gatti (2022), 23–43; **Prejudice only social**, McCullough (2008), 204–6; Kocjan (2018), 54; **'Fame and glory'**, Kocjan (2018), 53.

221 **Only one visual image:** Two other pieces have been seen as female gladiators, Gatti (2022), 37–9; the identification of a bronze statuette as a female Thracian rests on the curved object in her left hand; it could equally be a *strigil* (oil scraper), and mark her as an athlete; she lacks the belt, helmet, shield and greaves of a *Thraex*, the strapping on her left knee fits the gymnasium as well as the arena; the 'female breasts' of a pair of gladiators on an oil lamp look more like the 'man boobs' of tubby male gladiators; **Halicarnassus relief**, Coleman (2000), 487–500; **Two plausible suggestions**, Coleman (2000), 495–7.

222 **A few, scattered references:** Brunet (2004), 152–64, collects the evidence; Vesley (1998), 92, considers them 'widespread and numerous'; it must depend on your expectations, and points of comparison; **AD 19 law**, Brunet (2004), 161–2; McCullough (2008), 198, thinks the bans on women on stage of 23 and 22BC might have included the arena; **Cassius Dio**, 66.25.1; 76.16.1; **Inscription from Ostia**, *AE* 1977 No. 153; **Postdate Severus**, Coleman (2000), 498, 'may belong to the third century'; usually dated to the second century, but only because of Severus' ban, Brunet (2004), 156; McCullough (2008), 200.

222 **Combat was highly gendered:** Sidebottom (2004), 24–8, gives a brief overview; ***Iliad***: 6.492; **Statius**, *Silv*. 1.6.53–6; **Martial**, *de Spect*. 7; usually taken as a reference to beast-hunting, not gladiators, presumably because of the woman who kills a lion in the following poem, *de Spect*. 8.

223 **Other, less elevated, reasons: Titillation**, Coleman (2000), 499; **Watching naked women**, **Sinful**, John Chry., *In Matt. Hom.* 7.6; **Enjoyable**, Martial, *de Spect.* 30; with Coleman's commentary (2006).

223 **A final, equally lowbrow, motive: Dwarfs**, Brunet (2004), 145–52; **Statius**, *Silv.* 1.6.57–64; **Pygmies**, Clarke (2007), 106–7; Plate 6; **Disabled, Caligula**, Suet. *Cal.* 26.5; **Commodus**, CD 73.20.3; **Children and *Erotes***, Dunbabin (1978), 85–7; **Amusing**, Brunet (2004), 150, denies female gladiators were the subject of laughter.

224 **A key attraction: Paradoxical *Virtus***, Kocjan (2022), 54; **Disapproval stronger towards elite women**, Gatti (2022), 40; for McCullough (2008), 204-6, no disapproval of non-elite women in the arena.

224 **Female gladiators were so rare: *Gladiatrix* a modern invention**, McCullough (2008), 198.

The Laws of the Fight

225 ***Leges pugnandi***: (Ps.-)Quint., *Major Declamations* 9.9.6, the lawcourt is fictitious; Carter (2006/7), 97–114, is the essential modern study.

225 **On the Zliten mosaic: Referees**, MacLean (2014), 582; like trainers in the Schools, referees were ex-gladiators, quite likely the roles might be combined; ***Satyricon***, Petr. *Sat.* 45.

225 **To the finger:** Not necessarily of the left hand, as is sometimes claimed; ***Missio***, Release from the fight, and back to their *Ludus*, not release from being a gladiator, on which see below, Chapter 12, *The Future of the Gladiator*; **'For their life'**, Carter (2015), 42; **Marcus Aurelius**, CD 72.29.3; **'Sharp weapons'**, *Conta* Carter (2006)A, 161–75; ***Sine missio***, Fagan (2011), 195; *contra* Carter (2006/7), 101; and Potter (2011), 217; in Greek *Apotomos* meant the same, the arguments of Carter (2015), 39–52, against this are unconvincing; **Augustus**, Suet. *Aug.* 45, the wording of which might imply that he banned *other people* from giving Games *sine missione*, i.e. not the emperor himself.

226 **Certain types of gladiators: Pairings**, Coulston (2009), 199; our impressions of the popularity of pairings might be skewed by genre, the *Murmillo* tends to fight a *Thraex* or *Provocator* in art, but a *Retiarius* in literature, Futrell (2006), 96; ***Essedarius***, Dunkle (2008), 113–4; ***Equites* dismount**, Dunkle (2008), 99–101; **Spartaks fresco**, Jacobelli (2003), 73–6; **Isidore of Seville**, *Orig.* 18.53.

Andabata: Junkelmann (2010), 524; Cic. *Ad Fam*. 7.10.2.

227 Distinctive style of fighting: Artemidorus, Above, Chapter 4, *Dreams About Gladiators*.

227 Expected rhythm: Petr. *Sat. 36;* **Like oratory**, Quint. *Inst. Orat.* 5.13.54; **Crowd shout advice**, Tert. *Ad Mart*. 1.2; **Graceful**, Cic. *Orat*. 228; **Lack of initiative**, Petr. *Sat*. 45.

227 What were the moves: **'First stance'**, Coulston (2007), 34–51.
What happened after: Experimental archaeology, Junkelmann (2000), in German, is the definitive study; see also, in English, Junkelmann (2000)B, 113–7; Junkelmann (2010), 512–32; and Coulston (2007), 34–51; and Coulston (2009), 195–210.

228 What *could* have been done: Battle in Papua New Guinea: Meggitt (1977), 64.

The Mind of the Gladiator

229 Polemo was a sophist: Phil. *VS* 541, Polemo uses the term *Agon*, meaning here a contest in oratory, see below for *Agon* as athletic, and by extension gladiatorial contests; **Speaker in courtroom**, (Ps.-) Quint. *Major Declamations* 9.7.1–5; **Placidianus**, Lucil. 4.176–81; discussed by Potter (2011), 193–4; **Anger dangerous**, Sen. *De ira* 1.11.1; **Counsel in the sand**, Toner (2014), 82

229 A tombstone, even if small: Kontokosta (2021), 334–6, is a valuable overview; this section draws heavily on Hope (1998), 179–95; Hope (2000), 93–113; Carter (2009), 298–322; Mann (2009), 272–97; Coleman (2019), 1–36; **Several hundred**, Potter (2011), 259, usefully analyses two hundred and fifty-nine; Coleman (2019), estimates a total of 'approaching five hundred'.

229 Small, poorly cut: Hope (1998), 184.

230 Buried with their own kind: Gladiator cemeteries, Carter (2009), 307, n.31; Kontokosta (2021), 335; **Horatius Balbus' cemetery**, *CIL* 11.6528; Edwards (2007), 107–8.

230 The primary identity: Not generic *Gladiator*, Hope (2000), 101; **Abbreviated specific type**, Hope (1998), 187–8; **M. Antonius Exochus**, *CIL 6.10194*; Fagan (2011), 323; compare P(ublius) Folius Potitus Thraex, *AE* 1985.777.

230 **'Skilled and successful fighter': Victories recorded, less often pardons**, Coleman (2019), 4–5; **Evocations of age at death**, Hope (2000), 102.

231 **The terrible irony:** Coleman (2019), 14–5.

231 **Not the only identity: Husband, son, brother etc**, Potter (2011), 259, wives put up 115, out of 175 where it is known who erected the tombstone; ***Collegium***, *ILS* 5084; 5084a; Dunkle (2008), 152; on possible functions of a *Cryptiarius*, see above, Chapter 5, *Security*; **Dog owner**, Coleman (2019), 16, n.43; **Slave owner**, *CIL* 5.5933; Fagan (2011), 323.

232 **Previous Identities: Names**, Meilesis/Mestrianos, Carter (2006/7), 107; **Hometown, Nîmes**: Hope (1998), 182–6.

232 **Groups higher up the pyramid: Gladiators as soldiers in the Latin West**, Hope (2000), 105; 110–2; Coulston (2009), 198; **Trophies at Pompeii**, Jacobelli (2003), 67, Figure 55; ***Contubernales*, *coarmiones*, etc**, Fagan (2011), 323; gladiators used comparable military terms in the Greek East, Coleman (2010), 426–7, the differences between the two halves of the empire was not absolute, and should not be overstated.

233 **In the Greek East: Athletes**, Carter (2009), 298–322; Mann (2009), 272–97; Concannon (2014), 193–214; **Apollonius**, Carter (2009), 310.

233 **Athletes in the Greek world: Athlete-style honour, Thessalonica**, Mann (2009), 285; **Seven cities**, Robert (1940), No. 90; Futrell (2006), 138.

234 **The famous heroes of myth: Odysseus and Miletus**, Robert (1950), No. 331; Coleman (2010), 428, is more circumspect, 'the stress on friendship as a value of the gladiatorial barracks is clear, whether an erotic element is implied or not'.

235 **Claimed to have surpassed them: Melanippus**, Robert (1940), No. 298; reordered here to make easier to follow in English; discussed by Carter (2009), 307–9; and Concannon (2014), 203–4; **Carpophorus**, Mart. *Spect.* 17; 26; 32; Above, Chapter 8, *Events*.

235 **Traditional religious beliefs: *Dis Manibus***, Carter (1999), 263; **Ritual formulas**, Price (1984).

236 **Morally good: *Bene merenti***: e.g. *CIL* 10.72.97; 5.3466; Fagan (2011), 323–4; limitation of his 'worthiness' to being 'a good comrade who bravely faced his death in the arena', Hope (2000), 105, seems uncertain; **Merciful, M. Antonius Exochus**, *CIL* 6.10194; Fagan (2011), 323; **Emperor gives decision to victor**, CD 78.19.3–4; **'Saved'**

opponents, Carter (2006/7), 107–8, gives examples; **Boxer,** Dio Chry. *Orr.* 28; and 29.

236 Gladiators frequently spoke: Composition of epitaphs, Hope (2000), 94.

237 The very quality of mercy: Diodorus the wretched, Robert (1940), No. 79; discussed by Carter (2011)A, 63–69; and Coleman (2019), 18–9.

237 Something similar: Urbicus, *CIL* 5.5933; Fagan (2011), 323.

238 Another gladiator: Victor, Robert (1940), No. 34; Carter (2006/7), 109–10.

238 The gladiator talks to us: *Find your own star*, *CIL* 5.3466; Fagan (2011), 324.

Mass Combat

238 ***The gladiator takes counsel*****: Show at Pompeii,** *CIL* 4.3884; **Trajan,** CD 68.15; **Gladiator who fought three times,** *CIL* 6.10194.

239 A bout lasted: Combat studies, Goldsworthy (1996), 224.

239 Mass combats: Dunkle (2008), 190–201, gives a good overview, with source references, although he treats battles on land and water as separate phenomena; Coleman (1993), 48–74, is the essential study of *Naumachiae*; **Venues, including practicalities of flooding amphitheatres**, Coleman (1993), 50–60; **Scaled-down warships,** No ancient visual image of a *Naumachia* has been securely identified, Coleman (1993), 70–1; Augustus said thirty war galleys – triremes, rowed on three levels, and biremes, rowed on two – plus smaller craft featured on a purpose-dug lake 1,800 feet long, and 1,200 broad in his *Naumchia* of 2BC; the *Olympias*, a full-scale reconstruction of an Athenian trireme is 115 feet long and occupies 33 feet laterally with its oars extended, Morrison, Coates, and Rankov (2000), 270, Fig. 80; thirty of those would leave just 100 feet of clear water across the width of Augustus' lake, not nearly enough space for any manoeuvre; **Hundreds, sometimes thousands**, Numbers are prone to inflation in ancient sources: to praise the generosity of a 'good' emperor, and to condemn the profligacy of a 'bad' one; Julius Caesar, probably staging the first mass combat in 46BC, pitted two forces of 500 infantry, thirty cavalry and twenty elephants against each other, Suet. *Jul.* 39.3;

Augustus boasted 3,000 combatants, as well as the rowers, in his *Naumachia* in 2BC; **Philip the Arab**, Aur. Vic. 28.1.

239 **Often repeated, the modern assertion: All die**: e.g. Wiedemann (1992), 89–90; Kyle (1998), 93; Dunkle (2008), 193; **Not all die, Claudius**, Tac. *Ann.* 12.56; **Domitian**, CD 57.8.2–3.

240 **The creative reworking of history: Battles in Greek novels, Persians v Egyptians**: Chariton 7.5–6; **Aethiopians versus Persians**, Heliodorus 9.14–22; **Greeks versus Tyre**, Chariton 7.3–4; as far as I am aware there is no general study; for an insightful analysis of the 'battle piece' in ancient historians, Lendon (2017), 39–64; and (2017)A, 145–67.

241 **The uncertain result: Romans in mass combats, harmless, Ausonius**: *Mos.* 208–19; **Horace**, *Epist.* I.18.58–66.

242 **Only twice: Romans in mass combats, fixed, Sextus Pompey**, CD 48.18.1–19.1.

242 **After the invasion of Britain: Romans in mass combat, fixed, Claudius**, Suet. *Claud.* 21.6.

243 **A different theatre of history: Types of gladiators as defeated foes**, Junkelmann (2000)A, 37; Dunkle (2008), 22–3.

243 **Augustus professionalised the Roman army**: Keppie (1984), 145–71; **Perception of empire as armed camp**, Sidebottom (2007)A, 3–6.

243 **Not just for Roman consumption: Barbarian envoys, Frisians**: Tac. *Ann.* 13.54.4; **Martial**, *Spect.* 3; **Dacians versus Suebi**, CD 51.22.6–8.

244 **The gladiators called *Gregarii*: Edict of Marcus Aurelius**, Lines 35–44; text, Oliver, and Palmer (1955), 332; translation, Potter (2010) A, 368–9.

244 **Copied the emperor**: e.g. Herodian, 5.2.3–4.

245 **Another explanation: Marcomannic Wars**, Roth (2017), 1030–3; **Antonine plague**, Sidebottom (2020), 13–4, for a very brief overview; **Gladiators conscripted into army**, Toner (2014), 25.

245 **Conscripting gladiators: Publius Rutilius**, VM 2.3.2; **Gladiators in real battle**, Tac. *Ann.* 3.43; *Hist.* 2. 23; 34–6.

245 **The paradox: Barbarians and Romans as individuals and groups**, Vegetius, *Mil.* 1.1; Milner (1996), 2, n.6.

246 **Ended the Marcomannic wars: Five *Retiarii***, Suet. *Cal.* 30.

Defeat, Death and Victory

246 **The man giving the Games:** Dunkle (2008), 134–6; **Financial consequences**, Above, Chapter 1, *Backgrounds*.

247 **The opinion of the crowd: Handkerchiefs**, Martial, 12.29.7–8; **Togas**, Martial, 13.99; **Shouts**, *ILS* 5134, a graffiti with *Missos* in the plural, and *Iuglula* misspelt as *Iugla*; Balsdon (1969), 300, n.300, provides further ancient references; **Quarrel in crowd**, Pet. *Sat*. 45.

247 **The crowd on his side: Showmanship, Taunt of *Retiarius***, Festus, *Gloss. Lat*. 285.12–16; **Endurance**, Sen. *Constant*. 16.2; **Pleading**, (Ps.-)Quint. *Major Declamations* 8.9; **Counterproductive**, Cic. *Mil*. 92; Cagniart (2000), 616; **Send attendant**, Cic. *Tusc*. 2.17; **'In the savage arena'**, *Anth. Lat*. 415.27–8.

247 **All eyes are on: Clear hand gesture, Scholarly orthodoxy**, Corbeill (1997), 1–21, is always cited; e.g. by Dunkle (2008), 134; **Thumb turned**, Juv. 3.36–7; Prudentius, *C. Symm*. 2.1097–9.

248 **The thumb turns: *missio*: Gate of Life**, Bomgardner (2000), 137.

248 **The thumb turns: *Iugula*: Perpetua**: Musurillo (1972), 130–1.

248 **Expected to die well:** Toner (2014), 91–2; **As Cicero put it**, *Tusc*. 2.41; **Death of Cicero**, Wright (2001), 436, n.3, gives the sources; **Seneca**, *Ep*. 30.8; Cagniart (2000), 607–18.

249 **Method of killing varied:** Toner (2014), 64; **York**, Above, Chapter 2, *Sex*; **Poses in art**, Coulston (2009), 195–210; **Ephesus**, Above, Chapter 1, *Diet and Body Shape*; **Helmets depersonalise**, Above, *Introduction: Twenty-Four Hours in the Colosseum*; **No eye contact**, Kanz, and Grossschmidt (2006), 215; **Seneca**, *Ira* 2.8.2; **Fatal blow to 'dear friend'**, *SEG* 30, 1514; Coleman (2010), 427.

249 **Meant to be quick: Mutilation after medieval battles, Visby**, Keegan (1976); **Towton**, Fiorato, Boylston, and Knusel (2000); **Quick death for gladiators, Ephesus**: Kanz, and Grossschmidt (2016), 216; **Carthage**, Musurillo (1972), 130–1; not every skeleton in the York cemetery was decapitated with one blow, one took eleven cuts, Hunter-Mann (2015), 9.

250 **Gods of the Underworld:** Above, Chapter 7, *The Procession*; **Ephesus square traumas**, Kanz, and Grossschmidt (2006), 212, Table 2; 214.

250 **A palm branch:** Carter (2009)A, 438–41; **Dishes and contents**, Coleman (2006), commentary on Martial, *Spect*. No. 17, suggests the dish

might be full of wine; ***Rudis***, Usually thought to be a wooden sword, like those used in training, but probably the wooden staff of a referee, Coleman (2006), commentary on Martial, *Spect*. No. 31.

250 **The applause of the crowd:** ***Le gladiateur dans sa gloire***: Robert (1940), 47; **Lap of honour**, Suet. *Cal*. 32.2.

11. *Solis Occasus* (Sunset)

Gifts

252 **At the Saturnalia:** Statius, *Silv*. 1.6; the year is uncertain; **By the next day**, Stat. *Silv*. 1, pr. 31–3.

253 **The usual time for gifts: Seneca,** *Ep*. 74.7.

253 **Domitian's early morning gifts: Geographic sweep of empire**, Simon (2008), 785.

253 **In other shows:** ***Sparsio massilium***, Nibley (1945), 515–43; Simon (2008), 763–88; ***Missilia***, Simon (2008), 770–1; **Gifts in other shows**, Simon (2008), 772–3; **Sell tokens**, *Dig*. 18.1.8.1.

254 **'Threw' gifts:** ***Linea dives***, Killeen (1959), 185–8; **Two images**, Coleman (2010)A, 658; **Painting from Pompeii**, Day (2017), 178, Fig. 12.1.

254 **Such munificence: North African show,** *CIL* 8.7960; **Political philosophy and gifts**, Sidebottom (2006), 117–57, for an introduction.

255 **Despite an underlying ideology: Heliogabalus**, Her. 5.6.9; HA *Helio*. 22.1–3.

255 **Did the senators catch gifts: Not scramble for figs and nuts**, Epict. 4.7.22–4; **Extra tokens for elite**, Suet. *Dom*. 4.5; **Complain if not get their share**, Symm. *Ep*. 9.153; cf. Comm., *Instruct*. 2.34; **Plebs enjoy humiliation of elite**, Yavetz (1969), 114–6.

Politics and the Crowd

256 **The extraordinary growth: Cicero,** *Sest*. 106; 115, translation Gardner (1958); **Letters**, Wiedemann (1992), 167, n.2, provides the references.

257 **The people were sovereign:** Beard, and Crawford (1985), 40–59, is an excellent introduction to Republican politics; Nicolet (1980), 207–381, goes into much more detail; Wirszubski (1950) remains fundamental.

257 **Constitution of the Roman Republic': 'Mixed', Polybius**: P.S. Derow, in: *OCD*, 4th ed. (Oxford, 2012), 1174–5, for a succinct introduction; Walbank (1972) remains my favourite overview; neither take quite the line advanced here.

258 **Most of the twentieth century: 'Oligarchic' Republic**, Exemplified in the works of Sir Ronald Syme, especially in his classic *The Roman Revolution* (1939).

258 **The oligarchic interpretation:** Replaced by **'Democratic' Republic**, Four articles were fundamental; two by Millar (1984), 1–19; and (1986), 1–11; and one each by Lintott (1987), 34–52; and North (1990); the new consensus established by Millar (1998).

259 **Uncertainties and problems: People demand Augustus take more overt power**, Yavetz (1969), 26.

The Emperor and the Crowd

260 **'Long ago': *Bread and circuses***, Juv. 10.77–81; this section is much indebted to Yavetz (1969); also useful are Gunderson (1996), 113–51; and Edmondson (2002), 9–29.

260 **Emperor was expected to attend:** Suet. *Aug*. 45.1; *Tib*. 47.1; **Visibility**, Suet. *Ner*. 12.2; Pl. *Pan*. 51.4–5; **Pay attention**, Suet. *Aug*. 45.1; HA, *Marc*. 15.1; **Enter into the spirit**, Suet. *Claud*. 21; *Tit*. 8.2.

261 **Crowd made their wishes known: Chants**, Roueché (1984), 181–99; **Divine inspiration**, CD 76.4.5–6

261 **Specific to the show: Colosseum**, Mart. *Spect*. 23; with commentary by Coleman (2006); **Polycarp**, Musurillo (1972), 4–5; **Tetrinius**, Suet. *Cal*. 30.2; **Lion trainer**, CD 72.29; **Presiding magistrates not to free slaves at demand of crowd**, *Dig*. 40.9.17 pr.

261 **Motivated by self-interest: Price of grain**, Tac. *Ann*. 6.13; **Lower taxes**, Jos. *JA* 19.24–6.

262 **More altruistic: Tiberius and comic actor**, Suet. *Tib*. 47; **and the statue**, Pl. *NH* 34.62.

262 **Into the realm of politics: Julia**, CD 55.13.1; **Octavia**, Tac. *Ann*. 14. 60–1; **Cleander**, CD 73.13; Herodian places the outcry in the theatres, 1.12.5.

262 **On a few, rare occasions: End the wars**, CD 76.4.1–6.

263 **Renouncing their allegiance: Macrinus**, CD 79.20.1–2.

263 Extraordinary act of dissent: Acclaim Constantine, Lactant. *De mort. pers.* 44.

263 Conversation was not one way: Emperor 'talks' to crowd, Fagan (2011), 180–1; **Hadrian**, CD 69.6.1–2; he was less civil at the Circus, where he rejected a request by a placard, CD 69.16.3.

264 The crowd could turn nasty: Hiss and jeer, Cic. *Sest.* 126; **Throw fruit, not stones**, Macrob. *Sat.* 2.6.1; **Soldiers at the Circus**, Suet. *Aug.* 14.

264 Full-scale riot: Yavetz (1969), 24–37; **Clement**, *Protr.* 3.11.77; **Philostratus**, *VA* 1.15.

264 Generally more quiescent at the amphitheatre: Not numbers, Above, Chapter 6, *Popularity*; **Not social mix and seating**, *pace* Fagan (2011), 198; and Toner (2014), 42; **Not intrinsic interest in entertainments**, *pace* Toner (2014), 77; **Not frequency or duration**, *pace* Fagan (2011), 151.

265 A prosaic reason: Soldiers provide security, Above, Chapter 6, *Anticipation*; **Praetorians inside, urban cohorts outside**, is the conclusion of Bingham (1999), 369-79; **Fucine Lake**, Tac. *Ann.* 12.56.

12. *Vesper* (Evening)

In the gloom . . .

266 Dung heap of Romulus: Cic. Att. 2.1.8

Magic and Medicine

266 Long since left the arena: Father Dis/Mercury/Charon, Above, Chapter 7, *The Procession*; **Gate of Death**, Only known from two references to the same event, where the helmet of Commodus is carried out through the *Porta Libitiensis*, HA, *Com.* 16.7; CD 73.21.3, but we assume that one gate was so designated in most amphitheatres; ***Spoliarium***, Kyle (1998), 158–9; **Ill-fitting equipment**, (Ps.-)Quint. *Major Declamations* 9.8.10.

267 Attempts to identify the *Spoliarium*: Curator of the *Spoliarium*, *CIL* 6.10171; **Praeneste**, *CIL* 14.3014.

267 Gladiators who had a wife: Diodorus and Miletus, Above, Chapter 10, *The Mind of the Gladiator*.

267 Not all were so lucky: Magic, Two wonderfully written ways into the subject are MacMullen (1966), 95–162; and Nixey (2024), 53–74; a more conventional introduction is H.S. Versnel, in: *OCD*, 4th ed. (Oxford, 2012), *s.v. magic*, 884–5.

267 Two strange modern fantasies: Sweat as aphrodisiac, Fallacy explored and exposed by Paule (2024), 227–36; **Hairpins**, e.g. Sky HISTORY TV channel, https://www.history.co.uk/articles/18-surprising-facts-about-the-gladiators.

268 Hair parted by a spear: Plut. *Mor.* 285B–D; he went for just one reason in *Rom.* 15; Ovid. *Fast*. 2.560; Festus 55.3 L.

268 Superstition and magic: Otherness of both, Ogden (2008), esp. 77–114.

268 Another story: Faustina and the gladiator: HA *Marc.* 19.

269 The moment of conception: Heliodorus, *Aeth*. 4.8.

269 Very specific use: Although sometimes mentioned in scholarly works, e.g. Toner (2014), 57, I have not come across any ancient reference to the blood of a gladiator curing impotence.

269 The liver of a gladiator: Scrib. Larg. *Compos*. 12–18; liver at 17; fawn at 13; translation by I.T. Jocks (2020) online at https://theses.gla.ac.uk/82178/.

270 The blood of a gladiator: Moog, and Karenberg (2003), 137–43; **Tertullian**, *Apol*. 9.10–12; actually the blood of the guilty (*noxii*), on vagueness of Christian terminology for the Games, Above, Chapter 1, *Food and Participants*; **Pliny the Elder**, *NH* 28.2; **Celsus**, *Med*. 3.23.7.

270 Consumed there and then: Aretaeus of Cappadocia, *Treatment of Chronic Diseases* 7.4.7–8.

270 Magic and medicine overlapped: Barton (1994), 133–68

271 Gate of Life: Like the Gate of Death (*Porta Libitiensis*), the *Porta Sanavivaria* is only mentioned twice in our sources, both times in the *Passion of Perpetua and Felicitas*, set in Carthage, Musurillo (1972), 118–9; 128–9; again we generalise, although not all amphitheatres can have had both, for example that at Dorchester in Britain had only one entrance to the arena, Wilmott (2008), 103–8; **Galen**, On his career, briefly Boudon-Millot (2024), 23–42; and a full-length biography by Mattern (2013), with vivisection of monkey at 83–4.

271 Galen learned much: Dissection of human corpses rare, Mattern (2013), 71–3; **Celsus**, Scarborough (1971), 104; **Galen's surgical**

techniques at Pergamum, Mattern (2013), 93–6; and, more generally, Bliquez (2024), 206–26.

272 **Inflated impression of its efficacy: Rely on *lanista***, Scarborough (1971), 102; citing Eppictetus 3.15, which might carry that implication; note also that even in the upmarket school at Pergamum, Galen claimed that before his time the gladiators were treated by both physicians and *didaskoloi* (trainers), Mattern (2013), 93.

272 **Roman medicine in general: Ephesus injuries**, Kanz, and Grossschmidt (2016), 216; compare the various healed injuries in the York cemetery, Hunter-Mann (2015), 9.

272 **Always the danger of infection: Galen and wine**, Mattern (2013), 93; **Vitalis**, *CIL* 2.1070; translation by Fagan (2011), 324.

The Future of the Games

This section draws heavily on Ville (1960), 273–335; Wiedemann (1992), 128–64; Bomgardner (2000), 197–227; Dunkle (2008), 201–6; and Epplett (2016), 146–66; also particularly interesting is Potter (2010) B, 596–606, although his contention that those *damnatio ad ludum* were not gladiators is unconvincing.

273 **Constantine:** *CT* 15.12.1; Eus. *Vit. Const.* 4.25.1.

273 **Limits of the power of any emperor:** Remember the ruling of Marcus Aurelius and the Gallic martyrs, above, Chapter 1, *Backgrounds*; scholars have pointed out that Constantine's ruling was a rescript, and thus argued that its effect was always intended to be limited, e.g. Bomgardner (2000), 205; **Antioch**, Lib. *Or.* 1.5; Potter (2021), 186–7, noting that the Praetorian prefect of the eastern provinces in AD238 was none other than the man who had received Constantine's rescript; **Hispellum and Volsinii**, *CIL* 11.5265*;* **Carthage and Rome**, August. *Conf.* 6.7–8; Lane Fox (2015), 150; 166; **Valentinian**, *CT* 9.40.8; 11; Potter (2010)B, 602; **Apamea**, Zoz. 4.37; **Prudentius**, *C. Symm.* 2.1126–9; Wiedemann (1992), 152–3; ***Theodosian Code***, T. Honoré, in: *OCD*, 4th. Ed. (Oxford, 2012), *s.v. Theodosian Code*, 1458; **Medallions**, Wiedemann (1992), 158.

274 **Christians' relationship: Tertullian, *On the Spectacles***, Above, Ch. 6, *Popularity*.

274 **Another paradox: Christians invest more religious significance than pagans**, e.g. Tert., *De Spect.* 12.

274 **Human sacrifice: Jupiter Latiaris**, Rives (1995), 74–7.

275 **Christians developed an aggressive ideology: Martyrs as Athletes**, Edwards (2007), 211; Potter (2021), 183–5; **Martyrs as gladiators**, Thompson (2002), 42–3; Toner (2014), 60; **Perpetua**, Musurillo (1972), 116–9; **Goad beasts**, Eus. *HE* 3.36 (Ignatius); **Perfume**, Musurillo (1972), 14–5 (Polycarp); Eus. *HE* 1.35; (martyrs of Lyons); **Christ/God as *Editor***, Cyp. *Ep*. 7.2-3; or as *Summa Rudis*, Musurillo (1972), 118–9 (Perpetua); **Judgement Day as Games**, Tert. *De Spect*. 30.1–2; Musurillo (1972), 10–1 (Polycarp); and Cyprian, *Ep*. 8; **Arena shapes Hell**, Wiedemann (1992), 150.

275 **Eventually came to an end: *Codex Iustinianus***, T. Honoré, in: *OCD*, 4th ed. (Oxford, 2012), *s.v. Justinian's codification*, 780–1; **Constantine's rewritten words**, *CJ* 11.44.1.

276 **Wild-beast shows continued:** Until the mid-sixth century, Bomgardner (2000), 201; **Public executions continued**, Last recorded condemnation *ad Bestias* AD 568, Wiedemann (1992), 155, n.69; *ad Flammas* continued for centuries; **Range of methods and crimes increased**, MacMullen (1990), 204–17.

276 **Far from easy: Three Latin epitomes**, Aurelius Victor, the anonymous *Epitome* preserved with Victor, and Eutropius; **Two Greek overviews**, Zozimus (sixth century), and Zonaras (twelfth century); **'Epigraphic habit'**, MacMullen (1982), 233–46; **Archaeology and end of Gladiatorial Games**, Christie (2009), 221–33; Milliman (2021), 194–206.

277 **'Third Century Crisis':** Drinkwater (2005), 28–66, is the best attempt to impose a narrative on the refractory sources; **Not 'total crisis'**, Sidebottom (1998), 2792–803; **Lack of money**, e.g. Epplett (2016), 158; and Potter (2021), 188; **Beast-fights**, Last recorded in AD 537, Epplett (2016), 165; **Chariot racing**, Lasts centuries longer; **Traditionalism of 'barracks emperors'**, MacMullen (1976).

277 **A better approach: Shrinking numbers of local elite**, MacMullen (1988), *s.v.* Index, *Curiales (bouleutai): diminishing numbers*; **Not need to compete with each other**, Inspired by Wilmott (2008), 50–6, on British elite not buying into amphitheatres in the first place.

277 **Elite attitudes to munificence: Christianity**, Bomgardner (2000), 207.

278 **Christians later claimed the credit: Telemachus**, Later invention argued by Ville (1960), 326–31; not followed by Weidemann (1992),

158; Bomgardner (2000), 206–7, 206–7; and Epplett (2016), 157–8, all of whom treat the story as, more or less, historical.

The Future of the Gladiator

278 Returned to their *Ludus*: *Armamentarium*, Dunkle (2008), 57; **Ash in wine after fight**, Pl. *NH* 36.203; **Massage**, MacLean (2014), 581.

279 The *Rudis*: Ville (1981), 325–9; Dunkle (2008), 71; this was not the wooden training sword of the same name; instead it was the stick or rod carried by referees; a clear indication that referees were ex-gladiators.

279 A more realistic hope: Chances of death in a fight, Careful study, Ville (1981), 318–21; **Often followed**, e.g. Futrell (2006), 143–4; **One in six**, Hopkins, and Beard (2005), 89; **One in twenty**, Dodge (2011), 30: actually 5–10 per cent.

279 The evidence consists: Numbers of gladiators, Guesses, Hopkins, and Beard (2005), 92: 16,000; Toner (2014), 57: 20,000; **Unknowable**, Because we do not know how many *familiae* there were at any point, and it may have varied widely over time, nor the average number of gladiators in a *familia*, which will also have differed widely; my figure of over half a million assumes no fatalities at all, so is a massive underestimate.

280 Another problem: Bias of tombstones, cf. Toner (2014), 64–5.

280 The chances of survival: One extreme, Suet, *Ner.* 12, in a litany of mainly deplorable eccentricities; **The other at Miturnae**, *ILS* 5062, these were matches *sine missione*, for which the giver had sought the emperor's permission; the inscription implies their rarity; **Mesonius inscription**, *CIL* 4.2508; translated by Fagan (2011), 319–21.

280 How often he fought: Modern estimates, Once a year, Balsdon (1969), 301–2; under twice a year, Hopkins, and Beard (2005), 88; minimum of twice a year, Wiedemann (1992), 120; two or three times a year, Toner (2014), 64–5; **Bato**, CD 78.6.2; cf. Suet. *Cal.* 35.4; **Exochus**, *ILS* 5088; see above, Ch.10, *The Mind of the Gladiator*; **Trajan's Games**, CD 68.15.1; ***Suppositicii***, Dunkle (2008), 69–70; **Hermes**, Mart. 5.24.8; **Iuvenus**, *ILS* 5107.

281 Spanish cattle-rustlers: Above, Ch.2, *The Oath*.

282 Temptation to generalise: The jurist Ulpian, *Coll.* 11.7.4, says that men condemned to gladiatorial schools *may* be awarded the *rudis* after three years, and *may* be freed after five, not they all are; **Dozens of**

victories, Ville (1981), 321–2; a few claimed over a hundred, like Asteropaeus with 107, *CIL* 6.1421; of course such men probably re-enlisted.

282 **Constantine, always a savage-minded:** *CT* 9.18.1; Later Christians, if they had bothered when rewriting history, could have pointed to this ruling of AD315 coming ten years before his supposed abolition of gladiators; Above, *The Future of the Games*; **Venusia**, *ILS* 5083a; text and translation, Fagan (2011), 321–2; the inscription only lists victories, not any grants of *missio*, so those who had only won once or twice may have had more fights.

282 **World War One Pilots: Life expectancy**, Hart (2005), 355; quote on novices at 63; **Effects**, Yeates (1934); Lewis (1936).

282 **Far more likely to survive: *Palas* system**, Above, Ch.5, *Security*.

283 **Whatever his status: Pagan afterlife**, **Hades**, A. Henrichs, in: *OCD*, 4th ed. (Oxford, 2012), *s.v. Hades*, 640–1; **Eastern gladiators as heroes**, Above, Ch.10, *The Mind of the Gladiator*; **Achilles**, Hom. *Od*. 11.488–91.

283 **Consolation from popular philosophy:** Above, Ch.5, *Gladiator Suicides*; **Graffito about Seneca**, Above, Ch.6, *Opposition and Justification*; **Seneca**, *Ep*. 54; **Lucretius**, *De Re. Nat*. 3.910–1

284 **The stars enjoined fatalism: Astrology**, Long ago Thorndike (1913), 415–35; and MacMullen (1990)B, 218–24, showed how astrological literature could be used by historians; R.L. Beck, in: *OCD*, 4th ed. (Oxford, 2012), *s.v. astrology*, 187-8, gives a very brief introduction; and a more extended one at Beck (2007); Barton (1993), 27–94, is rewarding, but asks a lot from its reader.

284 **Firmicus Maternus:** Dykes (Minneapolis, 2023) is the only modern translation of the whole *Mathesis*; there is a need for a scholarly one with a commentary; likewise a discussion of the arena in the work; **Pose as amateur**, Firm. Mat. 1, *pref.* 1; 14; **Sicily**, Firm. Mat. 1, *pref.* 5–8.

284 **The stars at your birth: Horoscopes of Gladiators**, **Volunteers and condemned**, Firm. Mat. 8.8.12.4–5; also 7.7.24.2–3; **Death, victories, and fame**, Firm. Mat. 8.8.7.14; also 3.3.4.57; 7.7.26.2; 8.8.10. 8–9; 8.8.17.5–6; 8.8.24.28.

Ave atque vale

Catullus, 11.

Bibliography

Entries in *The Oxford Classical Dictionary* (4th ed., 2012) are not listed here.

Adams (1982): J.N. Adams, *The Latin Sexual Vocabulary* (London, 1982)

Aldrete (2014): G.S. Aldrete, 'Urban Sensations: Opulence and Ordure', in: Toner (2014)A, 45–67

Alföldy (1985): G. Alföldy, *The Social History of Rome* (Eng. tr., London, and Sydney, 1985)

Alföldy (1995): G. Alföldy, 'Eine Bauinschrift aus dem Colosseum', *ZPE* 109 (1995), 195–226

Anderson (1985): J.K. Anderson, *Hunting in the Ancient World* (Berkeley, 1985)

Aymard (1951): J. Aymard, *Essai sur les chasses romaines des origins à la fin du siècle des Antonins* (Paris, 1951)

Balsdon (1969): J.P.V.D. Balsdon, *Life and Leisure in Ancient Rome* (London, 1969)

Balsdon (1979): J.P.V.D. Balsdon, *Romans and Aliens* (London, 1979)

Barchiesi, and Scheidel (2010): A. Barchiesi, and W. Scheidel (eds.), *The Oxford Handbook of Roman Studies* (Oxford, 2010)

Barrett (2020): A.A. Barrett, *Rome is Burning: Nero and the Fire That Ended a Dynasty* (Princeton, and Oxford, 2020)

Barton (1993): C.A. Barton, *The Sorrows of the Ancient Romans: The Gladiator and the Monster* (Princeton, 1993)

Barton (1994): T.S. Barton, *Power and Knowledge: Astrology, Physiognomics, and Medicine under the Roman Empire* (Ann Arbor, 1994)

Beard (1980): M. Beard, 'The sexual status of Vestal Virgins', *JRS* 70 (1980), 12–27

Beard (2008): M. Beard, *Pompeii: The Life of a Roman Town* (London, 2008)

Beard (2014): M. Beard, *Laughter in Ancient Rome: On Joking, Tickling, and Cracking Up* (Berkeley, Los Angeles, and London, 2014)

Beard (2023): M. Beard, *Emperor of Rome: Ruling the Ancient Roman World* (London, 2023)

Beard, and Crawford (1985): M. Beard, and M. Crawford, *Rome in the Late Republic* (London, 1985)

Beard, and Henderson (2001): M. Beard, and J. Henderson, *Classical Art: From Greece to Rome* (Oxford, 2001)

Beck (2007): R. Beck, *A Brief History of Ancient Astrology* (Malden, MA, and Oxford, 2007)

Belayche (2021): N. Belayche, '*Assiduo sono* and *furiosa tibia* in Ovid's *Fasti*: Music and Religious Identity in Narratives of Processions in the Roman World', in: Nuño, Esquerra, and Woolf (2021), 366–88

Berns, and Ekinci (2015): C. Berns, and H. Ali Ekinci, 'Gladiatorial Games in the Greek East: a complex of reliefs from Cibyra', *Anatolian Studies* 65 (2015), 143–79

Berry, and Laurence (1998): J. Berry, and R. Laurence (eds.), *Cultural Identity in the Roman Empire* (London, and New York, 1998)

Betts (2017): E. Betts (ed.), *Senses of the Empire: Multisensory Approaches to Roman Culture* (London, 2017)

Bingham (1999): S. Bingham, 'Security at the Games in the Early Imperial Period', *Echos du Monde Classique* 18.3 (1999), 369–79

Birley (1988): A.R. Birley, *Septimius Severus: The African Emperor* (2nd ed., London, and New York, 1988)

Birley (1997): A.R. Birley, *Hadrian: The Restless Emperor* (London, and New York, 1997)

Bliquez (2024): L.J. Bliquez, '*Galenus Chirurgus*: Galen as Surgeon', in: Singer, and Rosen (2024), 206–26

Le Bohec (1994): Y. Le Bohec, *The Imperial Roman Army* (Eng. tr., London, 1994)

Bomgardner (1992): D.L. Bomgardner, 'The Trade in Wild Beasts for Roman Spectacles: A Green Perspective', *Anthropozoologica* 16 (1992), 161–6

Bomgardner (2000): D.L. Bomgardner, *The Story of the Roman Amphitheatre* (London, and New York, 2000)

Bomgardner (2009): D.L. Bomgardner, 'The Magerius Mosaic Revisited', in: Wilmott (2009), 165–77

Boudon-Millot (2024): V. Boudon-Millot, 'Galen: Life and Works', in: Singer, and Rosen (2024), 23–42

Bowersock (1969): G.W. Bowersock, *Greek Sophists in the Roman Empire* (Oxford, 1969)

Bowman, Garnsey, and Cameron (2005): A.K. Bowman, P. Garnsey, and A. Cameron (eds.), *The Cambridge Ancient History, Volume XII: The Crisis of Empire, A.D. 193–337* (Cambridge, 2005)

Bradley (1989): K.R. Bradley, *Slavery and Rebellion in the Roman World 140BC–70BC* (London, 1989)

Bradley (2021): M. Bradley, 'The Triumph of the Senses: Sensory Awareness and the Divine in Roman Public Celebrations', in: Nuño, Esquerra, and Woolf (2021), 125–40

Brettler, and Poliakoff (1990): M.Z. Brettler, and M. Poliakoff, 'Rabbi Simeon ben Lakish at the Gladiator's banquet: Rabbinic Observations on the Roman Arena', *Harvard Theological Review* 83.1 (1990), 93–8

Brice, and Slootjes (2015): L.L. Brice, and D. Slootjes (eds.), *Aspects of Ancient Institutions and Geography* (Leiden, 2015)

Brunet (2004): S. Brunet, 'Female and Dwarf Gladiators', *Mouseion* 4.2 (2004), 145–70

Brunt (1990): P.A. Brunt, 'Laus imperii', in: P.A. Brunt, *Roman Imperial Themes* (Oxford, 1990), 288–323 (originally published in P.D.A. Garnsey, and C.R. Whittaker, *Imperialism in the Ancient World* [Cambridge, 1978], 159–91)

Butler, and Nooter (2018): S. Butler, and S. Nooter (eds.), *Sound and the Ancient Senses* (London, 2018)

Cagniart (2000): P. Cagniart, 'The Philosopher and the Gladiator', *CW* 93.6 (2000), 607–18

Campbell (1984): J.B. Campbell, *The Emperor and the Roman Army* 31BC–AD235 (Oxford, 1984)

Campbell (2002): B. Campbell, *War and Society in Imperial Rome 31BC–AD284* (London, and New York, 2002)

Caplan (2000): J. Caplan (ed.), *Written on the Body: The Tattoo in European and American History* (Princeton, 2000)

Carr (1976): R. Carr, *English Fox Hunting: A History* (London, 1976)

Carter (2001): M. Carter, 'Artemidorus and the ἀρβήλας Gladiator', *ZPE* 134 (2001), 109–115

Carter (2001)A: M. Carter, 'The Roman Spectacles of Antiochus IV Epiphanes at Daphne, 166 BC', *Nikephoros* 14 (2001), 45–62

Carter (2003): M. Carter, 'Gladiatorial Ranking and the "SC de Pretiis Gladiatorum Minuendis" (CIL II 6278+ILS 5163)', *Phoenix* 57.1/2 (2003), 83–114

Carter (2004): M. Carter, '*Archiereis* and Asiarchs: A Gladiatorial Perspective', *GRBS* 44 (2004), 41–68

Carter (2006): M. Carter, 'Buttons and Wooden Swords: Polybius 10.20.3, Livy 26.51, and the Rudis', *CPhil* 101.2 (2006), 153–60

Carter (2006)A: M. Carter, 'Gladiatorial Combat with "Sharp" Weapons (tois othesi siderois)', *ZPE* 155 (2006), 161–75

Carter (2006/7): M. Carter, 'Gladiatorial Combat: The Rules of Engagement', *CJ* 102.2 (2006/7), 97–114

Carter (2008): M. Carter, '(Un)Dressed to Kill: Viewing the *Retiarius*', in: Edmondson, and Keith (2008), 113–35
Carter (2009): M. Carter, 'Gladiators and Monomachoi: Greek Attitudes to a Roman "Cultural Performance"', *The International Journal of the History of Sport* 26.2 (2009), 298–322
Carter (2009)A: M. Carter, 'Accepi ramum: Gladiatorial Palms and the Chavagnes Gladiator Cup', *Latomus* 68 (2009), 438–41
Carter (2011): M. Carter, 'A Doctor Secutorum and the Retiarius Draukos from Corinth', *ZPE* 126 (2011), 262–8
Carter (2011)A: M. Carter, 'Blown Call? Diodorus and the Treacherous Summa Rudis', *ZPE* 177 (2011), 63–9
Carter (2014): M. Carter, 'Romanization through Spectacle in the Greek East', in: Christesen, and Kyle (2014), 619–32
Carter (2015): M. Carter, 'Bloodbath: Artemidorus, Αποτομοσ Combat, and Ps.-Quintilian's "The Gladiator"', *ZPE* 193 (2015), 39–52
Carter (2018): M. Carter, '*Armorum Studium*: Gladiatorial Training and the Gladiatorial *Ludus*', *BICS* 61.1 (2018), 119–31
Carucci (2019): M. Carucci, 'The Spectacle of Justice in the Roman Empire', in: Hekster, and Verboven (2019), 212–33
Cecconi (2002): G.A. Cécconi, *Commento storico al libro II dell'epistolario di Q. Aurelio Symmace: Con introduzione, testo, traduzione e indici* (Pisa, 2002)
Chamberland (2021): G. Chamberland, 'Imperial Spectacle in the Roman Provinces', in: Scanlon, and Futrell (2021), 378–88
Chaniotis (2018): A. Chaniotis, 'Nessun dorma! Changing nightlife in the Hellenistic and Roman East', in: Chaniotis, and Derron (2018), 1–58
Chaniotis, and Derron (2018): A. Chaniotis, and P. Derron (eds.), *La Nuit: Imaginaire et Réalités Nocturnes dans le Monde Gréco-Romain* (Vancouver, 2018)
Christesen, and Kyle (2014): P. Christesen, and D.G. Kyle (eds.), *A Companion to Sport and Spectacle in Greek and Roman Antiquity* (Malden, MA, Oxford, and Chichester, 2014)
Christie (2009): N. Christie, 'No More Fun? The Ends of Entertainment Structures in the Late Roman West', in: Wilmott (2009), 221–33
Claridge (2010): A. Claridge, Rome: *An Oxford Archaeological Guide* (2nd ed., Oxford, 2010)
Clarke (1998): J.R. Clarke, *Looking at Lovemaking: Constructions of Sexuality in Roman Art, 100BC–AD250* (Berkeley, Los Angeles, and London, 1998)
Clarke (2003): J.R. Clarke, *Roman Sex 100BC–AD250* (New York, 2003)
Clarke (2003)A: J.R. Clarke, *Art in the Lives of Ordinary Romans: Visual Representation and Non-elite Viewers in Italy, 100BC–AD315* (Berkeley, Los Angeles, and London, 2003)

Clarke (2007): J.R. Clarke, *Looking at Laughter: Humor, Power, and Transgression in Roman Visual Culture, 100BC–AD250* (Berkeley, Los Angeles, and London, 2007)

Coarelli (2007): F. Coarelli, *Rome and Environs: An Archaeological Guide* (Eng. tr., Berkeley, and Los Angeles, 2007)

Coleman (1990): K.M. Coleman, 'Fatal Charades: Roman Executions Staged as Mythological Enactments', *JRS* 80 (1990), 44–73

Coleman (1993): K.M. Coleman, 'Launching into History: Aquatic Displays in the Early Empire', *JRS* 83 (1993), 48–74

Coleman (2000): K.M. Coleman, '*Missio* at Halicarnassus', *HSCP* 100 (2000), 487–500

Coleman (2006): K.M. Coleman, *M. Valerii Martialis Liber Spectaculorum* (Oxford, 2006)

Coleman (2010): K.M. Coleman, 'Valuing others in the gladiatorial barracks', in: Rosen, and Sluiter (2010), 419–45

Coleman (2010)A: K.M. Coleman, 'Spectacle', in: Barchiesi, and Scheidel (2010), 651–70

Coleman (2012): K.M. Coleman, 'Feral attraction: animal "stars" in the Roman arena', *Omnibus* 63 (2012), 13–6

Coleman (2019): K.M. Coleman, 'Defeat in the Arena', *GR* 66.1 (2019), 1–36

Concannon (2014): C.V. Concannon, '"Not for an Olive Wreath, but Our Lives": Gladiators, Athletes, and Early Christian Bodies', *JBL* 133. 1 (2014), 193–214

Cook (2012): J.G. Cook, 'Crucifixion as Spectacle in Roman Campania', *Novum Testamentum* 54 (2012), 68–100

Corbeill (1997): A. Corbeill, 'Thumbs in Ancient Rome: "Pollex" as Index', *MAAR* 42 (1997), 1–21

Coulston (2007): J. Coulston, 'By the sword united: Roman fighting styles on the battlefield and in the arena', in: Molloy (2007), 34–51

Coulston (2009): J. Coulston, 'Victory and Defeat in the Roman Arena: The Evidence of Gladiatorial Iconography', in: Wilmott (2009), 195–210

Crane (2015): D. Crane, *Went the Day Well? Witnessing Waterloo* (London, 2015, published in paperback as *Witnessing Waterloo: 24 Hours, 48 Lives, A World Forever Changed*, London, 2016)

Crouch (2005): D. Crouch, *Tournament* (London, and New York, 2005)

Cunliffe (1988): B. Cunliffe, *Greeks, Romans and Barbarians: Spheres of Interaction* (London, 1988)

Curry (2008): A. Curry, 'The Gladiator Diet', *Archaeology* 61.6 (2008), 28–30

Dalby (2000): A. Dalby, *Empire of Pleasures: Luxury and Indulgence in the Roman World* (London, and New York, 2000)

Dalby (2003): A. Dalby, *Food in the Ancient World from A to Z* (London, and New York, 2003)

D'Angour (2018): A. D'Angour, 'Hearing Ancient Sounds Through Modern Ears', in: Butler, and Nooter (2018), 31–43

Davison (1989): D.P. Davison, *The Barracks of the Roman Army from the 1st to the 3rd Centuries AD* (Oxford, 1989)

Day (2017): J. Day, 'Scents of place and colours of smell: Fragranced entertainment in ancient Rome', in: Betts (2017), 176–92

Dodds (1951): E.R. Dodds, *The Greeks and the Irrational* (Berkeley, 1951)

Dodds (1965): E.R. Dodds, *Pagan and Christian in an Age of Anxiety* (Cambridge, 1965)

Dodge (2011): H. Dodge, *Spectacle in the Roman World* (Bristol, 2011)

Dodge (2021): H. Dodge, 'The Colosseum', in: Scanlon, and Futrell (2021), 412–25

Dowden (2003): 'The value of sleep: Homer, Plinies, Posidonius, and Proculus', in: Wiedemann, and Dowden (2003), 141–63

Downie (2014): J. Downie, 'Narrative and Divination: Artemidorus and Aelius Aristides', *Archive für Religionsgeschichte* 15.1 (2014), 97–116

Drinkwater (2005): J. Drinkwater, 'Maximinus to Diocletian and the "crisis"', in: Bowman, Garnsey, and Cameron (2005), 28–66

Dunbabin (1978): K. Dunbabin, *The Mosaics of Roman North Africa* (Oxford, 1978)

Dunbabin (1999): K. Dunbabin, *Mosaics of the Greek and Roman World* (Cambridge, 1999)

Dunkle (2008): R. Dunkle, *Gladiators: Violence and Spectacle in Ancient Rome* (Harlow, 2008)

Dunn (2019): D. Dunn, *In the Shadow of Vesuvius: A Life of Pliny* (London, 2019)

Dunn (2024): D. Dunn, *The Missing Thread: A New History of the Ancient World through the Women Who Shaped It* (London, 2024)

Edmondson (1996): J.C. Edmondson, 'Dynamic Arenas: Gladiatorial Presentations in the City of Rome and the Construction of Roman Society during the Early Empire', in: Slater (1996), 69–112

Edmondson (2002): J.C. Edmondson, 'Public Spectacles and Roman Social Relations', in: *Ludi Romani: espectáculos en Hispania Romana: Museo Nacional de Arte Romano, Mérida, 29 de julio-13 de octubre, 2002* (Mérida, 2002), 9–29

Edmondson, and Keith (2008): J. Edmondson, and A. Keith (eds.), *Roman Dress and the Fabrics of Roman Culture* (Toronto, 2008)

Edwards (2007): C. Edwards, *Death in Ancient Rome* (New Haven, and London, 2007)

Ekirch (2005): A.R. Ekirch, *At Day's Close: Night in Times Past* (New York, 2005)

Epplett (2001): C. Epplett, 'The Capture of Animals by the Roman Military', *GR* 48.2 (2001), 210–22

Epplett (2014): C. Epplett, 'Roman Beast Hunts', in: Christesen, and Kyle (2014), 505–19

Epplett (2014)A: C. Epplett, 'Spectacular Executions in the Roman World', in: Christesen, and Kyle (2014), 520–32

Epplett (2016): C. Epplett, *Gladiators and Beast Hunts: Arena Sports of Ancient Rome* (Barnsley, 2016)

Erdkamp (2013): P. Erdkamp (ed.), *The Cambridge Companion to Ancient Rome* (Cambridge, 2013)

Ewigleben (2000): C. Ewigleben, '"What these Women love is the Sword": The Performers and their Audiences', in: Köhne, and Ewigleben (2000), 125–39

Fagan (2011): G.G. Fagan, *The Lure of the Arena: Social Psychology and the Crowd at the Roman Games* (Cambridge, 2011)

Fagan (2015): G.G. Fagan, 'Training Gladiators: Life in the *Ludus*', Brice, and Slootjes (2015), 122–44

Finley (1974): M.I. Finley (ed.), *Studies in Ancient Society* (London, and Boston, 1974)

Fiorato, Boylston, and Knüsel (2000): V. Fiorato, A. Boylston, and C. Knüsel (eds.), *Blood Red Roses: The Archaeology of a Mass Grave from the Battle of Towton AD 1461* (Oxford, 2000)

Fournie, and Parissaki (2018): J. Fournie, and M.-G.G. Parissaki (eds.), *Les communautés du Nord égéen au temps de l'hégémonie Romaine. Entre ruptures et continuités* (Athens, 2018)

Frayn (1995): J.M. Frayn, 'The Roman meat trade', in: Wilkins, Harvey and Dobson (1995), 107–14

Fuhrmann (2012): C.J. Fuhrmann, *Policing the Roman Empire: Soldiers, Administration, and Public Order* (Oxford, 2012)

Futrell (1997): A. Futrell, *Blood in the Arena: The Spectacle of Roman Power* (Austin, 1997)

Futrell (2006): A. Futrell, *The Roman Games: Historical Sources in Translation* (Malden, MA, 2006)

Futrell (2021): A. Futrell, 'Sex in the Arena', in: Scanlon, and Futrell (2021), 676–92

Gibson (1996): B.J. Gibson, 'Statius and Insomnia: Allusion and Meaning in *Silvae* 5.4', *CQ* 46.2 (1996), 457–68

Gilhus (2006): I.S. Gilhus, *Animals, Gods and Humans: Changing Attitudes to Animals in Greek, Roman and Early Christian Ideas* (London, and New York, 2006)

Ginzburg (1980): C. Ginzburg, *The Cheese and the Worms: The Cosmos of a Sixteenth-Century Miller* (Eng. tr., Baltimore, 1980)

Goldsworthy (1996): A.K. Goldsworthy, *The Roman Army at War, 100BC–AD200* (Oxford, 1996)

Gonlin, and Nowell (2017): N. Gonlin, and A. Nowell (eds.), *Archaeology of the Night: Life after Dark in the Ancient World* (Colorado, 2017)

González (1986): J. González, 'The Lex Irnitana: a New Copy of the Flavian Municipal Law', *JRS* 76 (1986), 147–243

Gordon (2009): R. Gordon, 'Animal-lore and the role of animals' (Review of Gilhus [2006]), *JRA* 22 (2009), 637–42

Green (1996): C.M.C. Green, 'Did the Romans hunt?', *CA* 15.2 (1996), 222–60

Griffin (1976): M. Griffin, *Seneca: A Philosopher in Politics* (Oxford, 1976)

Griffin (1986): M. Griffin, 'Philosophy, Cato, and Roman Suicide', *GR* 33.1 (1986), 64–77; *GR* 33.2 (1986), 192–202

Griffin, and Barnes (1989), M. Griffin, and J. Barnes (eds.), *Philosophia Togata* (Oxford, 1989)

Gruen (1990): E. Gruen, *Studies in Greek Culture and Roman Policy* (Berkeley, Los Angeles, and London, 1990)

Gruen (1993): E. Gruen, *Culture and National Identity in Republican Rome* (London, 1993)

Gunderson (1996): E. Gunderson, 'The Ideology of the Arena', *CA* 15.1 (1996), 113-51

Gustafson (2000): M. Gustafson, 'The Tattoo in the Later Roman Empire and Beyond', in: Caplan (2000), 17–31

Hammer (2010): D. Hammer, 'Roman Spectacular Entertainments and the Technology of Reality', *Arethusa* 43.1 (2010), 63–86

Hammond (2020): M. Hammond, *Artemidorus: The Interpretation of Dreams* (Oxford, 2020)

Hannestad (1988): N. Hannestad, *Roman Art and Imperial Policy* (Aarhus, 1988)

Harris (2019): R. Harris, *The Second Sleep* (London, 2019)

Harris (2009): W.V. Harris, *Dreams and Experience in Classical Antiquity* (Cambridge, Mass., and London, 2009)

Harrisson (2013): J. Harrisson, *Dreams and Dreaming in the Roman Empire: Cultural Memory and Imagination* (London, 2013)

Hart (2005): P. Hart, *Bloody April: Slaughter in the Skies over Arras, 1917* (London, 2005)

Heffernan (2012): T.J. Heffernan, *The Passion of Perpetua and Felicity* (Oxford, 2012)

Hekster (2002): O. Hekster, *Commodus: An Emperor at the Crossroads* (Amsterdam, 2002)

Hekster, and Verboven (2019): O. Hekster, and K. Verboven (eds.), *The Impact of Justice on the Roman Empire* (Leiden, 2019)

Hill (2004): T. Hill, *Ambitiosa Mors: Suicide and Self in Roman Thought and Literature* (New York, and London, 2004)

Holloway (1991): R.R. Holloway, *The Archaeology of Ancient Sicily* (London, and New York, 1991)

Holmes (1985): R. Holmes, *Firing Line* (London, 1985, reprinted as *Acts of War: The Behaviour of Men in Battle*, London, 2003)

Hope (1998): V.M. Hope, 'Negotiating Identity and Status: The gladiators of Roman Nîmes', in: Berry, and Laurence (1998), 179-95

Hope (2000): V.M. Hope, 'Fighting for Identity: The Funerary Commemoration of Italian Gladiators', *BICS* 73 (2000), 93–113

Hope (2009): V.M. Hope, *Roman Death: The Dying and the Dead in Ancient Rome* (London, and New York, 2009)

Hopkins (1983): K. Hopkins, 'Murderous Games', in: K. Hopkins, *Death and Renewal: Sociological Studies in Roman History 2* (Cambridge, 1983), 1–30

Hopkins, and Beard (2005): K. Hopkins, and M. Beard, *The Colosseum* (London, 2005)

Hopkins, and Burton (1983): K. Hopkins, and G. Burton, 'Ambition and Withdrawal: The Senatorial Aristocracy under the Emperors', in: K. Hopkins, *Death and Renewal: Sociological Studies in Roman History 2* (Cambridge, 1983), 120-200

Hunink (2010): V. Hunink, 'Did Perpetua Write Her Prison Account?', *Folia philologica* 133, No.1/2 (2010), 147–155

Hunter-Mann (2015): K. Hunter-Mann, *Driffield Terrace: An Insight Report* (York, 2015)

Isaac (2004): B. Isaac, *The Invention of Racism in Classical Antiquity* (Princeton, and Oxford, 2004)

Jacobelli (2003): L. Jacobelli, *Gladiators at Pompeii* (Los Angeles, 2003)

Jacobelli (2021): L. Jacobelli, 'Pompeii and Games', in: Scanlon, and Futrell (2021), 488–97

Janni (1984): P. Janni, *La Mappa e il Periplo: Cartografia Antica e Spazio Odologico* (Rome, 1984)

Jansen (2003): G.C.M. Jansen, 'Social distinctions and issues of privacy in the toilets of Hadrian's Villa', *JRA* 16 (2003), 137–52

Jarman (2021): C. Jarman, *River Kings: The Vikings from Scandinavia to the Silk Roads* (London, 2021)

Jennison (1937): G. Jennison, *Animals for Show and Pleasure in Ancient Rome* (Manchester, 1937)

Jones (2019): A. Jones, 'Greco-Roman Sundials: Precision and Displacement', in: Miller, and Symons (2019), 125–57

Jones (1964): A.H.M. Jones, *The Later Roman Empire 284–602* (Oxford, 1964)

Jones (2021): C. Jones, *The Fall of Robespierre: 24 Hours in Revolutionary Paris* (Oxford, 2021)

Jones (1986): C.P. Jones, *Culture and Society in Lucian* (Cambridge, Mass., and London)

Junkelmann (2000): M. Junkelmann, *Das Spiel mit dem Tod: So kämpften Roms Gladiatoren* (Mainz, 2000; republished, with additions, as *Gladiatoren: Das Spiel mit dem Tod* [Mainz, 2008])

Junkelmann (2000)A: M. Junkelmann, '*Familia Gladiatoria*: The Heroes of the Amphitheatre', in: Köhne, and Ewigleben (2000), 31–74

Junkelmann (2000)B: M. Junkelmann, 'Gladiatorial and military equipment and fighting technique: a comparison', *JRMES* 11 (2000), 113–7

Junkelmann (2010): M. Junkelmann, 'Gladiators in action: recent work on practical aspects of gladiatorial combat', *JRA* 23 (2010), 512–32

Kanz, and Grossschmidt (2006): F. Kanz, and K. Grossschmidt, 'Head injuries of Roman gladiators', *Forensic Science International* 160 (2006), 207-16

Kanz, and Grossschmidt (2009): F. Kanz, and K. Grossschmidt, 'Dying in the Arena: The Osseus Evidence from Ephesian Gladiators', in: Wilmott (20), 211–20

Keegan (1976): J. Keegan, *The Face of Battle* (London, 1976)

Kelly (2015): G. Kelly, Review of Salzman, and Roberts (2011), *CR* 65.1 (2015), 161–3

Keppie (1984): L. Keppie, *The Making of the Roman Army from Republic to Empire* (London, 1984)

Ker (2004): J. Ker, 'Nocturnal Writers in Imperial Rome: The Culture of *Lucubratio*', *CPhil* 99.3 (2004), 209–42

Ker (2019): J. Ker, 'Diurnal Selves in Ancient Rome', in: Miller, and Symons (2019), 184–213

Ker (2023): J. Ker, *The Ordered Day: quotidian time and forms of life in ancient Rome* (Baltimore, 2023)

Killeen (1959): J.F. Killeen, 'What was the *Linea Dives* (Martial, VIII, 78, 7)?', *AJPhil.* 80.2 (1959), 185–8

Kocjan (2018): T. Kocjan, 'A Woman's Virtus? Perceptions of the Female Gladiator', *Chronica* 8 (2018), 49–56

Köhne, and Ewigleben (2000): E. Köhne, and C. Ewigleben (eds.), *Gladiators and Caesars: The Power of Spectacle in Ancient Rome* (English tr., London, 2000)

Koloski-Ostrow (2015): A.O. Koloski-Ostrow, *The Archaeology of Sanitation in Roman Italy: Toilets, Sewers, and Water Systems* (Chapel Hill, 2015)

Kontokosta (2021): A.H. Kontokosta, 'Contests in Context: Gladiatorial Inscriptions and Graffiti', in: Scanlon, and Futrell (2021), 330–41

Kyle (1998): D.G. Kyle, *Spectacles of Death in Ancient Rome* (London, and New York, 1998)

Kyle (2021): D.G. Kyle, 'Animal Events', in: Scanlon, and Futrell (2021), 254–65

Lane Fox (1986): R. Lane Fox, *Pagans and Christians in the Mediterranean World from the Second Century* AD *to the Conversion of Constantine* (Harmondsworth, 1986)

Lane Fox (1996): R. Lane Fox, 'Ancient hunting: from Homer to Polybios', in: Salmon, and Shipley (1996), 119–53

Lane Fox (2015): R. Lane Fox, *Augustine: Conversion and Confessions* (London, 2015)

Laurence (1994): R. Laurence, *Roman Pompeii: Space and Society* (London, and New York, 1994)

Laurence (2013): R. Laurence, 'Traffic and Land Transportation in and near Rome', in: Erdkamp (2013), 246–61

Laurence (2017): R. Laurence, 'The sounds of the city: From noise to silence in ancient Rome', in: Betts (2017), 13–22

Lendon (2017): J.E. Lendon, 'Battle Description in the Ancient Historians, Part I', *GR* 64.1 (2017), 39–64

Lendon (2017)A: J.E. Lendon, 'Battle Description in the Ancient Historians, Part II', *GR* 64.2 (2017), 145–67

Lewis (1936): C. Lewis, *Sagittarius Rising* (London, 1936)

Lindberg (2019): N. Lindberg, 'The Emperor and his Animals: The Acquisition of Exotic Beasts for Imperial *Venationes*', *GR* 66.2 (2019), 251–63

Lindström (2010): T.C. Lindström, 'The animals of the arena: how and why could their destruction and death be endured and enjoyed?', *World Archaeology* 42.2 (2010), 310–23

Line (2022): P. Line, 'The elephants who appealed to the gods: animal agency in the Roman arena and the human perception of it', *Trace: Journal for Human Animal Studies* 8 (2022), 6–31

Linn (2014): J. Linn, *The Dark Side of Rome: A Social History of Nighttime in Ancient Rome* (DPhil thesis, Santa Barbara, 2014)

Lintott (1987): A. Lintott, 'Democracy in the Middle Republic', *ZRG* 104 (1987), 34–52

Lintott (1993): A. Lintott, '*Imperium Romanorum: Politics and Administration* (London, and New York, 1993)

MacKinnon (2006): M. Mackinnon, 'Supplying Exotic Animals for the Roman Amphitheatre Games: New Reconstructions Combining Archaeological, Ancient Textual, Historical and Ethnographic Data', *Mouseion* 6.2 (2006), 137–61

MacKinnon (2021): M. Mackinnon, 'Animal Supply', in: Scanlon, and Futrell (2021), 545–56

MacLean (2014): R. MacLean, 'People on the Margins of Roman Spectacle', in: Christesen, and Kyle (2014), 578–89

MacMullen (1966): R. MacMullen, *Enemies of the Roman Order: Treason, Unrest, and Alienation in the Empire* (Cambridge, Mass., and London)

MacMullen (1974): R. MacMullen, *Roman Social Relations* 50BC to AD284 (New Haven, and London, 1974)

MacMullen (1976): R. MacMullen, *Roman Government's Response to Crisis AD 235–337* (New Haven, and London, 1976)

MacMullen (1982): R. MacMullen, 'The Epigraphic Habit in the Roman Empire', *AJPhil* 103 (1982), 233–46

MacMullen (1984): R. MacMullen, *Christianizing the Roman Empire AD100–400* (New Haven, and London, 1984)

MacMullen (1988): R. MacMullen, *Corruption and the Decline of Rome* (New Haven, and London)

MacMullen (1990): R. MacMullen, *Changes in the Roman Empire: Essays in the Ordinary* (Princeton, 1990)

MacMullen (1990)A: R. MacMullen, 'Judicial Savagery in the Roman Empire', in: MacMullen (1990), 204–17 (originally published in *Chiron* [1986])

MacMullen (1990)B: R. MacMullen, 'Social History in Astrology', in: MacMullen (1990), 218–24 (originally published in *Ancient Society* [1971])

Magowan (2017): S.R. Magowan, *Approaching Sleep and Dreams in Early Greek Thought* (PhD thesis, Royal Holloway, London, 2017)

Mann (2009): C. Mann, 'Gladiators in the Greek East: A Case Study in Romanization', *International Journal of the History of Sport* 26.2 (2009), 272–97

Mattern (1999): S.P. Mattern, *Rome and the Enemy: Imperial Strategy in the Principate* (Baltimore, and London, 1999)

Mattern (2013): S.P. Mattern, *The Prince of Medicine: Galen in the Roman Empire* (Oxford, 2013)

Maxfield (1981): V.A. Maxfield, *The Military Decorations of the Roman Army* (London, 1981)

McCullough (2008): A. McCullough, 'Female Gladiators in Imperial Rome: Literary Context and Historical Fact', *CW* 101.2 (2008), 197–209

Meggitt (1977): M. Meggitt, *Blood Is their Argument: Warfare Among the Mae Enga Tribesmen of the New Guinea Highlands* (Palo Alto, 1977)

Meijer (2004): F. Meijer, *The Gladiators: History's Most Deadly Sport* (London, 2004)

Mennen (2011): I. Mennen, *Power and Status in the Roman Empire, AD 193–284* (Leiden, and Boston, 2011)

Millar (1981): F. Millar, 'The world of the *Golden Ass*', *JRS* 71 (1981), 63–75

Millar (1984): F. Millar, 'The Political Character of the Classical Roman Republic, 200–151 BC', *JRS* 74 (1984), 1–19

Millar (1986): F. Millar, 'Politics, Persuasion and the People before the Social War (150–90BC)', *JRS* 76 (1986), 1–11

Millar (1998): F. Millar, *The Crowd in Rome in the Late Republic* (Ann Arbor, 1998)

Miller, and Symons (2019): K.J. Miller, and S.L. Symons (eds.), *Down to the Hour: Short Time in the Ancient Mediterranean and Near East. Time, Astronomy, and Calendars* (Leiden, and Boston, 2019)

Milliman (2021): P. Milliman, 'The Decline and Fall of Spectacle', in: Scanlon, and Futrell (2021), 194–206

Milner (1996): N.P. Milner, *Vegetius: Epitome of Military Science* (2nd ed., Liverpool, 1996)

Mitchell (2012): J.M. Mitchell, 'The Case of the Strangled Saxons', CA Conference Paper, online at https://www.academia.edu/1804521/The_Case_of_the_Strangled_Saxons_CA_Conference_paper_2012

Molloy (2007): B. Molloy (ed.), *The Cutting Edge: Studies in Ancient and Medieval Combat* (Stroud, 2007)

Momigliano (1971): A. Momigliano, 'Popular religious beliefs and the late Roman historians', *Studies in Church History* 8 (1971), 1–18

Moog, and Karenberg (2003): F.P. Moog, and A. Karenberg, 'Between Horror and Hope: Gladiator's Blood as a Cure for Epileptics in Ancient Medicine', *Journal of the History of Neurosciences* 12.2 (2003), 137–43

Morrison, Coates, and Rankov (2000): J.S. Morrison, J.F. Coates, and N.B. Rankov *The Athenian Trireme: The History and Reconstruction of an Ancient Greek Warship* (2nd ed., Cambridge, 2000)

Musurillo (1972): H. Musurillo, *The Acts of the Christian Martyrs: Introduction, Texts, and Translations* (Oxford, 1972)

Neubauer et al. (2014): W. Neubauer, C. Gugl, M. Scholz, G. Verhoeven, I. Trinks, K. Löcker, M. Doneus, T. Saey, and M. van Meirvenne, 'The discovery of the school of gladiators at Carnuntum, Austria', *Antiquity* 88 (2014), 173–90

Nibley (1945): H. Nibley, '*Sparsiones*', *CJ* 40.9 (1945), 515–43

Nicolet (1980): C. Nicolet, *The World of the Citizen in Republican Rome* (Eng. tr., London, 1980)

Nissin (2015): L. Nissin, 'Sleeping Culture in Roman Literary Sources', *Arctos* 49 (2015), 95–133

Nixey (2024): C. Nixey, *Heresy: Jesus Christ and the Other Sons of God* (London, 2024)

North (1990): J.A. North, 'Democratic politics in Republican Rome', *P&P* 126 (1990), 3–21 (republished in Osborne [2004], 140–58)

Nuño, Esquerra, and Woolf (2021): A.A. Nuño, J.A. Esquerra, and G. Woolf (eds.), *Sensorium: The Senses in Roman Polytheism* (Leiden, and Boston, Mass., 2021)

Oakley (1985): S.P. Oakley, 'Single Combat in the Roman Republic', *CQ* 79.2 (1985), 392–410

Ogden (2008): D. Ogden, *Night's Black Agents: Witches, Wizards and the Dead in the Ancient World* (London, and New York, 2008)

Oliver, and Palmer (1955): J.H. Oliver, and R.E.A. Palmer, 'Minutes of an Act of the Roman Senate', *Hesperia* 24.4 (1955), 320–49

Olshanetsky (2023): H. Olshanetsky, 'Were there Jewish Gladiators? A re-evaluation of the available archaeological and textual evidence', *Atiquot, the Science of Ancient Warfare and Defense* 111 (2023), 119–48

Osborne (2004): R. Osborne (ed.), *Studies in Ancient Greek and Roman Society* (Cambridge, 2004)

Osgood (2022): J. Osgood, *Uncommon Wrath: How Caesar and Cato's Deadly Rivalry destroyed the Roman Republic* (Oxford, 2022)

Paule (2024): M. Paule, 'Blood, Sweat, and Sex: A Note on the Erotic Power of Gladiator Sweat', *Preternature* 13.2 (2024), 227–36

Pelling (1988): C.B.R. Pelling, *Plutarch: Life of Antony* (Cambridge, 1988)

Pelling (1997): C.B.R. Pelling, 'Tragical Dreamer: Some Dreams in the Roman Historians', *GR* 44.2 (1997), 197–212

Peyrefitte (1989): A. Peyrefitte, *The Collision of Two Civilisations: The British Expedition to China in 1792–4* (Eng. tr., London, 1989)

Plass (1995): P. Plass, *The Game of Death in Ancient Rome: Arena Sport and Political Suicide* (Madison, Wisc., 1995)

Potter (2010): D.S. Potter, 'Entertainers in the Roman Empire', in: Potter, and Mattingly (2010), 280–349

Potter (2010)A: D.S. Potter, 'Appendix: Two Documents Illustrating the Imperial Control of Public Entertainments', in: Potter, and Mattingly (2010), 351–71

Potter (2010)B: D.S. Potter, 'Constantine and the Gladiators', *CQ* 60.2 (2010), 596–606

Potter (2011): D.S. Potter, *The Victor's Crown: A History of Ancient Sport from Homer to Byzantium* (London, 2011)

Potter (2021): D.S. Potter, 'Roman Games and Spectacle: Christian Identity and the Arena', in: Scanlon, and Futrell (2021), 182–93

Potter, and Mattingly (2010): D.S. Potter, and D.J. Mattingly (eds.), *Life, Death, and Entertainment in the Roman Empire* (2nd ed., Ann Arbor, 2010)

Price (1984): S.R.F. Price, *Rituals and Power: The Roman Imperial Cult in Asia Minor* (Cambridge, 1984)

Price (1986): S.R.F. Price, 'The Future of Dreams: From Freud to Artemidorus', *P&P* 113 (1986), 3–37 (republished and revised in Osborne [2004], 226–59)

Rawlings (2007/9): L. Rawlings, 'Hannibal the cannibal? Polybius on Barcid atrocities', Cardiff Historical Papers: https://orca.cardiff.ac.uk/id/eprint/3875/

Rawson (1987): E. Rawson, '*Discrimina Ordinum*: The *lex Julia theatricalis*', *PBSR* 55 (1987), 83–114

Rawson (1989): E. Rawson, 'Roman Rulers and the Philosophic Advisor', in: Griffin, and Barnes (1989), 233–57

Rea (2016): J.A. Rea, 'Transforming civic space into sacred space in the "Passio" of Perpetua and Felicitas', *The Classical Outlook* 91, No.2 (20160, 46–50

Rendina (2022): S. Rendina, 'A Proconsul's Black Humour: Arrius Antoninus and his Culture in Tertullian's *Ad Scapulam*', *Rivista Storica dell' Antichitá* 52 (2022), 209–16

Rich, and Shipley (1993): J. Rich, and G. Shipley (eds.), *War and Society in the Roman World* (London, and New York, 1993)

Richardson (1992): L. Richardson, *A New Topographical Dictionary of Ancient Rome* (Baltimore, and London, 1992)

Riggsby (1997): A.M. Riggsby, '"Public" and "Private" in Roman culture: the case of the *cubiculum*', *JRA* 10 (1997), 36–56

Rives (1995): J. Rives, 'Human Sacrifice among Pagans and Christians', *JRS* 85 (1995), 65–85

Rives (1999): J. Rives, *Tacitus:* Germania (Oxford, 1999)

Robert (1940): L. Robert, *Les gladiateurs dans l'Orient grec* (Paris, 1940)
Robert (1950): L. Robert, 'Monuments de gladiateurs', *Hellenica* 8 (1950), 39–72
Romm (2014): J. Romm, *Dying Every Day: Seneca at the Court of Nero* (New York, 2014)
Rose (2005): P. Rose, 'Spectators and Spectator Comfort in Roman Entertainment Buildings: A Study in Functional Design', *PBSR* 73 (2005), 99–130
Rosen, and Sluiter (2010): R.M. Rosen, and I. Sluiter (eds.), *Valuing Others* (Leiden, 2010)
Roth (2017): J.P. Roth, 'Marcus Aurelius and Europe, c.165-80', in: Whitby, and Sidebottom (2017), 1030–3
Roueché (1984): C. Roueché, 'Acclamations in the Later Roman Empire: New Evidence from Aphrodisias', *JRS* 74 (1984), 181–99
Rutledge (2001): S.H. Rutledge, *Imperial Inquisitions: Prosecutors and Informants from Tiberius to Domitian* (London, and New York, 2001)
Sabin, van Wees, and Whitby (2007): P. Sabin, H. van Wees, and M. Whitby (eds.), *The Cambridge History of Greek and Roman warfare: Volume II: Rome from the Late Republic to the Late Empire* (Cambridge, 2007)
Sacks (1990): K. Sacks, *Diodorus Siculus and the First Century* (Princeton, 1990)
de Ste Croix (1974): G.E.M. de Ste Croix, 'Why were the early Christians persecuted?', in: Finley (1974), 210–49
Salmon, and Shipley (1996): J. Salmon, and G. Shipley (eds.), *Human Landscapes in Classical Antiquity: Environment and Culture* (London, and New York, 1996)
Salzman, and Roberts (2011): M.R. Salzman, and M.J. Roberts, *The Letters of Symmachus. Book 1* (Atlanta, 2011)
Saul (1986): N. Saul, *Scenes from a Provincial Life: Knightly Families in Sussex, 1280–1400* (Oxford, 1986)
Scanlon, and Futrell (2021): T.F. Scanlon, and A. Futrell (eds.), *The Oxford Handbook of Sport and Spectacle in the Ancient World* (Oxford, 2021)
Scarborough (1971): J. Scarborough, 'Galen and the Gladiators', *Episteme* 2 (1971), 98–111
Schmeling (2011): G. Schmeling, *A Commentary on The Satyrica of Petronius* (Oxford, 2011)
Schmitz (1997): T. Schmitz, *Bildung und Macht: zur sozialen und politischen Funktion der zweiten Sophistik in der greichischen Welt der Kaiserzeit* (Munich, 1997)
Scioli, and Walde (2010): E. Scioli, and C. Walde (eds.), *Sub imagine somni: Nighttime phenomena in Greco-Roman culture* (Pisa, 2010)

Scobie (1986): A. Scobie, 'Slums, Sanitation, and Mortality in the Roman World', *Klio* 68 (1986), 399–433

Scobie (1988): A. Scobie, 'Spectator Security and Comfort at the Gladiatorial Games', *Nikephoros* 1 (1988), 191–243

Sharland (2005): S. Sharland, 'Saturnalian Satire: Proto-carnivalesque reversals and inversions in Horace, "Satire" 2.7', *Acta Classica* 48 (2005), 103–20

Shaw (1993): B.D. Shaw, 'The Passion of Perpetua', *Past & Present* 139 (1993), 3–45

Shaw (2001): B.D. Shaw, *Spartacus and the Slave Wars: A Brief History with Documents* (Boston, and New York, 2001)

Sherwin-White (1967): A.N. Sherwin-White, *Racial Prejudice in Imperial Rome* (Cambridge, 1967)

Sidebottom (1990): H. Sidebottom, *Studies in Dio Chrysostom On Kingship* (DPhil thesis, Oxford, 1990)

Sidebottom (1993): H. Sidebottom, 'Philosophers' attitudes to warfare under the principate', in: Rich, and Shipley (1993), 241–64

Sidebottom (1996): H. Sidebottom, 'Dio of Prusa and the Flavian Dynasty', *CQ* 46.2 (1996), 447–56

Sidebottom (1998): H. Sidebottom, 'Herodian's Historical Methods and Understanding of History', *ANRW* II.34.4 (1989), 2775–836

Sidebottom (2004): H. Sidebottom, *Ancient Warfare: A Very Short Introduction* (Oxford, 2004)

Sidebottom (2005): H. Sidebottom, 'Roman Imperialism: The Changed Outward Trajectory of the Roman Empire', *Historia* 54.3 (2005), 315–30

Sidebottom (2006): H. Sidebottom, 'Dio Chrysostom and the development of *On Kingship* literature', in: Spencer, and Theodorakopoulos (2006), 117–57

Sidebottom (2007): H. Sidebottom, 'Severan historiography: evidence, patterns, and arguments', in: Swain, Harrison, and Elsner (2007), 52–82

Sidebottom (2007)A: H. Sidebottom, 'International Relations', in: Sabin, van Wees, and Whitby (2007), 3–29

Sidebottom (2014): H. Sidebottom, 'Rome in Crisis', *BBC History Magazine* (September, 2014), 24–8

Sidebottom (2017): H. Sidebottom, 'The Dacian Wars, 84–106', in: Whitby, and Sidebottom (2017), 1016–20

Sidebottom (2018): H. Sidebottom, *The Last Hour* (London, 2018)

Sidebottom (2020): H. Sidebottom, 'Fire from innermost depths: How the ancients experienced plague', *TLS* 6116 (19 June, 2020), 13–4

Sidebottom (2022): H. Sidebottom, *The Mad Emperor: Heliogabalus and the Decadence of Rome* (London, 2022)

Sidebottom (2024): H. Sidebottom, 'How Jesus was nearly swept away by a wave of unpleasant tales', *Daily Telegraph* (25 February, 2024)

Simon (2008): I. Simon, 'Un aspect des largesses imperials: les *sparsiones* de *missilia* à Rome (1er siècle avant J.-C. – IIIe siècle aprés J.-C.)', *Revue Historique* 310.4 (2008), 763–88

Simpson (2000): C.J. Simpson, 'Musicians and the Arena: Dancers and the Hippodrome', *Latomus* 59.3 (2000), 633–639

Singer, and Rosen (2024): P.N. Singer, and R.M. Rosen (eds.), *The Oxford Handbook of Galen* (Oxford, 2024)

Slater (1996): W.J. Slater (ed.), *Roman Theatre and Society: E. Togo Salmon Papers I* (Ann Arbor, 1996)

Smith (1998): R.R.R. Smith, 'Cultural Choice and Political Identity in Honorific Portrait Statues in the Greek East in the Second Century AD', *JRS* 88 (1988), 56–93

Smith (1999): R.R.R. Smith, 'Late Antique Portraits in a Public Context: Honorific Statuary at Aphrodisias in Caria, AD 300-600', *JRS* 89 (1999), 155–89

Smith, and Niederhuber (2023): R.R.R. Smith, and C. Niederhuber, *Commodus: The Public Image of a Roman Emperor* (Wiesbaden 2023)

Sogno (2016): C. Sogno, 'The Letter Collection of Quintus Aurelius Symmachus', in: Sogno et al. (2016), 175–89

Sogno et al. (2016): C. Sogno et al. (eds.), *Late Antique Letter Collections: A Critical Introduction and Reference Guide* (Berkeley, 2016)

Sorabji (1993): R. Sorabji, *Animal Minds and Human Morals: The Origins of the Western Debate* (London, 1993)

Spaeth (2010): B.S. Spaeth, '"The Terror that Comes in the Night": The Night Hag and Supernatural Assault in Latin Literature', in: Scioli, and Walde (2010), 231–58

Spencer, and Theodorakopoulos (2006): D. Spencer, and E. Theodorakopoulos (eds.), *Advice and Its Rhetoric in Greece and Rome* (Bari, 2006)

Stafford (2003): E. Stafford, 'Brother, Son, Friend, and Healer: Sleep the God', in: Wiedemann, and Dowden (2003), 71–106

Steger (2017): B. Steger, *Piazza Armerina: La villa romaine de Casale en Sicile* (Paris, 2017)

Sticka (2017): S. Sticka, *Segmented Sleep in First-Century Roman Society* (MA thesis, Brandeis University, 2017)

Storey (2017): G.R. Storey, 'All Rome Is at My Bedside: Nightlife in the Roman Empire', in: Gonlin, and Nowell (2017), 307–31

Stothard (2010): P. Stothard, *On the Spartacus Road: A Spectacular Journey through Ancient Italy* (London, 2010)

Stothard (2023): P. Stothard, *Palatine: An Alternative History of the Caesars* (London, 2023)

Streinu (2018): M.C. Streinu, 'Gladiators and Imperial Cult in Roman Thrace', in: Fournie, and Parissaki (2018), 357–62

Swain (1996): S. Swain, *Hellenism and Empire: Language, Classicism, and Power, AD 50–250* (Oxford, 1996)

Swain (2007): S. Swain (ed.), *Seeing the Face, Seeing the Soul: Polemon's Physiognomy from Classical Antiquity to Medieval Islam* (Oxford, 2007)

Swain, Harrison, and Elsner (2007): S. Swain, S. Harrison, and J. Elsner (eds.), *Severan Culture* (Cambridge, 2007)

Syme (1939): R. Syme, *The Roman Revolution* (London, Oxford, and New York, 1939)

Talbert (2000): R.J.A. Talbert (ed.), *Barrington Atlas of the Greek and Roman World* (Princeton, and Oxford, 2000)

Thébert (1987): Y. Thébert, 'Private Life and Domestic Architecture in Roman Africa', in: Veyne (1987), 313–409

Thompson (2002): L.L. Thompson, 'The Martyrdom of Polycarp: Death in the Roman Games', *The Journal of Religion* 82.1 (2002), 27–52

Thonemann (2020): P. Thonemann, *An Ancient Dream Manual: Artemidorus' The Interpretation of Dreams* (Oxford, 2020)

Thonemann (2020)A: P. Thonemann, 'Introduction', and 'Notes', in: Hammond (2020), xi–xxx; 233–303

Thorndike (1913): L. Thorndike, 'A Roman Astrologer as a Historical Source: Julius Firmicus Maternus', *CPhil.* 8 (1913), 415–35

Toner (1995): J. Toner, *Leisure and Ancient Rome* (Cambridge, 1995)

Toner (2009): J. Toner, *Popular Culture in Ancient Rome* (Cambridge, and Maldon, MA, 2009)

Toner (2014): J. Toner, *The Day Commodus Killed a Rhino: Understanding the Roman Games* (Baltimore, 2014)

Toner (2014)A: J. Toner (ed.), *A Cultural History of the Senses in Antiquity* (London, 2014)

Toynbee (1973): J.M.C. Toynbee, *Animals in Roman Life and Art* (London, 1973)

Tuck (2021): S.L. Tuck, '*Ludi* and *Factiones* as Organizations of Performers', in: Scanlon, and Futrell (2021), 534–544

Urbainczyk (2008): T. Urbainczyk, *Slave Revolts in Antiquity* (Berkeley, and Los Angeles, 2008)

Van Hooff (1990): A.J.L. van Hooff, *From Autothanasia to Suicide: Self-Killing in Classical Antiquity* (London, 1990)

Veyne (1987), P. Veyne (ed.), *A History of Private Life, Volume 1: From Pagan Rome to Byzantium* (Eng. tr., Cambridge, Mass., and London, 1987)

Vierow (1999): H. Vierow, 'Feminine and Masculine Voices in the "Passion of Saints Perpetua and Felicitas"', *Latomus* 58 (1999), 600–619

Ville (1960): G. Ville, 'Les Jeux de gladiateurs dans l'empire chrétien', *Mélanges d'archéologie et d'histoire* 72 (1960), 273–335

Ville (1981): G. Ville, *La Gladiature en occident des origines a la mort de Domitien* (Rome, 1981)

Vincent (2017): A. Vincent, 'Tuning into the past: Methodological perspectives in the contextualised study of the sounds of Roman antiquity', in: Betts (2017), 147–57

Vout (2022): C. Vout, *Exposed: The Greek and Roman Body* (London, 2022)

Walbank (1972): F.W. Walbank, *Polybius* (Berkeley, and Los Angeles, 1972)

Walde (2011): C. Walde, Review of Harris (2009), *CR* 61.1 (2011), 208–11

Wallace-Hadrill (1994): A. Wallace-Hadrill, *Houses and Society in Pompeii and Herculaneum* (Princeton, 1994)

Watson, and Watson (2014): L. Watson, and P. Watson, *Juvenal Satire 6* (Cambridge, 2014)

Weaver (1972): P.R.C. Weaver, *Familia Caesaris: A Social Study of the Emperor's Freedmen and Slaves* (Cambridge, 1972)

Webster (1985): G. Webster, *The Roman Imperial Army* (3rd ed., London, 1985)

Welch (1994): K. Welch, 'The Roman Arena in Late-Republican Italy', *JRA* 7 (1994), 59–80

Welch (2007): K. Welch, *The Roman Amphitheatre from its Origins to the Colosseum* (Cambridge, 2007)

Wellesley (2000): K. Wellesley, *The Year of the Four Emperors* (3rd ed., London, and New York, 2000)

Whitby, and Sidebottom (2017): M. Whitby, and H. Sidebottom (eds.), *The Encyclopedia of Ancient Battles* (3 vols., Chichester, 2017)

Wiedemann (1992): T. Wiedemann, *Emperors and Gladiators* (London, and New York, 1992)

Wiedemann, and Dowden (2003): T. Wiedemann, and K. Dowden (eds.), *Sleep* (Bari, 2003)

Wilkins, Harvey, and Dobson (1995): J. Wilkins, D. Harvey, and M. Dobson (eds.), *Food in Antiquity* (Exeter, 1995)

Willis (2008): S. Willis, *Fighting at Sea in the Eighteenth Century: The Art of Sailing Warfare* (Woodbridge, 2008)

Wilmott (2008): T. Wilmott, *The Roman Amphitheatre in Britain* (Stroud, 2008)

Wilmott (2009): T. Wilmott (ed.), *Roman Amphitheatre and Spectacula: a 21st-Century Perspective* (Oxford, 2009)

Wilson (2018): A. Wilson, 'Roman Nightlife', in: Chaniotis, and Derron (2018), 59–89

Wilson (1983): R.J.A. Wilson, *Piazza Armerina* (London, Toronto, Sydney, and New York, 1983)

Wilson (2004): R.J.A. Wilson, 'On the Identification of the Figure in the South Apse of the Great Hunt Corridor at Piazza Armerina', *Sicilia Antiqua* 1 (2004), 153–70

Wilson (2020): R.J.A. Wilson, Review of Steger (2017), *BMCR* 2020.03.17

Wirszubski (1950): Ch. Wirszubski, *Libertas as a Political Idea at Rome During the Late Republic and Early Principate* (Cambridge, 1950)

Woolf (1998): G. Woolf, *Becoming Roman: The Origins of Provincial Civilization in Gaul* (Cambridge, 1998)

Woolf (2006): G. Woolf, *Et Tu, Brute? The Murder of Caesar and Political Assassination* (London, 2006)

Wright (2001): A. Wright, 'The Death of Cicero. Forming a Tradition: The Contamination of History', *Historia* 50 (2001), 436–52

Yavetz (1969): Z. Yavetz, *Plebs and Princeps* (Oxford, 1969)

Yeates (1934): V.M. Yeates, *Winged Victory* (London, 1934)

Illustration Credits

1. Marble relief at Pompeii. Mondadori Portfolio/Contributor/Getty.
2. Gladiators fighting. Pictorial Press Ltd/Alamy Stock Photo.
3. The *cena libra*. Erdal Şükrü Akan/Alamy Stock Photo.
4. Funerary relief. Public domain.
5. The Zliten mosaic. Public domain.
6. Terracotta lamp. Public domain.
7. Amphitheatre at Pompeii. Public domain.
8. Gladiators grappling. Public domain.
9. Relief from Smyrna. UrbanImages/Alamy Stock Photo.
10. Cross-section of the Colosseum. Illustration © Darren Bennett at DKB Creative Ltd.
11. Social structure of the Roman Empire. Illustration © Darren Bennett at DKB Creative Ltd.
12. Magerius mosaic. Public domain.
13. Terracotta relief. NurPhoto SRL/Alamy Stock Photo.
14. Great Hunt (I). Public domain.
15. Great Hunt (II). Public domain.
16. Great Hunt (III). Public domain.
17. Types of gladiators. Illustration © Darren Bennett at DKB Creative Ltd.
18. Gladiators receiving the decision of the *editor*. Public domain.
19. Relief from Halicarnassus. Public domain.
20. Gladiator in the 'first position'. Danita Delimont/Alamy Stock Photo.

Index

About the Author

Harry Sidebottom teaches classical history at Oxford University and is the bestselling author of fifteen novels. His debut trade non-fiction book, *The Mad Emperor: Heliogabalus and the Decadence of Rome*, was published in 2022 and was a Book of the Year in the *Spectator*, the *Financial Times* and *BBC History*.